DISCOVERING NEW WORLDS

GARLAND MEDIEVAL CASEBOOKS
(VOL. 2)

GARLAND REFERENCE LIBRARY OF THE HUMANITIES
(VOL. 1436)

GARLAND MEDIEVAL CASEBOOKS
Joyce E. Salisbury, Series Editor

1. *Sagas of the Icelanders: A Book of Essays*
   John Tucker

2. *Discovering New Worlds: Essays on Medieval*
   Exploration and Imagination
   Scott D. Westrem

DISCOVERING NEW WORLDS
*Essays on Medieval
Exploration and Imagination*

edited by
Scott D. Westrem

GARLAND PUBLISHING, INC. • NEW YORK & LONDON
1991

Library of Congress Cataloging-in-Publication Data

Discovering new worlds : essays on medieval exploration and
imagination / edited by Scott D. Westrem.
    p. cm. — (Garland reference library of the humanities ; vol.
1436. Garland medieval casebooks ; vol. 2)
    Includes bibliographical references and index.
    ISBN 0–8153–0102–2 (alk. paper)
    1. Geography, Medieval. I. Westrem, Scott D., 1953– .
II. Series: Garland reference library of the humanities ; vol.
1436. III. Series: Garland reference library of the humanities.
Garland medieval casebooks ; vol. 2.
G89.D57 1991
910'.9—dc20   91–12450
                                                  CIP

The illustration on the front cover is a woodcut from *Myrrour of the Worlde*
(Westminster: Caxton, 1481), sig. d.6.r (used with permission from the
James Ford Bell Library of the University of Minnesota).

Printed on acid-free, 250-year-life paper
Manufactured in the United States of America

Table of Contents

List of Illustrations

Preface

Anniversaries offer convenient opportunities to remember important occasions, so it is no surprise that both the general public and the scholarly community have been marking, already for several years, the event of 12 October 1492, and the bequest that is ours because of that day. By mid-February 1988, popular and academic interest had already manifested itself at the successful exhibition "Encountering the New World, 1493-1800: Rare Prints, Maps, and Illustrated Books from the John Carter Brown Library" at the IBM Gallery of Science and Art in midtown Manhattan. A judicious assessment of Columbus's discovery and its legacy, however, depends on an understanding of the sophisticated medieval world from which he, together with his contemporaries, inherited both theory and impetus to undertake the bold action whose quincentenary is so widely being observed.

This is almost the last mention that Columbus will get in this book, although the broad semantic register of its title echoing in various of its essays will undoubtedly conjure the man from time to time. Remembered here instead are admirals of other seas—diplomats and pilgrims, chroniclers and poets, cartographers and missionaries—who, over the course of a millennium, added new territory to the map of human discourse. From Egeria in the fourth century to Dante in the fourteenth, these discoverers contributed greatly to what we know and how we think today.

This volume would not exist were it not for an anniversary. In celebration of its twenty years as an independent entity within The City University of New York, Lehman College, the only four-year public institution of higher education in the Bronx, hosted a series of academic meetings, including an interdisciplinary conference entitled "Imagining New Worlds: Factual and Figural Discovery During the Middle Ages," on 12-14 May 1989, which was attended by over 125 medievalists from around North America. While not a collection of conference papers, this gathering of articles has its genesis in that event and its wide-ranging discussions, to which each essayist here contributed formally.

Having chaired the committee that organized the conference, I must acknowledge a considerable debt to several colleagues at Lehman, medievalists whose ideas, wit, and dedication during eighteen months of planning turned a moment's fancy into an exciting reality: Herbert Broderick, Ana Diz, Reginetta Haboucha, Michael Paull, Daniel Rubey, and Larry Sullivan. A most faithful adviser and supporter throughout this period was Vice President for Institutional Advancement Emita B. Hill, whose office provided critical financial backing for the project. I am also grateful to Provost Melvyn Nathanson and Acting Dean of Arts and Humanties Jacob Judd for underscoring the College's commitment to a medieval conference at a time when New York State schools are being forced to sacrifice many academic programs. Fellow members of the Department of English offered welcome encouragement. Veronica Cash, in the manner of a good medieval text, generously gave instructive, pleasant help. Anne Perryman and her staff in Lehman's Office of College Relations, aided by Richard Hussey and his skilful team of printers, worked tirelessly to produce imaginative announcements and programs. In addition, a generous grant from the L. J. Skaggs and Mary C. Skaggs Foundation proved crucial to the conference's success.

In preparing this volume, I put my family and friends through tough exercises in forbearance: I appreciate their constancy. The collection itself benefited greatly from Professor Joyce Salisbury's editorial suggestions. At Garland Publishing, Vice President Gary Kuris offered valuable, enthusiastic support for this project, and Chuck Bartelt cheerfully lent her technical expertise in the production of the final copy.

It may seem hyperbolic to speak in the same breath of the twentieth anniversary of a fairly small public school and the quincentenary of a landmark date in history. Yet Lehman College, like hundreds of other institutions in this country, exists because of faculty members, administrators, and staff who are committed to continue—indeed, to enlarge—the mission of a medieval university by giving students from a remarkable range of social, ethnic, religious, and national backgrounds a chance to discover what for many are only dimly imagined worlds of opportunity. It is to such colleagues that this book is dedicated.

Scott D. Westrem
Lehman College of The City University of New York
14 January 1991

Introduction:
"From Worlde into Worlde"

Scott D. Westrem

We have it on good authority that humanity encountered its first new world east of Eden, a remove in space so far removed from us in time that our mental map records it only in the archipelago of archetypes. Even a poetic genius such as Milton invoked the aid of a Muse and the Paraclete to imagine the transition from Paradise to the land of Nod. It is a characteristic of the modern world, however, that we turn our attention to the future rather than the past: having watched, on television, men walking on the moon, we survey distant planets with half a notion to visiting them ourselves some day. It is tempting to adopt the hyperbole of a United States president who dismissed millennia of human discovery and concluded that, in going where no one had gone before, the Apollo 11 astronauts were the chief players in "the greatest week in the history of the world since the Creation."[1]

As a technological achievement, the lunar landing was, indeed, very good; it has unquestionably contributed to our fund of knowledge. Despite the mission's data and photographs, however, it has not markedly altered the way we look at the world. Radical shifts—great alterations—in human perspective are rare. For almost two thousand years, Western geographers conceived of the Earth as a sphere with three continents in sensible balance. The idea of a fourth land mass—an antipodean *terra australis*—was certainly alive, but it was a subject for intellectual speculation rather than actual investigation, a hypothesis to be defended or denounced by means of a logical application of theology and philosophy. Certainly Christopher Columbus was not seeking

Scott D. Westrem is Assistant Professor of English at Lehman College of The City University of New York (see Notes on Contributors, p. 223).

ix

empirical evidence of it when he set sail in 1492, and even after his return more than a decade passed before a map bore the revolutionary words "mundus novus."[2]

In the modern lexicon, the sense of unexpectedly-found literal territory is the primary connotation of "New World," but this does not sum up the phrase's meaning; the adventurous do not always go out after actual continents. We speak metaphorically of how unfamiliar cultures, representational schemes, and ideas make a whole world of difference to us when we encounter them. The heavens may be new territory for astronauts, but they certainly belonged to the medieval world; indeed, Dante described them—and hell—so graphically that readers of his capacious poem have mistaken his figural journey for fact. The essays collected in this volume attempt to give some shape to the character of medieval discovery (even to question whether it has any shape at all); in so doing, they also give definition to the human imagination, in which inquiry and gullibility, anxiety and creativity all pitch their tents.

An example of an unusual linguistic reversal, the phrase "new world" was, in fact, a metaphor long before it denoted the Americas.[3] As the Mongols invaded Russia and eastern Europe, beginning in the late 1230s, the pope, the king of France, and other leaders of Latin Christendom recognized the need to face the fact of the Orient. Missionary diplomats who journeyed during the next two decades to the khan's capital at Karakorum found the governmental and spiritual terrain as rugged as the route, and they reported bleakly on the possibility of establishing either political or religious missions in a place that was culturally so remote from home.[4] Not even experience tempered their sense of alienation; the Franciscan Peregrine had been in China for more than a decade when, writing as bishop of the great port city of Zaytun (Ch'uan-chou-fu) in January 1318, he described himself as "in another world . . . desiring to hear news from the world of the faithful."[5] Jordan of Severac, who became bishop of Columbum (Quilon) around 1329 after some eight years as a Dominican missionary on the Malabar coast, recalls the different skin color, clothing styles, and dietary preferences of the people he lived among, expressing his feeling of estrangement more generally: "Every thing is a marvel in this India! Verily it is quite another world!"[6] Several Europeans of this period wrote vividly—if not always reliably—about Asia, describing teeming cities, opulent land, forbidding mountains and deserts, and people almost universally ignorant of over twelve hundred years of Christian history. These accounts capture the disorientation of entering a different space and a different time, of being taken out of context, of crossing "from worlde into worlde."[7]

It would be hard to find a better avatar of such transit than the indefatigable and largely forgotten Franciscan missionary, William of Rubruck, who acquired a rich understanding of the mundane on his tedious and momentous journey east to Mongolia in 1253. He also experienced a sense of profound displacement—for example, when he entered an encampment of Asians for the first time. "[W]hen I came among them," he later wrote France's Louis IX, "it seemed indeed to me as if I were stepping into some other world."[8] At the time, he was still in the Crimea. In a thorough, observant letter to the king, Friar William does his best both to comprehend and to make comprehensible the outlandish things he saw in *quoddam aliud seculum*—some other world. From him the West heard its first mantra, found out about Buddhist belief in reincarnation, got word of Chinese ideographs and paper money, received its earliest lesson in the agglutinate language family, learned that the Volga and the Don do not merge and that the Caspian Sea is landlocked, and obtained one of its first detailed accounts of life in the Orient.[9] William even expressed what has become the traveler's quintessential cliché: recording his delight in the colorful design and tent-bearing carts of a Mongol settlement, he laments to his reader, the king, "The only way I can describe it to you is by sending a picture, which I'd do, if I could only draw."[10]

The Mongols, for their part, were apparently just as bewildered by William and the culture he brought with him. A Franciscan totally devoted to the Order's rule, he went shoeless during much of his grueling, six-month journey to the great khan. Standing barefooted in the Christmas snow waiting for an imperial audience, he and his companion were surrounded by men who, he writes, "gazed at us as if we were monsters," wondering what country it was where men had no need of their feet. Asians marveled at the beautifully illuminated manuscripts William was carrying, several of which a military governor forced him to hand over as hospitality gifts. In the Mongol capital, caught up in a squabble among Muslims, Buddhists, and Christians of various Eastern rites—all of them vying to become the khan's spiritual guide—William coached a team of Nestorians in the tactics of debate as if he were teaching students at the University of Paris. His

demonstration of the rationality of Christian dogma, and his hopes of
converting the crowd, came to a quick halt when opponents and
audience, unaccustomed to scholastic argument and unimpressed by
Catholic orthodoxy, started singing and then got drunk.[11]

William of Rubruck's account of his movement "from worlde
into worlde" poignantly captures the perspective of a Westerner looking
at the threatening and novel East. It also occasionally suggests the
point of view of an Asian looking at an alien, as if about to say, like
Prospero to Miranda—or a Carib to Columbus—"'Tis new to thee."
William ranks among the few Europeans of his time who lived long
enough in an Oriental society to form a knowledgeable impression of it
and then return home to tell the tale. But he would be an unusual man
in any era. A traveler to unfamiliar countries who was simultaneously a
theologian, geographer, rhetorician, philosopher, linguist, sociologist,
and skilful raconteur: no wonder he was polymath Roger Bacon's ideal
informant about Asia and the Mongols, that dimly understood people
who so forcefully challenged thirteenth-century Europe.

For us as well travelers like William provide the most obvious
—if not always the most reliable—witness to medieval European
attitudes about another world.[12] He was, of course, hardly the first
person interested in the Orient, nor was Mongol or Chinese territory the
Christian imagination's single fixation. By 1241, when the khan's
forces were fighting in Poland and Hungary, the crusaders had already
been pursuing their own agenda in the eastern Mediterranean for almost
150 years. Like pilgrims, who throughout the Middle Ages alternately
streamed and trickled to the shrines of the Holy Land, Christian warriors
brought home from the Levant (sometimes called Outremer) the tales
and cultivated tastes of a foreign way of life.[13] By the mid-1300s,
enough missionaries and merchants had written reports of their
experiences in the East for the knight John Mandeville (or someone
using this pseudonym) to borrow wholesale from a stack of existing
travel narratives, geographies, and histories, and to compile an account
of what he claimed was his own journey, undertaken over the course of
some thirty-three years. This urbane and concertedly tolerant account so
expertly blended the pilgrim's detail, the historian's anecdote, and the
traveler's rare experience that it became one of the most widespread and
widely-copied books of the late Middle Ages.[14]

While Europeans did not immediately change their way of life in
light of new information brought back from the East, they showed,

during the first five hundred years of this millennium, a gradual evolution from indifference to preoccupation with the Orient. The popularity of *Mandeville's Travels* is some testimony to this.[15] But travel books were not alone in feeding this interest. Among the intellectual contributions of the twelfth-century renaissance were several works that describe the Earth and its place in the cosmos; probably the most widespread and enduring of them was the *Imago mundi*, which Honorius Augustodunensis finished (at least in its first draft) around 1110, and which survives in at least 150 manuscripts. This book and others like it—Lambert of Saint-Omer's *Liber floridus* (c. 1120), Sacrobosco's *De sphaera* (c. 1220), and, later, Pierre d'Ailly's *Imago mundi* (1410)—recorded and sustained informed opinion, serving as authorities for travelers and explorers during the Age of Discovery.[16] In addition, a quasi-scientific text, which appeared around 1165, continued to intrigue readers for over four hundred years. This was the *Letter of Prester John*, a relatively brief epistolary description of Indian wonders written, in all probability, by a Levantine adventurer but claiming to be a message from no less than an emperor—and a Christian of unusual sacerdotal virtue at that. Marco Polo heard about him, Mandeville claims to have been his mercenary, and Henry the Navigator made his discovery a matter of official policy.[17]

Medieval cartographers combined in varying degrees travel reports, the authority of theologians and cosmographers, and common hearsay in order to produce graphic schemes of the Earth. One standard representation, the T-O map, is found occasionally in manuscript copies of medieval books with some geographical content, such as the *Etymologies* of Isidore of Seville (d. 636). The T-O map takes its name from its basic outline—a circle with an inscribed diameter and, at a right angle to it, a single radius; this design, resembling the letter T within a letter O, gave Asia one-half of the Earth's land mass, with Africa and Europe splitting the other half between them. East was often (but by no means always) shown at the top, with Jerusalem frequently (but not consistently) at the center. Scholars today, having learned that medieval maps operate within their own symbol systems, are providing an imaginative counterweight to earlier dismissals of the *mappaemundi* as "non-scientific . . . monstrosities" of "complete futility."[18] One particularly interesting area of research in medieval cartography is the relationship between word and picture, between presumed fact and figure.[19] Even portolan charts, which show coastlines and had a much more pragmatic purpose, were often the decorated products of skilled craftsmen. (Examples of a T-O map and a portolan chart appear as Plates 1 and 2, following this page.[20]) Not limited to mapmaking, artists also expressed in stone how they conceived distant people and lands, as evidenced in the stunning tympanum of the Church of the Madeleine at Vézelay with its border inhabited by what St. Augustine termed the "monstrous races of humans." Similar representations are found in manuscript illuminations of the travel books of Polo and Mandeville, as well as of works of apocalyptic literature.[21]

Remote animal and human populations acted as powerfully attractive magnets for the medieval imagination, which devised a bizarre zoology for *terrae incognitae*. Bestiaries from Scandinavia to Iberia describe the physical and moral attributes of animals as familiar as ants and as fantastic as manticores. Other sources—among them accounts by actual travelers, such as John of Plano Carpini, and experienced theologians, including Jacques de Vitry, bishop of Acre in the early 1200s—soberly report the existence of such humanoid monsters as one-eyed cannibals who lope into harbors to fetch fresh sailors on shipboard, and one-legged hoppers whose huge foot serves as an umbrella on hot days. These peculiar peoples were, in Rudolf Wittkower's words, "stock features of the occidental mentality," and they formed part of "the western idea of India for almost two thousand years."[22]

Medieval Europeans demonstrated their capacity to wonder about inward space as well as the unknown physical world; indeed, they produced some of the greatest literary works in human history when they entered the mythopoetic dimension of figural discovery. It is a commonplace to note that the world was "read" during the Middle Ages as if it were the text of God, but this literacy of the mundane expressed itself in various ways. Dante, for example, borrowed from European and Middle Eastern pilgrimage models to create hellish, purgatorial, and paradisal geographies that accommodate human souls. Chaucer's band of pilgrims sets out from a particular English inn early one April morning, is transported en route by the Squire to Chingis Khan's court "in the land of Tartarye," and, finally, becomes an emblem of Everyman's "viage" to the celestial Jerusalem. Popular *chansons de geste* offered an idealized world, presenting such an appealing picture of coherence and chivalry that people in later centuries have dreamed of recreating it. Literary utopias and works such as *The Land of Cockaigne* represent even wilder speculations in which ideals are challenged or even

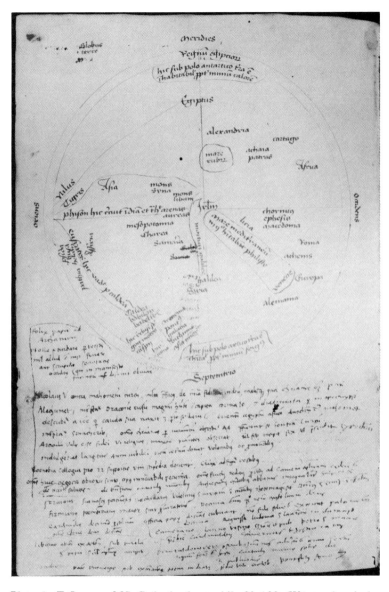

Plate 1. T-O map, MS Cod. theol. et phil. 2° 100 (Württembergische Landesbibliothek, Stuttgart), fol. 3v.

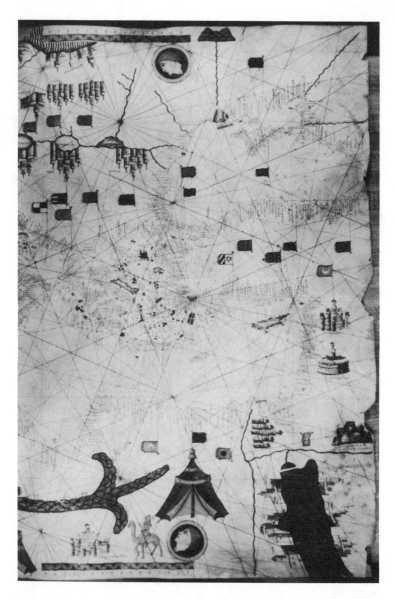

Plate 2. Portolan chart, drawn by Peter Roselli at Majorca in 1466 (James Ford Bell Library of the University of Minnesota).

dismissed.[23] The way in which a medieval text reflects in a little space
the limitless outside world has also attracted the attention of modern
critics; in Jurij Lotman's formulation, "historical and ethnical linguistic
models of space become the bases of organization for the construction
of a 'picture of the world'—an integral conceptual model inherent to a
given type of culture."[24]

This more abstract kind of discovery applies to the marketplace
of ideas as well. In the early twelfth century, students and professors
from throughout Europe began trekking to Bologna, Paris, and Oxford
to learn about the place human beings occupy in several worlds—
terrestrial and celestial, natural and spiritual. The broad provenance of
the population of these academic guilds gave them the name
"university"; this institution made a whole world of difference in the
development of Western civilization.[25] During the 1200s, a gradual
reintroduction of forgotten knowledge radically changed Western
thought as Arabic translations of Plato, Aristotle, and other giants of
the Classical Age were Latinized. Much of this astounding renovation
of thought came via communities of Muslim, Jewish, and Christian
scholars in Spain, where, simultaneously, a gradual *Reconquista*
brought about a new political, literary, and religious order.[26]

This cross-cultural contact helped bring about the transfer of
scientific and technological knowledge to Western Europe. Travelers'
needs also coaxed the innovative into developing navigational equipment, more efficient and maneuverable ships, and useful sea charts.
Thus, medieval science actually made it possible to visit new worlds.
Furthermore, better understanding of the human body—that "little world
made cunningly"—coincided with the establishment of new institutions
in the West to promote health, such as hospitals, medical schools, and
competency examinations.[27]

Cosmographers, cartographers, poets, professors, translators,
scientists, even many travelers—these largely represent the literate
during the Middle Ages and, therefore, a decided minority of the population. To be sure, there were "ditch diggers and alewives" who, like the
educated members of medieval society, believed the Earth was spherical;
at the same time, others thought nothing of the sort, as C. S. Lewis
pointed out, "not because they thought it was flat but because they did
not think about it at all."[28] Still, the discovery of America almost 500
years ago did more than create a sensation in European capitals. The
very fact of a fourth continent, according to William C. Spengemann,

"gradually removed the world as a whole from the authoritatively defined state of being it had enjoyed before 1500 and thrust it into a highly uncertain state of becoming." The medieval view of the world— conceived, in Spengemann's words, "as a complete, timeless, and fully comprehensible entity in an immutable divine order"—no longer had currency.[29]

****

The essays in this volume supply details and analysis that a survey cannot provide; they fill in the contours of several literal and metaphoric worlds that have been merely sketched above. The topics taken up here range from serious efforts by thirteenth-century European intellectuals to develop an understanding of the Mongols to the poetry of anonymous wags giddily heaping up lies about the communism of Cockaigne. Contributors to this book imagine many "new worlds," extending from Asia to Arabic cartography, from Aristotle's apodictic demonstration to Dante's poetic imagination.

The Old World of medieval Europe, not surprisingly, is also a subject for interpretation. Several writers describe a subtle arrogance in the West's efforts to contain its own cultural anxieties by attempting to comprehend—and thus intellectually to dominate—the East, systematiz- ing its biology, scandalizing its people, and syncretizing its religious diversity into one great fellowship of Christian love. Other writers maintain that acquisitive expansionism came later to Europe: they hold that pilgrims did not look on landscapes with an eye to capturing them in word or in deed, that chroniclers were not concerned with the "potential" of developing uncultivated plots of land, that popes actually worked to establish in canon law even an "infidel's" natural right to possess and to keep land. At least two essayists question the accuracy of speaking, as Spengemann does, of "a reigning conception of the world" current during the Middle Ages, or, as I have done with some reservation, of "the medieval imagination."[30] They imply that it is we, in fact, who need to discover something, that we are alienated from our settings and mired in a desire to impose our systems on foreigners.

Happily, a few clichés about the Middle Ages, ones that come out of their cages with unfortunate regularity, are kept in confinement by these essayists. Medieval sailors are not afraid of falling off the edge of the Earth—indeed, the world is round even for a geographical and theological conservative like Dante.[31] Life was not cheap and the age was not dark, as is evidenced by the author of *Mandeville's Travels.* Every human event was not watched throughout Latin Christendom—certainly not at the court of Frederick II Hohenstaufen—as a step in the choreography of divine drama. In addition, assumptions great and small are challenged in these essays: several dispute the prejudice that medieval Europeans considered everyone from other continents and other faiths to be subhuman; one analyzes the knotty problem of legitimizing on moral grounds an invading force's acquisition of land. Still others offer sophisticated explanations of the "lies" told by travelers to the Orient or of the apparent myopia of pilgrims in the Holy Land. Certain imbalances are also redressed. While Wittkower's study of medieval Europe's fascination for Asian exotica has been justly praised—the careful, experienced traveler John of Plano Carpini testifies to the existence in the East of cynocephalics, cyclopedes, and other "monsters" because he unquestioningly accepts the tradition that Wittkower traces[32]—this reading of the medieval imagination is too pat. Contributors to this volume fit other pieces into the mosaic: cartographers who charted genuine coastlines, clerics who wrote real Asians into canon law, and men and women who undertook actual journeys to achieve forgiveness from sins of which they were profoundly conscious. Discovering new worlds does not necessarily mean overwhelming them; imagining new worlds does not by definition mean fantasizing them. This book, as a whole, hopes to redress oversimplifications about the Middle Ages, especially the general assumption that medieval people suffered from "ignorance of a confined space," a malady from which the human race recovered in 1492.[33]

****

Contributors to this volume have widely differing interpretations of the words in its title. Mary Campbell, in fact, calls into question the very possibility of speaking of "discovering" in a medieval context, where travelers, unlike post-Columbian explorers, give little emphasis to their own perception—and, by extension, cognitive possession—of foreign, unfamiliar territory. Indeed, for many years it has been a widely-held belief among scholars that travel accounts written before the fifteenth century are practically devoid of landscape description. Campbell challenges this conclusion in her examination of several pilgrimage narratives of the early Middle Ages. Admitting that these accounts of travel to an "exotic" land provide only a modicum of topographical detail, she argues that medieval travelers to the Holy Land placed surroundings in historical, rather than personal, perspective: they viewed places through the lens of Scripture, with the result that locale became a kind of objective correlative for sacred occasion. As a result, landscape, a phenomenon of the present tense in modern travel literature, receded into the past—and away from both writer and reader—in pilgrimage accounts. Campbell also demonstrates that the relationship between the viewer and the view changed over the course of time. In the fourth century, the pilgrims Paula and Egeria arrive at particular places remembering so vividly the biblical events that occurred there that the scenery seems to be illuminated exclusively by history. By the late 600s, however, events can be distinguished from places as time separates the devout pilgrim from the sacred moment; thus, a visitor such as Arculf, the bishop of Gaul, is easily distracted from the Holy Land's vistas by its bounty of blessed detail—memorial stones, lithic footprints, pulverized remnants of saints. Campbell's analysis of what she calls "exotic travel writing" is steeped in grammar, and, as a result, she offers a novel, rhetorical approach to old texts that traditionally have been explicated with lengthy glosses on archaeological digs, Bible verses, and measurements of distance. Because Campbell ambitiously tries to see space and to hear words with the eyes and ears of a citizen of an earlier millennium, her essay appropriately comes first in a collection whose subject is human exploration and imagination.

By contrast, the landscape is lush in the literary tradition that James Romm investigates. Letters purportedly describing the wonders of India circulated widely in medieval Europe. One, styled as a report from the field by the conquering hero Alexander the Great to his philomathic teacher Aristotle, describes the extravagant botany and zoology that the West has traditionally located in Africa and Asia. The *Epistola Alexandri ad Aristotelem* appeared at roughly the same time that Egeria was describing the Holy Land; it draws not on the Bible but on a variety of classical sources that seek to identify, to catalogue, and occasionally to determine the origins of diverse, unruly life forms in exotic parts of the world. Romm's thesis incorporates a pun: the wonder letter attributed to Alexander—like others attributed during the Middle Ages to the traveler Fermes and the potentate Prester John—is "oriented" toward making etiological and taxonomic sense of the East's infinite variety. A text of this kind, he argues, met the West's political and scientific needs; indeed, it gave the West a noble warrior who was also an inquisitive investigator, one who applied the lessons and furthered the research of his "master" Aristotle. But, Romm concludes, the *Epistola*'s intellectually aggressive attempt to cultivate—and, thus, to acculturate—the jungle of Indian biology ultimately fails when Alexander, whose army is encamped near a pond, cannot contend with the plethora of peculiar life-forms that emerge to attack his soldiers. Western scientific theory, its vocabulary nearly depleted and the appearance of animalian novelties accelerating, collapses, a victim of its own need for neat categories.

Another method that medieval Europe employed to bring the Orient under control is the subject of Gregory G. Guzman's essay on the Mongols' alleged practice of cannibalism; his study demonstrates that Bishop Peregrine was not alone in considering Asia to be "another world." In a detailed analysis of six Latin sources from the mid-1200s—three records of eye-witness reports by travelers, and three accounts by clerics with access to reliable information—Guzman argues that descriptions of the Mongols as customary and/or ritual eaters of human flesh derived not from observation but from a complicated network of sacred and secular literary texts to which medieval writers appear to have added little, if any, information. First of all, the accusation is uniquely European: no other people who came under Mongol attack during the thirteenth century mention the repellent practice, and surviving articles of Chingis Khan's law code are silent on the issue. Moreover, as Guzman shows, the accusations, all of which are based on second- or third-hand reports, resemble each other semantically and hark back to pejorative treatments of threatening barbarians that are as old as Homer and Herodotus in the classical tradition and the ambiguous adversaries Gog and Magog in the Judeo-Christian. The complicated Alexander Romance tradition also depicts dangerous cannibals inhabiting the vast, obscure stretches of northern Asia. Applying the ancient scandal of cannibalism to an unknown people served to assuage significant anxiety in Europe in the mid-thirteenth century—indeed, assured a nervous public of the inevitable triumph of Christianity as promised in biblical eschatology. Unwittingly, the West curbed its understanding of Asia by superimposing myth onto fact and distorting valuable information. At the same time, Guzman maintains, Latin Europe, in its preoccupation with the Mongols, however derivative and misguided its ideas may have

been, signals its emergence from centuries of geographical isolation
into an arena where it would quickly become a major political player.

An intriguing and hitherto unnoticed superimposition of myth
onto myth prompts Vincent DiMarco to study the marriage of the
classical legend of the Amazons to Judeo-Christian apocalyptic prophecies concerning the people of Gog and Magog. DiMarco reconstructs
the development of a late medieval story, preserved in such works as
Mandeville's Travels, depicting the Queen of the Amazons standing
guard over strategic gates that hold back savage adversaries whose eventual escape will initiate the end of the world. This image is tarnished,
however, as the plot is gradually rewritten to allow for the spiritual
seduction of the queen and her warrior women by the heterodoxy of
Antichrist. In a way this may seem to be occasioned by dramatic
necessity—prisoners must either defeat or suborn their guards if they are
to escape—but DiMarco sees in this anti-conversion the strains of antifeminism, just as he recognizes anti-Semitism in the legend's
association of Gog/Magog with the ten lost tribes of the Jews. Like
Romm and Guzman, he moves through a complex of texts, discovering
both false leads and direct contributions to a convergence of sacred and
secular tales. Once again, medieval geography has been construed to
accommodate the coincidences of literary traditions. DiMarco's detailed
analysis incorporates unstudied pictorial evidence from manuscripts and
early printed books.

The work that triggered DiMarco's inquiry comprises Iain
Higgins's: *Mandeville's Travels*, which has probably inspired as great a
range of reactions from scholars as any medieval work has done, is here
understood to be a text that both celebrates Asian diversity and tries to
bring it under some measure of control. Higgins approaches this text
with an understanding of its extremely complicated history of transmission and translation; he is also able to apply modern theories in the
history of ideas. Although he has reservations about oversimplification,
he poses that the medieval Christian world generally shared a sense of
community—an "imagined" common culture. In addition, its members
were psychologically capable of entertaining "imaginary" contacts with
other communities. Perhaps the most remarkable example of this
phenomenon is Sir John Mandeville, whom Higgins regards as the
product of an anonymous writer's imagination, but who, in any event,
is someone not unlike William of Rubruck standing barefooted in the
snow at Karakorum—a European capable of assuming the perspective

of a foreigner. The *Travels* is remarkable for locating virtue at the margins of the Earth, which is more than can be said for the treatises by the missionary friars of the mid-1200s. Indeed, not only are these far-flung people pious, they are rational: even heliolaters and pygmies are imagined as part of an intelligent, diverse humanity, implicitly reproving a Laodicean Europe.[34] Moreover, Higgins observes, a tolerant attitude toward foreign cultures did not require a traveler's experience but rather an imagination's vitality. Yet, he concludes, even universalism may be ethnocentric. The audience for this book was, in fact, the increasingly divided and isolated Latin Christendom of the fourteenth century. The *Mandeville*-author's unusual and anachronistic attention to Prester John emblematizes for Higgins the book's nostalgia for the eventual Christianization of the global community. Thus, the *Travels* is the product of a paradoxical imagination that is both generally tolerant and subtly superior.[35]

Medieval Europeans appear less given to ethnocentrism or paranoia in James Muldoon's analysis of several thirteenth-century texts that demonstrate the Latin Church's effort to formulate a practical approach to non-Christians. This approach can be documented in works that arise out of a context different from that of literary and polemical writings, and that enable Muldoon to argue, as Higgins does for *Mandeville's Travels*, that medieval Europeans believed all the world's inhabitants possessed reason and souls. In this analysis, Innocent IV's canon law commentary upholding the right of "infidels" to possess property and his two letters to the great khan (delivered by John of Plano Carpini in 1246) presuppose that rationality is common to all humans. The pope, while defending his own right to call a crusade, nevertheless argues that, according to natural law, people may own land and choose rulers regardless of their religious conviction; he also dispenses with threats of damnation and catalogues of miracles, making a logical—even empirical—appeal to the khan to convert to Christianity. Similarly, Muldoon believes, Plano Carpini's report to the pope emphasizes the Mongols' organization and discipline, subtly underscoring their acumen.[36] Muldoon offers a valuable lesson in historiography as well. He suggests that frequently-quoted observations of chroniclers and moralists, who often wrote with disputatious intent, do not necessarily reflect the attitudes of medieval Europeans generally. He cautions that the sum of the surviving manuscripts of any one work does not necessarily equal its influence: in the undemocratic world of ideas, popularity

does not always dictate policy. Muldoon thus challenges the
assumption that medieval churchmen—or the conquistadores of later
centuries, whose attendant missionaries were well-versed in Innocent's
commentary—considered the inhabitants of the Indies to be subhuman.

In an essay that assesses one cultural world's debt to another,
Marina Tolmacheva examines evidence of Ptolemy's geographical data
and theory, as well as his cartography, in three influential Arab works
of the ninth and tenth centuries (A.D.). Her study is a reminder of the
linguistic and technical sophistication that today's scholars may need in
order to discover solutions to problems in medieval studies.
Tolmacheva's concern grows out of a well-known conundrum: maps in
the so-called "Ptolemaic tradition" extend the east coast of Africa
significantly toward the Orient, often showing the Indian Ocean to be
an enclosed sea. These representations seem so distorted to the modern
eye that some historians of geography have maintained that Ptolemy
himself could not have been responsible for them. Tolmacheva traces
Ptolemy's legacy in early Arabic geographical writings, some of which
acknowledge a debt to him but, nevertheless, record latitude and
longitude coordinate data that vary greatly from his (and from each
other's). She shows that these discrepancies need not have been caused
by phenomena that have been advanced by scholars—that Arab
geographers had independent and more trustworthy sources of data, used
a different prime meridian as a basis for their other calculations, or
shared Ptolemy's difficulty in measuring longitude. Instead, she
contends, in a written tradition in which numbers were represented
orthographically by Arabic alphabetical characters, scribal error must
have been frequent and significant. Her careful comparison of medieval
data lends support to the hypothesis that Ptolemy was indeed interested
in describing unknown places and that he could have been at least partly
responsible for a cartographical tradition that departs radically from our
understanding of the east African and south Asian coastlines.

The Islamic world's contributions to intellectual history also
underlie Laurie Shepard's investigation of how the rediscovery of
Aristotle, via Arab channels and the translations of Michael Scot,
affected rhetoric during the first half of the thirteenth century at the
court of Frederick II of Hohenstaufen, one of medieval Europe's most
celebrated international arenas. In her analysis of selected imperial and
papal letters, Shepard notices similarities in style and intention—the
diction is ornamented, the purpose is to establish or to counter a legal

charge—but she also detects very different interpretations of causation in the world of human affairs. In excommunicating Frederick in 1227, for example, Gregory IX offered an historical event, the defeat of a Crusader army in the Holy Land, as a manifestation of God's clear disapproval of the emperor; in his defense, Frederick reinterpreted the same event, attributing the military fiasco to such particular circumstances as poor tactics. Shepard contends that this unusually mundane explanation is a conscious attempt to apply Aristotle's theory of apodictic (or scientific) demonstration, according to which a specific cause can be linked to a specific effect only when incontravertible proof can be advanced.[37] The world of contingencies found in letters composed at the imperial chancery, she argues, is very different from the world of moral absolutes evident in the epistolary style of the papal court (although Muldoon's study of Innocent IV's method of argumentation suggests that these worlds did not long follow totally separate orbits). Shepard thus helps to chart the origins of a new method of interpretation by means of which Latin Europe gradually discovered new ways of assessing the surrounding world.

Monika Otter's essay likewise concerns the appropriation of ideas and language. She investigates the rhetorical strategies used by historical writers in the medieval English tradition to describe and to justify the acquisition of territory in Britain by a series of heroic figures—Trojan, Saxon, and Norman. Beginning with Geoffrey of Monmouth's *Historia regum Britanniae* and including works in Middle English and Anglo-French, Otter examines how texts render land "gaainable"—a term that in her broad lexicon means arable, attractive, and available—and how they legitimize territorial possession. Her study thus recalls Muldoon's. Otter's argument reveals an intriguing circularity in her contention that each text's conqueror/hero, claiming land ultimately by putting it to cultivation, resembles each text's historian/writer, plowing through the fields of his predecessors, making furrows with his own quill, sowing ink. Geoffrey, who depicts Brutus as justifiably taking land away from giants whom the Trojans drive literally in the earth, himself appears to get some of his source material out of thin air, a maneuver that Otter considers to be a bold challenge rather than sly mendacity. In turn, Geoffrey becomes the giant on whose shoulders other historians, in medieval fashion, will stand indebted. So too the anonymous author of *Fouke le Fitz Waryn* is a squatter calling attention to his acquisition and redistribution of other poets' turf, and Laȝamon, fingering lovingly the leaves of his collected books, mirrors his own Brutus, in love with the land he beholds. In this sense, Otter imaginatively farms the plot of writers who are out after "gaainable" texts.

The two final essays describe what are perhaps the most otherworldly worlds in this volume, yet their subjects and their purposes could hardly be more dissimilar. Louise Vasvari finds in a literary landscape, which she calls the "carnivalesque," a deliberate inversion of the social order and a ludicrous atmosphere that are uncharacteristic of arcadian or utopian fantasy lands. These latter places enable audiences to escape from the moral weaknesses of the present into the landscape of a nostalgic past or a designed future. The fabulous geography of a work like *The Land of Cockaigne*, on the other hand, offers a province of material abundance in which the socially honored values of truth, moderation, chastity, and peace are lampooned—even ridiculed—under rules that award the laurel wreath to the most fallacious description of unbridled consumption, sex, and even violence. Vasvari echoes Ernst Curtius in recognizing the distinctiveness of "topsy-turvy literary genres" that present "the world upside-down," but she rejects his sober reading of this kind of expression as a "denunciation of the times" or as "age's criticism of youth," celebrating instead the carnivalesque's dimension of fun.[36] At the same time, her contention that verbal games form variations of an "antigenre" suggests the *Cockaigne*-world's subversion of medieval order by radical rhetoric. Unsurprisingly then, Vasvari, like Shepard, notices important shifts in language, observing that the rhetorical authority extended to lies and oxymorons in these medieval fantasies releases the signifier from the signified, creating a temporary arena of pure linguistic freedom and play.[39] In uncovering what might be called a carnivalization of language in some medieval works, Vasvari has landed at the textual antipodes of the pilgrimage accounts in Mary Campbell's study.

Finally, Peter Hawkins explores Dante, a geographical conservative in his prose writings, who, as a poet of cosmic fiction, audaciously established a terrestrial location for Purgatory and then condemned Ulysses to hell for having the boldness to approach it, who outmaneuvered the Apostle Paul by being caught up into heaven and electing to make his vision public. And yet, Dante was a poet whose geographical manipulations represent only one facet of his genius for innovation. Hawkins himself is innovative in his treatment of what is probably the most heavily annotated and analyzed poem in world literature. He departs, for example, from the scholarly mainstream that regards the famous Ulysses episode (*Inferno* 26) to be principally a demonstration of Dante's essential orthodoxy, by pointing out the potential trespass of the scene's very conception and by reading it in the context of Dante's later comparisons of himself to a navigator and to Jason (*Paradiso* 2 and 25). Hawkins moves from history and geography to linguistics and poetics, noting that in Dante's eyes verse could be as dangerous an occupation as ocean discovery. This poet sees himself not plowing land, like Laȝamon or Jason, but sailing the sea; and he cautions, in what seems a warning of bizarre arrogance, that only a few should dare to follow in the wake of his enterprise, as if reading were as perilous as setting forth westward to seek Cathay.

Hawkins's essay will also recall other territory covered in this volume. In contending that the Ulysses canto describes the triumph of pilgrim over explorer, Hawkins discusses the character and efficacy of religious travel, and reviews the reception of classical texts in Christian Europe. Dante's radical inventiveness prompts him to rewrite Virgil and Ovid—even to turn the world on its head (or, at least, to re-landscape Eden and to crown Mt. Purgatory with it). While some contributors to this collection conclude their studies noting a text's final ambiguity or paradox—Latin Europe, for example, is finally unable to contain Asia's exoticism or its own anxieties; the Carnival that everyone champions inevitably capitulates to Lent—Hawkins shows that Dante reaches the dearest metaphor of his imagination: home port. As Dante enters into the ultimate, unmediated experience of the Empyrean (and, simultaneously, the last lines of his *Commedia*), his vision dissolves in a flash of light when, as Egeria the pilgrim had so earnestly desired, the place at last becomes the event, space and time merge, and *saeculum* becomes unequivocal and univocal.

NOTES

1. "Nixon Sees Crew," *New York Times*, 25 July 1969, late city ed.: 1. It certainly was a great week for rhetoric. The previous Sunday, Richard Nixon placed what he called "the most historic telephone call ever made" to tell the astronauts on the moon that, as a result of their achievement, "the heavens have become a part of man's world" ("Men Walk on Moon," *New York Times*, 21 July 1969, late city ed.: 1).

2. Cartographers took their nomenclature from the popular letter *Mundus novus*, published around 1500, and attributed to Amerigo Vespucci; see Francesco Rosselli's world map, produced at Florence around 1507 (Kenneth Nebenzahl, *Atlas of Columbus and the Great Discoveries* [Chicago: Rand McNally, 1990], pp. 56-57 and plates 17B-17C). In this same year, the cosmographer Martin Waldseemüller used Vespucci's first name—rather than his book's title—to identify part of the unexpected hemisphere, but many years passed before "new world" disappeared from the chart. Some sixteenth-century maps labeled the lands "terra inventa," a locution that accords with Edmundo O'Gorman's intricate semantic argument against speaking of the "discovery" of the New World; see *The Invention of America* (Bloomington, Ind.: Indiana Univ. Press, 1961), first published in Spanish in 1958. Marcel Bataillon disputes O'Gorman's thesis in "The Idea of the Discovery of America Among the Spaniards of the Sixteenth Century," in *Spain in the Fifteenth Century, 1369-1516: Essays and Extracts by Historians of Spain*, ed. [John] Roger [Loxdale] Highfield, trans. Frances M. López-Morillas (London: Macmillan, 1972), pp. 426-64.

3. Two excellent studies of the semantic range of "world" and its literary applications, are C. S. Lewis's *Studies in Words*, 2nd ed. (Cambridge, Eng.: Cambridge Univ. Press, 1967), pp. 214-68; and Donald R. Howard's *The Three Temptations: Medieval Man in Search of the World* (Princeton: Princeton Univ. Press, 1966), esp. pp. 257-301.

4. The subject of many investigations, this chapter of world history has been intelligently rehearsed recently by J. R. S. Phillips, *The Medieval Expansion of Europe* (Oxford: Oxford Univ. Press, 1988), pp. 59-101; Phillips offers an extensive bibliography. Reports and letters by many of the Franciscans involved in this enterprise are available in the careful Latin critical edition of Anastasius van den Wyngaert, *Itinera et Relationes Fratrum Minorum Saeculi XIII et XIV*, vol. 1 of *Sinica Franciscana* (Quaracchi-Florence: Collegium S. Bonaventurae, 1929). The best English translation of most of these accounts is "by a nun of Stanbrook Abbey" in Christopher Dawson, ed., *The Mongol Mission* (London: Sheed and Ward, 1955), a work republished as *Mission to Asia* (New York: Harper and Row, 1966), and as Medieval Academy Reprints for Teaching 8 (Toronto: Univ. of Toronto Press, 1980).

5. Wyngaert, *Itinera et Relationes,* p. 365 ("in mundo alio . . . cum desiderio nova de mundo fidelium audiendi"); Dawson, *The Mongol Mission,* p. 232. For brief appraisals of the letter and its writer, see Wyngaert, pp. 359-64 and Dawson, pp. 222-23.

6. Henry Yule, ed. and trans., *Mirabilia Descripta: The Wonders of the East*, Hakluyt Society, 1st ser. 31 (London, 1863; repr. New York: Franklin, 1970), p. 37. Jordan sees marvels everywhere he looks—and his looks went everywhere—as may be inferred from the title of his book, which Yule dates to around 1330.

7. These words are themselves taken out of context from a thirteenth-century prose work based on the treatise *De anima* by Hugh of St. Victor: they translate "in saecula saeculorum," a locution for eternity that the *Book of Common Prayer* still occasionally renders "world without end"; see *Sawles Warde*, ed. R. M. Wilson, Leeds School of English Language Texts and Monographs 3 (Leeds: Titus Wilson, 1938), p. 36 (Royal MS 17. A. 27, line 344).

8. Wyngaert, *Itinera et Relationes,* p. 171; Dawson, *The Mongol Mission,* p. 93.

9. Although William's letter to King Louis probably reached a limited number of people and survives in only a few manuscript copies, he was befriended by Roger Bacon, who credits William for contributing information about the East to his own, influential *Opus maius* (1268); see John Henry Bridges, ed., *The* Opus Majus *of Roger Bacon,* 2 vols. with supplement (Oxford, 1897; repr. Frankfurt: Minerva, 1964), 1:305.

10. Wyngaert, *Itinera et Relationes,* pp. 230, 295, 231 and 271, 218-19, 199, 211, 173; Dawson, *The Mongol Mission,* pp. 139, 192, 140 and 171-72, 131-32, 116, 125; the final quotation is my own translation.

11. Wyngaert, *Itinera et Relationes,* pp. 245, 204 and 316, 293-97; Dawson, *The Mongol Mission,* pp. 150, 120 and 210, 189-94.

12. The language of this sentence echoes the title of Mary B. Campbell's provocative study, *The Witness and the Other World: Exotic European Travel Writing, 400-1600* (Ithaca: Cornell Univ. Press, 1988), in which William's account is discussed on pp. 112-21. One of the themes of her book, the traveler's movement in space and time, also figures in her study of early medieval pilgrimage accounts in this volume on pp. 3-15. Gregory G. Guzman, in his essay here (pp. 31-68), analyzes allegations by William and several other thirteenth-century European clerics with first-hand knowledge of Asia that the Mongols practiced cannibalism.

13. The complicated relations of medieval Christians, Muslims, and Jews in the Holy Land are expertly detailed by Steven Runciman, *A History of the Crusades,* 3 vols. (Cambridge, Eng.: Cambridge Univ. Press, 1951-54); and Hans Eberhard Mayer, *The Crusades,* 2nd ed. (Oxford:

Oxford Univ. Press, 1988). James Muldoon, in an essay in this collection (pp. 115-24), examines Pope Innocent IV's legal and diplomatic approaches toward non-Christian non-Europeans during the 1240s.

14. A medieval cleric could, of course, demonstrate intellectual sophistication by "borrowing" from a written authority, which, in any event, often took precedence over an individual's experience. Thus, the copying method employed by the author of *Mandeville's Travels* does not necessarily undermine the credibility of his claims; they may be disputed on other, better grounds. For a general discussion of the *Travels* and its dissemination, see Josephine Waters Bennett, *The Rediscovery of Sir John Mandeville*, The Modern Language Association of America Monograph Series 19 (New York: MLA, 1954). Iain Higgins studies the book's fascination with diversity and its portrayal of Asia (he also cites many other relevant sources) in his article on pp. 91-114.

15. Donald Lach traces this growing interest in *The Century of Discovery*, vol. 1 (in two books) of *Asia in the Making of Europe* (Chicago: Univ. of Chicago Press, 1965), pp. 20-86. Lach concludes that "the European image of Asia" was "compounded of a mixture of fact, theory, and myth," but that this view of "an imaginary East" was no longer possible after 1500 (pp. 85, xvi).

16. See Valerie I. J. Flint, ed., "Honorius Augustodunensis. *Imago mundi*," *Archives d'Histoire Doctrinale et Littéraire du Moyen Age* 57 (1982): 7-153; Albert Derolez, ed., *Liber floridus colloquium* (Ghent: Story-Scientia, 1973); Lynn Thorndike, ed. and trans., *The Sphere of Sacrobosco and Its Commentators* (Chicago: Univ. of Chicago Press, 1949); and Edmond Buron, *Imago mundi, de Pierre d'Ailly . . . texte latin et traduction française des quatre traites cosmographiques de d'Ailly et des notes marginales de Christophe Colombe*, 3 vols. (Paris: Maisonneuve frères, 1930). The *Imago mundi* manuscript tally is my own. Although Honorius may have revised his book—Flint speaks of three "editions" of the work—he almost certainly made no significant changes in the section on geography (Book 1).

17. See Vsevolod Slessarev, *Prester John: The Letter and the Legend* (Minneapolis: Univ. of Minnesota Press, 1959); see also the opinionated historical and historiographical study by L. N. Gumilev, originally published in Russian in 1970, *Searches for an Imaginary Kingdom: The Legend and Kingdom of Prester John*, trans. R. E. F. Smith (Cambridge, Eng.: Cambridge Univ. Press, 1987). Another complicated text in the epistolary science tradition, Alexander's famous (and pseudonymous) letter to Aristotle, is examined by James Romm in his essay on pp. 16-30 in this volume.

18. The opinion was C. Raymond Beazley's, in *The Dawn of Modern Geography*, 3 vols. (London, 1897-1903; repr. New York: Peter Smith, 1949), 3:528. One of the most significant recent events in geo- and cartographical research is the publication of *Cartography in Prehistoric, Ancient, and Medieval Europe and the Mediterranean,* ed. J. B. Harley and David Woodward, vol. 1 of *The History of Cartography* (Chicago: Univ. of Chicago Press, 1987). In his essay, "Medieval *Mappaemundi*," Woodward provides a historical review of medieval maps and their Classical antecedents (pp. 286-370). Professor Woodward's distinguished presentation ("Cartography and the Abstraction of the World Picture") at the Lehman College conference, described in the Preface, was based on material that will appear in future volumes of the *History* series. The connection between Ptolemy and early Arab geography is studied by Marina Tolmacheva here on pp. 125-41.

19. See Jörg-Geerd Arentzen, *Imago Mundi Cartographica: Studien zur Bildlichkeit mittelalterlicher Welt- und Ökumenekarten unter besonderer Berücksichtigung des Zusammenwirkens von Text und Bild*, Münstersche Mittelalter-Schriften 53 (Munich: Fink, 1984); and Anna Dorothee von den Brincken, "Mappa mundi und Chronographia," *Deutsches Archiv für die Erforschung des Mittelalters* 24 (1968): 118-86.

20. The T-O map in Plate 1, drawn around 1440, is found on fol. 3v of MS Cod. theol. et phil. 2° 100 (Württembergische Landesbibliothek, Stuttgart); in the fifteenth-century the manuscript belonged to the library of the Benedictine foundation at Komburg. The map is contemporaneous with the text that follows it—a copy of Honorius Augustodunensis's *Imago mundi* (see above, n. 16); most of the map's place names are also found in Honorius's text. As in many medieval *mappaemundi*, Jerusalem is at the center of this map, but the orientation of the scheme is to the south, which is more typical of Arabic cartography. An inscription at the top describes the "Antarctic Pole," which is uninhabitable on account of its great heat. A circular Red Sea is located in Africa (in the upper-right-hand quadrant), and a tubular Mediterranean extends through most of Europe from Jerusalem to its terminus, which is marked Venice. Gog and Magog are noted to be enclosed in the Caspian Mountains at the lower left. The written text, added to the map in a later hand, contains excerpts from an anti-Islamic treatise written in 1456 by Pope Calixtus III (1455-1458), and here attributed to his predecessor, Nicholas V (1447-1455).

Plate 2 shows detail (approximately one quarter) of a portolan chart drawn by Peter Roselli at Majorca in 1466; it is now at the James Ford Bell Library of the University of Minnesota. The coastlines of the eastern Mediterranean and the Black Sea are easily distinguished, as are islands in the Aegean and a rather flattened Cyprus. The many names of coastal towns accentuate the dividing line between water and land. The round building at the right-hand edge of the map marks Jerusalem (it is labeled "Sant sapulcra"); below it is a rather indistinct Mt. Sinai, to the left of which is Cairo, designated by a multi-towered fortress flying a flag with three crescent moons. Below this great city, a vividly scarlet Red Sea appears (incorrectly) to be dotted with major ports. At the top left are more fortresses, marking cities along the banks of the Danube, which empties into the Black Sea. For many medieval geographers, this river served as the border between the known world and the dimly-understood northern (Scythian) regions, inhabited by monstrous humans and other perils.

I am greatly indebted to the Württembergische Landesbibliothek and the James Ford Bell Library of the University of Minnesota for permission to print these maps.

21. Augustine's phrase is in *City of God*, 16.8; see the standard work by John Block Friedman, *The Monstrous Races in Medieval Art and Thought* (Cambridge, Mass.: Harvard Univ. Press, 1981), esp. pp. 77-79. Professor Friedman's intriguing lecture at Lehman's conference, "The Iconography of Medieval World Maps," was based on his ongoing, detailed examination of Western cosmography and teratology. Vincent DiMarco, in his essay in this volume, traces apocalyptic elements that enter the Amazon legend during the later Middle Ages, and he examines pictorial representations that associate the warrior women with Gog and Magog (see pp. 69-90).

22. Rudolf Wittkower, "Marvels of the East: A Study in the History of Monsters," in *Allegory and the Migration of Symbols* (New York: Thames and Hudson, 1987); this article was first published in 1942. See also Friedman, *Monstrous Races* (above, n. 20); Beryl Rowland, *Animals with Human Faces: A Guide to Animal Symbolism* (Knoxville: Univ. of Tennessee Press, 1973); several articles in Gabriel Bianciotto and Michel Salvat, ed., *Epopée animale, fable, fabliau*, Actes du IVe Colloque de la Société Internationale Renardienne, Publications de l'Université de Rouen 83 (Paris: Presses Universitaires de France, 1984); and Jan Ziolkowski, "Avatars of Ugliness in Medieval Literature," *Modern Language Review* 79 (1984): 1-20.

23. John G. Demaray believes that Dante's fictive world explicates "key 'words' in God's Worldly Book" and that the poet "was deeply mindful of and influenced by the literature and lore of the long pilgrimage"; see *The Invention of Dante's* Commedia (New Haven: Yale Univ. Press, 1974), pp. 4, 47. On the image and motivations of *homo viator*, see Jonathan Sumption, *Pilgrimage: An Image of Mediaeval Religion* (London: Faber and Faber, 1975). In essays in this volume, Peter S. Hawkins elaborates on the world that Dante both inherited and

created (pp. 193-220; in this context, see esp. p. 215, n. 14), and Louise O. Vasvari reviews examples of the "carnivalesque" turning of the real world on its head for purposes different from those of utopian literature (pp. 178-92).

24. *The Structure of the Artistic Text*, trans. Ronald Vroon and Gail Vroon, Michigan Slavic Contributions 7 (Ann Arbor: Univ. of Michigan Press, 1977), p. 218. Monika Otter, in her essay on pp. 157-77, argues that descriptions, found in a variety of literary histories, of the acquisition by foreigners of arable land in Britain acquire particular resonance given their authors' appropriation of material.

25. See Woodward, "Medieval *Mappaemundi*," p. 306 (above, n. 18); and Jozef Ijsewijn and Jacques Paquet, ed., *The Universities in the Late Middle Ages*, Mediaevalia Lovaniensa, 1st ser. 6 (Louvain: Louvain Univ. Press, 1978), esp. Paquet, "Aspects de l'Université Médiévale," p. 4.

26. Derek W. Lomax, *The Reconquest of Spain* (London: Longman, 1978). The famous confluence of cultures at the court of Frederick II Hohenstaufen is the arena for Laurie Shepard's study of the effect that newly-recovered Aristotelian texts had on imperial epistolary style; see pp. 142-56 of this volume.

27. See Lynn Thorndike, *Medieval Technology and Social Change* (New York: Galaxy, 1966); David C. Lindberg, ed., *Science in the Middle Ages* (Chicago: Univ. of Chicago Press, 1978); Madeleine Pelner Cosman, "Machot's Medical-Musical World," in *Machot's World: Science and Art in the Fourteenth Century*, ed. M. P. Cosman (New York: New York Academy of Sciences, 1978); and Thomas Goldstein, *The Dawn of Modern Science: From the Arabs to Leonardo da Vinci* (Boston: Houghton Mifflin, 1980). Marina Tolmacheva's essay in this volume has already been mentioned (see above, n. 18).

28. *The Discarded Image* (Cambridge, Eng.: Cambridge Univ. Press, 1964), p. 20.

29. *The Adventurous Muse: The Poetics of American Fiction, 1789-1900* (New Haven: Yale Univ. Press, 1977), p. 6; the introduction and chapter one, "The Poetics of Adventure" (pp. 1-67), take up issues that relate to medieval thought.

30. Spengemann, *The Adventurous Muse*, p. 14. Speaking casually about "world-views" may betray the resilience and richness of another culture, especially when we do so, however subtly, to characterize an earlier age as homogeneous and therefore lackluster. We are convinced that we live in a "new world," but we are uncertain when it began. It is

tempting to inch its discovery closer to ourselves in time, relishing the idea that the complications of the universe have only recently dawned on people. Spengemann, whose subject is the influence of travel literature and the aesthetics of Romanticism on American literature, speaks of "the elegantly simple cosmology of the late Middle Ages" and "Columbus's elegantly simple view of the world" (pp. 6, 23).

31. John Noble Wilford, an experienced student of science and author of a book entitled *The Mapmakers*, simply propagated familiar poppycock by allowing his laudatory review of Harley and Woodward's landmark work on medieval cartography (see above, n. 18) to appear under the headline "When the Earth Was Flat" in *The New York Times Book Review* on 4 October 1987, p. 4.

32. John reports on a number of monsters (or "monstrous" behaviors); see Wyngaert, *Itinera et Relationes*, pp. 54-55, 60-63, 73-75 (and 111); Dawson, *The Mongol Mission*, pp. 20, 23-25, 30-31 (and 58).

33. R. W. Southern attributes Western Europe's disregard for the Islamic world over the course of four centuries (from 700 to 1100) to the "ignorance of a confined space." He argues further that Latin Christendom intellectually broke out of this confinement in the twelfth century, when creative minds turned their attention to the world around them, but these thinkers were themselves limited by an "ignorance of the triumphant imagination" and remained unable to appreciate Muslim culture. See *Western Views of Islam in the Middle Ages* (1962; repr. Cambridge, Mass.: Harvard Univ. Press, 1978), p. 14.

34. Higgins thus focuses attention on the more representative anthropological character of *Mandeville's Travels* and sounds a helpful counterpart to the common notion—echoed elsewhere in this volume—that the *Travels* is a collection of fanciful or mendacious stories, heavy on the monsters.

35. In a similar vein, Southern describes the "spirit of detachment" found in nineteenth-century European treatments of Islam, calling it "a product of superiority and of the conviction that there was nothing to fear" (*Western Views*, p. 4).

36. One might speculate, however, that repeated warnings by Franciscans of a renewed Mongol attack may have been meant to remind readers that liberal attitudes about land rights were not shared by the khan. On Plano Carpini's insistence that the Mongols intended to conquer the West, see Wyngaert, *Itinera et Relationes*, pp. 64, 84, 86, 93, 94, 95, 98-99, 101, 122; Dawson, *The Mongol Mission*, pp. 25, 38, 39, 43, 44, 45, 48, 50, 65. Wyngaert himself suggests that Plano Carpini was

trying to stimulate unity among the quarreling lords of Europe (p. 10). In addition, Innocent's rational presentation of the Faith to the khan and a general Mongol rejection of the papal offer—the Mongols were, after all, men of ultimatums—may explain why William of Rubruck, who summarized his mission in a plaintive sentence ("There we baptised in all six souls"), passionately appeals for a crusade against the Mongols (Wyngaert, pp. 244, 322-23; Dawson, pp. 150, 213-14). Intellectual rejection may hurt more than physical attack.

37. Shepard points out that apodictic demonstration is implicitly or explicitly taken up in many of Aristotle's works. In his recent biography, *Frederick II: A Medieval Emperor* (London: Allen Lane, 1988), David Abulafia paraphrases the "Prooemium" to the *Constitutions of Melfi*, an important text for Shepard's argument, noting hesitantly that in it "we perhaps see the influence of Aristotelian ideas," yet he goes on to say that Frederick's optimistic view of government cannot have its source "in a close reading of Aristotelian texts (Aristotle's political and ethical works not yet being available in the west)" (pp. 205, 207). Shepard, on the other hand, maintains that Frederick's rhetoric could certainly have derived its character from already translated texts of natural philosophy. Abulafia's index does not even contain an entry for Aristotle.

38. See *European Literature and the Latin Middle Ages*, trans. Willard R. Trask, Bollingen Series 36 (New York, 1953; repr. Princeton: Princeton Univ. Press, 1973); Curtius describes a literary topos where "the whole world is topsy-turvy," where "the world upside down" is created in part by "stringing together *impossibilia*" (p. 96). His dour perspective colors the entire discussion on pp. 94-98.

39. One might argue, however, that the relationship between signifier and signified is never stronger than when absurdity seeks to unbind them: a marzipan roof implicitly reminds a peasant of his empty stomach and leaky thatch.

Discovering New Worlds

"The Object of One's Gaze":
Landscape, Writing, and
Early Medieval Pilgrimage

Mary B. Campbell

"So gaze on Holy Jerusalem and view this Sion. For it stands
for us as an allegory of Paradise."
—Fretellus, *Liber locorum sanctorum*

Geographical discovery is an ambiguous concept, at home largely in a
nest of other concepts and practices unknown to the writers and travelers
of the European Middle Ages and only barely accessible to the
"discoverers" of the Age of Discovery itself. The most famous
Discovery of them all, the Discovery of America, has been the subject
of intense debate among historians and geographers: *Who* discovered
America? Who discovered what we now think of as *America*? For
whom was it a *discovery*?[1] As Wilcomb Washburn put the question in
1962, does "discovery" mean "uncovering land that was 'hidden' to us,
but known to exist? Or does it mean reaching, by calculation or by
chance, lands never known before?"[2] In its usual, quasi-technical sense,
the word refers to a public event, and postulates a community *to* which
a place has been "discovered." For the Carib Indians, Columbus's
landfall on San Salvador was no discovery.

In an almost purely rhetorical aside, Washburn remarks, "Indeed,
one might say that discovery is a personal accomplishment. Nothing
can be discovered for us; we must discover it. . . ."[3] His remark begs

Mary B. Campbell is Assistant Professor of English and American Literature
at Brandeis University (see Notes on Contributors, p. 221).

3

the question he is trying to consider, and Washburn leaves it behind. But from a literary point of view it is suggestive: we identify moments of discovery in travel accounts since Columbus by a certain rhetoric— by a subject-centered burst of landscape description in the explorer's text. It is to such textual traces of discovery that Keats alludes when he tells us that, on first looking into Chapman's Homer, he felt "like stout Cortez when with eagle eyes / He star'd at the Pacific."

Discovery itself is not my topic here; I am concerned with the rhetorical practice of landscape description in accounts of exotic travel. Looking over the medieval corpus, we find neither traces of discovery nor even a flourishing tradition of the sort of *topographia* that later travelers would employ to signal or represent discovery. These absences seem to me to be connected. The *topographia* of medieval exotic travel writing is concerned with matters other than the "personal accomplishment" of visual perception, and visual perception itself is not connected to ideas of domination or possession. "I came, I saw, I conquered" puts looking/seeing at the center of the imperial gesture. When, in the thirteenth century, William of Rubruck effectively "discovers" the Caspian Sea (Isidore had authoritatively proclaimed it not a sea but a gulf of the ocean), he does not offer a view of it but merely says that "it takes four days to go around," and promises to "tell you of it later." When he gets around to telling, even this most proto-modern of medieval travelers simply locates it in reference to surrounding mountain chains and a river.[4] Two centuries later we discover at last the language of discovery, in the *Letter to Sanchez* of Christopher Columbus. Cuba comes to us as the Admiral's experience of trees "flourishing and adorned as they usually are in Spain in the month of May. . . . The nightingale chattered, and other sparrows . . . in the month of November where I myself went strolling among them."[5]

I want to take a brief look in this essay at some of Christian Europe's earliest exotic travel accounts, to examine and correct what for many readers is an impression of scenic emptiness. While these accounts offer only the barest minimum of vista, and seem oblivious to even a personalized notion of "discovery," they do in fact present landscapes—in passages that obscure the immediate object of the writer's attention no more and no less than does the vivid mimesis of the awestruck mountain climber in the modern world. To see this we might begin by considering what the word "landscape" encompasses in its largest sense.

The project of landscape—both of perceiving it and representing it—has a psychological dimension that must not be overlooked if we are to see anything but absences in early medieval travel literature. It is a dimension illustrated more clearly by accounts of pilgrimage outside Europe than by any other subgenre of the literature. Travel to the Holy Land is travel into the blatantly sublime, and for the European pilgrim it is exotic travel, too. Thus these early accounts negotiate with especially clear intensity the conditions of desire and alienation that frame our perception of the space around us.

The exotic landscape is simply the hyperbole of landscape in general—a word defined in the OED as "the object of one's gaze." From Rockefeller Center to the Grand Canyon to the Kasbah, when I take up my pen to describe my surroundings I describe what is outside and other than myself—the surround by means of which developmental psychologists define the process of individuation. Compared to my original assumption that the whole world is part of me, any surround seen as separate from me—as the object rather than the subject of my senses—is alien, other. My own apartment illustrates me, perhaps, but that is as much of geographical space as I can easily subdue to my narcissism. The landscapes of the most nostalgic genres of imaginative literature, pastoral and romance, have tended to recreate the female body from whom our original alienation was the most traumatic (but with whom that alienation was normally resolved in love). Nature is domesticated by the figure of the Lady or the Mother, and populated by the female spirits of trees and waters.[6]

For the actual traveler in truly alien territory the drama of alienation is palpably renewed, and domestication is trickier. For one thing, the generic appeal of the travel account lies partly in the *frisson* of alienation: we read for wonders and absurdities, for a comfortably vicarious experience of *estrangement*. I need scarcely point out that in this the modern reader is no different from the medieval consumer of *Wonders of the East* or *Mandeville's Travels*, or the earlier Greek devourers of the fabulous *Indika* of Ktesias.

But most early medieval travel literature was pilgrimage literature (as indeed most nonofficial distant travel was pilgrimage). A certain sobriety is bound to be part of the decorum of the literature, while the writer's impulse, as traveler, to domesticate is complicated by the hierarchical difference in status between Home and the Holy Land. ("For it stands for us as an allegory of Paradise.") This particular exotic landscape ought not be rendered grotesque, and would not be overtly domesticated until Blake's astonishing *Jerusalem* turned it, by Romantic fiat, into the English Midlands.

With these problems of genre and decorum in mind, let me give a brief sketch of what the pilgrim writers did with their material in a general way. I will finish with some closeups of actual passages of *topographia*, which by then we should be able to see as containing more than the absence of the picturesque.

Considering the relative sizes of figure and landscape in most medieval painting and calendar illustration, it is an easy guess that the medieval travel writer will be more concerned with the divine and human than with the natural or ecological. Places are almost always "places where" someone once did or said something; geography tends to be history; description then comes in the form of narration. Where the historical human figure is absent, human artifacts take their places and descriptions of communal rituals of devotion take the place of historical anecdote. Sacred history and a limited sort of ethnography provide the matter of description, despite the fact that what the traveler is traveling *in* is a landscape and what he is traveling between are places.

The sensuous impression of a place is particularly avoided. Palestine has little significant present tense, and the significance of its past tense is overwhelming—we might say blinding. Place description, *ekphrasis* in general, is a matter of present tenses, even if it is the imaginary and data-less present tense of formulaic epithets. Therefore we tend not to *see* place description in the tissue of anecdote and scriptural quotation that constitutes these pilgrimage accounts.

It is a cliché that soldiers overseas like to look at the moon because their lovers back home can see the same moon: one feature of the alien landscape is not alien, one feature of home is still present in the new surround and shared with those who are distant. Scripture provides this mediating function for the medieval writer on Palestine. When a place is located or defined by anecdote, that anecdote is usually familiar to the Christian reader from the Bible (or apocrypha); often it is quoted directly. This maneuver at one stroke domesticates the place thus "described" *and* provides the thrill of strangeness: the pilgrim writer can actually say "I am here"—here in that place purely heard of or meditated on till now, here in the pages of a Book. Tired of describing Sinai and unable to remember "so many details," Egeria stops, advising her reader to look them up "in the holy books of Moses, [where] she will perceive, carefully written, all that was *done there*" (emphasis added).[7]

I want to concentrate on sizable passages from three works in particular: the letter of Jerome's disciple Paula to Marcella, Egeria's *Peregrinatio* (both written in the late fourth century), and Adamnan's account of Arculf's pilgrimage (written in the late seventh century). All are Latin accounts by devout and educated members of their respective elites—a Roman aristocrat, a (probably) Gallician nun with imperial connections,[8] a Merovingian bishop, and the famous abbot of Iona. I will quote and comment on them in chronological order, as a shift is observable within the fixed scheme of Holy Land *topographia*—a shift in the direction of a Palestinian present tense. But, as we will see, it is a subtle shift. The present tense of Adamnan is still a *memorial* present; it focuses on ruins, monuments, and miraculous repetitions of the sacred past.

Here is Paula writing to Marcella, whose arrival in Palestine she is eagerly awaiting:

> VII: We shall go to Nazareth, and, according to the interpretation of its name, shall behold the flower of Galilee. Not far from thence will be seen Cana, wherein the waters were turned into wine. We shall go on to [Mt. Tabor], and shall see the tabernacles of the Savior, not, as Peter would have built them, with Moses and Elias, but with the Father and the Holy Spirit. Thence we shall come to the Sea of Gennesareth, and shall see the five and four thousand men in the desert fed with five and seven loaves. . . . We shall also see Capharnaum, that familiar witness of the miracles of our Lord.[9]

Most of the descriptive passages in Paula's letter are in the future tense, many in the interrogative mode ("when shall we behold . . . ?"). This is partly due to the fact that she is writing a letter of friendship, trying to include her interlocutor in the text. But it is suitable to her express decorum, too: about the grotto of Bethlehem she says, "That manger, wherein the babe wailed, is better honored by silence than by imperfect speech." Rather than itemize its features, she goes on to say (again in the interrogative) what is missing: "Where are spacious porticoes? Where are gilded ceilings?"[10] The only feature offered in the indicative is the long-vanished tableau of the Nativity, which we are invited to reimagine: "Behold, in this little nook of the earth the Founder of the heavens was born; here He was wrapped in swaddling clothes, beheld by the shepherds, shown by the star, adored by the wise men."[11]

As in the paragraph about Galilee, the visualizable details are iconographic epitomes of sacred history. The landscape of Palestine has simply been replaced by the events of the gospel. Paula is overwhelmed by her topic and by the earlier and sacred books for which this landscape was the *mis-en-scène*.

In a peculiar instance of the return of the repressed, this replacement of *topographia* by sacred *historia* is reversed when it comes to visual representation. According to E. D. Hunt, an iconography of biblical episodes had developed by the sixth century in which the episodes are represented, "not in any idealized portrayal of a scene contemporary with the episodes themselves, but *as they actually appeared to the early pilgrims*." He notes as the "most familiar instance . . . the *ampullae* in which sixth-century pilgrims carried back their holy oil to the West from Jerusalem, where the centre-piece of the portrayals of the Nativity, Crucifixion, and Resurrection is in each case the appropriate contemporary memorial—the 'aedicules' over the cave in Bethlehem and over the Tomb on Golgotha, and the actual wooden relic of the cross."[12] Such souvenirs, however, were themselves an aid to remembrance: they would function for their original owners to catalyze memories of their Holy Land experiences of remembering.

Egeria's *peregrinatio* takes a less evasive approach than Paula's letter. The only extant manuscript is a long fragment, opening in the middle of a paragraph about her party's approach to Mt. Sinai across a long flat valley. She goes on:

> This valley is certainly vast, extending to the mountain of God. As far as we could judge with our eyes and as the guides told us, it is around sixteen miles long; and they said it is four miles wide. We had to cross this valley in order to be able to climb the mountains. This is the vast and very flat valley where the children of Israel tarried during those days when the holy man Moses climbed the mountain of God; and he was there for forty days and forty nights. This is also the valley where the calf was made, and to this day its location is shown, for a large stone set there stands on the very spot. Furthermore, at the head of this same valley is the place where God spoke twice from the burning bush to the holy man Moses as he was grazing his father-in-law's flocks.[13]

Egeria has Paula's custom of providing anecdotal rather than topographical detail, but she does offer a minimum visual outline, on which she in fact expands somewhat in the following paragraphs. Most of her expansion takes the form of recapitulation or even pure repetition, but she does indicate the way in which the "mountain of God" dominates the others on the flanks which, paradoxically, hide it. She considers this topographic fact a miracle, and the miracle is offered as proof of the mountain's identity as Sinai. The attributes she points to are of extremity, and she usually points to them in superlatives, often in abstract value judgements ("This place is very beautiful"). She tells us that the plain is "ingens et planissima" three times in the first two paragraphs. What we get, then, are the physical details most suitable to the familiar events of which this landscape was the scene—details which express the hugeness and importance of those events. Topography here is not invisible background, as in Paula, but mirror. God would not have spoken to Moses on a foothill.

For both women, the surround is of supreme importance. But neither considers herself to be in a foreign country interesting in part by reason of its visible foreignness. It is not Palestine but the Holy Land they write of, and even the Holy Land is a witness to something else. Paula's phrase for Capharnaum—"that familiar witness of the miracles of our Lord"—pinpoints the object of these gazes—the vanished past, what Eliade calls *illud tempus* or mythic time, the time from which our (historical) time is separated.

This vanished or invisible past will remain the object of the traveler's attention when secular travel begins to be written up, from the time of the First Crusade. Myth, legend, long-remembered prodigy will fill the pages not devoted to contemporary chronicle, and contemporary events themselves will often be seen as fulfillments of scriptural prophecy. The wars and feats of Alexander and Prester John will take over when the traveler moves beyond the borders of scriptural territory. At long last (in the eighteenth century), the focus of awe will become the land itself; the sublimity of mountains will replace the sublimity of the God who spoke from them or the conqueror who passed across them, when the "real" sources of sublimity have become a matter of guess or invention. The eighteenth-century admirer of a mountain admires his own capacity for impression, describes his linguistic mastery of it, worships his own "human" spirit, conquers his own experience. The covert object of *his* description—himself—is as apparently absent as the Christian pilgrim's object. (Wordsworth comments brilliantly on this by climaxing his self-describing poetic account of the French Alps, book six of *The Prelude*, with the absence of the Simplon Pass: the Jerusalem of this secular traveler's Holy Land.)

Arculf provides Adamnan with more copious physical detail than we get from the firsthand accounts of Paula and Egeria. Here is a little piece of humanized landscape on top of the Mount of Olives:

> On all Mt. Olivet no place appears to be higher than that from which the Lord is said to have ascended to heaven. A great round church stands there, which has within its circuit three arched porticoes roofed in over. Now of this round church the central area lies wide open to heaven under the clear air without roof or vaulting, and in its eastern portion an altar is erected which is sheltered by a narrow covering. The reason the central area has no vaulting placed over it is this: so that, from the place where the divine feet rested for the last time when the Lord was raised up to heaven in a cloud, there should always be an open passage leading to the ethereal regions for the eyes of those who pray there. Because, when this basilica . . . was being built, the place of the Lord's footprints . . . could not be incorporated in a pavement with the rest of the floor. For the ground (unwont to bear anything human) would reject whatever was laid upon it, casting the marble into the faces of those who were laying it. Nay more, so lasting is the proof that the dust was trodden by God that the imprints of the feet are visible; and, though crowds of the faithful daily plunder the earth trodden by the Lord, still the spot suffers no perceptible damage, and the ground goes on keeping the semblance . . . of footprints.[14]

Though the footprints were there in her time, Egeria says only of Mt. Olivet that this is the mountain from which the Lord ascended and that the church on the site is "very beautiful." She reports no miracles and pays no attention to architecture. But the terminus of Adamnan's description is the concrete representation of those same footprints Egeria and Paula inscribe in their accounts by means of biblical epitome and imagined tableau. Adamnan goes on to describe the pilgrims' habit of taking away particles of the dust in which the footprints lie, and that description necessitates a few more details about the physical site. The chapter on Olivet ends with the account of a yearly miracle on the day of the Ascension, and the optical illusion of a mountain on fire created by the lamps ritually lighted there behind glass shutters on that day. The narrative of miracle and ritual motivates and takes over from *descriptio*, and both miracle and ritual memorialize the event of which these footprints are the "witness."

The landscape once displaced by memory and imagination of event is now fetishized and fragmented into dust—stolen, hoarded, maybe even sold. Where Paula had stood on a holy site and "remembered," Arculf stands and touches. It is not really that he sees and reports more landscape but that he responds to the more literal tableaux and memorials erected since the time of Egeria and Paula. The Holy Land has become, so to speak, more of a zoo and less of a wildlife preserve. Less of the ineffable is left to the pilgrim's imagination. Indeed, a little less of the actual Palestine is left: an increasing reification of its sites has concentrated attention on its actual matter (earth from the Holy Land was considered a potent relic), even as the resident holy men of earlier days have tended to give place to their own fetishized remains.[15]

This process had in fact begun even before the time of Paula's and Egeria's visits, with the monumentalizing campaign of Constantine in the early fourth century. According to Eusebius's account of the building of a church on the site of the Resurrection, Constantine, "being inspired with holy zeal . . . issued orders that, having dug up the soil to a considerable depth, they should transport to a far-distant spot the actual ground, earth and all, inasmuch as it had been polluted by the defilements of demon worship."[16] The process is so far advanced as to have turned a corner into sympathetic magic by the time the "Piacenza Pilgrim" (c. 570) reports this of another set of Christ's footprints, on the stone "witness box" in the Praetorium, where he was tried by Pilate: "From this stone where he stood come many blessings. People take 'measures' from the footprints, and wear them for their various diseases, and they are cured."[17]

With soil so sacred and so defiled, and sites so transcendently referential, it is small wonder that our texts avoid the business of vistas. Palestine dissolves under the gaze of these "inspired" travelers into fetishized matter or spiritual hallucination. The landscape they offer us is as nostalgic and desirable as any landscape of romance, any picturesque nineteenth-century evocation of Roman ruins, any American tourist's account of a trip to the mother country. Any landscape both alien and longed-for recapitulates the first we lost and, in so doing, learned to love. Description of it rarely renders physical space transparently or innocently. The difference between the vivid picturesque of modern travel writing and the invisible sublime of the pilgrims lies in the writer's sense of what his environment stands in for, what it can return to her, what she has been divided from.

The pilgrim texts suggest above all a *temporal* alienation, a sense of being cut off from biblical *time*. Paula wonders "when will that day come, when we shall be able . . . to behold Amos the prophet even now lamenting on his rock with his shepherd's bugle-horn?"[18] The moods and tenses of her *verbs* are what matter here, not the preeminent nouns and adjectives of the picturesque. From a writing desk in Palestine, Paula evokes a past more vivid than the literal surround of her present; she imagines this past in the future tense—a future she describes as "even now." In this extremely complex perceptual present, Amos *is* the "object of [her] gaze." When she delivers her details in the interrogative future, she reflects the apocalyptic hopes of an era which expected the Second Coming to take place in this landscape.[19] Adamnan, with his perpetual footprints, is simpler and sadder: *his* present tense maintains an unerasable past which, though visible, appears to be over.

The vast landscapes in which medieval Holy Land pilgrimage was conducted grew more and more restricted in the *itineraria*, as the distance in time increased between the events of Christ's lifetime and the pilgrim's historical moment. An emphasis on ruins and monumentalia went hand in hand with an increasingly systematized labeling and linking of the holy places, and the eventual attachment to them of specific indulgences for the pilgrim who visited them. The Holy Land became increasingly a pointillistic collection of officially administered sites, which clustered ever closer together as new sites were identified and old ones conveniently relocated. Place description becomes more and more detailed in regard to these highly charged sites, while the spaces between clusters drop almost out of view. Significant travel can be measured in paces:

> As we went down from the choir, on the left of the stairs by which we went down is one wall of a well (and the other is joined to the choir-screen): over this well the star stood which led the Magi from the east. From the well to the place where our Lord was born is one-and-a-half paces. Then from this place, where it pleased our Lord to be born, to the Manger

is three paces. And there are twelve steps by which we went down to the Manger. [. . .] When I had done all this and measured everything I was happier than ever before.[20]

In this eighth-century text we get an eerie verbal prefiguring of modern snapshot *itineraria*, similarly keyed to prescribed (and usually urban) sites, which similarly stand in for historical events and times that feel somehow more "real" than the unphotographed surround. But the eighteenth century has left its mark on the modern tourist, the gaze of whose camera is not focused on the after all rather frequently photographed pigeons of St. Mark's, but on the domestic human figures of the wife and kids. Here we are in front of Rheims Cathedral. Here we are at the Tower of London. Here we are on Calvary. Such photographs testify to the grim possibility that what *we* feel divided from is human history, and ourselves.

NOTES

1. The classic text on these questions is Edmundo O'Gorman, *The Invention of America* (Bloomington, Ind.: Indiana Univ. Press, 1961).

2. "The Meaning of 'Discovery' in the 15th and 16th Centuries," *American Historical Review* 68 (1962): 12.

3. Washburn, "The Meaning of 'Discovery'," p. 12.

4. William of Rubruck, "The Journey of William of Rubruck," trans. "a nun of Stanbrook Abbey," in *Mission to Asia*, ed. Christopher Dawson, Medieval Academy Reprints for Teaching 8 (Toronto: Univ. of Toronto Press, 1980), p. 116. This book was first published under the title *The Mongol Mission* (London: Sheed and Ward, 1955), and was originally reprinted as *Mission to Asia* in 1966 (New York: Harper and Row).

5. Christopher Columbus, *Epistola de insulis nuper inventis* (Rome: S. Plannck, after April, 1493).

6. On Nature and the female in classical and vernacular European literature, see Carolyn Merchant, *The Death of Nature: Women, Ecology and the Scientific Revolution* (San Francisco: Harper and Row, 1980).

7. Egeria, *Itinerarium Egeriae*, ed. E. Franceschini and R. Weber, Corpus Christianorum, Series Latina 175 (Turnhout: Brepols, 1953), 5.8. The translation is from George Gingras, *Egeria: Diary of a Pilgrimage*, Ancient Christian Writers: The Works of the Fathers in Translation 38 (New York: Newman Press, 1970), p. 57.

8. But see the informed opinion of Hagith S. Sivan in her recent article, "Holy Land Pilgrimage and Western Audiences: Some Reflections on Egeria and Her Circle," *Classical Quarterly* 38[2] (1988): 528-35.

9. "Ibimus ad Nazareth et iuxta interpretationem nominis eius 'florem' uidebimus Galilaeae. Haud procul inde cernetur Cana, in qua aquae in uinum uersae sunt. Pergemus ad Itabyrium et ad tabernacula saluatoris, non, ut Petrus quondam uoluit, [eum] cum Moysi et Helia, sed cum Patre cernemus et Spiritu sancto. Inde ad mare Gennesareth, et de quinque et septem panibus uidebimus in deserto quinque et quattuor milia hominum saturata. Videbitur . . . Capharnaum quoque signorum Domini familiaris. . . ." Considered as a letter of Jerome, the women's spiritual patron in the Holy Land, this document appears as Letter 46 in *Saint Jerome: Lettres*, ed. and trans. Jerome Labourt (Paris: Société d'Éditione "Les Belles Lettres," 1951). The translation is from the "Letter of Paula and Eustochium to Marcella," trans. Aubrey Stewart, Library of the Palestine Pilgrims' Text Society (London, 1889; repr. New York: AMS Press, 1971), 1:15.

10. "Letter of Paula," pp. 11-12.

11. "Letter of Paula," p. 12. "Et illud praesepe in quo infantulus uagiit, silentio magis quam in firmo sermone honorandum est. Vbi sunt latae porticus? ubi aurata laquearia? . . . ecce in hoc paruo terrae foramine caelorum conditor natus est. Hic inuolutus pannis, hic uisus a pastoribus, hic demonstratus ab stella, hic adoratus a magis" (Jerome, *Lettres*, 46:11).

12. E. D. Hunt, *Holy Land Pilgrimage in the Later Roman Empire, A.D. 312-460* (Oxford: Clarendon Press, 1982), pp. 104-05.

13. Gingras, *Diary of a Pilgrimage*, pp. 49-50. "Vallis autem ipsa ingens et ualde, iacens subter latus montis Dei, quae habet forsitan, quantum potuimus uidentes estimare aut ipsi dicebant, in longo milia passos forsitan sedecim, in lato autem quattuor milia esse appellabant. Ipsam ergo uallem nos trauersare habebamus, ut possimus montem ingredi. 2. Haec est autem uallis ingens et planissima, in qua filii Israhel commorati sunt his diebus, quod sanctus Moyses ascendit in montem Domini et fuit ibi quadraginta diebus et quadraginta noctibus. Haec est autem uallis, in qua factus est uitulus, qui locus usque in hodie ostenditur: nam lapis grandis ibi fixus stat in ipso loco. Haec ergo

uallis ipsa est, in cuius capite ille locus est, ubi sanctus Moyses, cum pasceret pecora soceri sui, iterum locutus est ei Deus de rubo in igne" (*Itinerarium Egeriae*, 2.1-2).

14. "In toto monte Oliueti nullus alius locus altior esse uidetur illo de quo Dominus ad caelos ascendisse traditur, ubi grandis eclesia stat rotunda, ternas per circuitum cameratas habens porticos desuper tectas. 2. Cuius uidelicet rotundae eclesiae interior domus sine tecto et sine camera ad caelum sub aere nudo aperta patet; in cuius orientali parte altare sub angusto protectum tecto constructu existat. 3. Ideo itaque interior illa domus cameram supra collocatam non habet ut de illo loco in quo postremum diuina institerant uestigia cum in caelum Dominus in nube sublatus est uia semper aperta et ad ethera caelorum directa oculis in eodem loco exorantium pateat. 4. Nam cum haec . . . basilica fabricaretur, idem locus uestigiorum Domini . . . contenuari pauimento cum reliqua stratorum parte non potuit, siquidem quaecumque adplicabantur insolens humana suscipere terra respueret in ora adponentium excussis marmoribus. 5. Quin etiam calcati Deo pulueris adeo perenne est documentum ut uestigia cernantur impressa, et cum cotidie confluentium fides a Domino calcata diripiat, damnum tamen arena non sentit et eandem adhuc sui speciem ueluti inpraesis signata uestigiis terra custodit." *Adamnan's* De locis sanctis, ed. and trans. Denis Meehan, Scriptores Latini Hiberniae 3 (Dublin: Dublin Institute for Advanced Studies, 1958), 23.1-5. Meehan's edition of *De locis sanctis* prints the Latin text and his English translation on facing pages.

15. For earth as a relic, see Hunt, *Holy Land Pilgrimage*, pp. 129-30.

16. Extracted from Eusebius, *Historia ecclesiastica*, in "The Churches of Constantine at Jerusalem," ed. and trans. John H. Bernard, Library of the Palestine Pilgrims' Text Society (London, 1890; repr. New York: AMS Press, 1971), 1:3.

17. "Travels from Piacenza," in John Wilkinson, *Jerusalem Pilgrims before the Crusades* (Warminster, Eng.: Aris and Phillips, 1977), p. 84. Elsewhere, the Piacenza Pilgrim records his experience of sitting on the couch at Cana, "where the Lord attended the wedding. . . . On it (undeserving as I am) I wrote the names of my parents" (p. 79).

18. "Ergone erit illa dies, quando nobis liceat . . . Amos prophetam etiam nunc bucina pastorali in sua conspicere rupe clangentem?" (Jerome, *Lettres*, 46:13).

19. See Hunt, *Holy Land Pilgrimage*, pp. 3, 156.

20. "Jacinthus the Presbyter: Pilgrimage," in Wilkinson, *Jerusalem Pilgrims*, p. 123.

Alexander, Biologist:
Oriental Monstrosities and the
Epistola Alexandri ad Aristotelem

James Romm

Among the most popular fragments of the Alexander legend transmitted
by late antiquity to the Middle Ages is the *Epistola Alexandri ad
Aristotelem*, a pseudonymous letter from Alexander to his teacher
Aristotle describing the wonders of India. Based on a Greek epistle
inserted into the so-called Alexander Romance of the second/third
centuries A.D., the *Epistola* came to enjoy an immense currency in late
antique and medieval culture, circulating in an independent text in Latin
and in several vernacular languages (including an Anglo-Saxon version,
which appears to be the earliest Alexander text in England).[1] The
influence of the *Epistola* becomes even more striking, moreover, if we
consider its connection with other, similar wonder-letters, including the
letter of Pharasmanes (or Fermes) to Hadrian,[2] first attested around the
eighth century, and the more famous letter of Prester John, which swept
Europe in the twelfth. Even if not lineal descendants,[3] these later
epistles share with the *Epistola Alexandri* a common geographical
orientation in that all purport to describe the wonders of the East for the
benefit of the political and scientific leaders of the West.

It is, in fact, in this shared "orientation"—the word inevitably
becomes a *double entendre* here—that we should base our reading of the
Indian wonders epistles and our explanation of their longevity and wide

James Romm is Assistant Professor of Classics at Bard College (see Notes
on Contributors, p. 222).

diffusion. The *Epistola Alexandri*, for example, addresses itself to one of the western world's principal concerns about the East: the kaleidoscopic diversity of oriental wildlife, a phenomenon which seemed to contravene many deeply held Greco-Roman conceptions regarding the coherence of the natural world. The *Epistola* and related texts work to restore this natural order by casting Alexander as a crusading biologist, extending the reach of Hellenic rationality into the region that had most resisted its incursions; and close behind him stands his teacher Aristotle, the great scientist who, more than any other individual, had secured man's cognitive dominion over nature.[4] Through Alexander's agency Aristotle was, in effect, put in charge of a natural environment that would otherwise have seemed dangerously disorganized and unintelligible to western eyes.

To put the *Epistola* into a more complete context, however, we must begin at the roots of the Hellenic experience of India, and of Africa as well—since those two regions are frequently treated as a single land mass by ancient geographic writers. Thus when Pliny the Elder, for example, observes that "India and Africa are especially noted for wonders," we sense that he is discussing, if not a single place, at least a single literary tradition.[5] Both continents formed worlds unto themselves, defined by the peculiar character of plant and animal life; by the bizarre behavior of streams, springs, and rivers; and by alien races of men; and both became the locus of a genre of descriptive literature which specializes in such exotica. As a result, this literature, though known collectively as the Indian wonders or wonders of the East, often includes Africa as well, as in the following example from Herodotus's *Histories*:

> The land westward of Libya is extremely hilly, and wooded, and filled with wild beasts; in this region there are giant snakes, and bears, and vipers, and asses with horns [i.e. unicorns], and dog-headed men, and headless men with eyes in their breasts (thus they are described by the Libyans), and wild men, and wild women, and other beasts in huge numbers, not at all fabulous. (4.191)

The aim of such quasi-scientific literature is, to quote Jean Céard's analysis in *La Nature et les Prodiges*, to portray a region in which "la nature paraît . . . jouer avec la distinction des espèces. . . . Livrée à une fécondité inépuisable, elle s'amuse à créer de nouvelles formes, à diversifier ses oeuvres, elle s'abandonne à une séduisante et terrible anarchie."[6] That is, these accounts depict the landscapes of the far East and South as "free-play" zones in which nature's generative force was unleashed in all its wonderful, and terrible, power. The Greeks, in fact, coined a proverb to express their sense of how nature had run riot in distant lands: *Aei ti pherei Libué kainon*, 'Libya always brings forth some strange, new thing.'[7] Although in its immediate application this saying refers to Africa and not India, we should understand *Libué* metonymically for both the South *and* East,[8] the two regions in whose tropical landscapes nature seemed to exfoliate in a limitless series of new and unexpected forms. To judge by its use in a comedy by the fourth-century poet Anaxilas, moreover, the proverb seems to represent a resigned shrug of the shoulders, a layman's acknowledgment that certain phenomena transcend the scientist's power to explain them: "The arts, like Libya, produce some new beastie [*thérion*] every year," perhaps an equivalent for our "that's progress for you."[9]

Despite this etiological confusion, though, there were those who attempted to explain in rational, scientific terms why *aei ti pherei Libué kainon*. Aristotle, for instance—whose system does not easily tolerate open questions in matters of causation—analyzes the phenomenon in the *De generatione animalium*, in a discussion of the process by which two members of different species can interbreed to produce a third type:

> The proverbial expression about Libya, that 'Libya always nurtures some new thing,' has been coined because of the tendency for even heterogenous creatures to interbreed there. On account of the paucity of water, different species encounter one another at the few places which possess springs, and there interbreed. (*GA* 746 b 7-13)

The same theory of poolside miscegeny is adduced in an interpolated section of Aristotle's *Historia animalium*, as part of an explanation for the fact that "in Libya all creatures are exceedingly diverse in form" (*polumorphotata, HA* 606 b 17). And finally, a similar (but less well articulated) theory regarding the proliferation of southern and eastern wildlife is put forward in the first century B.C. by Diodorus Siculus:

> [In the eastern portion of Arabia] arise goat-stags and antelopes and other types of biformed creatures, in which parts of animals which differ widely by nature are combined. . . . For it seems that the land which lies closest to the equator takes in a

> great deal of the sun's most generative force, and thus gives
> rise to species of fine beasts. It is for this reason that croc-
> odiles and hippopotami arise in Egypt, and in the Libyan
> desert a huge number of elephants and variegated snakes . . .
> and likewise in India, elephants of exceptionally great
> number and bulk, as well as strength. (2.51.2-4)

Unscientific though such explanations may appear from our perspective, they nevertheless succeed in their primary goal: connecting the biological diversity of Asia and Africa to an indigenous climatic feature, the heat of the sun.[10]

While a handful of thinkers like Aristotle may have puzzled over the cause of "Libyan" diversity in nature, however, other naturalists and ethnographers were content to leave it a mystery. For them, the awe which such diversity could inspire could only be dampened by etiological or teleological explanations, and the eastern landscape assumed its most striking aspect when presented as an inexplicable or incomprehensible fact. Hence the format in which the Indian wonders are typically recorded is that of the catalogue: bare, reductive lists which strive for impressive panoramic effects but avoid all discussion of cause.[11] To this tradition belong the great *Indika* of Ktesias of Knidos in the early fourth century, and, insofar as we can judge, the writings of the historians who accompanied Alexander into the East or who followed in his footsteps: Megasthenes, Deimachus, Onesicritus, and others.[12] From this school as well come such encyclopedic efforts as the medieval bestiary, derived from the late Greek *Physiologus*, and their descendants in the *Liber monstrorum* and *Liber creaturarum*.

The great encyclopedia which collects and subsumes all Greek pseudoscience, Pliny's *Natural History*, would seem at first glance to be a part of this catalogic tradition; in fact it contains the longest of the extant wonder-lists, compiled in Book 7 under the rubric we looked at earlier ("India and Africa are especially noted for wonders"). But Pliny, interestingly enough, also reintroduces Aristotelian etiology into his retelling of the wonders of the East; and the context in which he does this will be important for later Indographic literature, especially the *Epistola Alexandri ad Aristotelem*. Hence it is in Pliny that we may trace the next step in the evolution of our central text.

Readers of the great wonder-catalogue of *Natural History* 7 are struck first of all by its extreme density and lack of elaboration. Here Pliny does not bother to explain or even comment on the phenomena he recounts, but simply tosses each new item paratactically into the great grab bag of wonders.[13] Moreover the pace of the list is frenetic, even when measured against Pliny's normally clipped and unceremonious prose style; the reader scarcely has time to absorb any single item before being hurried on to the next:

> There are satyrs in the easternmost mountains of India (in the region said to belong to the Catarcludi); this is a very fast-moving creature, going at times on all fours and at other times upright, in human fashion; because of their speed only the older and sick members of the tribe can be caught. Tauron says that the Choromandi tribe are forest-dwellers, have no power of speech yet shriek horribly, have shaggy bodies, grey eyes, and dog-like teeth. Eudoxus says that in equatorial India the men have cubit-long feet, while the women have such small ones they are called the Sparrowfeet. Megasthenes says that a race living among the Nomad Indians has only holes instead of nostrils, and is club-footed; they're called the Sciritae. (7.2.24-5)

This mad dash through the oriental landscape continues, without pause, for more than seven pages of octavo text, before Pliny finally draws breath and moves, in a more sober frame of mind, to a discussion of his next topic.

The effect created by this hypertrophy of facts and images is not only striking in itself but crucial to the larger goals of the *Natural History*, to judge by the programmatic introduction and conclusion with which Pliny frames it. He prefaces this catalogue by remarking on the kaleidoscopic diversity of these two lands, which he compares to a leopard's spots and the variegated features of the human face; it is at this vast diversity, he says, and not at individual phenomena, that we must look when we consider the wonders of the East (7.1.6-7). He then repeats this idea at the end of the wonders-catalogue, suggesting that only by surveying the whole of nature can we experience its truly awesome multiplicity:

> In her cleverness nature has created these and other, similar things as playthings for herself, and as miracles for us. Moreover who has the power to list the individual things she creates every day, nay, almost in every hour? Let it suffice that her power is revealed by the fact that the races of men are among her marvels. (7.2.32)

The Indian landscape, as Pliny sees it, only exemplifies the near-infinite diversity inherent in all natural forms, a diversity which Pliny celebrates as the source of a sublime sense of wonder.[14]

In the eighth book of the *Natural History,* Pliny again turns his attention to the wonders of Asia and Africa, this time in connection with the animal kingdom rather than the family of man. Here too the frenetic pace of the wonder-catalogue is often felt driving the narrative forward, as for example in chapters 30 and 31,[15] where Pliny retails many of the animal legends made famous by Ktesias's *Indika*.[16] However, Pliny, surprisingly enough, sees himself as the direct heir not of Ktesias but rather of Aristotle. In discussing the African lion, for instance (8.17.44), Pliny pauses to comment on the Greek adage "Libya always produces something new," and repeats Aristotle's theory that the random gatherings of species by scarce watering holes accounts for this wide array of hybrids.[17] Directly following this discussion, moreover, Pliny goes on to cite Aristotle more explicitly, rejecting a piece of lore concerning the lion in the following terms:

> Aristotle relates a different account; and his opinion I see fit to place first, since I shall follow him in the greater part of these inquiries. When Alexander the Great became inflamed with a desire to learn the nature of the animal world, and assigned this pursuit to Aristotle, a man who excelled in every field of study, then it was ordered to the many thousands of men in the territory of all Asia and Greece to obey him: All those to whom hunting, birding, and fishing gave sustenance, and all who were in charge of pens, flocks, beehives, fishponds, and aviaries, were not to let any living thing escape his notice. And by questioning these men he laid the foundations for those nearly fifty brilliant volumes on biology. These have been summarized by me, along with some items that their author was ignorant of; I ask that my readers give them a warm reception, and, with my guidance, wander at leisure amid the universal works of nature and the central passion of the most illustrious of all rulers. (8.17.44)

This collaboration between Aristotle and his one-time student, Alexander, implies that Aristotle (rather than Ktesias) had been in possession of full and accurate knowledge concerning the wonders of the East; and Pliny, as the heir to that knowledge, takes upon himself the mantle of lofty scientific authority that it confers.

The legend recounted here by Pliny has only the most tenuous basis in historical fact, as I have discussed elsewhere.[18] Although Aristotle probably did serve as tutor to the adolescent Alexander at the request of the latter's father, Philip of Macedon, the relationship between the two men had probably been severed well before Alexander had come to control much of Asia. Whatever the story's veracity, though, it is important for our purposes that Pliny has used it to make tractable the otherwise chaotic disarray of the wonders of the East. Through the legendary partnership of Alexander and Aristotle, Pliny asserts, a cognitive dominion over the East has been established by the West, allowing the penetrating light of Hellenic science to be shone under every rock and into every dark, forbidding thicket.

I have dwelt at some length on Pliny because I believe he provides our best glimpse of the imaginative context in which the *Epistola Alexandri ad Aristotelem*, and other late antique Alexander texts, must be read.[19] Here, in particular in the *Epistola*'s sentimental prologue, the partnership of Alexander and Aristotle is staged as a kind of high scientific drama taking place against the backdrop of the remote and terrifying East. The two men have been paired up as an immensely powerful research team, the greatest of explorers serving as the collecting and investigating arm of the greatest of zoologists, extending the reach of empirical science into regions where it had never before been able to go. But in this case the drama also becomes a horror story, in that the Aristotelian system does not stand nearly so firm as it had for Pliny. Instead, nature shows the dark side of her wondrous diversity: a nightmarish power which threatens at every moment to overwhelm the recording scientist.

We should look first of all at the form in which these letters were originally circulated. The Alexander epistles, although known to the Middle Ages largely by way of those which found their way into the Alexander Romance, seem, according to our best evidence, to have originally formed a book-length collection of letters, perhaps an epistolary novel.[20] Thus, although the longest of these epistles, the text on which I have chosen to focus this discussion, was eventually published in Greek in the β version of the Alexander Romance (II.17ff.)[21] and in a separate Latin edition, probably in the second or third century A.D., we should nevertheless bear in mind that it was part of a much larger epistolary tradition focused on the scientific partnership of Alexander and

Aristotle. In fact the Alexander who speaks in the *Epistola Alexandri* describes it as one of a series:

> In my previous letters I have already spoken to you concerning the eclipses of the sun and moon, the fixed position of the stars and the presages of the weather; I sent these to you after setting them out in a careful exposition, and now I shall combine with them these new accounts and set down everything on paper. (3)[23]

Extrapolating from this statement we may perhaps reconstruct the original setting of the *Epistola* as a compendious cycle of missives from Alexander to Aristotle, examining all aspects of the "New World" in the East from the perspective of Old World biology and teratology.

This reconstruction is supported, moreover, by the degree to which the *Epistola*, and the other letters describing Alexander's journeys into the land of wonder, portray their hero not only as a military conqueror but also as a beleaguered champion of experimental science.[24] He constantly expresses a "desire" [*pothos*][25] to see new lands and new creatures, and refuses to allow even the most dire warnings and portents to deter him from this quest. And when he does encounter such novelties his first impulse is to investigate, experiment, or take samples for later study. In an episode described in a letter home to his mother, for example, Alexander, after coming upon a species of tree which grows tall in the morning but shrinks to invisibility in the afternoon, orders his men to collect its sap (an effort cut short by an unseen hand which attacks the army with whips and threats).[26] In another extraordinary episode, Alexander, having come upon a primitive man in the Indian wilds, conducts a crude test to determine its sexual taxonomy:

> He ordered a beautiful young girl to be brought, and when she was brought Alexander said to her: "Approach that wild man so that you may observe his condition and see whether he has an entirely human character in him." This she did, and when the man turned around and saw her, he picked her up and straightaway began to eat her. . . . (II.33)

Although his efforts ultimately end in a grisly failure, the episode is nevertheless significant in that it casts Alexander as Aristotle's investigating arm—the same role as that created for him by Pliny's *Natural History*.[27]

The prologue to the *Epistola* gives a clearer sense of the terms in which this communiqué between field researcher and laboratory scientist was conceived. Here Alexander expresses himself nostalgically to his former teacher, and lays out his scientific objectives:

> I am always in mind of you, my dearest teacher and nearest to my heart (after my mother and sisters), even amidst the hazards of war and the many dangers that threaten us; and since I know that you are dedicated to philosophy, I decided I must write to you concerning the lands of India and the condition of the climate and the innumerable varieties of serpents, men and beasts, in order to contribute something to your research and study by way of my acquaintance with new things [*per novarum rerum cognitionem*]. For although your prudence is wholly self-sufficient, and your system of thought, so fitting both for your own age and for future times, needs no support, nevertheless I thought I had better write to you about what I have seen in India . . . so that you would know of my doings (you always follow them so closely) and so that nothing here would be foreign to your experience [*ne quid inusitatum haberes*]. (1)

As a good Aristotelian, Alexander realizes that unaccustomed phenomena (*inusitata*) pose an innate threat to his master's taxonomic system, and so, having uncovered a vast array of such novelties, he feels the need to get them transcribed and categorized. There is even a certain urgency in his tone, as revealed in his repetition of the phrase "I thought I had better write to you"—a formula that will recur several times in the body of the letter.

Having thus opened by informing Aristotle that the reigning taxonomy will need to be revised (while tactfully reassuring him that the system as a whole remains valid), Alexander goes on to express the overhelming sense of wonder and confusion his new discoveries have inspired:

> As I see it, these things are worthy of being recorded, whether singly or in great, manifold groups; for I would never have taken it from anyone else that so many wonders could exist, unless I myself had first examined them all right in front of my own eyes. It's amazing how many things, both evil and good, the earth produces, that mother and common parent of beasts and fruits, of minerals and animals. If it were permitted

> to man to survey them all, I would think that there would hard-
> ly even be enough names for so many varieties of things. (2)

Here Alexander, in tones reminiscent of Pliny's seventh book,
envisions the natural kingdom as a totality, awesome in the near-
infinite range of its creations. For Alexander, though, this totality has
become more threatening than it had been for Pliny, in that the
parameters of taxonomy here seem to be stretched to the breaking point.
Indeed, by suggesting that man's supply of "names" [*nomina*] may not
be large enough to denominate nature's bounty, Alexander poses a
rather serious challenge to Aristotle, who often refers to his own
taxonomic categories as "names" [*onomata*]. In other words, the
Aristotelian system may be in danger of overload as it tries to absorb
all oriental anomalies, and Alexander, the man of action who carries
that system forward into the world, seems afraid that he will ultimately
be unable to hold together the rapidly diverging poles of theory
and experience.

The shaky sense of control Alexander reveals in this prologue
becomes even more tenuous as his army moves across the Indian
frontier, encountering swarms of hostile beasts and monsters at every
juncture. In the first long episode of the *Epistola*, for example,
Alexander, whose army has been chronically short of fresh water,
decides to bivouac his army beside a stagnant pool. His mistake
becomes apparent, however, when swarms of scorpions arrive to drink
at the pool and commence stinging the soldiers with their barbed tails
(17). No sooner have these pests been driven off than others arrive, so
that the night becomes a long series of horrific incursions of beasts:[28]

> At the fifth hour of the night the trumpet signalled that those
> awake on watch should take their rest; but suddenly white
> lions, the size of bulls, arrived. . . . Also boars of immense
> size . . . together with spotted lynxes, tigers, and fearsome
> panthers, gave us a fight worse than any previous plague. And
> then a huge flock of bats, similar to doves in their form, flung
> themselves into our mouths and faces, attacking the soldiers'
> limbs with their man-like teeth. In addition one beast of a
> new type appeared, larger than an elephant, and equipped with
> three horns on its forehead, which the Indians call a *denti-
> tyrannus*; it has a head like a horse but black in color. This
> beast, having drunk water, spotted us and made a charge at our
> camp. . . . (18-20)

This night of terrors sees the entire panoply of the Indian wonders ranged against Alexander's troops, many of whom are wounded or killed as a result. It is as if Pliny's wonder-catalogue in the seventh book of the *Natural History* had been brought terrifyingly to life, and Alexander set down in the midst of its chaotic diversity. The connection to Pliny becomes even more striking, in fact, when we take account of the setting for this zoological Walpurgisnacht: beside a watering-hole, ancient science's primary locus, as we have seen, for the generation of new animal forms.

In fending off the swarming creatures that surround the watering-hole, then, Alexander is acting out his role as champion of Aristotelian biology, putting to rout the taxonomic disorder exemplified by that environment and making the world safe for Hellenic science. If the *Epistola*'s prologue shows us an Alexander struggling hard to hang onto his endangered Aristotelianism, then the first major episode of the narrative thrusts him into a seething stewpot of animal miscegeny where that system is put most severely to the test. The Alexander of the *Epistola* is thus depicted as both a heroic and a tragic figure: his noble efforts on behalf of rationalism are, within the landscape constructed by the letter's author, doomed to failure. In the letters of Alexander to Aristotle we see the very paragon of western humanity reduced to a powerless and uncomprehending being, unable to apply in the New World the comfortable theories developed in the Old.

NOTES

1. This translation was known in England as early as the eighth or ninth century, according to Kenneth Sisam (*Studies in the History of Old English Literature* [Oxford: Clarendon Press, 1953], p. 83 n. 3). The text (bound into the Beowulf codex, British Library MS Cotton Vitellius A.xv) has been edited by Stanley Rypins, *Three Old English Prose Texts*, EETS, o.s. 161 (London: Oxford Univ. Press, 1924), pp. xxix-xliii and 1-50. For the transmission, see George Cary, *The Medieval Alexander* (1956; repr. Cambridge, Eng.: Cambridge Univ. Press, 1967), pp. 14-16; and Friedrich Pfister, "Auf den Spuren Alexanders in der älteren englischen Literatur," reprinted in *Kleine Schriften zum Alexanderroman*, Beiträge zur klassischen Philologie 61 (Meisenheim am Glan: Hain, 1976), pp. 200-05.

2. Text by Henri Omont, *Bibliothèque de l'école des Chartres* 74 (1913): 507-15. This letter, like the *Epistola Alexandri*, seems to have been translated into Latin from some late Greek original. See also the Letter of Premo to the emperor Trajan, published by Edmond Faral (*Romania* 43 [1914]: 199 ff.).

3. Cary, without citing evidence, states that the *Epistola* was "used in the Letter of Prester John" (*Medieval Alexander*, p. 15).

4. As the Asian queen Kandaké remarks in the Alexander Romance (3.22), not only by might but also by mind did the Greco-Roman world strive to conquer the East. For other examples of the intellectual and spiritual encounters between eastern and western societies, see the legends discussed in two articles in *Revue de l'histoire des réligions* by André-Jean Festugière—"Trois rencontres entre la Grèce et l'Inde" (1942-43): 32-57, and "Grecs et sages orientaux" (1945): 29-41. For a brief survey, see also Jean W. Sedlar, *India and the Greek World* (Totowa, N.J.: Rowman and Littlefield, 1980), ch. 10.

5. Similarly in the case of the *mappa mundi* described by Herodotus in the *Histories* (4.37-42), India (or the somewhat larger province of Asia) and Africa are paired as twin "down-under" landmasses which by their antipodal position stand in opposition to northerly, and normative, Europe. On this confusion, see Sedlar, *India*, p. 9.

6. Travaux d'Humanisme et Renaissance 158 (Geneva: Droz, 1977), p. 14. For a survey of the whole tradition from its origins to the Renaissance, see Rudolph Wittkower, "Marvels of the East," *Journal of the Warburg and Courtauld Institutes* 5 (1942): 159-97. John Block Friedman's book *The Monstrous Races in Medieval Art and Thought* (Cambridge, Mass.: Harvard Univ. Press, 1981) focuses in particular on the anthropological dimension of the wonders. For the grounding of these texts in actual experiences of India, see Jean Filliozat, "La valeur des connaissances greco-romaines sur l'Inde," *Journal des Savants* (1981): 97-136; and Albrecht Dihle, "Die fruchtbare Osten," *Rheinisches Museum* n.f. 150 (1962): 97-110, reprinted in *Antike und Orient: Gesammelte Aufsätze* (Heidelberg: Winter, 1984), pp. 47-61.

7. The saying is cited twice in Aristotle's works (*Historia animalium* 607 a 4 ff. and *De generatione animalium* 746 a 35-36) in ways that imply a certain popular currency. See Athenaeus's *Deipnosophistae* 14.18.10-12, and Eustathius on *Od.* 1.66.29. The saying later came to be particularly associated with evil schemes and contrivances; see Zenob. 2.51 and Diog. 1.68 in vol. 1 of Ernst Leutsch and Friedrich G. Schneidewin, *Paroemiographi Graeci* (Göttingen: Vandenhoeck and Ruprecht, 1839).

8. It bears noting that the saying is used by Aristotle to explain both African *and* Asian creatures (see below).

9. *Hyakinthos Pornoboskos* fr. 27, in vol. 3 of August Meineke, *Comicorum Graecorum Fragmenta* (1840; repr. Berlin: de Gruyter, 1970). See also the explanation of the proverb *Libukon thérion* in Apostolius 10.75 (Leutsch and Schneidewin, *Paroemiographi Graeci,* 2:507).

10. See Pliny, *NH* 6.35.187: "There is nothing surprising in the fact that monstrous forms of animals and men arise in the extreme reaches of [Africa], because of the molding power of fiery motility in shaping their bodies and carving their forms."

11. Mary Campbell's analysis of the medieval wonders texts in *The Witness and the Other World: Exotic European Travel Writing, 400-1600* (Ithaca: Cornell Univ. Press, 1988), esp. pp. 57-75, helps to elucidate the importance of their catalogic form. See also Nicholas Howe, *The Old English Catalogue Poems,* Anglistica 23 (Copenhagen: Rosenkilde and Bagger, 1985), esp. ch. 1.

12. See Paul Pédech, "Le paysage chez les historiens d'Alexandre," *Quaderni di Storia* 3 (1977): 125: "La peinture de cette nature, avec ces grandes fleuves, ses forêts immenses, ses animaux inconnus et sa végétation exubérante renouvelait dans la littérature grècque un genre hérité d'Hérodote: l'exotisme."

13. Indeed, the run-on quality of this list is such that its Renaissance editors, who elsewhere divided up the *Natural History* into fairly brief chapters for reference purposes, were unable to find any convenient break and subsumed the entire list within a single, gigantic chapter.

14. On this passage, see Céard, *La Nature* (above, n. 6), p. 16.

15. Examined in detail by Ermino Caprotti, "Animali Fantastici in Plinio," in *Plinio e la natura,* ed. A. Roncoroni (Como: Camera di commercio, industria, artigianato e agricoltura di Como, 1982), pp. 42-46.

16. For Pliny's dependence on Ktesias, see Céard, *La Nature,* p. 14.

17. Cf. 6.35.187; Céard, *La Nature,* p. 16.

18. "Aristotle's Elephant and the Myth of Alexander's Scientific Patronage," *American Journal of Philology* 110 (1990): 566-75.

19. On the Alexander legend's enduring power to define the Indian landscape for later Greek civilization, see Dihle, "The Conception of India

in Hellenistic and Roman Literature," *Antike und Orient*, pp. 89-97 (see above, n. 6).

20. Such is the belief of Reinhold Merkelbach, *Die Quellen des griechischen Alexanderromans*, 2nd ed. (Munich: Beck, 1977), p. 56 n. 32; and Lloyd L. Gunderson, *Alexander's Letter to Aristotle about India*, Beiträge zum klassischen Philologie 110 (Meisenheim am Glan: Hain, 1980), p. 86. The arguments surrounding the origin and accretion of the Alexander Romance as a whole are beyond the scope of this study, but it seems clear in every account of this process that the miracle letters were originally a separate element, deriving more from the stream of folk tale and oral saga than from historiography. See B. Berg, "An Early Source of the Alexander Romance," *Greek, Roman and Byzantine Studies* 14 (1973): 382. Erwin Rohde believes the letters to represent the oldest stratum of the novel (*Der griechische Roman*, 3rd ed. [Leipzig: Breitkopf und Härtel, 1914], p. 187).

21. A different Indian journey is described in a letter addressed jointly to Aristotle and Olympias, contained in the β recension of the Romance (II.23-31), and then twice in the Γ recension, once in a greatly expanded version of the β narrative (II.36-42). For the relationship between the independent Latin letter and the Greek version contained in the novel, see Merkelbach, *Quellen*, pp. 193-98.

22. There is no good evidence as to how early its Greek original should be dated. Gunderson (*Alexander's Letter*, p. 119) argues that this *Ur*-letter is in fact very nearly contemporary with Alexander himself, since the prophecies which it supplies about the fate of his sisters would only have rung true in the twenty years or so after his death. The opinion is seconded by Merkelbach (*Quellen*, pp. 60-62), who also supposes that the historical details of the prophecy would only be intelligible to an audience very close to the actual events. However, see the review of Gunderson by A. Cizek, *Gnomon* 54 (1982): 810.

23. Citations are page numbers from Walther W. Boer's text (*Epistola Alexandri ad Aristotelem ad Codicum Fidem Edita* [The Hague: Excelsior, 1953]), largely because these are conveniently keyed to Gunderson's English translation. A better text for Latinists is that of Michael Feldbusch (*Der Brief Alexanders an Aristoteles über die Wunder Indiens*, Beiträge zur klassischen Philologie 78 [Meisenheim am Glan: Hain, 1976]), which is laid out so as to permit a synoptic comparison of the *Epistola* with other, related Alexander narratives.

24. The tradition is admirably summarized and catalogued by Gunderson, *Alexander's Letter*, pp. 32-33 and ch. 4, as a series of "miracle letters" which "report as many remarkable experiences as possible. The setting is always in distant lands. There Alexander and his soldiers

fight with monsters and undergo thrilling adventures, they see strange peoples, weird customs, and march through uninhabitable deserts. This is teratological literature" (p. 33). See also the useful catalogue provided by Rohde, *Der griechische Roman*, p. 187 n. 1.

25. See Victor Ehrenberg, *Alexander and the Greeks* (Oxford: Blackwell, 1938), ch. 2.

26. Γ recension of the Alexander Romance, II 36. See the edition by Helmut Engelmann, *Der griechische Alexanderroman Rezension Γ Buch II*, Beiträge zum klassischen Philologie 12 (Meisenheim am Glan: Hain, 1963).

27. See also the legend of the bathyscaph expedition discussed by David J. A. Ross, *Alexander and the Faithless Lady: A Submarine Adventure* (London: Birkbeck College, 1967).

28. On this episode see A. Cizek, "Ungeheuer und magische Lebewesen in der *Epistolae Alexandri ad Magistrum Suum Aristotelem de Situ Indiae*," *Third International Beast Epic, Fable and Fabliau Colloquium, Münster 1979: Proceedings*, ed. Jan Goossens and Timothy Sodmann (Cologne: Böhlau, 1981), pp. 78-94, esp. pp. 83-89.

Reports of Mongol Cannibalism in the Thirteenth-Century Latin Sources: Oriental Fact or Western Fiction?

Gregory G. Guzman

Contact between Christian Europe and Mongol Asia in the thirteenth and fourteenth centuries constitutes an important and little-known chapter of world history. Within a few decades of the great Mongol conquests of the 1200s, the European horizon grew to encompass the whole of Eurasia, from the Black Sea to the Pacific Ocean. The Mongol invasion of eastern Europe in 1241 traumatized Western Christians, who saw the existence of their civilization threatened by unknown Asian people. For several decades the West was unsure who the Mongols were and what their future military intentions were toward Europe.

Prior to the mid-thirteenth century, medieval Europe was very ignorant of Asia beyond the Muslim Middle East. The Latin West accepted many Greek and Roman myths and legends about far-off places and peoples and fused them with Alexander Romances and apocalyptic biblical traditions. Many Christians viewed the Mongol invasion as punishment for sin and, possibly, the beginning of the end of the world, especially when placed into the context of the final release of the unclean biblical nations of Gog and Magog.[1] Thus the Mongol conquests forced Europeans to become aware of the peoples of central and east Asia. However, in the early stages of its inquiry, the West did not receive a very accurate view of them because it was initially dependent on vague oral accounts and rumors for its information. No reliable eyewitness accounts were written by Westerners until after the Mongol expansion had nearly reached its limit.

Gregory G. Guzman is Professor of History at Bradley University (see Notes on Contributors, p. 221).

Pope Innocent IV was the first Western leader far-sighted enough to send envoys to the Mongols in order to find out *who* they were and *what* their intentions were toward Europe. One of these early envoys, the Franciscan John of Plano Carpini, in 1247 wrote the first eye-witness description by a European of these central Asian conquerors; the Dominican Simon of Saint-Quentin supplied the second in 1248. Vincent of Beauvais incorporated a good portion of the reports of John and Simon into his *Speculum historiale*, one part of his famous encyclopedia, the *Speculum maius*; this increased the audience and impact of both accounts. William of Rubruck's later narrative (c. 1255) never acquired wide circulation and prestige, but he and his predecessors provided the Western Christians with one of the first reliable eye-witness accounts of the geography and peoples of central and east Asia.[2]

One seldom-studied aspect of Mongol behavior recorded by John, Simon, William, and three other mid-thirteenth-century authors— Archbishop Peter of Russia, C. de Bridia, and Matthew Paris—raises questions of accuracy, however, and this aspect will be the focus of this study's analysis and evaluation. All six of these Latin sources clearly call the Mongols *cannibals*. This claim is all the more extraordinary in light of the fact that these Western texts are the only extant sources that repeatedly accuse the Mongols of eating human flesh.[3] Chinese, Tibetan, and Muslim sources never do so, even though they had more direct and longer-lasting contact with the Mongols than the Europeans did. These six Western accounts of Mongol cannibalism have been dismissed as untrue, fanciful, and even wildly imaginative, based on the assumption that had the Mongols actually practiced cannibalism, it would have been recorded in the written sources of all of the civilized peoples who had witnessed it.[4]

In attempting to explain the report of cannibalism in these six thirteenth-century Latin accounts, one must first identify and investigate the probable sources of this information. Instead of merely stating that the accounts are wrong, it is more helpful to show how they fuse classical legends, Alexander Romances, biblical exegesis, and/or allegations of Asian ritual cannibalism—in other words, how they continue centuries of Western and Middle Eastern literary tradition. This study will reveal that medieval European reports of Mongol cannibalism are a confused mixture of sacred, profane, and purely legendary history.

Before examining the Latin sources that are the focus of this study, it will be helpful to define the three types of cannibalism—survival, customary, and ritual—that will be mentioned throughout it.[5]

Survival Cannibalism occurs among all peoples in emergencies. Numerous records report starving peoples eating other humans in besieged cities during wars, in life raft situations, and at other times of critical hunger.

Customary Cannibalism is the social practice of eating other human beings as a regular source of food.[6] Few people admit to being cannibals themselves because the practice is regarded as the inverse of humanity, as a sign that one is a savage barbarian. For Westerners, one principal way to denigrate and dehumanize people is to call them barbarians in general and cannibals in particular.

Ritual Cannibalism is the most complex and sophisticated form; in this type of cannibalism, small amounts of human flesh are consumed, not because they provide needed nourishment, but because they pass on virtue, strength, wisdom, and legitimacy. In some cases, a strong, healthy son places a morsel of his own flesh in a stew or soup in order to impart his youthful vigor to an enfeebled parent who consumes it. More frequently sources report the opposite: that a son consumes a small portion of a dead parent to legitimize the continuity of the family bloodline—to symbolize the passing on of the elder's virtue, strength, and wisdom to the next generation. Here cannibalism is the result of ritual rather than hunger.[7]

The second issue that must be addressed is whether or not the Mongols viewed themselves as cannibals. Remnants of the *Yassa*, the basic law and criminal code of the Mongols decreed by their founder, Chingis Khan, represent the most obvious document to examine for proscriptions (or allowances) of cannibalism.[8] Prohibition in the *Yassa* would indicate that cannibalism was practiced by the Mongols; deeply entrenched practice would be suggested by repeated prohibitions. On the whole, the *Yassa* was harsh in terms of physical punishments and generous with the death penalty.[9] There are no references to cannibalism in *Yassa* articles preserved.[10] In short, cannibalism was not a legal issue among the Mongols, presumably because it was not practiced.

Thus it is surprising and puzzling that thirteenth century Latin sources record examples of all three types of cannibalism: survival, customary, and ritual. Each author explains the Mongol practice of cannibalism differently, and, as a result, all three types are represented in the Western accounts, as a chronological survey of relevant passages in the sources will reveal.[11]

The earliest Latin source to label the Mongols as cannibals is a short letter written by a Russian Archbishop named Peter. It was written between 1241 and 1244, but it did not become widely publicized until the Council of Lyons, called in 1245 by Pope Innocent IV.[12] Archbishop Peter's letter contains the following statement: "[The Mongols][13] eat the flesh of horses, dogs, and other abominable meats, and in times of necessity, even human flesh, not raw however, but cooked."[14] The qualifying phrase "in times of necessity" indicates that this is an example of survival cannibalism. The revealing description at the end of the sentence, "not raw . . . but cooked," makes the Mongols appear better than animals eating raw meat; they are at least human enough to cook it first.

John of Plano Carpini, leader of one of the four papal embassies sent to the Mongols in 1245, provided another Latin account of Mongol cannibalism. As was mentioned earlier, this portly, sixty-year-old Italian Franciscan wrote the first Western European eye-witness account of the Mongols upon his return from Karakorum in 1247.[15]

In chapter 4 of his *Ystoria Mongalorum*, Friar John writes:

> Their food consists of everything that can be eaten, for they eat dogs, wolves, foxes and horses and, when driven by necessity, they feed on human flesh. For instance, when they were fighting against a city of the Kitayans, where the Emperor was residing, they besieged it for so long that they themselves completely ran out of supplies and, since they had nothing at all to eat, they thereupon took one out of every ten men for food.[16]

Chapter 5 records:

> While this army, that is to say the army of the Mongols, was returning, they came to the land of Burithabet, which they conquered in battle. The inhabitants are pagans; they have an incredible or discreditable custom, for when anyone's father pays the debt of human nature, they collect all the family together and eat him; we were told this for a fact.[17]

Friar John describes survival cannibalism in the first example and ritual cannibalism in the second. In the latter, Friar John's claims are less forceful for two reasons. Since most scholars identify Burithabet with

Tibet,[18] John may not be describing Mongol practices in this passage. Moreover, in his remark that "we were told this for a fact," he does not claim to have witnessed the practice himself.

Another Franciscan, who called himself C. de Bridia, produced in 1247 what is thought to be an abbreviated version of John of Plano Carpini's account, based on an oral version of the trip. Known as the *Tartar Relation*, the title given it in 1965 by the editors of *The Vinland Map and the Tartar Relation*, it appears to have gone unnoticed between the mid-fifteenth century and the late 1950s.[19] Although the Vinland Map has been regarded by some to be a forgery, the *Tartar Relation* is an important commentary on the Plano Carpini mission to central Asia and on the history of the Mongols during the period of their great expansion.[20] Only two manuscript copies of *The Tartar Relation*, are known,[21] so its spread and influence is not likely to have been great.

C. de Bridia mentions the eating of human flesh four times. In paragraph 9 he writes:

> At last, after a long war, he [Chingis Khan] put the emperor's army to flight and beleaguered the emperor himself in his very strong capital city, until the besiegers were compelled by extreme famine to eat one man in each platoon of ten, with the exception of Chingis himself.[22]

In paragraph 13 he reports similarly of Chingis: "At last after toiling continuously on his journey for three more months through the desert, he ordered them, as food was running short, to eat one man in every ten."[23]

Paragraph 19 states that:

> On their way home from this country the Tartars conquered the country known as Burithebet. Burith means wolf [in Turkish], and this name suits the natives well, since it is their custom when their father dies to collect the whole family and eat his body, like ravening wolves.[24]

Finally, in paragraph 54, he comments about the Mongols generally: "They eat immoderately all forms of unclean food, wolves, foxes, dogs, carrion, afterbirths of animals, mice, and, when necessary, human flesh."[25] C. de Bridia thus repeated information about Mongol cannibalistic practices to his fellow Europeans.

In 1248 Simon of Saint-Quentin produced the fourth European eye-witness account of the Mongols. A Dominican, he was part of Friar Ascelin's embassy, which Pope Innocent IV sent to the Mongols in 1245. Simon's independent report is entitled *Historia Tartarorum*. No complete manuscript copies are extant; it is known only through excerpts that Vincent of Beauvais incorporated into the last three books of his *Speculum historiale*.[26]

Simon mentions cannibalism four separate times in the *Historia Tartarorum* as recorded in Book XXX of the *Speculum historiale*. In chapter 77, entitled "Their [Mongol] Cruelty and Deceit," he states:

> They devour human flesh like lions, but prefer it roasted by fire rather than boiled. They do this sometimes out of necessity, sometimes out of pleasure, and sometimes in order to strike fear and terror in the people who will hear of it. Also they exalt and glory in the killing of men, and they are greatly delighted in a large number of dead men.[27]

Here survival cannibalism appears to be outweighed by the Mongols' desire to introduce terror tactics into their arsenal.

Toward the end of chapter 78, entitled "Their Food," Simon (or possibly Vincent) repeats one sentence—"They devour human flesh like lions, but prefer it roasted by fire rather than boiled"[28]—then continues:

> When they capture anyone very hostile and inimical toward them, they all gather together in one place to consume him in revenge of the rebellion made against them, and avidly drink his blood as if they were infernal bloodsuckers. When they lacked food, as in the siege of a certain Kimoran [Khitan or Chinese] city, one of every ten men was taken to be eaten.[29]

According to the first sentence, cannibalism was practiced to terrorize belligerent people and, thus, to deter them from thinking of rebellion. Since the last sentence, describing survival cannibalism for military expediency, is so similar to John of Plano Carpini's earlier statement, scholars generally assume that it was inserted here for emphasis by Vincent, who openly admitted using John's history to supplement Simon's.[30]

In the last few sentences of chapter 86, entitled "Their Death and Burial Practices," Simon reports that:

> There are also other Mongols, some among them even Christians but very evil, whose sons, when they see their fathers growing old and becoming burdened by old age, give them some fat food, like tails of rams and the like; having overwhelmed them with food, they can easily suffocate them. When the fathers have been killed in such a manner, the sons burn their bodies and collecting their ashes they guard these as something precious. From that time, when the sons eat their daily food, they sprinkle some of the ashes on their food.[31]

This unusual example of ritual cannibalism, which starts with euthanasia, is reported only in Simon's history.

And finally, in chapter 89, which deals with the Mongol conquest of Persia, Simon introduces the story of Alexander's Gates, which shut in evil barbarians:

> They have only this writing that the famous Alexander forced some unclean and horrible people, who lived near the Caspian Mountains and who ate other humans and even each other, to live within those mountains. He also built gates which are called until today the Gates of Alexander, and the Mongols have broken one of these.[32]

Curiously enough, Simon goes on to observe that he has inserted this story in his history despite the fact that he doubts its veracity since no Dominicans in the city of Tiflis could find any Georgians, Persians, or Jews who knew anything about Alexander's Gates.

As noted above, William of Rubruck, like Friar John, was a well-known Franciscan who traveled to Karakorum between 1253 and 1255. Despite the assumptions of some scholars, he was not an envoy for either the pope or King Louis IX of France; he was a friar out to preach, to make converts, and to provide religious services to the Christians living among the Mongols. William wrote a letter, entitled *Itinerarium,* to King Louis detailing his travels and observations. In chapter 26 he describes:

> the Tebec, men whose custom it was to eat their deceased parents so as to provide them, out of filial piety, with no other sepulchre than their own stomachs. They have stopped doing this now, however, for it made them detestable in the eyes of all men. Nevertheless they still make fine goblets out of their parents' skulls so that when drinking from these they

> may be mindful of them in the midst of their enjoyment. I was
> told this by one who had seen them.[33]

William is thus the second Western traveler to admit that he did not
personally observe what he reported but that he repeats information
obtained orally from a third party.

Matthew Paris is the last of the six Latin authors who call the
Mongols cannibals. In contrast to the other writers, he was a sedentary
Benedictine monk who spent most of his adult life writing at the
monastery of St. Albans, near London. He never traveled to the central
Asian steppes; so far as anyone knows, he never saw a Mongol! It is
still not certain what his sources were. Nevertheless, in at least two of
his works he made some of the most intriguing and detailed comments
about Mongol cannibalism to circulate in medieval Europe.

Under the year 1241 in his *Chronica majora*,[34] Matthew
recounts that:

> an immense horde of that detestable race of Satan, the Tartars,
> burst forth from their mountain-bound region. . . . The men
> are inhuman and of the nature of beasts, rather to be called
> monsters than men, thirsting after and drinking blood, and
> tearing and devouring the flesh of dogs and human beings.[35]

Under the year 1243 Matthew states that:

> The Tartar chiefs, with the houndish cannibals their
> followers, fed upon the flesh of their carcasses, as if they had
> been bread, and left nothing but bones for the vultures. But,
> wonderful to tell, the vultures, hungry and ravenous, would
> not condescend to eat the remnants of flesh, if any by chance
> were left. The old and ugly women were given to their dog-
> headed cannibals—anthropophagi as they are called—to be
> their daily food; but those who were beautiful, were saved
> alive, to be stifled and overwhelmed by the number of their
> ravishers, in spite of all their cries and lamentations. Virgins
> were deflowered until they died of exhaustion; then their
> breasts[36] were cut off to be kept as dainties for their chiefs,
> and their bodies furnished a jovial banquet to the savages.[37]

This graphic description of Mongol eating habits depicts them as
savages who include sexual abuse in their cannibalistic practices.
Preservation of certain human body parts as delicacies appears particularly disgusting and grotesque. It is followed by this notice under the

year 1244: "They eat the flesh of horses, dogs, and other abominable meats, and, in times of necessity, even human flesh, not raw, however, but cooked; they drink blood, water, and milk."[38] Matthew says that he received this last information from Archbishop Peter of Russia; this is textually evident in Archbishop Peter's memorable descriptive phrase, "not raw . . . but cooked."[39]

Matthew's final coverage of Mongol cannibalism is contained in the *Additamenta*.[40] Under the year 1242, Matthew records that:

> They do not eat men, but they devour them; they eat frogs and snakes. . . . They are terrible in person, furious in aspect, their eyes show anger, their hands are rapacious, their teeth are bloody, and their jaws ever ready to eat the flesh of men, and to drink human blood.[41]

Matthew had written a few lines earlier in the *Additamenta*: "I asked where this country was, and they told me it was beyond the mountains, and lies near a river which is called Egog, and I believe that people [the Mongols] to be Gog and Magog."[42] Matthew presents this information as a letter written in 1241 from an unnamed Hungarian bishop to William of Auvergne, the Bishop of Paris.

A few other mid-thirteenth-century texts[43] refer briefly to cannibalism among the Mongols, but their information comes primarily from the accounts of John of Plano Carpini, William of Rubruck, and Matthew Paris. Roger Bacon, for example, openly admits that he is blending the accounts of Friars John and William.[44] This concludes the summary of the six major Latin sources which describe various types of cannibalism practiced by the Mongols.

Before attempting to decide whether these reports of Mongol cannibalism in the Latin texts are factual or imaginary, one must first determine the likely, if not the actual, sources of as much of this information as possible. This requires going beyond these six sources and examining the literary tradition these well-educated clerical authors knew and continued. Two such traditions—the European and the Middle Eastern—influenced the medieval West generally and these six clerical authors particularly. They encouraged them to invoke Greek and Roman, as well as Judeo-Christian and Alexander Romance, traditions in labeling all Northern and Eastern nomads as barbarians and cannibals. In other words, these well-read clerics merely did what secular and sacred literary tradition encouraged them to do: they called the Mongols—the contemporary barbarian threat—cannibals because earlier writers had treated barbarians the same way.

Thus, it is appropriate to survey briefly and chronologically the more significant authors in the European and Middle Eastern literary traditions, focusing especially on how they described and treated the barbarians of their respective ages. In the West, the tendency to associate foreigners with inhuman behavior is as ancient as Homer's *Odyssey* in which the Cyclopes and the Laestrygonians are portrayed as cannibals. In Book IX, Ulysses relates that:

> [The Cyclops] jumped up, and reaching out towards my men, seized a couple and dashed their heads against the floor as though they had been puppies. Their brains ran out on the ground and soaked the earth. Limb by limb he tore them to pieces to make his meal, which he devoured like a mountain lion, never pausing till entrails and flesh, marrow and bones, were all consumed. . . . When the Cyclops had filled his great belly with this meal of human flesh, he washed it down with unwatered milk . . . .[45]

In describing the Laestrygonian chief Antiphates in Book X, Homer has Odysseus remember that "he gave my men a murderous reception, pouncing on one of them at once with a view to eating him for supper."[46] Later some of Odysseus's men are captured by Laestrygonians who "carried them off to make them their loathsome meal."[47]

Both the Cyclopes and the Laestrygonians are presented as types of monsters and/or animals who regularly ate human flesh—customary cannibalism; their monstrous physical features and their practice of cannibalism definitely placed them on a lower level than the so-called civilized Greeks. The thirteenth-century horror is different in that the Mongol "cannibals" have a normal human shape, but they are not stationary and isolated—they are on the move and, thus, seriously threaten Western civilization.

In the fifth century B.C., Herodotus, the Father of Western History, continued the Greek practice of calling barbarians cannibals in his treatment of the Scythians and other tribes in the North in Book IV of his *History of the Persian Wars*. In chapter 18 Herodotus writes: "Above this desolate region dwell the Cannibals, who are a people apart, much unlike the Scythians."[48] His comments on Northern barbarian eating practices in chapter 26 are particularly relevant to this discussion:

> The Issedonians are said to have the following customs.
> When a man's father dies, all the near relatives bring sheep to
> the house, which are sacrificed, and their flesh cut in pieces,
> while at the same time the dead body undergoes the like
> treatment. The two sorts of flesh are afterwards mixed
> together, and the whole is served up at a banquet. The head of
> the dead man is treated differently: it is stripped bare,
> cleansed, and set in gold. It then becomes an ornament on
> which they pride themselves, and [it] is brought out year by
> year at the great festival which sons keep in honor of their
> father's death . . . .[49]

Here Herodotus describes a unique mixture of customary and ritual
cannibalism occurring together.

Herodotus observes in chapter 100: "As for the inland boundaries
of Scythia, if we start from the Ister [Danube], we find it enclosed by
the following tribes, first the Agathyrsi, next the Neuri, then the Man-
eaters, and last of all the Black-cloaks."[50] In chapter 106 he reports that
the "manners of the Man-eaters are more savage than those of any other
race. . . . Unlike any other nation in these parts, they are cannibals."[51]
Finally, in chapter 125, he refers to "the Scythians [who] led the way
into the land of the Man-eaters with the same result as before."[52]

The Roman writers continued the tradition started by the earlier
Greek authors. Pliny, in his *Natural History*, states that:

> We have pointed out that some Scythian tribes, and in fact a
> good many, feed on human bodies—a statement that perhaps
> may seem incredible if we do not reflect that races of this
> portentous character have existed in the central region of the
> world, named Cyclopes and Laestrygones, and that quite
> recently the tribes of the parts beyond the Alps habitually
> practiced human sacrifice, which is not far removed from
> eating human flesh. . . . According to Isogonus of Nicaea the
> former cannibal tribes whom we stated to exist to the north,
> ten days' journey beyond the river Dnieper, drink out of
> human skulls and use the scalps with the hair on as napkins
> hung round their necks.[53]

Like Herodotus, Pliny claims that various Northern barbarians practice
cannibalism and drink out of human skulls, but he maintains that the
Scythians are cannibals as well, which Herodotus did not. Such
information from Pliny may have given rise to William of Rubruck's
later story of barbarians drinking out of their parents' skulls.[54]

Middle Eastern literary traditions were the source of many religious and apocalyptic themes in the Western clerical authors. Much medieval symbolism had its roots in the revealed religious traditions of the Middle East; the Judeo-Christian conflict between good and evil was transformed, to a certain degree, into the conflict between sedentary civilized peoples (representing God and goodness) and the cannibalistic barbarians (representing Satan and wickedness). Within this context, the barbarians are frequently cast in the role of the precursors of the end of the world—as the heralds of the Antichrist. Nomadic barbarians and evil might win temporary victories, but, for the Judaic-Christian believers, sedentary peoples and goodness will eventually triumph in the end.[55]

The origin of this religiously based symbolism goes back to Genesis 10:1-5, where Magog is mentioned as one of the sons of Japhet and as the representation of a people or country.[56] Ezekiel 38:1-23 and 39:1-6 take the story further, introducing Gog as a ruler in the land of Magog, located far away in the North, where the geographical horizon of the known civilized world had expanded by then. Gog and Magog emerges as the name of unclean people who are represented as Northern barbarians. A third biblical reference is in Revelation 20:7-10 where Gog and Magog are mentioned along with and as part of the release of Satan from his prison; thus Gog and Magog emerge as a symbol of imprisoned Northern barbarians, as a symbol of evil, and as a symbol of all future enemies of the Kingdom of God.[57] This idea is succinctly expressed by Andrew Runni Anderson:

> The term Gog and Magog has . . . become synonymous with barbarian, especially with the type of barbarian that bursts through the northern frontier of civilization. . . . The legend of Alexander's Gate and of the enclosed nations is in reality the story of the frontier in sublimated mythologized form.[58]

Later authors, including Josephus, equated Gog and Magog with the Scythians.[59] The invasions of Rome by Germanic tribes prompted some Christian writers to link the Goths etymologically to Gog in the Bible.[60] Gog and Magog as symbols of Scythians and evil Northern barbarians were fused with another legend in a fifth-century Syrian apocalyptic vision, in which Alexander the Great confines unclean peoples (Gog and Magog, Scythians, and symbolically all Northern barbarians) in the mountains (Caucasus) behind iron gates (sometimes called the Caspian Gates). This Syrian vision, with its classical allusions to people like Alexander, next appears in a sixth century Syrian compilation called the *Christian Legend Concerning Alexander*.[61] In this version, Alexander is portrayed as a champion of God and a most Christian ruler. Instead of building gates, he encloses unclean barbarians in the mountains by praying to God to move together two mountains called the Breasts of the North—the *Ubera Aquilonis*.[62] The *Christian Legend* influenced the *Koran* (Sura 28), the seventh-century Syrian *Pseudo-Callisthenes*, and another work called the *Revelations* of Pseudo-Methodius.[63]

Professor David J. A. Ross, the dean of scholars doing research on Alexander,[64] has proven that the legend of Alexander enclosing Gog and Magog and unclean barbarian peoples was passed into the Western literary tradition primarily through Pseudo-Methodius.[65] This fusion of Western classical traditions and Middle Eastern religious symbolism began to have eschatological implications, as Alexander was presented as a prefiguration of Christ's Second Coming—as one battling evil and the Antichrist.[66] However, by the thirteenth century, Latin authors, while fully aware of the religious overtones of the Alexander legend, were more clearly interested in the natural and geographical aspects of the story. They wanted to know the location of the Gates of Alexander and the Breasts of the North; they wondered if the Mongols could be identified with Gog and Magog, who had supposedly broken out of Alexander's prison.[67] While Jews presented Alexander as a champion of Jehovah, Muslims associated him with their mysterious early hero Dulcarnian, and Christian historians viewed him as a secular forerunner of Christ, the later Western sources treat Alexander as a hero, who encounters exciting adventures on his travels.[68]

This overview of the classical, Judeo-Christian, and Alexandrian literary traditions prepares the way for the examination of specific references to "cannibalistic" Northern barbarians. In turn, this should shed light on the Middle Eastern stories that lie behind the Latin accounts. This examination will stress the changing identity of Gog and Magog, as well as descriptions of the eating habits of the various invading barbarian tribes over the course of several centuries.

As early as the late fourth century, the *Sermo de fine extremo* records one of the earliest fusions of the legend of Alexander's Gate and of Gog and Magog. It also makes a revealing comment on the eating habits of Northern barbarians: "They [the Huns] eat the flesh of infants and drink the blood of women."[69]

The blending of the Alexander Romance, the biblical legend of Gog and Magog, and cannibalistic barbarians continued in the sixth century with the Syrian *Christian Legend Concerning Alexander*.[70] This work, an adapted translation from the Greek Alexander Romance (Pseudo-Callisthenes, redaction ∂*) became in its turn the principal source for the Muslim *History of Dulcarnian*.[71] Before it was lost, the Arabic text served as the intermediary between the Syrian version and the Ethiopian *History of Alexander*, which contains one of the most graphic and gruesome of all medieval descriptions of barbarian behavior:

> They never cook their meat, but eat it raw, without any cooking whatsoever. If they find the blood of a man which hath been shed, they drink it, the flesh of reptiles is their food. . . . God sendeth them to attack the nation which merits punishment, for they are merciless. When the moment hath arrived for them to go forth to war, they take a pregnant woman and strip her naked. Then they light a huge fire and set her in front of the fire until the child is cooked in her womb. Then they rip open her belly, and take out her child and place it in a large trough and flood it with water. They light a fire under the trough and make the water in it boil until the flesh is entirely dissolved in the water. They next take some of this water and sprinkle it over their beasts and over their weapons of war. Through this water, if a man should fight against a hundred thousand [enemies] he would be able to conquer them and to slay them. This cometh to pass because this work is of the DEVIL, whom they serve.[72]

This quotation, from this ongoing fusing of Middle Eastern religious texts, clearly illustrates both the cruel behavior attributed to the Northern barbarians as well as their direct association with the devil and evil. Thus it is easy to see why Christian eschatologists would associate their release from Alexander's enclosure with the coming of Antichrist and the end of the world.

The Greek Alexander Romance is erroneously attributed to the peripatetic philosopher Callisthenes in one manuscript copy.[73] Since the mid-nineteenth century, scholars have credited a writer known only as Pseudo-Callisthenes for this version of the story, on which were based a number of translations and/or adaptations, such as the seventh-century Syrian *History of Alexander the Great*. This Syrian text contains the following description of Northern barbarians:

> These were the peoples that were confined within the gates
> that King Alexander built to exclude them because of their un-
> cleanness. For they ate things polluted and base, dogs, mice,
> serpents, the flesh of corpses, yea unborn embryos as well as
> their own dead. Such were all of their practices which King Al-
> exander beheld, and since he feared that these nations might
> come forth upon the civilized word, he confined them.[74]

Instead of cooking an embryo and using its magical powers for military success, the barbarians now eat it.

Another manuscript version of the Greek Alexander Romance text includes the following assertion in a letter from Alexander to his mother, Olympias, Queen of Macedonia: "And I found there also many peoples that ate the flesh of human beings and drank the blood of animals (and beasts) like water; for their dead they buried not, but ate."[75] To prevent such wicked peoples from polluting others, Alexander successfully prayed that God would move two great mountains—the Breasts of the North—together to enclose these evil peoples; he then sealed the entrance with an iron gate—the famous Gates of Alexander.[76]

Another text in this tradition is the *Book of the Cave of Treasures*. While it is attributed to Ephraem the Syrian of the fourth century, Sir Ernest A. Wallis Budge dates the earliest extant manuscript to the sixth century.[77] *The Cave of Treasures* starts out to be a history of the world from creation to the Crucifixion of Christ, but it goes on to include a series of legends, idle stories, and vain fables.[78] It is a type of religious wonder book. In discussing Alexander observing the unclean barbarian children of Japhet, *The Cave of Treasures* says:

> They were more wicked and unclean than all [other] dwellers
> in the world; filthy people of hideous appearance, who ate
> mice and the creeping things of the earth, and snakes and
> scorpions. They never buried the bodies of their dead [but ate
> them].[79]

The text then reports that Alexander shut these evil barbarians in the northern mountains by praying to God to move two high mountains called "the Children of the North."[80] At the end of the world:

> suddenly the gates of the north shall be opened, and the hosts
> of the nations that are imprisoned there shall go forth. The
> whole earth shall tremble before them. . . . They will eat dead
> dogs and cats; they will give mothers the bodies of their

children to cook, and they will eat them before them without
shame. They will destroy the earth, and there will be none
able to stand before them.[81]

Another offshoot of the Alexander legend, entitled *Revelations*,
purports to be by St. Methodius, an early bishop of Patara, and is often
referred to as the *Pseudo-Methodius*.[82] This quasi-historical account was
written in Syriac in the last decade of the seventh century (691/692) and
ends with prophecies about the end of the world.[83] The Latin text,
which was made soon after the original composition, contains the following description of Northern barbarians, who are called "descendants
of the sons of Japheth":

> [W]hen he [Alexander] saw their moral impurity he shuddered.
> For they ate in cups every kind of defiled and filthy thing,
> that is, dogs, rats, serpents, dead men's flesh, aborted and
> unformed bodies, and those which are not yet formed in the
> womb in their essential features, . . . both those of beasts of
> burden and also every type of unclean and untamed beast.
> Moreover, they do not even bury their dead but often eat
> them.[84]

The Syrian Christian Alexander Romance started by Ephraem the
Syrian and continued in Pseudo-Methodius's *Revelations* also gave rise
to the legend included in Solomon of Basra's *Book of the Bee*.[85]
Solomon discusses barbarian cannibalism in chapter 54, entitled "Of
Gog and Magog, who are imprisoned in the North." He reports that:

> [Alexander] saw in the confines of the East those men who are
> the children of Japhet. They were more wicked and unclean
> than all (other) dwellers in the world; filthy peoples of
> hideous appearance, who ate mice and the creeping things of
> the earth and snakes and scorpions. They never buried the
> bodies of their dead, and they ate as dainties the children
> which women aborted and the after-birth. . . . [Alexander] shut
> them up within the confines of the North. This is the gate of
> the world on the north. . . .[86]

In a later prophetic passage, Solomon states that:

> suddenly the gates of the north shall be opened and the hosts
> of the nations that are imprisoned there shall go forth. The
> whole earth shall tremble before them. . . . They will eat the

flesh of men and drink the blood of animals; they will devour the creeping things of the earth, and hunt for serpents and scorpions and reptiles that shoot out venom and eat them. They will eat dead dogs and cats, and the abortions of women with the after-birth; they will give mothers the bodies of their children to cook, and they will eat them before them without shame. They will destroy the earth, and there will be none able to stand before them. . . . [A]nd by the command of God one of the hosts of the angels will descend and will destroy them in one moment.[87]

According to Solomon, aborted fetuses and children are not merely eaten, but are regarded as delicacies by the barbarians.

It was the Pseudo-Methodius version of Gog and Magog that was readily accepted by Europe, and it was the one that directly entered the Western literary tradition as early as the eleventh century.[88] Its influence on the West was tremendous because of its message. Christendom was repeatedly threatened with new perils and barbarian invasions through-out the medieval centuries—earlier by Germans, Magyars, and Vikings; now by Turks, Mongols, and others. In its darkest hour of need and despair, Christendom found in Pseudo-Methodius not only hope but an explanation, even an assurance, of final victory over Gog and Magog and over the might of the Antichrist.[89]

Meanwhile in early medieval Europe, several Christian authors continued the classical tradition of associating barbarians with cannibalism. They preferred Solinus's third-century adaptation of Pliny to the *Natural History* itself. Solinus's *Collection of Wonderful Things* stressed unusual events, fables, and marvels.[90] He brought together a body of alleged travelers' tales that became the basis of geographical assumptions for over a millennium. He took three-quarters of his material from Pliny, leaving out the scientific base and keeping only the marvels. His book became a principal source of geographic lore for Isidore of Seville and Hrabanus Maurus; many of his picturesque narrations were transferred almost in their entirety to medieval maps as late as the Ebstorf and Hereford maps in the thirteenth century.[91]

Isidore of Seville, in his influential *Etymologies* (c. 630), discusses barbarian peoples, such as Scythians, Goths, and Magog (whom he calls the son of Japhet), concluding: "Some among them cultivate the fields; others, inhuman and bloodthirsty, live on human flesh and blood."[92]

Isidore's contemporary, Aethicus Ister, in commenting on the monstrous and evil people of Gog and Magog, writes in his *Cosmography* (c. 650) that they "ate everything abominable—the fruit of human abortion, the flesh of children, beasts of burden, bears, vultures, also plovers and kites, owls and bison, dogs and monkeys."[93]

Two centuries later, in the encyclopedic *De universo* (c. 850), Hrabanus Maurus, talking about Scythia, Goths, and Magog (the son of Japhet), obviously echoes Isidore: "Some cultivate the fields; others, inhuman and bloodthirsty, live on human flesh and blood."[94]

Thus classical literary tradition, which viewed barbarians as cannibals, began to be fused with the biblical tradition and the legends of Gog and Magog from the Middle East, which contained more specific stories of barbarian cannibalism. The medieval tradition of spreading fables and marvels grew because it was fueled by copyists of classical Western curiosities and of Middle Eastern religious and geographical legends and apocalyptic literature. This led to a series of similar descriptions of fabulous peoples and their unusual customs in natural histories, cosmographies, and encyclopedias written during the ensuing centuries.[95]

During the eleventh century, in his *History of the Archbishops of Hamburg-Bremen*, Adam of Bremen lists various races of peoples, including "those who are given the name Anthropophagi and they feed on human flesh."[96] Adam goes on to report about the peoples living in the north lands:

> where hordes of human monsters prevent access to what lies beyond. There are Amazons, and Cynocephali, and Cyclops who have one eye on their foreheads; there are those Solinus calls Himantopodes, who hop on one foot, and those who delight in human flesh as food, and as they are shunned, so may they also rightfully be passed over in silence.[97]

The tradition of barbarian cannibalism is also evident on two thirteenth-century *mappaemundi*—the Ebstorf and the Hereford maps. Written comments on these world maps describe various mountains, cities, regions, and peoples in their appropriate geographical areas. The Ebstorf Map[98] describes a northern island named Taracontum as being inhabited by "the Turci, part of the stock of Gog and Magog; [they are] a barbaric and morally unclean tribe, the most savage of all cannibals who eat the flesh of youths and the premature offspring of men."[99] The practice of eating "the fruit of human abortion" is found in only one earlier Western text—Aethicus Ister's *Cosmography*.[100] The map also says: "Here Alexander enclosed the peoples Gog and Magog who the Antichrist will have as his companions. They eat human flesh and drink human blood."[101]

Jane A. Leake claims that the Hereford *mappa mundi* is the peak of medieval travel and geographic literature, because this single work is very complete and graphic in representing medieval views of the world's human and physical geography.[102] As was earlier the case with the Scythians, the far North is again depicted as the land of the fabulous and marvelous—and of the cannibalistic barbarians. One inscription records:

> The Essedones[103] live here and they have this custom. At the funeral of parents, they attend singing, and having assembled a crowd of friends, they tear the body into pieces, and after mixing it with the flesh of sheep, they have a meal, believing the body is better eaten by them than by worms.[104]

Another inscription on the map reads:

> Here there are savages who feed on human flesh and drink human blood, accursed sons of Cain. God shut them in through the agency of Alexander the Great; for when an earthquake occurred, the king saw mountains torn from the earth and thrown up as a barrier against them, and where the mountains were lacking, he himself surrounded them with an impassable wall.[105]

The map continues: "Those enclosed are said to be the same people who Solinus called Anthropophagi, among whom the Essedones are counted; at the time of the Antichrist, they will erupt and persecute the whole world."[106] Here the unclean nations of the North are not only enclosed by Alexander, but they are specifically associated with the descendents of Cain. Since Cain was cursed by God, so are all the savage barbarians of the North, who are associated with the symbolic peoples of Gog and Magog and the biblical Antichrist.[107]

Given these literary traditions, it is no surprise that the invading Mongols, who represented the next barbarian threat to the security of the Christian West, were immediately labeled as cannibals by some of the earliest Latin authors to write descriptions of them.[108] Thus it is time to return to the Latin texts written in the mid-thirteenth century by

Archbishop Peter, John of Plano Carpini, C. de Bridia, Simon of Saint-Quentin, William of Rubruck, and Matthew Paris in order to come to some conclusions about their accuracy and reliability.

First, claims of Mongol cannibalism in these six sources must no longer be attributed to the wild dreams and overactive imaginations of their authors. Classical and religious traditions as old as Homer and the Old Testament refer to barbarian invaders as unclean peoples and cannibals. As these legends were fused, cannibals symbolically called Gog and Magog were equated with invaders from the North and the East who would herald the coming of Antichrist and the end of the world.

All six thirteenth-century authors were well-educated clerics. They are likely to have read all they could on geographical information and foreign peoples before they traveled into the world of the Mongols or began to write their histories. Given the contents of their accounts, it is not far fetched to assume that sedentary historians like Matthew Paris simply copied what they read and that the eye-witness envoys saw what they expected to see in barbarian society. They equated the Mongols with the barbarian invaders in the earlier records and described them in the standard literary terms reserved for such peoples—unclean, cruel, and cannibalistic. By following written authorities whom they respected and possibly feared to contradict, these six Latin authors participated in a self-fulfilling prophecy—they recorded observations and evidence in order to get the expected result.[109]

References to Mongol cannibalism in mid-thirteenth-century texts offer little if any new information; most of the details are found, in one form or another, in earlier literary works. These six descriptions are a composite or eclectic continuation of some of the earlier sources—a confused mixture of sacred, profane, and purely legendary history.

The six Latin sources analyzed here describe all three types of cannibalism defined earlier. Five of the six authors record examples of survival cannibalism; this kind is probably the most common and most easily understood and forgiveable of the three types. Customary cannibalism, the most disgusting and indefensible type, is reported only twice—by Simon of Saint-Quentin and Matthew Paris. It should be added that these two sources also contain the longest and most detailed accounts of cannibalism.

Many of the earlier literary sources mention ritual cannibalism. This type is reported in four of the six Latin sources; only Archbishop Peter and Matthew Paris do not speak of it. As the most complex of the three types, it is the most difficult to understand. Since it was usually part of funeral rites, it had deep religious and symbolic implications and overtones. Because this practice was apparently new to the Western Christian mentality, the clerical authors evidently failed to grasp all of the ramifications. Indeed, the Western eye-witnesses consistently failed to clarify that only a small piece of flesh was consumed at these funeral rites; their accounts imply, if not openly state, that the entire body was eaten as a source of nourishment. They ignored the ritual aspect, as well as the filial piety and respect involved, and focused instead on the eating of the body as food. It is likely that the Western authors made an honest mistake—one based more on ignorance and poor comprehension than on hatred and malice.

Western writers may also have seen a parallel between Mongol cannibalism and the medieval Christian doctrine of transubstantiation, first officially defined in 1216 at the Fourth Lateran Council. As active clergymen, all six must have been aware of Christian liturgical references to eating the body and drinking the blood of Christ in the Mass. Claims that the Mongols or other oriental peoples practiced cannibalism—especially ritual cannibalism—may have come a little too close for comfort, and the six Western clerics may have responded by being unnecessarily harsh and even inaccurate when placed in the uncomfortable position of observing a religious and ritual custom conceptually similar to their own sacred practice. But this suggestion is speculative, for there is no textual evidence to support it.

Two final matters for discussion have no ready explanations. First, one cannot help but notice that earlier descriptions of eating unborn human fetuses and embryos have no analogues in the thirteenth-century accounts of Mongol customs. Why were such dramatic and despicable practices, guaranteed to ensure the hatred and condemnation of their civilized Christian audience, left out of the Western reports, if, indeed, the authors were exposed to and familiar with the earlier literary traditions and their standard description and condemnation of barbarians? The only explanation that might possibly account for this omission is again more speculative than demonstrable. It is possible that the six celibate clergymen were so religiously oriented and so far removed from physical sexuality that such explicit sexual and medical references made them feel uncomfortable and possibly even sinful.[110] Since they may have felt ill at ease in reporting something with such delicate sexual overtones and possibly fearing further questions on the topic, they may have opted not to record this aspect of Mongol behavior, regardless of whether or not it was contained in their written or oral sources.

In this regard, it is also important to remember that the oral sources of the Christian envoys to the Mongols knew that these Europeans were eager for information about the Mongols. The conquered people among the Mongols[111] may have fed them some tall tales, myths, and distortions, in order to get back at the Mongols—by providing as much negative publicity as they could for the Western accounts. The Western envoys frequently say they received their information from individuals living among the Mongols; at the end of one of the earlier quotations, Friar John said, "We were told this for a fact" and Friar William said, "I was told this by one who had seen them."[112] No Europeans ever claimed to have personally witnessed an act of Mongol cannibalism. The Latin accounts thus reported what they were told to be true—what they believed to be true; the Latin accounts are thus only as good as their oral sources.

The second item, one that is even more difficult to explain, is Matthew Paris's description of the Mongols' eating female breasts or nipples as delicacies; this phenomenon is so unique and disgusting that it is not readily forgotten. Such behavior is not specifically recorded in any earlier literary source originating either in Europe or in the Middle East. It is even more puzzling when one recalls that Matthew himself was not an eye-witness traveler to the Mongols; he never left western Europe. At present, there is no known source from which Matthew directly copied this strange and unusual story—or most of his Mongol information for that matter. The only possible source might be Solomon of Basra's *Book of the Bee* which records that aborted children were eaten as dainties by the barbarian cannibals. This does not account, however, for replacing children with breasts as the delicacy preferred.

It is now appropriate to return to the question posed in the title of this study. Latin reports of Mongol cannibalism in the thirteenth century were not based on "Oriental Fact" because there is no concrete evidence whatsoever to support the claim that the Mongols ate other human beings. On the other hand, the reports were also not "Western Fiction" in the strict sense that they arose out of the wild dreams and overactive imaginations of the six authors. But they were fiction in that the classical and biblical literary traditions that gave rise to these six accounts were based more on myth, legend, and distortion than on actual events and evidence. The six Western authors passed on the literary tradition of their culture and society, even though it was based more on religious myth and symbolism than on actual people, events, and geography. The literary tradition of medieval Western civilization, and not the six individual authors, was at fault for seeing the rest of the world through the framework of the classical and biblical legends, myths, and literary accounts. The six reporters merely saw and wrote what they were expected to see, hear, and report. In short, the Western literary tradition and Christian society as a whole could not cut itself free of its early classical and biblical moorings; it did so very slowly and reluctantly. In a rapidly changing world, Western civilization preferred to retain its biblical and apocalyptic image of the world, because it foretold the eventual victory of good over evil—of Christianity over the unclean cannibalistic barbarian peoples who periodically disturbed the peace, order, and stability of western Europe. The old vision promised them not only safety and security here on earth, but eternal salvation in the afterlife.

It was a medieval practice to associate contemporary peoples and events with classical and biblical legend, myth, and history. Writers' respect for tradition precluded any sense that they might be stretching or distorting the facts. Ironically, then, medieval Europe's expanding geographical scope and knowledge of the physical world was curtailed by its superimposition of sacred and profane myths and legends on newly acquired information about the Orient. Names were changed and corrupted, monsters and bizarre behavior were added to acquired ethnology, and characteristics freely floated from one people to another. This resulted in distorted and confused reports because the two layers of information were often at odds with each other. Medieval writers preferred to save, reproduce, and believe the most imaginative and least accurate myths, fables, and legends; they preferred the most fanciful and dramatic stories to the most reliable and scientific facts.[113]

Early European-Mongol contacts form a fascinating, important chapter of world history. Unfortunately, it is one which is frequently overlooked by historians because the Latin sources recording this interaction are unorganized, and some are inaccessible to modern scholars. The documents and sources of these early exchanges between East and West are significant because they record the impact of European Christians and Asian Mongols on each other. They trace Europe's first contact with and reaction to a totally foreign civilization outside the traditional Mediterranean cultures which emerged from the breakup of the Roman Empire. Thus the Christian-Mongol interaction in the thirteenth century represents Europe's first true intercultural experience. Therefore this experience is critically important to understand the development of Western intellectual history, especially of the emergence of a Western world-view of mankind and history. Indeed, it was not exposure to foreign civilizations during the century after Columbus that ended the West's geographical isolation and began to broaden its intellectual horizons, but rather it was medieval Europe's thirteenth-century contacts with the Mongols.

NOTES

1. A biblical basis for the existence of Gog and Magog is established in Genesis 10:1-5, Ezekiel 38:1-23 and 39:1-6, and Revelation 20:7-10. For more information on these legendary and mythical peoples, see Andrew Runni Anderson, *Alexander's Gate, Gog and Magog, and the Inclosed Nations* (Cambridge, Mass.: Medieval Academy of America, 1932); Denis Sinor, "Góg és Magóg fia," *Irodalomtörtenet,* 14[1] (1957): 78-79; C. W. Connell, "Western Views of the Origin of the 'Tartars': an Example of the Influence of Myth in the Second Half of the Thirteenth Century," *Journal of Medieval and Renaissance Studies* 3 (1973): 115-37, esp. pp. 118, 126-33; Ian Michael, "Typological Problems in Medieval Alexander Literature: The Enclosure of Gog and Magog," in *The Medieval Alexander Legend and Romance Epic: Essays in Honour of David J. A. Ross,* ed. Peter Noble, Lucie Polak, and Claire Isoz (Millwood, N.Y.: Kraus, 1982), pp. 131-47; and Anna Dorothee von den Brincken, "Gog and Magog," in *Die Mongolen,* ed. W. Heissing and Cl. C. Muller (Innsbruck: Pinguin und Umschau, 1989), pp. 27-29.

2. For further discussion of the first Western envoys to the Mongols and the first Western accounts of the Mongols, see C. Raymond Beazley, ed. *The Western Texts and Versions of John de Plano Carpini and William de Rubruquis,* Hakluyt Society, extra ser. 13 (London: Hakluyt Society, 1903); Henry Yule, ed., *Cathay and the Way Thither,* 2nd ed., rev. Henri Cordier, 4 vols., Hakluyt Society, 2nd ser. 33, 37, 38, 41 (London: Hakluyt Society, 1913-16); Paul Pelliot, "Les Mongols et la Papauté," *Revue de l'Orient Chrétien,* 3rd ser. 23 (1922): 3-30; 24 (1924): 225-335; 28 (1931): 3-84; Anastasius van den Wyngaert, ed., *Itinera et Relationes Fratrum Minorum Saeculi XIII et XIV,* vol. 1 of *Sinica Franciscana* (Quaracchi-Florence: Collegium S. Bonaventurae, 1929); Giovanni Soranzo, *Il Papato, l'Europa cristiana e i Tartari: un seculo di penetrazione occidentale in Asia* (Milan: Univ. cattolica del Sacro Cuore, 1930); E. Vogelin, "The

Mongol Orders of Submission to European Powers, 1245-1255,"
Byzantium 15 (1940-41): 378-413; Leonardo Olschki, *Marco Polo's
Precursors* (Baltimore: Octagon, 1943); Christopher Dawson,
*Mission to Asia: Narratives and Letters of the Franciscan
Missionaries in Mongolia and China in the Thirteenth and Fourteenth
Centuries*, Medieval Academy Reprints for Teaching 8 (Toronto:
Univ. of Toronto Press, 1980), a book first published under the title
The Mongol Mission (London: Sheed and Ward, 1955), then reprinted
as *Mission to Asia* (New York: Harper and Row, 1966); Denis Sinor,
"Les relations entre les Mongols et l'Europe jusqu'à la mort d'Arghoun
et de Bela IV," *Cahiers d'histoire mondiale* 3 (1956): 39-62; ----, "The
Mongols and Western Europe," in *A History of the Crusades*, ed. K.
Setton (Madison: Univ. of Wisconsin Press, 1975), 3:513-44; Jean
Richard, *Simon de Saint-Quentin: Histoire des Tartares* (Paris: Libraire
Orientaliste Paul Geuthner, 1965); ----,"The Mongols and the Franks,"
Journal of Asian History 3 (1969): 45-57; ----, "Les Mongols et
l'Occident: Deux siècles de contacts, dans 1274," *Année charnière* 558
(1977): 85-96; Igor de Rachewiltz, *Papal Envoys to the Great Khans*
(Stanford: Stanford Univ. Press, 1971); Gregory G. Guzman, "Simon
of Saint-Quentin and the Dominican Mission to the Mongol Baiju: A
Reappraisal," *Speculum* 46 (1971): 232-49; ----, "Simon of Saint-
Quentin as Historian of the Mongols and Seljuk Turks," *Medievalia et
Humanistica*, n.s. 3 (1972): 155-78; ----, "The Encyclopedist Vincent
of Beauvais and His Mongol Extracts from John of Plano Carpini and
Simon of Saint-Quentin," *Speculum* 49 (1974): 287-307; ----, "John
of Plano Carpini," in *Dictionary of the Middle Ages*, gen. ed. Joseph
Strayer (New York: Scribners, 1986), 7:137-39; G. A. Bezzola, *Die
Mongolen in abendländischer Sicht (1220-1270): Ein Beitrag zur
Frage der Völkerbegegnungen* (Bern: Francke, 1974).

3. Mongol cannibalism in Western sources is briefly mentioned by
   Guzman, "Historian of the Mongols," pp. 159-60, esp. nn. 37-38;
   and Connell, "Western Views," p. 126.

4. Throughout the ancient and medieval periods, most sedentary
   historians were predisposed to portray all central Asian steppe
   nomads as barbarous, subhuman, and even monstrous. Thus, it has
   been argued, all sedentary writers would undoubtedly have included
   cannibalism if there had been any evidence to support such a clearly
   derogatory charge. The Christian label of cannibalism may thus be
   seen as another way to denigrate and condemn the Mongols—the
   latest wave of steppe nomads to invade the Latin West. For an
   introduction to the topic of barbarians and monsters, see Rudolf
   Wittkower, "Marvels of the East: A Study in the History of Monsters,"
   Journal of the Warburg and Courtauld Institutes 5 (1942): 159-97;
   Denis Sinor, "Foreigner—Barbarian—Monster," in *East-West in Art*,
   ed. Theodore Bowie (Bloomington, Ind.: Indiana Univ. Press, 1966),

pp. 154-73; Claude Kappler, *Monstres, démons et merveilles à la fin du Moyen Age* (Paris: Payot, 1980); John Block Friedman, *The Monstrous Races in Medieval Art and Thought* (Cambridge, Mass: Harvard Univ. Press, 1981); Gregory G. Guzman, "Were the Barbarians a Negative or Positive Factor in Ancient and Medieval History?" *The Historian* 50 (1988): 558-72; and Jill Tattersall, "Anthropophagi and Eaters of Raw Flesh in French Literature of the Crusade Period: Myth, Tradition, and Reality," *Medium Ævum* 57 (1988): 240-53.

5. Obviously, the medieval sources did not make these distinctions which approach cannibalism in modern sociological and anthropological terminology. They are used here to clarify the perspectives of ancient and medieval authors. See Tattersall, "Anthropophagi," pp. 240-41, 245.

6. See William Arens, *The Man-Eating Myth: Anthropology and Anthropophagy* (Oxford: Oxford Univ. Press, 1979). This book's provocative thesis denies the existence of customary cannibalism. Arens claims that no credible observer has ever documented cannibalism as a custom and that such reports of cannibalism are all second- or third-hand parties telling the recorder about it—in other words, our ancestors, our neighbors, our enemies (etc.) ate humans. Also see the interesting short article by Gina Kolata, "Are the Horrors of Cannibalism Fact—or Fiction?" *Smithsonian* 17 (1987): 150-70.

7. For the most detailed discussion of early ritual cannibalism in Asia (during the B.C. period), see Marcel Granet, *Chinese Civilization* (1930; repr. New York: Barnes and Noble, 1957), esp. pp. 216-18 and 222-25. Such practices continued in China into the Yüan Dynasty, according to reports of similar acts of filial piety. Court documents from the 1270s relate that a man named Tien-Erh Tu cut off part of his backside in an act of filial piety to enable his sick mother to regain her health. The Board of Census officially prohibited such bodily mutilation because it feared foolish people would follow such harmful practices. This example, and several others as well, was generously translated by Professor Ruby Lam of Wellesley College from the *Ta Yüan sheng-cheng kuo-ch'ao tien-chang* (Yüan ed.; repr. Taipei: National Palace Museum, 1972), ch. 33, 19a-19b.

8. The term *Yassa* itself means prohibition, regulation, or law; see Valentin A. Riasanovsky, *Fundamental Principles of Mongol Law*, Uralic and Altaic Series 43 (1937; repr. Bloomington, Ind.: Research Institute for Inner Asian Studies, 1965), p. 25.

9. While the *Yassa* is generally considered to be harsh and cruel, a recent study concludes that the law code enforced in China by the Yüan Dynasty was characterized by leniency, not harshness. But here the

law enforced was the Yüan codification of Chinese—not Mongol—law. See Paul Heng-chao Ch'en, *Chinese Legal Tradition Under the Mongols: The Code of 1291 as Reconstructed* (Princeton: Princeton Univ. Press, 1979), esp. pp. xiii-xix, 3-5, and 41-47.

10. For the most comprehensive overview of current study on the *Yassa,* see David Ayalon, "The Great Yasa of Chingiz-Khan: A Reexamination," *Studia Islamica* 34 (1971): 97-140(A) and 150-180(B). Also see George Vernadsky, "The Scope and Contents of Chingis-Khan's *Yassa*," *Harvard Journal of Asiatic Studies* 3 (1938): 337-60; Riasanovsky, *Principles of Mongol Law*, pp. 25-32; and D. O. Morgan, "The Great Yasa of Chinguiz Khan and Mongol Law in the Il Kanate," *Bulletin of the School of Oriental and African Studies* 49 (1986): 163-76. These four studies thoroughly cover what is known about the so-called fragments of the *Yassa* that are preserved in the records of the historians al-Maqrizi, al-Juwayni, and Rashid al-Din.

11. For the convenience of the reader, quotations will be given in English in the body of this text; sources for both the translation and the original Latin text will be given in the corresponding endnotes.

12. This letter was written shortly after the Mongol conquest of Kiev in December of 1240, but it took several years for it to reach western Europe. Heinrich A. Dörrie entitled it *Report on the Tartars* in his standard edition of the Latin text; see "Drei Texte zur Geschichte der Ungarn und Mongolen," *Nachrichten der Academie der Wissenschaften,* Göttingen phil.-hist. Klasse 6 (1956): 187-94, esp. p. 191. Dörrie presents parallel readings from the two extant texts of this letter; they are found in *Annales Burtinenses,* ed. Pauli, in MGH SS (1885), 27:474-75; and in Matthew Paris, *Chronica Majora,* ed. Henry Richards Luard, *Rerum Britannicarum Medii Aevi Scriptores* 57 (1877), 4:386-89. Also see *Annales de Burton, (A.D. 1004-1263)* in *Annales Monastici,* ed. Henry Richards Luard, *Rerum Britannicarum Medii Aevi Scriptores* 36 (1864), 1:271-75. The *Chronica Majora* assigns this letter to the year 1244, while the *Annales de Burton* lists it under the year 1245; thus this letter is not independent of the two larger collections. It is treated as a separate source here because it was written before the Council of Lyons. Very little is known about Archbishop Peter; see de Rachewiltz, *Papal Envoys,* p. 86; and Bezzola, *Mongolen,* pp. 110-18.

13. "They" most accurately renders the original here; the Mongols were called Tartars in almost all of the Latin sources. The term 'Tartar' was a corruption of *Tatar,* one of the several tribes that made up the Mongols; this term was then associated etymologically with *Tartarus,* a medieval Latin word for Hell. Thus the invading Tartars were viewed not only as steppe barbarian invaders, but also as messengers of

Satan, as precursors of the Antichrist coming from the land of Gog and Magog to punish Christians for their sins. The Tartars were, at one and the same time, all of these to the threatened Christians of medieval Europe. See Connell, "Western Views," pp. 117-18, esp. nn. 9 and 10, for a discussion of all of the references and intricacies of the meaning and use of the term 'Tartar'.

14. The English translation comes from J. A. Giles's translation of the *Chronicle* of Matthew Paris; see Giles, *English History from the Year 1235-1273* (London: George Bell, 1853), 2:29. For the Latin text, see Dörrie, "Drei Texte," p. 191.

15. John's report contains an accurate description of Mongol customs and a detailed account of Mongol military tactics and how best to oppose them. Friar John was as much a military spy for the threatened Christian West as a religious envoy for Pope Innocent IV. See above, n. 2, esp. Guzman, "John of Plano Carpini," pp. 137-39; Denis Sinor, "John of Plano Carpini's Return from the Mongols: New Light from a Luxembourg Manuscript," *Journal of the Royal Asiatic Society* (1957): 193-206; and John J. Saunders, "John of Plano Carpini: The Papal Envoy to the Mongol Conquerors who traveled through Russia to eastern Asia in 1245-47," *History Today* 22 (1972): 547-55.

16. The English translation, by "a nun of Stanbrook Abbey," is contained in Dawson's *Mission to Asia* (above, n. 2); for the passage quoted here, see p. 16. This is the only English translation based on the latest critical edition of John's text; for the Latin, see Wyngaert, *Itinera*, pp. 47-48.

17. Dawson, *Mission to Asia*, p. 23; Wyngaert, *Itinera*, pp. 60-61.

18. See Dawson, *Mission to Asia*, p. 23, n. 1.

19. R. A. Skelton, Thomas E. Marston, and George D. Painter, *The Vinland Map and the Tartar Relation* (New Haven: Yale Univ. Press, 1965). This edition has the Latin text and an English translation on facing pages.

20. Skelton, Marston, and Painter, *Tartar Relation*, pp. 21 and 40.

21. Skelton, Marston, and Painter, *Tartar Relation*, pp. 23 and 51; the editors of the *Tartar Relation* claimed that their copy was the only extant manuscript. This is not true because this author knows of the existence of at least one other manuscript copy of the *Tartar Relation,* and he is in the process of comparing the two Latin texts.

22. Skelton, Marston, and Painter, *Tartar Relation*, pp. 60-61.

23. Skelton, Marston, and Painter, *Tartar Relation*, pp. 64-65.

24. Skelton, Marston, and Painter, *Tartar Relation*, pp. 72-73.

25. Skelton, Marston, and Painter, *Tartar Relation*, pp. 96-97.

26. Simon's history remained virtually ignored until an edition of the Latin text, excerpted from Vincent's *Speculum historiale*, appeared; see Richard, *Simon de Saint-Quentin*. Simon's text has not yet been translated, but for several recent studies of Simon's account, see three articles by Guzman: "Dominican Mission," pp. 232-49; "Historian of the Mongols," pp. 155-78; and "Encyclopedist Vincent," pp. 287-307. (For Richard and Guzman, see above, n. 2.)

27. Translation by the author from the Latin text presented by Richard, *Simon de Saint-Quentin*, p. 38.

28. See the quotation documented in n. 27 and corresponding references.

29. Translation by the author; Richard, *Simon de Saint-Quentin*, p. 41.

30. See Richard, *Simon de Saint-Quentin*, p. 41, n. 2; and Guzman, "Encyclopedist Vincent," pp. 289 and 292-93.

31. Translation by the author; Richard, *Simon de Saint-Quentin*, p. 51.

32. Translation by the author; Richard, *Simon de Saint-Quentin*, p. 55.

33. Dawson, *Mission to Asia*, p. 142; n. 2 identifies the men of Tebec as Tibetans. For the Latin text, see Wyngaert, *Itinera*, p. 234.

34. The *Chronica majora* was originally finished in 1251, but additions to the text continued; the chronicle now covers the years 1236 to 1259. During the 1240s, Matthew wrote each annual entry within a year or two of the events themselves, according to internal evidence; see Richard Vaughan, *Chronicles of Matthew Paris: Monastic Life in the Thirteenth Century* (1984; repr. New York: St. Martin's, 1986), p. 7.

35. Giles, *English History*, 1:312-13; for the Latin text, see Luard, *Chronica Majora*, 4:76 (see above, nn. 12, 14).

36. The word given in the Latin text by Matthew is *papillis*. This word is usually translated 'nipples', while *ubera* usually means 'breasts'. Giles is here somewhat inaccurate in his translation of Matthew's text.

37. Giles, *English History*, 1:469-70; Luard, *Chronica Majora*, 4:273. Matthew says that this information comes from a letter written by Ivo of Narbonne; this letter is accompanied by a well-known illustration of Mongol cannibalism in Matthew's *Chronica* (Corpus Christi College [Cambridge] MS 16, fol. 166). For a discussion and reproduction of this famous illustration, see Suzanne Lewis, *The Art of Matthew Paris in the Chronica Majora* (Berkeley: Univ. of California Press, 1987), p. 286, fig. 180.

38. Giles, *English History*, 2:29; Luard, *Chronica Majora*, 4:388.

39. See nn. 12, 13, and 14 for the initial coverage of Archbishop Peter in this study.

40. The *Additamenta* is a type of appendix for documents to accompany the text of Matthew's *Chronica majora*.

41. Giles, *English History*, 3:451; Luard, *Chronica Majora*, 6:77. Matthew says that this information is contained in a letter to the Duke of Brabant from Henry Raspe, Landgrave of Thuringia and Count Palatine of Saxony.

42. Giles, *English History*, 3:449; Luard, *Chronica Majora*, 6:75.

43. See Luard, *Annales de Burton*, 1:273; Thomas of Cantimpré, *Liber de natura rerum*, ed. H. Boese (Berlin: de Gruyter, 1973), 1:98-99; and Roger Bacon, *Opus majus*, ed. Robert B. Burke (New York: Russell and Russell, 1962), 1:386.

44. Burke, *Opus majus*, 1:386.

45. Homer, *Odyssey*, trans. A. T. Murray, Loeb Classical Library (1919; repr. Cambridge, Mass.: Harvard Univ. Press, 1976), 1:323. The translation used here is by E. V. Rieu, *The Odyssey* (Baltimore: Penguin, 1946), p. 147.

46. Rieu, *Odyssey*, p. 158; Murray, *Odyssey*, 1:353.

47. Rieu, *Odyssey*, p. 158; Murray, *Odyssey*, 1:353.

48. Herodotus, *History of the Persian Wars*, trans. A. D. Godley, Loeb Classical Library (1921; repr. Cambridge, Mass.: Harvard Univ. Press, 1971), 2:219. The translation used here is by G. Rawlinson, *The Persian Wars* (New York: Modern Library, 1942), p. 298.

49. Rawlinson, *Persian Wars*, p. 300; Godley, *History*, 2:225.

50. Rawlinson, *Persian Wars*, p. 331; Godley, *History*, 2:303. In Greek, cannibals and/or man-eaters are called *anthropophagi*, a term that is carried over into some later Latin texts—such as those by Matthew Paris (n. 37), Pliny (n. 53), Adam of Bremen (n. 96), and others.

51. Rawlinson, *Persian Wars*, p. 333; Godley, *History*, 2:307.

52. Rawlinson, *Persian Wars*, p. 340; Godley, *History*, 2:325.

53. Pliny, *Natural History*, trans. H. Rackham, Loeb Classical Library (1938; repr. Cambridge, Mass.: Harvard Univ. Press, 1942), 2: 512-15. In this same passage, Pliny mentions "a certain large valley in the Himalayas," situtated "beyond the other Scythian cannibals."

54. See n. 33 for references and the discussion of a similar story in William of Rubruck's *Itinerarium*.

55. Michael, "Typological Problems," pp. 132-33.

56. For a discussion of these biblical references, see Anderson, *Alexander's Gate*, pp. 4-5; and Michael, "Typological Problems," pp. 132-33.

57. See n. 1 for a list of sources dealing directly with the legendary peoples of Gog and Magog.

58. Anderson, *Alexander's Gate*, p. 8; see also two articles by Denis Sinor: "Foreigner—Barbarian—Monster," p. 160 (see above, n. 4), and "The Barbarians," *Diogenes* 18 (1957): 59-60.

59. Josephus, *Jewish Antiquities*, trans. H. St. J. Thackeray, Loeb Classical Library (Cambridge, Mass.: Harvard Univ. Press, 1961), 4:59, 61 (for I:123 [vi. 1]). The Greek text is on facing pp. 58, 60.

60. The Visigoths and Ostrogoths were the two largest and most powerful early Germanic tribes with whom Rome had direct contact. See Michael, "Typological Problems," p. 133; and Jane A. Leake, *The Geats of Beowulf* (Madison: Univ. of Wisconsin Press, 1967), pp. 34-42. St. Ambrose, Jordanes, Orosius, and Isidore of Seville identified the invading Goths with Gog and Magog; on the other hand, St. Jerome and St. Augustine rejected the idea that Gog and Magog could be associated with any particular people. See Michael, "Typological Problems," p. 133; and Leake, pp. 35-39.

61. These Syrian accounts and legends have all been critically studied and translated by Sir Ernest A. Wallis Budge: *History of Alexander the Great, being the Syriac version of the Pseudo-Callisthenes*

(Cambridge, Eng., 1889; repr. Amsterdam: Philo Press, 1976), pp. lxxvii-lxxix; [Solomon of Basra's] *Book of the Bee*, in *Anecdota Oxoniensia* (Oxford: Clarendon Press, 1886), vol. 1, pt. 2; and *The Book of the Cave of Treasures* (London: Religious Tract Society, 1927). The latter was formerly attributed to Ephraem the Syrian. See also below, nn. 70-72 (and related discussion).

62. Budge, *Alexander*, pp. 153-55; Anderson, *Alexander's Gate*, pp. 24-25; Leake, *Geats of Beowulf*, pp. 38-39; and Michael, "Typological Problems," p. 133. Anderson and Michael report that the two mountains moved a distance of twelve cubits. The two mountains are sometimes called the Children of the North instead of the more usual designation as the Breasts of the North.

63. Anderson, *Alexander's Gate*, pp. 30-31; Michael, "Typological Problems," p. 133.

64. In addition to the already-mentioned references to Alexander in Budge, *Alexander*; Anderson, *Alexander's Gate*; Leake, *Geats of Beowulf*; and Michael, "Typological Problems," see the following list of major studies by David J. A. Ross: "A Check-list of Manuscripts of Three Alexander Texts," *Scriptorium* 10 (1956): 127-32; "A New Manuscript of Archpriest Leo of Napoli; Nativitas et Victoria Alexandri Magni," *Classica et Mediaevalia* 20 (1959): 98-158; *Alexander Historiatus* (1963; 2nd ed., Frankfurt am Main: Warburg Institute, 1988) and the Supplement in *Journal of the Warburg and Courtauld Institutes* 30 (1967): 283-88; *Illustrated Alexander-Books in Germany and the Netherlands* (Cambridge, Mass.: Modern Humanities Research Association, 1971); *Studies in the Alexander Romance* (London: Pindar Press, 1985). This last volume contains reprints of 23 of Ross's articles on the Alexander legend. Several important recent studies on the subject are contained in *The Medieval Alexander Legend and Romance Epic: Essays in Honour of David J. A. Ross* (see above, n. 1). A detailed study of the Alexander Romance must also include the works of George Cary, *The Medieval Alexander* (1956; repr. Cambridge, Eng.: Cambridge Univ. Press, 1967); Lionel Pearson, *The Lost Histories of Alexander the Great* (New York: American Philological Association, 1960); *Alexander the Great in the Middle Ages. Ten Studies on the Last Days of Alexander in Literary and Historical Writing*, ed. W. J. Aerts, J. M. Hermans, and E. Visser (Nijmegen: Alfa, 1978); K. deGraaf, *Alexander de Grote in de Spiegel Historiael* (Nijmegen: Alfa, 1983); *Vincent of Beauvais and Alexander the Great*, ed. W. J. Aerts, E. R. Smits, and J. B. Voorbij (Groningen: Forsten, 1986); and W. J. van Bekkum, "Alexander the Great in Hebrew Literature," *Journal of the Warburg and Courtauld Institutes* 49 (1986): 218-26.

65. Michael, "Typological Problems," p. 133; and Ross, *Alexander Historiatus* and the Supplement in *Warburg Journal*; see n. 64 for the full references.

66. See R. K. Emmerson, *Antichrist in the Middle Ages: A Study of Medieval Apocalypticism, Art, and Literature* (Seattle: Univ. of Washington Press, 1981).

67. Michael, "Typological Problems," pp. 133-34.

68. Michael, "Typological Problems," p. 144.

69. Translation by the author; Latin text in *Sancti Ephraem Syri Hymni et Sermones*, ed. T. J. Lamy (Malines: Dessain, 1889), 3:200. Lamy is the only scholar to attribute this sermon to Ephraem; most others have believed that the chief source of the sermon was the Syrian *Christian Legend Concerning Alexander*. For a discussion of this controversy, and for the Latin text taken from Lamy, pp. 197-200, see Anderson, *Alexander's Gate*, pp. 16-20, esp. n. 1 (on pp. 17-19).

70. This text was published by Budge as *The History of Alexander the Great, being the Syriac Version of the Pseudo-Callisthenes*, pp. 144-61; see n. 61 for the full reference.

71. Andrew Runni Anderson, "The Arabic *History of Dulcarnian* and the Ethiopian *History of Alexander*," *Speculum* 6 (1931): 434-45. This information is briefly summarized in Anderson, *Alexander's Gate*, pp. 30-31; Cary, *Medieval Alexander*, pp. 130-31; and Michael, "Typological Problems," pp. 133-34.

72. Budge, *The Life and Exploits of Alexander the Great, being a Series of Ethiopic Texts* (London: Clay, 1896), 2:232-33. Only 250 copies of this translation were published. A slightly revised edition came out shortly thereafter; see Budge, *The Alexander Book in Ethiopia: The Ethiopic Versions of Pseudo-Callisthenes* (London: Oxford Univ. Press, 1933), p. 139.

73. The fabulous Life or History of Alexander was not attributed to any one ancient or medieval author until Müller put the name Pseudo-Callisthenes on the title page of his 1846 edition; the original title of the work was the equivalent of *Historia Alexandri Magni*. For a discussion of this Müller misnomer and text, and for the Latin texts of the various versions of the Alexander Romance, see *Pseudo-Callisthenes Historia Fabulosa*, ed. Karl Müller, in *Arriani Anabasis et Indica*, ed. Fr. Dübner (1846; repr. Paris: Firmin-Didot, 1877). Also see *Historia Alexandri Magni (Pseudo-Callisthenes)*, ed. W. G. Kroll (1926; 2nd ed., Berlin: Weidmann, 1928); and *Res Gestae Alexandri*

Macedonis, ed. A. Mai (Milan: Regiis Typis, 1817) for the earliest translation of Pseudo-Callisthenes, attributed to Julius Valerius. The B. G. A. Kübler edition (Leipzig: Teubner, 1888) contains the standard Latin edition of the Valerius text. The most recent English translation of the above Alexander texts, by E. H. Haight, is based on the Kroll edition of 1926; see Pseudo-Callisthenes, *The Life of Alexander of Macedon*, Loeb Classical Library (New York: Longmans, Green, 1955), pp. 1-135. For a discussion of the inappropriateness of the term Pseudo-Callisthenes, see Anderson, *Alexander's Gate*, pp. 29-31. For a study of the sources and origin of Pseudo-Callisthenes, including a brief account of the history of the problem, a listing of the principal texts, and important studies devoted to the issue, see Friedrich Pfister, "Studien zum Alexanderroman," *Würzburger Jahrbücher* 1 (1946): 29-66. See also Cary, *Medieval Alexander*, p. 355, n. 5.

74. English translation by Anderson, *Alexander's Gate*, p. 36, and repeated in Leake, *Geats of Beowulf*, p. 39. The original Greek text is found in Müller, *Pseudo-Callisthenes*, p. 138.

75. Anderson, *Alexander's Gate*, p. 38; Müller, *Pseudo-Callisthenes*, p. 142.

76. Anderson, *Alexander's Gate*, pp. 39-41.

77. Budge, *Cave of Treasures*, p. xi (English translation from the Syriac text); and Anderson, *Alexander's Gate*, p. 44.

78. Budge, *Cave of Treasures*, p. xv.

79. Budge, *Cave of Treasures*, p. 265.

80. Budge, *Cave of Treasures*, p. 266. The mountains moved together until they were about twelve cubits apart.

81. Budge, *Cave of Treasures*, p. 267.

82. Pseudo-Methodius, *Methodii Revelationes*, ed. Ernst Sackur, in *Sibyllinische Texte und Forschungen* (Halle: Niemeyer, 1898). This Latin text includes the tradition of the Syrian *Book of the Bee* by Solomon of Basra; see Anderson, *Alexander's Gate*, pp. 43-50; and Leake, *Geats of Beowulf*, pp. 39-41. Also see the recent publication by G. J. Reinink, "Pseudo-Methodius und die Legende vom Römischen Endkaiser," in *The Use and Abuse of Eschatology in the Middle Ages*, ed. W. Verbeke, D. Verhelst, and A. Welkenhuysen (Leuven: Leuven Univ. Press, 1988), pp. 82-111.

83. St. Methodius was martyred in the early fourth century, and the *Revelations* cannot be dated before the seventh century—hence the use of the term 'Pseudo' before Methodius's name; see Anderson, *Alexander's Gate*, p. 44.

84. Leake, *Geats of Beowulf*, p. 40; for the Latin text, see Sackur, *Methodii Revelationes*, p. 72. This Latin text is reproduced in Anderson, *Alexander's Gate* (p. 46) and Leake (p. 40).

85. Anderson, *Alexander's Gate*, p. 37. The Nestorian bishop Solomon wrote his account in Syrian shortly after 1200; see Budge, *Book of the Bee*, p. iii, for the English translation from the Syriac text.

86. Budge, *Book of the Bee*, pp. 127-28.

87. Budge, *Book of the Bee*, p. 129.

88. The ∂-redaction of the Greek Alexander Romance was translated into Latin by Julius Valerius in the fourth century. While manuscripts of the full text are rare, the opposite is true for a very popular abbreviated version—the *Epitome* of Julius Valerius, probably made in the ninth century; see Cary, *Medieval Alexander*, pp. 11, 25; and Ross, *Alexander Historiatus*, p. 9. The traditions of this *Epitome* and Pseudo-Methodius remained separated, while the reverse is the case with the ∂-redaction of the Romance. It was translated into Latin by Archpriest Leo of Naples in c. 950; Leo entitled his version *Nativitas et victoria Alexandri Magni*. This translation represented the beginning of the large and complicated *Historia de preliis* tradition in the Latin West; see Wittkower, "Marvels of the East," p. 179; and Friedrich Pfister, *Der Alexanderroman des Archipresbyter Leo* (Heidelberg: Winter, 1913). Pseudo-Methodius's account of Gog and Magog was interpolated into the *Historia de preliis* (notably in the very popular first redaction) and became a permanent part of the Western literary tradition on Alexander—in the vernacular languages as well as in Latin. Pseudo-Methodius also influenced the Slavs in eastern Europe; see Samuel Hazzard Cross, "The Earliest Allusion in Slavic Literature to the *Revelations* of Pseudo-Methodius," *Speculum* 4 (1929): 329-39.

89. Anderson, *Alexander's Gate*, p. 49.

90. The composition of Solinus's work is traditionally dated c. A.D. 230-240. See Wittkower, "Marvels of the East," p. 167; and C. Raymond Beazley, *The Dawn of Modern Geography* (London, 1897; repr. New York: Peter Smith, 1949), 1:248. For the critical edition of the Latin text, see Theodor Mommsen, ed., *C. Iulii Solini Collectanea Rerum Memorabilium* (1895; 3rd ed., Berlin: Weidmann, 1958). The only

available English version is a facsimile of Arthur Golding's translation of 1587: *The Excellent and Pleasant Worke Collectanea Rerum Memorabilium*, ed. George Kish (Gainesville, Fla.: Univ. of Florida Press, 1955).

91. Beazley, *Dawn of Modern Geography*, 1:247-48; and Wittkower, "Marvels of the East," p. 167.

92. Leake, *Geats of Beowulf*, p. 35; for the Latin text, see Isidore of Seville, *Isidori Hispalensis Episcopi Etymologiarum sive Originum Libri XX*, ed. W. M. Lindsay (1911; repr. Oxford: Clarendon Press, 1985), vol. 2, 14.3.32. Lindsay's Latin text is reproduced in Leake, p. 34.

93. Translation by the author; for the Latin text, see Aethicus Ister, *Cosmographia*, ed. Heinrich Wuttke, in *Die Kosmographie des Istrier Aithikos im lateinischen Auszüge des Hieronymus* (Leipzig: Dyk, 1853), p. 18 [3.32]. Also see the discussion of Aethicus in Leake, *Geats of Beowulf*, pp. 55-63.

94. Leake, *Geats of Beowulf*, p. 68; for the Latin text, see Hrabanus Maurus, *De Universo*, ed. J. P. Migne, *PL*, SL, 2nd ser. (1852; repr. Paris, 1964), 111:342 [12.4]. The Latin text is reproduced in Leake, p. 67.

95. Wittkower, "Marvels of the East," p. 167.

96. Adam of Bremen, *History of the Archbishops of Hamburg-Bremen*, trans. Francis J. Tschan (New York: Columbia Univ. Press, 1959), p. 201. For the Latin text, see Adam of Bremen, *Gesta Hammaburgensis ecclesiae pontificum*, ed. G. Waitz, in MGH SS rer. Germ. (Hanover: Bibliopolii, 1876), 2:168 [4:19]. The translation is reproduced in Leake, *Geats of Beowulf*, p. 77.

97. Tschan, *History of the Archbishops*, p. 206; Adam of Bremen, *Gesta*, 2:173-74 [4:25]. The translation is reproduced in Leake, *Geats of Beowulf*, pp. 77-78.

98. This map is reproduced in Konrad Miller, *Mappaemundi: die ältesten Weltkarten* (Stuttgart: Roth, 1896), 4:3; and in Friedman, *Monstrous Races*, p. 83. This large map measured ten and one-half feet square and was made c. 1240 (before any of the Latin sources called the Mongols cannibals) near Luneburg in lower Saxony. It derives its name from the fact that it was discovered in a closet in the former Benedictine nunnery of Ebstorf. Unfortunately it was destroyed during the bombing of Hanover in 1943; see Friedman, p. 45.

99. Translation in Leake, *Geats of Beowulf*, pp. 90-91; for the Latin text, see Miller, *Mappaemundi*, 5:26, and Miller, *Die Ebstorfkarte, eine Weltkarte aus dem 13. Jahrhundert* (Stuttgart: Roth, 1900), p. 50. The Latin text is reproduced in Anderson, *Alexander's Gate*, p. 88; and Leake, p. 90.

100. For Aethicus, see above, n. 93. Miller, *Mappaemundi*, 5:26, also refers to chapter 32 of Aethicus's *Cosmography*.

101. Translation by the author; for the Latin text, see Miller, *Ebstorfkarte*, p. 61.

102. A more detailed discussion of this point of view can be found in Leake, *Geats of Beowulf*, p. 81. The Hereford Map is reproduced in Miller, *Mappaemundi*, 4:3; Leake, p. 69; and Friedman, *Monstrous Races*, p. 82. This large map measures 65 by 54 inches and is in the Hereford Cathedral. It was made in the late-thirteenth century by Richard of Haldingham, a cathedral canon from 1305 to 1313 (see Friedman, p. 45).

103. The Essedones are called Issedonians by Herodotus; see above, p. 41, and n. 49.

104. Translation by the author; for the Latin text, see Miller, *Mappaemundi*, 4:24; and W. L. Bevan and H. W. Phillott, *Mediaeval Geography: An Essay in Illustration of the Hereford Mappa Mundi* (London, 1873; repr. Amsterdam: Meridian, 1969), p. 61.

105. Leake, *Geats of Beowulf*, p. 90; Bevan and Phillott, *Mediaeval Geography*, p. 50. The first sentence is also translated in Friedman, *Monstrous Races*, p. 95. For the Latin text, see Vicomte de Santarem [Manuel Francisco de Baros], *Essai sur l'Histoire de la Cosmographie et de la Cartographie pendant le Moyen Age* (Paris: Maulde et Renou, 1850), 2:338; Miller, *Mappaemundi*, 4:25; Anderson, *Alexander's Gate*, p. 88; Leake, pp. 89-90; and Bevan and Phillott, pp. 50-51.

106. Translation by the author; for a loose translation, see Bevan and Phillott, *Mediaeval Geography*, p. 50. For the Latin text, see Miller, *Mappaemundi*, 4:25; Anderson, *Alexander's Gate*, p. 88; and Bevan and Phillott, p. 51.

107. Friedman, *Monstrous Races*, pp. 94-107, esp. p. 95 where Cain's descendents are said to retain his cannibalistic tendency.

108. Anderson, *Alexander's Gate*, p. 61; Anderson discusses the hosts of Gog and Magog and the Antichrist—and how they were identified with the Mongols in the mid-thirteenth century.

109. Wittkower, "Marvels of the East," pp. 195-96; and Tattersall, "Anthropophagi," pp. 240-41.

110. The Latin sources include only a few sentences on the subjects of sex and lust. This may be the result of the clergymen being reluctant to discuss sex—a topic generally taboo for celibate monks and friars. On the other hand, the Christian clerics probably viewed human sex and sexuality as a private and not a public act; thus such private behavior and practices were not viewed as a fitting topic for discussion and description—outside of the confessional. Such an approach and mentality would help to explain the paucity and brevity of sexual descriptions in the Latin sources. See Scott D. Westrem, "Medieval Western European Views of Sexuality Reflected in the Narratives of Travelers to the Orient," *Homo Carnalis, Acta* 14 (1987): 141-56.

111. The early Western envoys received the bulk of their information from European captives and others living among the Mongols. The following statement from Friar John of Plano Carpini is very revealing: "We picked up many other bits of private information about the Emperor from men who had come with other chiefs, a number of Russians and Hungarians knowing Latin and French, and Russian clerics and others, who had been among the Tartars, some for thirty years, through wars and other happenings, and who knew all about them, for they knew the language and had lived with them continually some twenty years, others ten, some more, some less. With the help of these men we were able to gain a thorough knowledge of everything. They told us about everything willingly and sometimes without being asked, for they knew what we wanted." See Dawson, *Mission to Asia*, p. 66; Wyngaert, *Itinera*, pp. 122-23. The early envoys' sources of information is an important topic and is currently under examination by the author.

112. See above, pp. 34, 37-38 (and pp. 58, 59 and nn. 17, 33).

113. See Leake, *Geats of Beowulf*, pp. 20, 53-54, 75, 78-79, 94-95; Wittkower, "Marvels of the East," pp. 167-69; and Tattersall, "Anthropophagi," p. 240.

The Amazons and the End of the World

Vincent DiMarco

Mandeville's account in the *Travels* of the traditional story of
Alexander's Gate, Gog and Magog, and the Enclosed Nations proceeds
along familiar and conventional lines, with one curious exception: the
fact that, in his narration, control over the fearsome hordes earlier
confined by Alexander the Great within the Caucasus is exerted by none
other than the Queen of the Amazons. It is she, we discover, who
exacts tribute from "the Iewes of x. lynages . . . that men clepen Goth
and Magoth," and she who guards the single mountain pass through
which they could pour forth.[1] Although I suspect that more than a few
readers are surprised, and perhaps some even dismayed, to learn that
only the Amazons protect us from the beginning of Armageddon,
Mandeville himself betrays no apprehension whatsoever in this regard:
while he prophesies that in the time of the Antichrist the savage tribes
will destroy Alexander's barrier, escape to join with Jews throughout
the world who have kept alive the hope of subjugating Christianity,
then effect a great slaughter of Christians, Mandeville makes no mention of how the Amazons might figure in that final eschatological
drama. Nor does his earlier description of the Amazons (Cotton version,
chapter 17)—one which follows the traditional account of Justin and
Orosius[2] to show that the Amazons murder the men of their tribe, spurn
marriage, mutilate their daughters, abandon or murder their male issue,
then embark on a career of invasion and warfare—in any way anticipate

Vincent DiMarco is Professor of English at the University of Massachusetts
at Amherst (see Notes on Contributors, p. 221).

or explain their function here as the temporary, yet crucially important defenders of Christendom against Antichrist's terrifying hordes. As a result, the Amazons' appearance in the Gog/Magog episode seems curiously isolated and inorganically conceived; it suggests itself either as Mandeville's original, not fully realized invention, or as a shard of some tradition with which he has come into contact, but which perhaps he does not fully understand or transmit clearly. In any event, it calls for some explanation.

It will not surprise readers of Mandeville—surely an armchair traveler if ever there were one—to discover that his depiction of the Amazons guarding Alexander's Gate is neither unique nor, for that matter, unprecedented. The immensely popular Middle English poem the *Prick of Conscience*, roughly contemporaneous with the *Travels*, likewise identifies the Amazon queen as guard, until the Last Days, of the enclosed forces of Gog/Magog. The author of this poem offers the two standard exegeses of Gog/Magog in this section: they represent either the actual forces of Antichrist who will war on the Church (as is prophesied in Revelation 20) or, in an echo of the equally traditional "etymological" interpretation favored by Jerome and Augustine, they are in a more general sense those sinful human beings through whom the devil works first secretly, and then openly, for the destruction of Christianity.[3] The *Prick of Conscience* in one respect may be said to favor the non-specific, allegorical explanation over the literal identification of actual tribes and races as the forces of Gog/Magog, for the description in the poem of Gog/Magog as merely "þe werst folk þat in þe world duels" is for this author an uncharacteristically loose rendering of his source, the *Compendium theologicae veritatis* of Hugh Ripelin of Strassburg (d. 1268), who also names the Amazon queen as guardian of Alexander's Gate but who, like Mandeville, explicitly identifies Gog/Magog with the Ten Lost Tribes of the Jews.[4] Such an identification, as we shall see, was a late-medieval anti-Judaic commonplace. In the *Compendium*, these Ten Tribes alone constitute Gog/Magog; to Mandeville they appear to be added to, or compose part of, the twenty-two peoples imprisoned by Alexander. These three texts show in their differences how adaptable was the rich store of commentary on the Book of Revelation, as well as the varying degree to which general allegorical exegesis could be concretized in specific racial or tribal terms to satisfy particular audiences. But how and why the Amazons were introduced in the Gog/Magog legend remain questions to which our texts supply no answers whatsoever.

The explanation may turn on certain geographical confusions and their resulting narrative coincidences. The Greek text of the *Alexander Romance* (mistakenly attributed to Pseudo-Callisthenes) immediately follows the episode in which Alexander peacefully subdues the Amazons with the narration of his enclosing "behind the gates he called Caspian" twenty-two barbarian tribes.[5] Similarly, the French text of the widely disseminated *Letter of Prester John* (fourteenth century), which draws on materials from the *Alexander Romance*, has Prester John relate his control over Gog/Magog—whom occasionally after warfare he lets out of confinement to clean up the battlefield by eating the corpses— immediately before describing his Amazon subjects.[6] One can imagine how such collocations might have coalesced and developed into a narrative that involved the Amazons more actively with their horrible "neighbors." Now, Alexander's meeting with the Amazons in the *Romance*, reported often with skepticism by Hellenistic historians, derives ultimately from an early romanticized history by Cleitarchus, extant only in fragments. The geographer Strabo alludes to the visit of the Amazon queen to Alexander during Alexander's campaign in Hyrcania, south of the Caspian; she came, Cleitarchus says, all the way from the Caspian Gates and the river Thermodon (south of the Black Sea).[7] Strabo, who knows how far it is from the Caucasus to Hyrcania, will have none of this; but behind Cleitarchus's fantastic geography lies a confusion of two of the geographical barriers associated with Alexander: one, the only "Caspian Gates" known to classical antiquity, located along Alexander's historical route about seventy miles southeast of Teheran (and hence not far distant from Hyrcania, where Alexander did in fact campaign); and another, in the central Caucasus, where Alexander never went, but which was close to one of the Amazons' traditional homelands, the region around the Thermodon in Cappadocia. Andrew Runni Anderson has documented the changing perception of the Gates' location; one contributing factor seems to have involved an attempt to rationalize the Amazons' appearance as far east as Hyrcania with the historical realities of various barbarian incursions through the Caucasus, closer to the Amazons' traditional stomping grounds.[8] Certainly by the time of Jordanes's *History of the Goths* (sixth century), the Amazons, the Caucasus, and Alexander's (unhistorical) activity there to hold in the barbarians have all been connected:

> After conquering various tribes in war and making others their
> allies by treaties, she [Marpesia, Queen of the Amazons] came
> to the Caucasus. There she remained for some time and gave
> the place the name Rock of Marpesia. . . . It is here Alexander
> afterwards built gates and named them the Caspian Gates,
> which now the tribe of the Lazi guard as a Roman outpost.[9]

Had Jordanes been more of a romancer, the Amazons might well have
been represented in his *History* as loyal subjects of Alexander faithfully
guarding the gates.

Indeed, one might think that two late-medieval vernacular
Alexander poems in which the Amazons are called upon to provide a
defense against Gog/Magog show just such a narrative in development.
In both the Middle English *Kyng Alisaunder* and its source, the Anglo-
Norman *Roman de toute chevalerie* of Thomas of Kent,[10] Alexander
turns from a projected invasion of western Europe when he learns of the
unnatural depravity of the tribes in the northern regions. Seeking to
teach those barbarians a salutary lesson, he calls upon tributary states to
augment his forces; among those who respond is the Queen of Scythia,
"þat nas neuer ouercome / Bot of Alisaunder," and "two quenes of
Amazoyne," each of whom brings thousands of maiden-warriors under
her banner. But this vignette, doubtless inspired by Alexander's earlier,
peaceful domination of the Amazons, fails to convince as an informing
model for the Amazons in their privileged role of opposition to the concentrated forces of Gog/Magog, as we see in Mandeville. For in these
two poems the Amazons are hardly more than stage machinery: they
constitute only a small part of the vast army assembled by Alexander
for the struggle against the demonic tribes; their participation in the war
is not specifically described; and there is no mention of who, if anyone,
is left to guard the gates Alexander is finally able to construct across the
Caspian mountains.

In fact, I believe that the legend of the Amazons guarding the
Gates develops rather differently, as an imaginative elaboration of historical conditions related to the various barbarian incursions across the
Caucasus over the course of centuries. The Roman historian Josephus,
treating of affairs in the early 70s A.D., at one point interrupts his
narrative with a digression on the nation of the Alans (the *Alani*),
living north of the Caucasus in the vaguely defined and mysterious land
of Scythia, who desired to invade Media, "with which intention they
treated with the king of Hyrcania; for he was master of that passage

which Alexander shut up with iron gates." They are allowed, for whatever reasons, to pass through Alexander's Gates in the central Caucasus; they plunder Media and Armenia before returning to their own country.[11] This was neither the first nor the last time the pass was opened to the rampages of the Alans: Strabo notes that during the reign of Augustus the Iberians (i.e. the Georgians) called upon the peoples north of the Caucasus as allies in time of trouble; Josephus records that in the early 30s of the first century A.D. the Iberians admitted the northern barbarians to fight the king of Parthia; Suetonius and Tacitus both tell of Nero's preparations to send a legion to "Alexander's Gate" (quoted as Nero's own words) to prevent an incursion of the Alans; and Dio Cassius relates the opening of the Gates to the Alans by Pharasmenes II of Iberia in 135.[12]

These Alans were often identified as Gog/Magog for the threat they posed to European civilization, just as later were the Huns, who at one point subdued and largely assimilated the Alans, and who became for the Middle Ages an even more fearsome candidate for such an identification. The Iberians/Georgians, however problematic their allegiance had been to the Roman empire, became staunch defenders of Christianity from the time of their conversion to the Greek Orthodox faith in the early fourth century, against the ravages of later invaders such as the "Saracens," the Turks, and the Mongols—all of whom, too, were regularly identified as Gog/Magog.[13] Hence the importance for our investigations of the accounts of these Georgians given by the thirteenth-century historian and propagandist for the Crusades, Jacques de Vitry:

> [T]hey are much dreaded by the Saracens, and have often by
> their inroads done great damage to the Persians, Medes, and
> Assyrians, on whose borders they dwell, being entirely
> surrounded by infidel nations. . . . Their noblewomen, like
> the Amazons [*more Amazonum*], bear arms in battle like
> knights.[14]

In a later passage Jacques describes the Georgians as inhabiting the region surrounding the Caspian mountains "in which the ten tribes who seek the coming of Antichrist dwell"; the Georgian women, he says, are "trained in the ways of chivalry for battle."[15] Here, as is obvious, the *Amazon-like* Georgian women are brought directly into the orbit of the enclosed nations and the final eschatological drama. It can be objected, of course, that Jacques draws only a comparison of Christian Georgian women to the heathen Amazons of old, rather than makes any literal identification of present-day Amazons fighting for Christianity against the demonic hordes. But as John Block Friedman has pointed out, Thomas of Cantimpré, whose encyclopedic *De naturis rerum* was completed 1237-40, expressed the matter somewhat differently, perhaps having caught the drift of Jacques's line of thought. Explicitly citing Jacques's *Historia*, Thomas drops all direct reference to the Georgians, and by so doing redefines the Amazons as contemporary Christian warriors living next to the enemy: "this most brave race of women . . . [are] called by the name of Christians. Against the Saracens they fight fiercely. And indeed it was not long ago that the Queen of the Amazons, coming in service from the regions of the east, gave herself title to the temple and sepulchre of the Lord."[16] What accounts for Jacques's figurative and Thomas's literal ennoblement of the Amazons, of all people, as Christianity's bulwark and last defense? On what basis can they be justified as the noble savage? The answer, interestingly enough, has to do with sexual intercourse: because, says Jacques (and, following him, Thomas) a great amount of energy is consumed in copulation, the relatively chaste Amazons (who restrict their sexual relations to only certain times of the year, and for the express purpose of propagation) "are more brave and more suited for fighting."[17]

Less than thirty years separate the composition of Thomas's encyclopedia from Hugh of Strassburg's *Compendium*, which, as the immediate source of the *Prick of Conscience*, alludes without explanation to the Amazon Queen as guarding the gates constructed by Alexander against Gog/Magog. I suggest that Mandeville's equally uncritical allusion reflects this same tradition as it had evolved and developed, and had recently been attached to the Georgian people as the avatars, either analogous or literal, of the Amazons of old. Is Mandeville aware that in speaking of the Amazon queen guarding the Gates his real subject is the Georgians as they had come to be represented by Jacques de Vitry? It would appear that he is, for in his description of the Georgian people earlier in the *Travels* (Cotton version, chapter 13), Mandeville, who has been following Jacques closely, leaves his source at that very point where Jacques describes the power of the Georgians over the infidels and compares the Georgian women to Amazons. I suggest that Mandeville departs from Jacques here because, as we discover later in the *Travels*, Mandeville knows that the Georgian nation at a time after Jacques wrote were conquered, and fell "in subieccioun of the Grete Chan." For that reason, they can hardly serve Mandeville as a fit model of Christians victorious over the demonic forces.[18]

At this point, however, I want to suggest that the conception of the Amazons as noble savages who could be imaginatively enlisted in the defense of Christendom does not exhaust the phenomenon of their representation in the eschatological drama of Gog/Magog. More specifically, I want to suggest that the traditional associations of the Amazons' history, which persistently embodies a threat to shared and accepted notions of natural hierarchy, values, and relations, would more generally have resisted assimilation to such a positive conception. I think this would be all the more true in a scenario imposed by a canonical biblical source—in this case, the Book of Revelation, which insists, through the inspired prophecy of John of Patmos, that Gog and Magog will in the time of the Antichrist break forth from the barriers later legend came to identify as those constructed by Alexander. No human activity will avail at that point: Antichrist will rise, draw unto him countless converts, then be destroyed by God as necessary prelude to the final Judgment and dissolution. There is, moreover, an "unnatural affinity" of the Antichrist, every detail of whose biography and career was understood to invert and parody Christ's life and ministry, to the Amazons, who customarily upset and subvert traditional sex roles and larger social relations.[19] All in all, it may be more useful to view the Amazons' apparently "innocent," even virtuous, participation in the Gog/Magog episode more suspiciously than Mandeville's *Travels* at first would seem to warrant.

The non-canonical eschatological tradition offers a hint of such an alternative conception in the motif of a woman's rule as one of the signs of the End. It is thus in the widely quoted and influential *Oracula Sibyllina* (3:57ff.) where Beliar, who like Antichrist will lure away many once faithful Jews through his marvels before he is destroyed in a divine conflagration, rises to power during the reign of an evil woman.[20] The author need not have the Amazons in mind here, of course. Apparently a disillusioned Egyptian Jew, he seeks merely to render Roman domination of his homeland in eschatological terms; the queen whose rule hastens this catastrophe is doubtless Cleopatra, who elsewhere in the work (8:194-97) is alluded to as "the abominable woman" who reigns before the "destroyer of all" comes to annihilate. But the ruling woman's presence here, like that of the "foul and alien

woman" in whose reign is prophesied the coming of the Antichrist in
the ninth-century Byzantine *Apocalypse of Daniel*,[21] contributes to the
representation of what 2 Esdras 9:3 describes as the "tumult of nations,
confusion of leaders, disquietude of Princes" that will characterize the
Last Days, a time so lacking in human sympathy that, as 1 Enoch 99:5
describes it, babies and children will be abandoned without qualm of
conscience, and relation will slay relation. Such motifs of inversion,
confusion, and the destruction that results from woman's rule are generally reminiscent of the Amazons. But we are on much firmer ground, I
believe, if we examine the connections of the Amazons and the various
tribes known to the classical and medieval world under the collective
term "Scythians."

Although Herodotus and Hippocrates distinguished the true
Scythians (i.e. Royal Scythians, corresponding to the *Scoloti*), a
nomadic race of the south Russian steppe, from all of their neighbors,
most classical and medieval sources uncritically grouped many of the
northern tribes under this designation, and came to view Scythia as a
vast land stretching across northern Europe and Asia, from Persia,
Albania, and the mouth of the Danube on the south to the Ocean Sea
on the north, and corresponding in every epoch to the lands that marked
the limits of colonization and "civilization."[22] Biblical scholars have
speculated that behind the prophet Ezekiel's description of Gog's army
(38:5) is an allusion to a Scythian incursion through the pass of
Derbend at the eastern end of the Caucasus in the early seventh century
B.C.[23] Josephus, who, as we have seen, speaks of Alexander's
enclosure of the wicked races, identifies the Scythians with
Gog/Magog, and this equation became standard with Jerome's important
commentary on Ezekiel.[24] But just as traditional and familiar to the
Middle Ages was the connection made by Justin and Orosius, et al., of
the Scythians and the Amazons. Indeed, the Amazon race sprung from
exiled Scythian women who, taking matters in their own hands when
their Scythian warrior-husbands were killed by Egyptians, murdered the
remaining men of their settlement on the Thermodon, overran their
neighbors, invaded both Europe and Asia, and succeeded in warfare
until, checked by Hercules's defeat of Hippolyte and Penthesilea's death
at Troy, they retreated to their own country, from which, centuries later,
their queen visited Alexander in the hopes of having his child. It is of
some interest, I think, that whereas the pagan Justin praises both the
Scythian men for their wise governance and the Amazon-Scythian

women for their bravery in war, the Christian Orosius denies the Amazons any heroic stature whatsoever, choosing instead to see in their rise to power an image of the barbarity of the time before Christ. The Scythians have become the Goths (*Getae*) who, Orosius notes, have chosen to live in peace with the Roman empire; is it not to be understood, he asks, as "the blessing of the Christian religion which unites all peoples through a common faith, that those men, whose wives destroyed the greater part of the earth with boundless slaughter, became subject to the Romans without a battle?"[25]

As is clear from this quotation from Orosius, the collective term "Scythians" was periodically redefined as the changing conditions of barbarian incursions warranted, and as a result various of the Scythian tribes came to be described as comprising the forces of Gog/Magog enclosed by Alexander. When Josephus speaks of the Alans behind the Iron Gates guarded by the King of Hyrcania he is speaking of a *Scythian* tribe; and we are not surprised to find in both the Greek *Alexander Romance* and the influential *Revelations* of Pseudo-Methodius that the Alans are formally listed in the company of Gog/Magog.[26] Later, at a time when writers could not be as sanguine as was Orosius concerning the threat posed by those latter-day Scythians, the Goths, that tribe too was identified with Gog (as in Ambrose, Isidore, Jordanes, the Talmud, etc.).[27] And coincident with this was the appropriation to *Gothic* history of the old story of the Amazons' origins, as we now find it in Jordanes and, among others, Trevisa's translation of Bartholomaeus Anglicus. Like the Scythians of an earlier time, the Goths came to be thought of as having produced the Amazons; and like the Scythians, the Goths came to be thought of as Gog/Magog.[28]

It may be objected that even an origin myth as often repeated as this need not "translate" into any active, on-going identification of the Amazons and the peoples they are supposedly protecting us from; but the example of the Huns, who for centuries were regularly identified as Gog/Magog or among their savage forces, shows that just such identifications were fostered and perpetuated, even by sober historians not uncritical of Amazon legends. Procopius, who in *Histories* makes what is for his time (sixth century) the familiar association of Alexander with the fortification of the Pass of Dariel in the central Caucasus, relates the familiar Amazon-origin story as one associated with the Hunnish peoples; at one time, he says, a force of warriors along with their

women went forth to the Thermodon; the men were killed; and the
women subsequently "put on manly valour, not at all of their own will,
and, taking up the equipment of arms and armour left by the men in the
camp and arming themselves in excellent fashion with this, they made a
display of manly vigour, being driven to do so by sheer necessity. . . ."
Though Procopius believes that these *Ur*-Amazons were later destroyed,
the present-day Huns offer to him convincing proof of the truth of the
old stories:

> For customs which are handed down to remote descendants
> give a picture of the character of former generations. I mean
> this, that on many occasions when Huns have made raids into
> the Roman domain and have engaged in battle with those who
> encountered them, some, of course, have fallen there, and
> after the departure of the barbarians the Romans, in searching
> the bodies of the fallen have actually found women among
> them. No other army of women, however, has made its
> appearance in any locality of Asia or Europe.[29]

Two centuries later, in the *Syriac Legend concerning Alexander
the Great*, the same connection is made explicitly in the biblical
context: when Alexander asks who should be enclosed, the threat is
defined as the Huns, among whose kings are Gog and Magog; their
women, he is further told, have one breast apiece and are more savage
fighters than even their spouses.[30] By the time of the Ethiopian version
of the *Alexander Romance* (fourteenth/sixteenth century), the Amazons
have been firmly established "on the other side," both literally and
symbolically: the women of Gog/Magog in this text are one-breasted,
fierce fighting Amazons; they drink the blood of the men they kill; and
God will in time send out these merciless, demoniacal hordes to chas-
tise the faithful despite Alexander's virtuous attempt to hold them in.[31]

The forces of Gog/Magog kept imprisoned by the Amazon queen
in Mandeville's casual reference are associated, as in the *Prick of
Conscience*, with the Ten Lost Tribes of the Jews, in a fashion that
may well surprise students of the Hebrew scriptural commentary, which
envisioned the return of the tribes in glory with the Messiah. Once
again, geographical coincidence may have played a part, since the Lost
Tribes were traditionally believed to have been banished to north-east
Media, i.e. the region around Alexander's historical gates, and other
Jews were early found in the Caucasus. Here, too, dwelt the Khazars,
who had been converted to Judaism and had also been identified with

Gog/Magog.[32] In the twelfth century, Peter Comestor's *Historia scholastica* has Alexander coming upon the Ten Tribes already enclosed in the Caucasus; he considers their plea for release, but decides to shut them in more securely. Their sometimes unclear relation to Gog/Magog was resolved by Hugh of Strassburg, Mandeville's indirect source, who in the *Compendium* equated the Jewish Messiah with the Antichrist of *Revelation*—for the true Messiah had of course already come—and likewise equated the Lost Tribes with Gog/Magog, whom Antichrist would lead in the Last Days.

These same motifs are evident in illustrations of manuscripts and early printed books, which also suggest how the legend of the faithless Amazon Queen became attached to traditional biblical exegesis. Plate 1 (plates follow page 80) is of fol. 134v (top) of the *Velislav Bible*, an illustrated Bohemian Bible produced c. 1340-50, which contains twenty-two scenes of Antichrist's life. The illustrations are heavily indebted to the *Compendium* of Hugh of Strassburg, which was a popular book in Bohemia. This illustration carries a close paraphrase of Hugh, which I translate as follows:

> Here Antichrist comes with kings and his prophets and apostles to Gog and Magog and those ten tribes which had been enclosed within the Caspian Mountains. They were not so shut in that they could not leave, but they were not permitted to by the Queen of the Amazons, under whose rule and ordinance they lived. In the time of the Antichrist they are to come out into Jerusalem with their army.[33]

In the illustration we see Antichrist preaching to Gog and Magog (right). The Amazon Queen has not yet assumed an iconographic presence, and exists only in the gloss taken over from the *Compendium*.

The next two illustrations (plates 2 and 3) form part of the pictorial "Life of Antichrist" interpolated in the series of illustrations of the Book of Revelation in the South German *Wellcome Apocalypse*, produced c. 1420-25. Fol. 11r (plate 2) shows (top) Antichrist marking a worshiper (as in Revelation 13:15-16); in the middle register, Antichrist sending his prophets into the world; and in the lower register, Antichrist's disciples preaching to the kings of Egypt and Libya and the Amazon Queen. The inscription reads in translation: "[And] another disciple [preaches to] the Queen of the Amazons and to the Jews, Gog and Magog, and they will go out at that time from the mountains, as says Jerome." As far as I know, Jerome never mentions the Amazon Queen—merely Antichrist's conversion of the kings of Egypt, Libya, and Ethiopia.[34]

The illustration immediately following in the manuscript (fol. 11v; here, plate 3) shows (top) all nations coming to worship Antichrist; (middle) the kings of Libya, Egypt, and Ethiopia worshiping him; and (bottom) Antichrist dispensing gifts and working conversions. In the top register the Amazon Queen, on horseback, is among those in attendance upon Antichrist. Behind her (to our right) are the forces of Gog/Magog, so identified by the inscription: "Then will come every race to see Antichrist and they will believe in him and they will be liberated from the Caspian Mountains. And the Queen of Amazonia will lead them."[35] What has happened by the time of the *Wellcome Apocalypse* is that the legend of the Amazon Queen's "innocent" involvement in guarding Gog/Magog, as communicated by the *Compendium*, has been brought into the context of Daniel 11, a key biblical text in the theology of the Antichrist, the standard exegesis of which text interpreted the homage paid by the kings of Egypt, Libya, and Ethiopia to the "king of the north" as a type of the rise of the Antichrist.[36] There is no intrinsic reason to identify the Amazons with the Ethiopians; but their inclusion here among those converted by the Antichrist was established, I suggest, on analogy to the Amazons' association with those tribes and races traditionally, and persistently, imagined as constituting the forces of Gog/Magog.

We find much the same in plate 4, a German blockbook produced c. 1456. After illustrations (fols. 6v, 7r top) of preaching to the kings of Egypt, Libya, and Ethiopia, we see (fol. 7r bottom) the Amazon Queen receiving Antichrist's instruction, along with "the Red Jews whom Alexander had enclosed in the Caspian Mountains. They will come out in Antichrist's time, as St. Jerome writes."[37]

The very next illustration in the blockbook (fol. 7v; here, plate 5) indicates the effect of Antichrist's teaching: we see the conversion of the Jews to the beliefs of Antichrist, together with the conversion of the Amazon Queen (second figure from the right). The inscription reads in translation: "And the Queen of the Amazons also draws to the Antichrist."[38]

Plate 6 returns us to Mandeville, through the late-fourteenth-century translation of the *Travels* by Otto von Diemeringen, Canon of Metz (1369-98). The illustration I have chosen is from the second

Plate 1. A scene from the life of Antichrist, *Velislav Bible* (State Library of the Czech Socialist Republic), fol. 134v.

Plate 2. Antichrist marking a worshiper, sending prophets into the world, and preaching to the kings of Egypt and Libya and the Amazon queen, *Wellcome Apocalypse* (Library of the Wellcome Institute for the History of Medicine, MS 49), fol. 11r.

Plate 3. All nations worship Antichrist; the kings of Libya, Egypt, and Ethiopia worship Antichrist; and Antichrist dispenses gifts and works conversions, *Wellcome Apocalypse* (Library of the Wellcome Institute for the History of Medicine, MS 49), fol. 12v.

Plate 4. The Amazon queen receives Antichrist's instruction, *Der Antichrist und die fünfzehn Zeichen: Faksimile-Ausgabe des einzigen erhaltenen chiroxylographischen Blockbuches* (Prestel-Verlag, Munich), fol. 7r.

Plate 5. The conversion of the Jews and of the Queen of the Amazons to the beliefs of Antichrist, *Der Antichrist und die fünfzehn Zeichen: Faksimile-Ausgabe des einzigen erhaltenen chiroxylographischen Blockbuches* (Prestel-Verlag, Munich), fol. 7v.

Plate 6. The Amazon queen receiving instruction from Antichrist's preacher, *[Itinerarium] Iohannes von Montewilla Ritter* (Strassburg: Johann Pruss, 1488), Book 2, chapter 5 (Yale Center for British Art, Paul Mellon Collection).

printed edition (1488), Book 2, chapter 5. The picture is of an obviously credulous Amazon Queen receiving instruction from Antichrist's preacher in a now familiar iconography. What is surprising, however, is that later in the text (Book 4, chapter 1) the traditional story of Alexander's mountain barrier is related, complete with reference to the installation of the Amazon Queen as (faithful) defender against the Jews, with an illustration of her positioned between the Gates and two Jews. It would appear that in the earlier section of von Diemeringen's translation the legend of the Amazon Queen's perfidy, which began somewhat as a gloss on the text, is asserting a life of its own. For the text of this chapter in Book 1 relates the familiar story of the origin of the Amazons and their early history, into which von Diemeringen has interpolated, without regard for context, that "she will be among the first to follow the Antichrist. The Queen will hear his sermon and believe in him."[39] Mandeville's *Travels*, it appears, has been rewritten to accommodate the inescapable and sinister implications of the legend of the Amazon Queen.

If these pages have succeeded in exposing the underside of an image of the Amazons as the virtuous protectors of Christendom from the forces that would engulf it, and have likewise suggested some of the processes by which a wholly contrary conception could have developed, we may want to speculate on the cause of such a transformation. We might approach an explanation through a partial analogy to the Jews who, as we have seen, are, like the Amazons, "grafted upon" the Gog/Magog legend. Anti-Judaism, like antifeminism, was endemic in the Church for a millennium before the Crusades; yet it is undeniable that the war for the Holy Land caused an upsurge of anti-Jewish feeling, not only as a result of the creation of a Christian mercantile class that came into competition with established Jewish commercial interests, but in the less tangible, yet no less real explosion of hostile feelings against the "other"—the non-Christian, the heathen, the infidel. It is during the Crusades, of course, that the Ten Tribes are firmly established as Gog/Magog.

And it is also the time when the Queen of the Amazons becomes Christendom's problematic guardian and protector. Is it too much to suggest that the contradictory conception of her that develops—as defender against the Jewish Gog/Magog or as convert of the Jewish Antichrist—reflects both the hopes and anxieties latent in Christianity's struggle for hegemony? Jacques de Vitry had looked hopefully to the

Georgian women of his own day and from them constructed a myth of Amazons who hold the line. But it was an unrealistic hope of deliverance, preservation, and aggrandizement, for the barbarians had been pouring through the gates for centuries, and it would not be long before the Holy Land itself was completely lost to the enemies of Christ. Indeed, Jacques himself left Acre permanently for Europe in 1225, weary and disillusioned. Jacques knew, on the very strength of Scripture itself, that the *ultimate* victory would be Europe's, however: Gog/Magog would be defeated, the Antichrist destroyed, the Jews converted to the True Faith. Indeed, he confidently says of the enemy Jews, whom he associates with Gog/Magog, that "they are as weak as women" and even that "they have a flux of blood every month."[40]

But if such are our adversaries, how much faith can we place in the woman guarding the Gates?

NOTES

Grateful acknowledgment for permission to reproduce plates is made to: the State Library of the Czech Socialist Republic (Plate 1, *Velislav Bible*, fol. 134v); Wellcome Institute Library, London (Plates 2-3, Wellcome Institute for the History of Medicine, MS 49, fols. 11r and 12v); Prestel-Verlag, Munich (Plates 4-5, *Der Antichrist und die fünfzehn Zeichen: Faksimile-Ausgabe des einzigen erhaltenen chiroxylographischen Blockbuches*, fols. 7r and 7v); and the Yale Center for British Art, Paul Mellon Collection (Plate 6, *[Itinerarium] Iohannes von Monteuilla Ritter* [Strassburg: Johann Pruss, 1488], Book 2, chapter 5).

1. *Mandeville's Travels*, ed. M. C. Seymour (Oxford: Clarendon Press, 1967), p. 192; this edition is based on British Library MS Cotton Titus C.xvi, which is a representative of the Cotton version, one of the four English prose recensions of the *Travels*. There are no significant variants in the Egerton version (*The Buke of John Maundeuill*, ed. George F. Warner [Westminster: Roxburghe Club, 1889], p. 131), and the incident is omitted in the Bodley version. The Defective version, which has yet to appear in a critical edition, identifies the guard as the "queyne of armony"; see *The Travels of Sir John Mandeville: Facsimile of Pynson's Edition of 1496, with an Introduction by Michael Seymour* (Exeter: Univ. of Exeter, 1980), sig. [H2v] (faulty pagination). No variants of significance appear in a rendering of the work into English verse, known as the Metrical version (*The Metrical Version of Mandeville's Travels*, ed. M. C. Seymour, EETS, o.s. 269 [London: Oxford Univ. Press, 1973], lines 2221 ff.).

2. The *Historiae Philippicae* of the Augustan historian Trogus Pompeius is known only from its abridgement by Justinus (third century?); for the Amazons (2.4), see *Justin, Cornelius Nepos; and Europius,* trans. John Selby Watson (London: George Bell, 1890), pp. 20-23. Justin was widely read in the Middle Ages, and much of his material, including the history of the Amazons, was incorporated by Orosius in his *Historiarum adversum paganos*; see *Pauli Orosii Historiarum adversum Paganos libri VII accedit eiusdem liber apologeticus,* ed. Carl Zangemeister, CSEL 5 (Vienna, 1882; repr. New York: Johnson Reprint Corporation, 1966), pp. 63-69 (1.14-16). Orosius was highly influential; see, for example, the account of the Amazons in *The Two Cities: A Chronicle of Universal History to the Year 1146 A.D. by Otto Bishop of Freising,* trans. Charles Christopher Mierow, ed. Austin P. Evans and Charles Knapp (New York: Columbia Univ. Press. 1928), p. 142, and *The Old English Orosius,* ed. Janet Bately, EETS, s.s. 6 (London: Oxford Univ. Press, 1980), pp. 28-31.

3. *The Prick of Conscience (Stimulus Conscientiae),* ed. Richard Morris (Berlin: Asher, 1864), p. 121 (lines 4457-66). Concerning the exegesis of Gog and Magog, see Richard K. Emmerson, *Antichrist in the Middle Ages: A Study of Medieval Apocalypticism, Art, and Literature* (Seattle: Univ. of Washington Press, 1981), pp. 42, 59, 85-87.

4. For the text of the *Compendium,* see *B. Alberti Magni opera omnia,* ed. S. C. A. Borgnet (Paris: Ludovicum Vines, 1895), 34:243-44 (7.11). For the author, see Georg Boner, "Ueber den Dominikaner-theologen Hugo von Strassburg," *Archivium Fratrum Praedicatorum* 24 (1954): 269-86; A. Taugel, "Ripelin [,] Hugues," in *Dictionnaire de théologie catholique* (Paris: Librairie Letouzey et Ané, 1937), 13[2]:cols. 2737-38; and Heribert Fischer, "Hugues Ripelin de Strasbourg," in *Dictionnaire de spiritualité* (Paris: Beauchesne, 1969), 7:894-96. Speaking of the *Compendium,* Joseph Schroeder, "Hugh of Strassburg," *Catholic Encyclopedia* (New York: Encyclopedia Press, 1914), 7:524 notes: "In the entire medieval literature there is probably no work whose composition has, till very recently, been attributed to so many different authors." The influence of the *Compendium* in Germany in the late Middle Ages is Georg Steer's subject in *Hugo Ripelin von Strassburg* (Tübingen: Niemeyer, 1981).

5. Noted by Andrew Runni Anderson, *Alexander's Gate, Gog and Magog, and the Inclosed Nations* (Cambridge, Mass.: Mediaeval Academy of America, 1932), pp. 36-37. The references are to 3.25-26 of *Pseudo-Callisthenes.*

6. See M. Gosman, ed. *La Lettre du Prêtre Jean: édition des versions en ancien français et en ancien occitan* (Groningen: Bouma, 1982), pp. 165-73.

7. *The Geography of Strabo*, trans. and ed. Horace Leonard Jones, Loeb Classical Library (London: Heinemann; New York: Putnam, 1928), 5:235-40 (2.5.3-5); see Andrew Runni Anderson, "Alexander at the Caspian Gates," *Transactions of the American Philological Association* 59 (1928): 130-63, esp. p. 133.

8. Anderson, "Alexander at the Caspian Gates," passim.

9. *The Gothic History of Jordanes*, trans. Charles Christopher Mierow (Cambridge, Eng.: Speculum Historiale; New York: Barnes and Noble, 1966), p. 64 (corresponding to 7.49). Jordanes sees a reference to this mountain in Virgil's description of Dido's reaction to Aeneas in the Underworld (*Aeneid*, 6.471): "Quam si dura silex aut stet Marpesia cautes" ("[she does not change her countenance more] than if she were set in hard flint or the Marpesian cliff").

10. *Kyng Alisaunder*, ed. G. V. Smithers, EETS, o.s. 227 (London: Oxford Univ. Press, 1952), pp. 311ff.; and *The Anglo-Norman Alexander (Le Roman de toute chevalerie) by Thomas of Kent*, ed. Brian Foster (London: Anglo-Norman Text Society, 1976), vol. 1, lines 6170-84.

11. *Wars of the Jews* (7.7), in *Josephus, Complete Works*, trans. William Whiston (Grand Rapids, Mich.: Kregel, 1960), p. 598. The incident is elaborated upon by Hegesippus, c. 390, in his adaptation of Josephus, in which version the Alans are said to be driven either by the effects of drought and famine or merely by a desire for plunder (*praedandi cupidine*); see *Hegesippi qui dicitur historiae libri V*, ed. Vincentius Ussani, CSEL 66 (Vienna: Hoelder-Pichler-Tempsky; Leipzig: Akademische Verlags-Gesellschaft, 1932), p. 405 (5.50); and Anderson, "Alexander at the Caspian Gates," p. 148. The translation of Josephus ben Gorion by Peter Morwyng mentions only the "great dearth and famine throughout al their [the Alans'] land" as motivation for their request to the "People of Hurkan"; see *A Compendious and most marueilous History of the latter tymes of the Jewes commune weale, . . . Translated into Englishe by Peter Morvvyng of Magdalen Colledge in Oxford* (London, 1558), fol. cclxv.

To have the Gates under the control of the king of Hyrcania may mean that Josephus has confused the Caucasian and Persian gates; but as Anderson notes, *Hyrcani* may have represented a transliteration of the Armenian word for the Iberians (i.e. the Georgians), who for centuries did in fact control the territory that bordered the Caucasian pass on the south ("Alexander at the Caspian Gates," pp. 147-48).

12. See Strabo, 11.500 ff.; Josephus, *Antiq.*, 18.4.6; Tacitus, *Annales*, 6.33; Seutonius, *Nero*, 19; and Tacitus, *Hist.*, 1.6, where the tribe is referred to as *Albanos*, (i.e. the Albanians, who were located on the west, not the north, shore of the Caspian Sea; but see Theodor

Mommsen, *Römische Geschichte* [Berlin: Weidmann, 1885], 5:339, n. 1; and Dio Cassius, 63.8.1). See also K. Czégledy, "Kaukázusi Hunok, Kaukázusi Avarok" [Caucasian Huns, Caucasian Avars], *Antik Tanulmányok* 2 (1955): 121-40, esp. pp. 128-31; and David Magie, *Roman Rule in Asia Minor to the End of the Third Century after Christ* (Princeton: Princeton Univ. Press, 1950), pp. 575, 621, 659-61, 1418, 1438. Dr. Laszlo Kurti of American University kindly translated Czégledy's study for me.

13. See the references conveniently assembled by Anderson, *Alexander's Gate*, pp. 12-14.

14. Jacques de Vitry, *Historia Iherosolymitana*, trans. Aubrey Stewart (*The History of Jerusalem A.D. 1180 by Jacques de Vitry*), Library of the Palestine Pilgrims' Text Society (London, 1896; repr. New York: AMS Press, 1971), 3:83-84 (ch. 49). The Old French translation of the *Historia* at this point reads: "Lor gentils femes selonc la maniere des Armanonienes vont en batailles ausi come li chevalier"; see *La Traduction de l'Historia Orientalis de Jacques de Vitry*, ed. Claude Buridant (Paris: Klincksieck, 1986), p. 127. Elsewhere in the Old French version (p. 152 [ch. 90]) they are called *Armazonum*.

15. Jacques de Vitry, *Historia Orientalis*, in *Gesta Dei per Francos*, ed. Jacques Bongars (Hanover: Typis Wechelianis apud Ioan. Aubrii, 1611), 1:1142: "Sunt autem *Georgiani* cultores Christi, ritus habentes Graecorum, Persis vicini, longo terrarum tractu a Terra Promissionis distantes, quorum dominiam extenditur vsque ad Caspios montes, in quibus decem tribus inclusae desiderant aduentum Antichristi; tunc etiam erumpent magnam stragem facturae. Georgiani bellicosi sunt homines. . . . Mulieres eorum equestris ordinis edoctae sunt ad praelium." Elsewhere (ed. Bongars, 1:1107 [ch. 90]), Jacques refers to the Amazons as "egregiae in armis & praeliis mulieres, iuxta montes Caspios. . . ."

16. The Latin text reads as follows: "ille feminarum populus fortissimus sit et Christiano nomini dicatus. Contra Sarracenos acerrime pugnat. Et quidem non est diu, quod ipsarum Amazonarum regina veniens a partibus orientis servitio se mancipavit templi et sepulchri dominici." See *Thomas Cantimpratensis Liber de Natura Rerum*, ed. H. Boese (Berlin: de Gruyter, 1973), 1:31 [1.26].

    Is it possible that behind this "reminiscence" is a reference to the great Georgian queen Tamar (Tamara, co-ruler with her father Giorgi III from 1156 to 1184, and sole ruler from 1184 to 1212), under whose rule Georgia achieved its greatest power and influence? For Tamar, see W. E. D. Allen, *A History of the Georgian People* (New York: Barnes and Noble, 1932), pp. 103-08; Ronald Grigor Suny, in *Dictionary of the Middle Ages*, gen ed., Joseph T. Strayer (New York: Scribners,

1988), 11:587 (s.v. "Tamar"); and I. Mantskhava, "The Golden Age of Georgia," *Asiatic Review* 37 (1941): 366-76.

17. See the valuable discussion by John Block Friedman, *The Monstrous Races in Medieval Art and Thought* (Cambridge, Mass.: Harvard Univ. Press, 1981), pp. 170-71. "Et quoniam ex frequenti usu libidinis multi spiritus consumuntur, quanto rarius coeunt, tanto prefate viragines fortiores sunt et magis ydonee ad pugnandum" (*Thomas Cantimpratensis*, ed. Boese, 1:98 [3.2]). In the passage referred to in the previous note (1.26), Thomas mentions the unusually strong bones of the Amazons: "Ossa masculorum fortiora sunt ossibus feminarum nisi tantum in genere Amazonarum mulierum, ubi fortitudo et robur feminarum prefertur fortitudini virorum. . . ." Thomas's sentiments would seem to be at variance with the Galenic theory that seed must be released periodically or else it will poison the womb and cause death by suffocation. The Old French versified moralization of *De naturis rerum* (late-thirteenth/early-fourteenth century) holds the Amazons up as models of chaste and virtuous sexuality; see Alfons Hilka, ed., *Eine altfranzösische moralisierende Bearbeitung des* Liber de Monstruosis Hominibus Orientis *aus Thomas von Cantimpré,* De naturis rerum *nach der einzigen Handschrift (Paris, Bibl. Nat. fr. 15106)*, in *Abhandlungen der Gesellschaft der Wissenschaften zu Göttingen*, Philologisch-Historische Klasse, 3rd ser. 7 (Berlin: Wiedmann, 1933), pp. 24-25 (lines 55-104).

18. *Mandeville's Travels*, ed. Seymour, p. 87: "There ben othere that men clepen Georgyenes that Seynt George conuerted, and him thei worschipen more than ony other seynt, and to him thei crien for help. And thei camen out of the reme of George. Theise folk vsen crounes schauen; the clerkes han rounde crounes, and the lewed men han crownes alle square. And thei holden Cristene law as don thei of Grece, of whom I haue spoken of before." Jacques de Vitry (ed. Bongars, 1:1095) writes: "Hi homines *Georgiani* nuncipantur, eo quod sanctum Georgium, quem in praelis suis contra gentem incredulam aduocatum habent & patronum, & tanquam signiferum, cum summa reuerentia colunt & adorant, & prae aliis sanctis specialiter honorant. Vtuntur autem Graeco idomate in scripturis diuinis & Graecorum consuetudinis in sacramentis obseruant. Clerici eorum rotundas habent *coronas*, laici vero quadratus. Quotiescuncque Dominicum Sepulchrum visitaturi peregre adueniunt, absque tributo aliquo cum erectis vexilillis ciuitatem sanctam ingrediuntur. Saraceni enim nullo modo molestare praesumunt, ne forte cum ad propria reuersi essent, aliis Saracenis sibi vicinis, vicem rependerent. Nobiles autem mulieres eorum more Amazonum tanquam milites armis vtuntur in praelis."

19. The parodic aspects of Antichrist's biography are discussed by Emmerson, *Antichrist*; note his index entry "Antichrist—as pseudo-Christ" on p. 346 (see above, n. 3). I owe the suggestion of the Amazons in a similar context to a perceptive comment of John Block Friedman, orally communicated. For a valuable caveat on reading typological associations into vernacular Alexander literature, see Ian Michael, "Typological Problems in Medieval Alexander Literature: The Enclosure of Gog and Magog," in *The Medieval Alexander Legend and Romance Epic: Essays in Honour of David J. A. Ross*, ed. Peter Noble, Lucie Polak, and Claire Isoz (Millwood, N.Y.: Kraus, 1982), pp. 131-47.

20. *Sibylline Oracles*, trans. J. J. Collins, in *The Old Testament Pseudepigrapha*, ed. J. H. Charlesworth (Garden City, N.Y.: Doubleday, 1983), 1:370. See also J. Jeanmarie. "Le règne de la Femme des derniers jours et le rajeunissement du monde," in *Mélanges Franz Cumont* (Brussels: Université libre de Bruxelles, 1936), pp. 297-304.

21. *Apocalypse of Daniel*, trans. G. T. Zevros, in Charlesworth, *Old Testament Pseudepigrapha*, 1:766 (6:10-11). See also Wilhelm Bousset, *The Antichrist Legend*, trans. A. H. Keane (London: Hutchinson, 1896), pp. 69-71, where reference is made to a *Vision of Daniel* in South Slavonic and Russian with a similar prediction of a ruling virgin who accepts the Antichrist.

22. See Jane A. Leake, *The Geats of Beowulf* (Madison: Univ. of Wisconsin Press, 1967), pp. 13-16; Friedman, *Monstrous Races*, pp. 84-85.

23. Anderson, *Alexander's Gate*, pp. 6-8.

24. *S. Hieronymi Presbyteri opera, pars I, opera exegetica 4, commentariorum in Hiezechielem libri XIV*, Corpus Christianorum, Series Latina 75 (Turnhout: Brepols, 1964), p. 535 (38.2).

25. *Paulus Orosius, The Seven Books of History against the Pagans*, trans. Roy J. Deferrai, The Fathers of the Church 50 (Washington, D.C.: Catholic Univ. of America Press, 1964), p. 37 (1.16); the original text is in *Pauli Orosii*, ed. Zangemeister, pp. 68-69. See also *The Old English Orosius*, ed. Bately, pp. 30-31 (see above, n. 2).

26. Anderson, *Alexander's Gate*, p. 12.

27. See Anderson, *Alexander's Gate*, pp. 9-12; and Leake, *Geats of Beowulf*, pp. 24-52.

28. Jordanes, *Get.*, 5.44; 7.49; and *On the Properties of Things: John Trevisa's Translation of Bartholomaeus Anglicus* De Proprietatibus

Rerum, gen. ed. M. C. Seymour (Oxford: Clarendon Press, 1975),
2:765-66. A recent discussion of this topic as regards Jordanes's
history is in Walter Goffart, *The Narrators of Barbarian History
(A.D. 550-800)* (Princeton: Princeton Univ. Press, 1988), pp. 80-82.

29. *Procopius*, trans. and ed. H. B. Dewing, in *History of the Wars, Books
    VII (continued) and VIII*, Loeb Classical Library (London: Heinemann;
    Cambridge, Mass.: Harvard Univ. Press, 1962), 5:77-79 (8.3.8-11).
    John Scylitzes mentions that warrior women's bodies were likewise
    found among the bodies of the slain Rus after a battle near the Danube
    against the Byzantine army; see H. R. Ellis Davidson, *The Viking
    Road to Byzantium* (London: Allen and Unwin, 1976), pp. 114-15.

30. Translated by Ernest A. Wallis Budge, *The History of Alexander the
    Great, being the Syriac version of the Pseudo-Callisthenes*
    (Cambridge, 1889; repr. Amsterdam: Philo Press, 1976), pp. 150-52.
    See also K. Czégledy, "The Syriac Legend concerning Alexander the
    Great," *Acta Orientalia* 7 (1957): 231-49, and, for a convenient list of
    texts that identify the Huns with Gog/Magog, Anderson, *Alexander's
    Gate*, p. 12.

31. *The Alexander Book in Ethiopia*, trans. Ernest A. Wallis Budge
    (London: Oxford Univ. Press, 1933), pp. 138-43. On the subject of
    cannibalism, see Jill Tattersall, "Anthropophagi and Eaters of Raw
    Flesh in French Literature of the Crusade Period: Myth, Tradition, and
    Reality," *Medium Ævum* 57 (1988): 240-53.

32. See Anderson, *Alexander's Gate*, pp. 58-59.

33. *Velislai Biblia Picta*, ed. Karel Stejskal (Prague: Pragopress, 1970),
    fol. 13v: "Ibi antichristus vadit cum regibus et suis prophetis et
    apostolis contra Gog et Magog. idem contra illas X. tribus, que clause
    sunt ultra montes Caspios. Non tamen ita clause sunt quoniam bene
    possent exire. Sed non permituntur a regina Amazonum, sub cuius
    regno et dicione uiunt. Isti tempore Antichristi sunt venturi in
    jherusalem cum suo exercitu." Dependence of the legends of the
    illustrations of the *Velislav Bible* on the *Compendium* was
    demonstrated by Karel Chytil, *Antikrist V Naukách a Uměni
    Středověku a Husitské Obrazne Antithese* (Prague: Nákladem České
    Akademie Císaře Františka Josefa, 1918). For the Antichrist
    illustrations in this Bible, as well as those in the *Wellcome
    Apocalypse* (below, n. 34), see the most valuable discussion by Jessie
    Jean Poesch, "Antichrist Imagery in Anglo-Norman Apocalypse
    Manuscripts" (Ph.D. diss., Univ. of Pennsylvania, 1966), pp. 291-
    319; and Emmerson, *Antichrist*, pp. 109-11, 125-26.

34. London, Wellcome Institute for the History of Medicine, MS 49, fol. 11r: "Primus discipulus praedicat regi Egypti. Glossa super Daniel 7. Convertet tres reges sub scriptos. Alius discipulos praedicat regi Libyae. Alius reginae Amazoniae et judeis gog et magog et exibiit illo tempore de montibus ut dicit Hieronimus."

35. London, Wellcome Institute for the History of Medicine, MS 49, fol. 11v: "Postea praedicabunt christianis Antichristum fore verum deum et ante illum nullum fuisse. Christianosque omnes Antichristos fuisse. Tunc veniet omnes gentes videre Antichristum et credent in eum et liberabuntur a montibus caspiis. Et regina Amazoniae praeceditque eos. . . ."

36. In his *Commentary on Daniel*, Jerome established the earlier identification (by Porphyry, et al.) of the "little horn" of Daniel 11 as Antiochus Epiphanius as a type of the Antichrist. Regarding Daniel 11:42-43 ("Et mittet manum suam in terras, et terra Ægypti non effugiet; et dominabitur thesaurorum auri et argenti, et in omnibus pretiosis Ægypti per Libyas quoque et Æthiopias transibit"), Jerome notes special relevance to the Antichrist, since in his wars with Egypt (the kingdom of the south [Daniel 11.5 ff.]) the historical Antiochus never subdued Libya or Ethiopia. See *S. Hieronymi Presbyteri opera,* pars I, opera Exegetica V: *Commentariorum in Danielem libri III<IV>*, Corpus Christianorum, Series Latina 75a (Turnholt: Brepols, 1964), p. 930. The typological reading of Daniel 11 is not in favor among modern commentators; Alexander A. Di Lella, trans., *The Book of Daniel,* Anchor Bible 23 (Garden City, N. Y.: Doubleday, 1978), remarks that the "Antichrist interpretation of these verses is exegetically witless and religiously worthless" (p. 303). But it was standard exegesis throughout the Middle Ages; see Emmerson, *Antichrist,* pp. 21, 24-26, 44-45, 60, 67, 121-22. Hippolytus, *De Antichristo,* 25, CSCO 264:64-65, precedes Jerome in the matter, and Nicholas of Lyre, *Glossa,* vol. 4, fol. 310r incorporates it into his widely read *Postilla* to the *Glossa Ordinaria.* But precisely at what point the Amazon queen is drawn into the exegesis of Daniel 11, I cannot yet determine.

37. *Der Antichrist und die fünfzehn Zeichen: Faksimile-Ausgabe des einzigen erhaltenen chiroxylographischen Blockbuches,* ed. H. Th. Musper (Munich: Prestel-Verlag, 1970), 1:10-11 (corresponding to 2:7r): "[Aber ein ander pot predigt der kunigin von amason vnd] den Roten Juden. dy der gros kunig alexander in den gepirgen Caspie beslossen het. dy kumen aus zu des endkristes zeyten als sanctus Jeronimus schreibet."

38. *Der Antichrist,* fol. 7v: "vnd zewcht dy kungin von Amason auch zu dem endkrist."

39. *[Itinerarium]* *Iohannes von Monteuilla Ritter* (Strassburg: Johann Pruss, 1488) 2.5: "Die würt mit den ersten syn die zü dem Antichrist ziehen. die künigin würt sin predig horen und an in glauben."

For von Diemeringen and his translation, see Malcolm Letts, *Sir John Mandeville: The Man and His Book* (London: Batchworth, 1949), pp. 135-43. In his 1927 University of Erlangen dissertation, Arthur Schoernes lists 27 manuscripts of this translation, only one of which (Berlin, Staatsbibliothek [Preußischer Kulturbesitz] MS Germ. Fol. 205) dates from before the fifteenth century (*Die Deutschen Mandeville-Versionen: Handschriftliche Untersuchungen*, pp. 13-30). Von Diemeringen's translation used the revised French text, incorporating material related to Ogier the Dane, which was produced at Liège c. 1390, as well as a Latin translation of the *Travels*. Von Diemeringen's work was in turn used by Vavrinec of Brezová for his (early-fifteenth-century) Czech translation of the *Travels*; see Frantisek Simek, ed., *Cestopis tzv. Mandevilla. Ceský preklad porizeny Vavrincem z Brezove* [Travel Account of the So-called Mandeville. Czech Translation by Vavrinec of Brezová] (Prague: Nákladem České akademie Císaře Františka Josefa pro vedy, 1911). An illustration of von Diemeringen at work on his translation can be found in British Library MS Add. 24189, reproduced in facsimile as *The Travels of Sir John Mandeville: A Manuscript in the British Library*, trans. Peter Kussi, ed. Josef Krása (New York: Braziller, 1983), a manuscript of twenty-eight full-page pictures that illustrate, without text, the first thirteen chapters of the Czech translation. For early printed texts of von Diemeringen's translation, see Letts, pp. 180-81.

40. Jacques de Vitry (ed. Bongars), *Historia Iherosolymitana*, 1:1096 (ch. 81): "Imbelles enim & imbecilles facti sunt quasi mulieres. Vnde singulis lunationibus, vt dicitur, fluxum sanguinis patiuntur."

Imagining Christendom
from Jerusalem to Paradise:
Asia in *Mandeville's Travels*

by Iain Higgins

"During the Middle Ages," Erich Auerbach once wrote, "all practical acquaintance with alien forms of life and culture was lost." As generalizations go, this is not a very helpful one, and it would be easy enough to challenge it. One could start, for example, with its grammatical expression and point to the stative passive "was lost," asking "by whom? where?"—even "when?"[1] For Auerbach's claim suggests that "the Middle Ages" should be regarded as a unified totality which occupied a precisely delimited and, what is more important, closed geographical, historical, and cultural space: western Europe, one would assume, between the end of the Roman Empire and the beginning of the Reformation, otherwise known as Latin Christendom. That, of course, is how many people have regarded the period, perhaps particularly during moments of conflict or crisis in their own time.[2] "Those were beautiful, brilliant times," wrote Novalis in 1799 in a tract on *Christendom or Europe*, times "when Europe was *one* Christian country. . . ." "We project dynamic polarities on history," D. W. Robertson, Jr. has more recently argued, calling them "class struggles, balances of power, or . . . conflicts between economic realities and traditional ideals," forgetting that "the medieval world with its quiet hierarchies knew nothing of these things."[3] Such visions as these of

Iain Higgins is Assistant Professor of English at the University of British Columbia (see Notes on Contributors, p. 222).

"beautiful, brilliant times" and "quiet hierarchies," depending as they do on the assumption that medieval Europe stands apart from the writer's own place and time by virtue of being a closed and unified cultural space, are clearly nostalgic to the point of naïveté, and one has a hard time taking them seriously.

Yet the interesting and perhaps ironic thing is that these naïve visions have more than a little in common with the ways in which many medieval Christian thinkers imagined their world. Ernst Kantorowicz, for instance, has argued that the Romantic and post-Romantic Myth of Medieval World Unity [his uppercase] had its origins in medieval thought, since medieval thinkers probably "found it easier than we do to acknowledge a [unified] totality, even an imaginary one," beginning as they did from "the Whole" rather than the separate parts and often within an eschatological framework.[4] Christendom was one such *a priori* totality, and it was in many respects a real one. It was after all a transnational community of men, women, and children acknowledging the same God, professing the same Faith, belonging to the same Church, claiming the same universality—and on occasion therefore persecuting the same heretics or fighting the same wars against other religious communities. But as Benedict Anderson would argue, this genuine and historically definable religious community must also be regarded as an imagined one. For, in his view, "all communities larger than primordial villages of face-to-face contact (and perhaps even these) are imagined"; and they are imagined precisely because the members of such communities, despite not actually knowing in any way most of their fellow-members, still have in their minds "the image of their communion." That image will of course differ from community to community, such that distinct communities are effectively distinguished from one another "not by their falsity/genuineness, but by the style in which they are imagined." "The great sacral cultures," for example— Anderson names the Ummah Islam, the Middle Kingdom, and Latin Christendom—"incorporated conceptions of immense communities." Imagining themselves as "cosmically central," partly on the basis of their relation to a sacred language and sacred texts, these communities grounded themselves in the belief that the world was "centripetal and hierarchical, rather than boundary-oriented and horizontal."[5]

Put thus, Anderson's definition of an immense sacral community seems vague, only a little more helpful than Auerbach's generalization. Yet if one compares the world depicted on our standard geopolitical maps with that depicted on certain medieval *mappaemundi* (e.g., the Ebstorf and Hereford maps), one can see exactly what Anderson means. The world on our maps usually appears as an arrangement of distinct and sovereign nation-states, thereby emphasizing the horizontally bounded parts in relation to the geographical whole; the world on the *mappaemundi*, by contrast, appears as the classical *orbis terrarum* (schematically depicting only the three continents of Asia, Africa, and Europe) transformed in such a way that Jerusalem occupies the exact center and the Earthly Paradise defines the eastern and topmost edge, while Christ either hovers over the whole (Hereford) or actually embodies it (Ebstorf).[6] The style in which the world is imagined on these medieval maps, then, suggests that their makers were concerned above all with "the Whole" and that they regarded everyone as potentially belonging to a Christendom which defined (though it did not in fact occupy) both center and periphery. To put it another way, Latin Christendom as represented on these maps can be thought of as being at once an imagined and an imaginary religious community—that is, a real community of believers projecting an image of their communion well past its actual boundaries in the world to a point at which it no longer has any basis in reality.

In the pages that follow I want to examine one version of this peculiar religious community: specifically, the version represented in the remarkable book usually known as *Mandeville's Travels* (c. 1360). Despite its modern title, this book is more than a simple *récit de voyages* (real, imagined, and imaginary); it is also a popular encyclopedia devoted to representing "a partie of custumes and maneres and dyuersitees of contrees" that lie "ouer the see" dividing "the west syde of the world" from "the gretter and the beste partie toward the est, that is clept Asye"—that is, the entire region bounded by Jerusalem and Paradise on the *mappaemundi* just mentioned.[7] Like many such medieval books, *Mandeville's Travels* is not content merely to describe the "diversities" of far countries; it also attempts to relate them to their counterparts at home, which of course requires the author to imagine home (Latin Christendom) in relation to the cultural and religious diversity found throughout the entire eastern or "upper" half of the world, parts of which are real (e.g., the Mongol empire) and parts imaginary (e.g., Prester John's land).

Moreover, since *Mandeville's Travels* was written at a moment when the sometimes fluid boundaries between Latin Christendom and the surrounding Christian and non-Christian world had been shrinking considerably after a period of unprecedented European expansion, and when Latin Christendom itself was growing increasingly divided, it is obviously a book conceived, produced, and distributed within an increasingly enclosed culture, if not quite a closed one.[8] In this respect, therefore, the book and the culture alike can be thought of as practically unacquainted with "alien forms of life and culture"—I say "book" rather than "author" because (for reasons given below) it is unclear whether its author had any acquaintance whatsoever with the world beyond Latin Christendom apart from that obtained through books and, possibly, *mappaemundi*. Insofar as the author lacked such practical acquaintance with the East, and in addition supplemented his account thereof with fictions of his own and others' making, his book can be thought of as depicting imaginary relations between cultures—that is, relations based on "images derived not from observation, experience, and perceptible reality but from a psychological urge," an "urge [that] creates its own realities which are totally different from the political realities" known through practical acquaintance, though not therefore less significant or influential.[9]

Defined more precisely, then, the aim of the present essay is as follows: to examine some of the ways in which *Mandeville's Travels* imagines the community of Christendom by focusing on its representations of other religious communities, real and imaginary, and specifically to consider the manner in which the book both acknowledges the irreducible diversity of the world and at the same time incorporates or appropriates that diversity into a totality coterminous with the work of a God "that in alle places is present and alle thinges conteynynge" (p. 230; Letts, p. 411). In order to carry out such an examination, of course, it will be necessary to regard *Mandeville's Travels* as representing "a certain *will* or *intention* . . . to incorporate what is a manifestly different . . . world," that will or intention being implied by the book's handling of the non-Christian world. To some extent, therefore, this essay can be thought of as a qualifying footnote to Edward W. Said's at once learned and polemical study of "the interrelations between society, history, and textuality" in those more recent writings emerging from what he calls "orientalism."[10]

Although their meanings will be clarified in the course of my analysis of *Mandeville's Travels*, it might helpful at this point to define very briefly the cognate terms "image," "imagining," "imagined," and "imaginary," none of which I am using in a strictly technical sense. By "image" I mean the *product* of representation (as, for example, the "image" of the Indian in popular Western novels), while by "imagining" I mean the *process* of representation (what, for instance, is selected or emphasized, what is not, and how and why?). By "imagined," used here largely of communities, I mean something made and specifically something made from what already exists (as, for example, the "imagined community" of Latin Christendom is made from the actual communion of medieval Christians), whereas by "imaginary," used here largely of relations between communities, I mean something made up, which even if it draws on what already exists cannot be considered as simply made from it (as, for instance, Prester John's land is made up, based at most on rumors of an Asian Christendom); the problem is, of course, that these two terms are not fully distinct, nor is the relation between them fully symmetrical: something made up is obviously also something made, although something made is not necessarily something made up. Still, I believe that there is useful and fairly clear distinction to be made between "imagined" and "imaginary" and that this distinction allows one to regard a work like *Mandeville's Travels* in an interesting way.

Very little, unfortunately, is known about the origins of *Mandeville's Travels*, except that it was compiled in French by an unknown author, and that immediately thereafter it was copied and recopied, translated and retranslated, such that it has come down to us in more than 250 manuscripts and various incunabular editions representing ten languages (French, English, Irish, Danish, Dutch, German, Czech, Italian, Spanish, and Latin). In compiling this book, the unknown author drew on a number of sources, amongst them the anonymous *Letter of Prester John*, Johannes Sacrobosco's *De sphera*, and Vincent of Beauvais's *Speculum historiale* and *Speculum naturale*. But he used these works mostly as supplements, as sources of scientific, historical, or legendary information. For the larger body of the book, the author turned to the accounts of two genuine travelers: William of Boldensele, a wealthy German Dominican who, sometime in 1336, wrote a detailed and orderly Latin account of his *peregrinatio* to the areas in and around the Holy Land; and Odoric of Pordenone, a rather undistinguished Franciscan who, in May of 1330, dictated to a fellow religious a sometimes confused and confusing Latin account of his wanderings in India and China during the previous decade or so. After splicing their accounts together and reworking them, the *Mandeville*-author presented them as the memoirs of an English knight errant, who emerges now and again from the text to recount some striking personal anecdote or other.[11]

The knight errant born of this curious literary union of pilgrim and missionary is of course none other than the famous (or infamous) John Mandeville, a fictional character long thought to have been the genuine author, but whose actual relation to the author seems likely to remain an unresolved problem. Also likely to remain open is the question whether or not its author traveled anywhere beyond a good library. Although it seems reasonable to suppose that he might at least have made the Jerusalem pilgrimage, the fact remains that his book is a compilation based on the travels of others and, as such, tells us nothing about his own practical acquaintance with far countries.[12] If it can tell us anything, then, the book may well tell us something about the ways in which its author imagined his community in relation to others, regardless of how he came to know, or know about, those other communities. At any rate, the *Mandeville*-author, in producing his apparently personal and definitely popular encyclopedia of the known and imagined world, was engaged in what Said has called "the central cultural activity": the "elaboration" of a few "principal, directive ideas" in order "to perpetuate a world view."[13]

Not surprisingly, given such uncertainties in our knowledge, recent readers of *Mandeville's Travels* have reacted quite differently to the knowledge that it is a compilation, variously describing it as "a rank literary imposture," "a romance of travel," the work of a "marvel-monger," "a summa of travel lore," "a rich index of a new sensibility," and the "first" instance of "realistic prose fiction . . . since Petronius."[14] Yet however one chooses to characterize this book, it is hard to deny that *Mandeville's Travels* often displays an almost un-medieval capacity to imagine lives radically different from those known within fourteenth-century Latin Christendom, and to do so sympathetically. While attempting, for instance, to prove not simply that the earth is a potentially circumnavigable sphere, but also that it might be inhabited virtually everywhere, the *Mandeville*-author has the narrator Sir John counter the obvious objection of the literal-minded:

> it semeth to symple men vnlerned that men ne mowe not go
> vnder the erthe, and also that men scholde falle toward the
> Heuene from vnder. But that may not be vpon less than wee

mowe falle toward Heuene from the erthe where wee ben. For fro what partie of the erthe that man duelle, outher abouen or benethen, it semeth alweys to hem that duellen that thei gon more right than ony other folk. And right as it semeth to vs that thei ben vnder vs, right so it semeth hem that wee ben vnder hem. (p. 135; Letts, p. 334)[15]

One's earthly situation, in other words, is not just relative; it is also "relativizing," since it helps shape one's knowledge of the world.

Nor is this moment of imagined and probably imaginary otherness, which comes as a digression in the *Mandeville*-author's rewriting of Friar Odoric's *Relatio*, merely an isolated example in the book. Throughout the *Travels*, one comes across both brief and extended remarks which, drawing strength from their frequency, leave the impression that the author was anything but narrow in his views. Even the pagan practice of heliolatry, to take a simple example, receives a considered response from him; significantly, this response comes in the context of an extended discussion of "the customs of the yles abouten Ynde" inserted into Odoric's narrative at the expense of the friar's longish history of four brother mendicants martyred for the faith in Thana, near Bombay:[16] "for [the sonne] is of so gret profite thei [the people of Thana] knowe wel that that myghte not be but that God loueth it more than ony other thing. . . . Therfore it is gode resoun, as thei seyn, to don it worschipe and reuerence" (p. 121; Letts, p. 323). Carefully refraining from actually approving such behavior, the *Mandeville*-author nevertheless treats it as motivated by both reason and piety and therefore as worthy of explanation rather than condemnation.

Of course, not all of these "relativizing" explanations necessarily come from the *Mandeville*-author himself. At least some of his striking capacity to imagine other lives and other ways seems to have been derived from the book's sources, although in the known sources that capacity appears only intermittently and sometimes merely by virtue of scribal interpolation. An excellent example of "relativism" derived from such intermittent and possibly scribal "relativism" can be found in the book's brief but striking account of the "Pigmans" who live near China, an account which derives from Odoric and is, as Henry Yule has remarked, "very confused in almost all versions" of the *Relatio*. The Latin and Italian texts of Odoric's account, for instance, generally offer the simplest possible sketch of the pygmies, as this Latin text shows:

[H]ii pigmei sunt magni tribus spansis, qui faciunt magna
opera Goton, id est bombicis, quam aliqui homines qui sunt in
mundo. Homines autem magni qui ibi sint filios generant qui
plus quam pro dimidietate similes illis pigmeis sunt qui sunt
ita parvi. Ideoque tot istorum parvorum ibi generantur et
nascuntur quod sine numero quasi sunt.

[These pygmies are three spans in height, and they do greater
work in cotton, as it is called, than any people in the world.
And the full-sized men who dwell there beget sons who are
more than half of them like those pygmies who are so small.
And for that reason so many of these small people are
begotten and born there that they are almost countless.]

In some Latin versions, however, this brief account concludes
with what may be an interpolated sentence; that sentence notes simply
that the pygmies "have rational souls like ourselves" ("habent autem
animam rationalem sicut nos").[17] This apparently trivial interpolation,
if that in fact is what it is, suggests that some of Odoric's readers were
capable of imagining beings in far countries as radically other and yet
still capable of salvation. Certain French texts, moreover, go even
further, if also in a slightly different direction, offering their audiences a
quick pygmy's-eye-view of the world. The translation of Odoric's book
made, for instance, in 1351, by Jean le Long of Ypres, after noting that
these tiny creatures have amongst them "grandes gens qui labourent les
terres et les vingnes," provides the following startling insight into their
world: "De ces grandes gens se truffent les pumeaux dessus dis, ainsi
que nous faisons en ces parties des gens qui sont grant oultre mesure de
raison. . . . Ilz sont droitement gens visans raison comme nous"; or, as
the translator of the Cotton version of *Mandeville's Travels* even more
forcefully renders it: "And of tho men of oure stature han thei als grete
skorn and wonder as we wolde haue among vs of geauntes yif thei
weren amonges vs. . . . And alle be it that the pygmeyes ben lytylle,
yit thei ben fulle resonable after here age and conen bothen wytt and
gode and malice ynow" (p. 152; Letts, p. 348).[18] Clearly, then,
whatever the ultimate source of this particular vision of otherness, the
Mandeville-author has preserved it in his own rewriting of Odoric's
relation, since it is consistent with the sort of imaginative
"relativism" just mentioned. Indeed, this fuller depiction of the pygmies
as creatures possessed of both their own view of things and enough
reason to be capable of salvation can stand as an exemplar of his

generally sympathetic, scholarly, and imaginative treatment of the world's diversity.[19]

But what concerns me here is not the *Mandeville*-author's treatment of diversity as such; rather, it is his version of Christendom as seen in the mirror of Asian diversity, a version to which I now want to turn for the remainder of this essay.

Towards the end of *Mandeville's Travels*, when Sir John is passing on information about some of the "yles [that] there ben in the lond of Prestre Iohn," he offers his audience a brief anecdote that purports to explain the origin of Prester John's name. Like many such anecdotes, this one also suggests something of the author's—or at least of the book's—own views on larger matters:

> I trowe that yee knowe wel ynow . . . wherfore this emperour is clept Prestre Iohn, but natheles for hem that knowen not I schalle seye you the cause. It was somtyme an emperour there . . . that hadde Cristene knyghtes in his companye, as he hath that is now. So it befelle that he hadde gret list for to see the seruise in the chirche among Cristene men. *And than dured Cristendom beyonde the see alle Turkye, Surrye, Tartarie, Ierusalem, Palestyne, Arabye, Halappee, and alle the lond of Egypte.* So it befelle that this emperour cam with a Cristene knyght with him into a chirche in Egypt, and . . . the bisshopp made ordres. And he beheld and listend the seruyse fulle tentyfly. And he asked the Cristene knyght what men of degree thei scholden ben that the prelate had before him. And the knyght answerde . . . that thei scholde ben prestes. And than the emperour seyde that he wolde no lenger ben clept kyng ne emperour but preest, and that he wolde haue the name of the firste preest that wente out of the chirche. And his name was Iohn, and so eueremore sithens he is clept Prestre Iohn.
>
> In his lond ben manye Cristene men of gode feyth and of gode lawe . . . and [thei] han comounly hire prestes that syngen the messe and maken the sacrement of the awtier of bred right as the Grekes don. But thei seye not so manye thinges at the messe as men don here. For thei seye not but only that that the Apostles seyden as oure lord taughte hem, right as Seynt Peter and Seynt Thomas and the other Apostles songen the mess, seyenge the *Pater Noster* and the wordes of the sacrement. But wee haue many mo addicouns that dyuerse popes han made that thei ne knowe not offe. (pp. 216-17, emphasis added; Letts, p. 402, omitting "Tartarie")

One of the two "grettest lordes vndir the firmament" (p. 196; not in Letts), according to the narrator, Prester John was a popular figure in late medieval writings dealing with Asia, having entered the imagination of Latin Christendom by means of a famous and fictional *Letter* (c. 1165) which circulated throughout Europe in both Latin and the vernacular. For this legendary king whose land was even "more ferr be many dredfulle iourneyes" than Cathay (p. 196; Letts, p. 384) offered European audiences not only the fascination of "Oriental mystery and grandeur"—which, after the latter part of the thirteenth century, they could likewise find in depictions of the Great Khan—but also, as the above quotation should suggest, the possibility of imagining an enormous Christian empire stretching from Europe, "the west syde of the world," through the Holy Land, "the herte and myddes of all the world," to farthest Asia, "the gretter and the beste partie" of "alle the world" (pp. 5, 1, 160; Letts, pp. 232, 229, 354).[20]

It is hardly surprising, then, that Prester John should appear in at least some of the precursors and sources of *Mandeville's Travels*, whatever their origin and ostensible purpose. This great Christian emperor figures, for instance, not only in the *Divisament dou monde* dictated by the merchant Marco Polo to the *romancier* Rustichello of Pisa, but also in the generally more sober accounts given by various missionaries, including John of Plano Carpini's *Ystoria Mongalorum* and William of Rubruck's *Itinerarium* and Odoric of Pordenone's *Relatio*. What is surprising, however, is that only Marco Polo's *Divisament* even remotely suggests that Prester John and his realm might be a distant mirror for Christian rulers, and, moreover, that none of these works, not even the militantly religious ones, seriously considers him as an agent of Christendom in Asia. Indeed, they hardly consider him at all. The diligent Friar John, for instance, has other matters to deal with—in particular, the readiness of the Mongols to wage war against Christendom—while the characteristically sceptical Friar William dismisses the received portrait of the great Christian king as the product of Nestorian lies (*Itinerarium*, ch. 17); moreover, and even more important in the present context, the generally credulous Friar Odoric does almost exactly the same thing, asserting that "not one hundredth part is true of what is told of him as if it were undeniable."[21]

By contrast, the *Mandeville*-author shows no such sceptical indifference towards Prester John. Rather, he presents this "grete emperour of Ynde" (p. 194; Letts, p. 383) as the model ruler of a model

Christian society which hardly suffers at all from its lack of some of the latest European articles of the Faith. In fact, not only do the temporal and spiritual powers know no separation in this far-off land, but the local subjects would seem to be as pure in belief as they are distant from Latin Christendom, for in the world according to *Mandeville's Travels*, the closer one is to the eastern edge of the *mappa mundi*, the closer one seems to be to the origins of things:[22]

> This Prestre Iohn hath vnder him many kynges and many yles and many dyuerse folk of dyuerse condicouns. And this lond is fulle gode and ryche, but. . . . the marchauntes comen not thider so comounly . . . as thei don in the lond of the Gret Chane, for it is to fer to trauaylle to. . . .
> . . . Prestre Iohn is Cristene and a gret partie of his contree also, but yif ["yit"?] thei haue not alle the articles of oure feyth as wee hauen. Thei beleuen wel in the Fader, in the Sone, and in the Holy Gost. And thei ben fulle deuoute and right trewe on to another. . . .
> This emperour Prestre Iohn hath eueremore vii. kynges with him to seruen him, and thei departen hire seruice be certeyn monethes. And with theise kynges seruen alleweys lxxii. dukes and ccc. and lx. erles. . . . And the partriark of Seynt Thomas is there as is the Pope here, and the erchebisshoppes and the bisshoppes and the abbottes in that contree ben alle kynges. And euerych of theise grete lordes knowen wel ynow the attendance of hire seruyce. (pp. 195-200; Letts, pp. 383-87)

There are probably any number of reasons for this discrepancy between *Mandeville's Travels* and the earlier writings just mentioned— some of them obviously have to do with the difference between "fact" and a form of "factual fiction"—but at least one of them has to do with the *Mandeville*-author's own historical situation. For unlike the traveling friars, this stay-at-home author, working, as I have said, probably in the late 1350s, had to have known that the Crusades and the mission to Asia alike had failed to fulfill the high hopes surrounding their launching; after all, his book begins by announcing that "it is longe tyme passed that ther was no generalle passage ne vyage ouer the see" (p. 3; Letts, p. 231) and eventually demonstrates in copious detail that Asia is full of diverse peoples of even greater piety and devotion than Christians, who, despite having had the benefit of the One True Faith, are now divided amongst themselves. To take just one example: after

describing the sufferings of Indian pilgrims who freely cast themselves
under a passing juggernaut, Sir John reflects briefly but pointedly on
the feebleness of the comparable European practice of *imitatio Christi*:
"And, schortly to seye you, thei suffren so gret peynes and so harde
martyrdomes for loue of here ydole that a Cristene man, I trowe, durst
not taken vpon him the tenthe part the peyne for loue of oure lord Ihesu
Crist" (p. 129; Letts, p. 329). Clearly, the *Mandeville*-author's manifestly anachronistic attraction to Prester John stems from a nostalgia for
the better days of Christendom, the days when it supposedly "dured . . .
beyonde the see" even as far as "Tartarie" and seemed possessed of an
Apostolic simplicity untouched by the "addicouns that dyuerse popes
han made" (pp. 216-17; Letts, pp. 402).

So far as one can tell, this nostalgia for a once large and
powerful Christendom seems to have led the *Mandeville*-author to
imagine its eventual return, indeed even to demand it on one or two
occasions. For one thing, his book begins with an impassioned exor-
dium calling on "eury gode Cristene man that is of powere and hath
whereof . . . [to] peynen him with alle his strengthe for to conquere
oure right heritage [i.e., the Holy Land] and chacen out alle the
mysbeleeuynge men" (p. 2; Letts, p. 230). And even if one has to
admit that this passion for a crusade wanes somewhat as the *Travels*
progresses, one has also to acknowledge that it never fully disappears,
since the book refers at least twice to "prophecies" regarding the
ultimate demise of the non-Christian lords of both the Holy Land and
central Asia (pp. 100-01, 181; Letts, pp. 305-06, 371). Moreover, the
agents of such a demise are on one occasion specifically shown to be
Christians. While explaining how the "Saracens" can be "lyghtly
conuerted," because "thei han many gode articles of oure feyth," Sir
John tells the following tale, which may well have its ultimate source
in Caesarius of Heisterbach's *Dialogus miraculorum* (4: 15):[23]

> And therfore I schalle telle you what the Soudan tolde me
> vpon a day in his chambre. . . . for he wolde speke with me in
> conseille. And there he asked me how the Cristene men
> gouerned hem in oure contree, and I seyde hem, 'Right wel,
> thonked be God'. And he seyde me:
> 'Treulych nay. For yee Cristene men ne recche right noght
> how vntrewely *ye* seruen God'. (p. 100, emphasis in original;
> Letts, pp. 305-06)

The Sultan then proceeds to castigate European Christians for numerous failings, condemning their drunkenness, excessive devotion to fashion, covetousness, lechery, adultery, and so on, before concluding with the following announcement:

> 'And thus for here synnes han thei [Cristene men] lost alle
> this lond that wee holden. For for hire synnes *here* God hath
> taken hem into oure hondes, noght only be strengthe of
> oureself but for here synnes. For wee knowen wel in verry
> soth that whan yee seruen God, God wil helpe you, and whan
> He is with you, no man may ben ayenst you. And that knowe
> we wel be oure prophecyes that Cristene men schulle wynnen
> ayen this lond out of oure hondes whan thei seruen God more
> deuoutly. But als longe as thei ben of foul and of vnclene
> lyvynge as thei ben now, wee haue no drede of hem in no
> kynde, for *here* God wil not helpen hem in no wise'. (p. 101,
> emphasis added; Letts, p. 306)[24]

And as if that were not enough, the book briefly entertains the possibility of a world-wide Christian empire. Having just told his audience of a miracle that preserved the early Christians against the evil designs of "a cursed emperour of Persie that highte Saures" (Shapur II, d. 379), Sir John offers the following pointed moral:

> Wherfore me thinketh that Cristene men scholden ben more
> deuoute to seruen oure lord God than ony other men of ony
> other secte. For withouten ony drede, ne were cursedness and
> synne of Cristene men, thei scholden ben lordes of alle the
> world. For the banere of Ihesu Crist is alleweys displayed and
> redy on alle sydes to the help of his trewe louynge seruauntes,
> in so moche that o gode Cristene man in gode beleeve scholde
> ouercomen and outchacen a m. [=1000] cursed mysbeleevynge
> men [this is then proved by reference to the Psalter]. (p. 188;
> Letts, p. 377)

Yet such was not to be, at least not in the latter part of the fourteenth century or in relation to Asia. For the Holy Land had been in Muslim hands since the end of the thirteenth century, and the hopes of a pan-Asian Christendom raised by the tolerant Mongol empire were dashed by the rise to power in 1360 of Timur, or Tamerlane, "one of the great destroyers in history."[25] It is perhaps no small irony that Timur was emerging as one of the forces that would break the fragile links between Europe and Asia at almost the very moment when the

Mandeville-author was compiling his often nostalgic book and perhaps imagining for just a moment a universal Christian community finally realized through the help of one of Timur's thirteenth-century predecessors:

> Vnder the firmament is not so gret a lord ne so myghty ne so riche as is the Grete Chane, nought Prestre Iohan that is Emperour of the High Ynde, ne the Sowdan of Babyloyne, ne the Emperour of Persye. Alle theise ne ben not in comparisoun to the Grete Chane nouther of myght ne of noblesse ne of ryaltee ne of richesse, for in alle theise he passeth alle erthely princes. Wherfore it is gret harm that he beleueth not feithfully in God. And natheles he wil gladly here speke of God. And he suffreth wel that Cristene men dwelle in his lordschipe, and that men of his feith ben made Cristene men yif thei wile thorghout alle his contree, for he defendeth no man to holde no lawe other than him lyketh. (p. 177; Letts, p. 368)[26]

Yet even if the *Mandeville*-author appears here to be naïvely or wilfully ignorant of the failure of the mission to Asia, despite having read at least some of the documents sent back to Europe (e.g., the shortened version of Friar John's *Ystoria Mongalorum* in Vincent of Beauvais's *Speculum historiale*), he was, as I have tried to show, by no means unaware of the difficulties posed for his imagined religious community by the practice of Christians themselves.

Indeed, it ought to be clear by now that one of his main intentions in depicting Asia was to reflect critically on the state of Latin Christendom, even though (and perhaps because) he probably had no genuine practical acquaintance with most or all of the Asian communities which he describes. Apparently motivated by more than just the desire to satisfy the medieval appetite for far-away "diversities"— though that is obviously no small part of what lies behind both the book and its remarkably favorable reception—the *Mandeville*-author has fashioned from his imagined encounter with the world beyond Christendom a sometimes fantastic mirror of his own world, and a mirror which he uses not only to point up the numerous practical failings within Latin Christendom itself, but also, if paradoxically, to affirm the ultimate superiority of that community by imagining it as somehow capable of containing all others—indeed, entitled to do this, whatever the practical impossibility of such an undertaking. It is hardly surprising, then, in such a speculative book as this, that that impossibility does not hinder the recognition of an already existing and almost universal religious community. In fact, towards the very end of his book, after having already demonstrated the greater piety of numerous Asian communities which lack the benefit of Christian revelation, the *Mandeville*-author offers his audience a final, reassuring account of the Christian God's mysterious omnipotence, an account that amounts to a description of an immense, imagined, and imaginary religious community; for he gives these distant and "dyuerse folk . . . of dyuerse beleeves" access to the One True God and therefore potentially to Christendom through both their "naturelle wytt" and the books of "Genesis, of the prophetes sawes, and . . . of Moyses," since "the prophete seyth, *Et metuent [D]eum omnes fines terre* [Psalm 67:7]" (p. 227; Letts, p. 410).[27] Thus, if there is any truth in what William Langland wrote of pilgrims like "Sir John Mandeville"—that they "Wenten forth in hire wey with many wise tales, / And hadden leve to lyen al hire lif after"[28]—then it is also true that some pilgrim-travelers, whether genuine or not, lied to a purpose.

Lies are tricky things, however, and their effects are unpredictable. Some two centuries later, for instance, one finds an Italian miller called Menocchio responding to them in a way that eventually got him into trouble. In a letter written from prison in 1584, he told his judges that it was partly his reading of *Mandeville's Travels* that had led him away from orthodoxy towards a "new world and way of life": "These have been the causes of my errors: . . . second, because I read that book of Mandeville about many kinds of races and different laws, which sorely troubled me. . . ." Fifteen years later, in 1599, convicted of relapsing into the heterodox beliefs to which "that book of Mandeville" had helped lead him, Menocchio was burnt at the stake. One of his heretical beliefs—still more tolerant than those of his "relativizing" text—was that "the majesty of God has given the Holy Spirit to all, to Christians, to heretics, to Turks, and to Jews; and he considers them all dear, and they are all saved in the same manner." It is worth noting that these words were uttered by someone having no practical acquaintance with alien forms of life and culture.[29]

NOTES

1. Erich Auerbach, *Mimesis: The Representation of Reality in Western Literature*, trans. Willard R. Trask. (1953; repr. Princeton: Princeton Univ. Press, 1968), p. 320. "Was lost" translates "ging . . . verloren" in the original German, a slightly different grammatical construction from the English stative passive, but one that likewise avoids the problem of agency (Auerbach's generalization is also slightly more nuanced than the translator's version of it): "Im Mittelalter ging sogar die praktische Kenntnis fremder Kulturkreise und Lebensbedingungen verloren" (*Mimesis: Dargestellte Wirklichkeit in der abendländischen Literatur*, 2nd ed. [Bern: Francke, 1959], p. 305).

2. It is worth recalling in this context the origins of Auerbach's *Mimesis*—in Istanbul during World War II—as he describes them at the end of that remarkable book (pp. 556-57).

3. Novalis's claim (emphasis in the original) is quoted on p. 76 of Ernst H. Kantorowicz, "The Problem of Medieval World Unity," in his *Selected Studies* (Locust Valley, N.Y.: J. J. Augustin, 1965), pp. 76-81; originally published in the *Annual Report of the American Historical Association for 1942* 3 (1944): 31-37. D. W. Robertson, Jr., *A Preface to Chaucer: Studies in Medieval Perspectives* (1962; repr. Princeton: Princeton Univ. Press, 1969), p. 51.

4. Kantorowicz, "Problem," pp. 76-78 (quotation from p. 78).

5. Benedict Anderson, *Imagined Communities: Reflections on the Origin and Spread of Nationalism* (London: Verso, 1983), pp. 15, 20, 22.

6. On these and related maps see the excellent study by David Woodward, "Medieval *Mappaemundi*," in *Cartography in Prehistoric, Ancient, and Medieval Europe and the Mediterranean*, ed. J. B. Harley and David Woodward (Chicago: Univ. of Chicago Press, 1987), pp. 286-370. It is important to note, incidentally, that Jerusalem comes to be placed at the exact center of the *mappaemundi* quite late (from the twelfth century on, and especially in the fourteenth and fifteenth centuries) and that this practice, which may have been a consequence of the Crusades, was by no means unique "for the entire medieval period, or even the most of it," as is often assumed (Woodward, pp. 341-42).

7. *Mandeville's Travels*, ed. M. C. Seymour (Oxford: Clarendon Press, 1967), pp. 15, 3, 5, 160; this text is the most recent critical edition of British Library MS Cotton Titus C.xvi. See also the French text in

Mandeville's Travels: Texts and Translations, ed. Malcolm Letts, 2 vols., Hakluyt Society, 2nd ser. 101-02 (London: Hakluyt Society, 1953) 2:239, 231, 232, 354. All further citations of *Mandeville's Travels* will be taken from this edition; for the reader's convenience, I shall also note the corresponding pages of the French text in Letts. Documentation from both editions will follow quotations in the body of the text. For further information on the *Travels*, see below, n. 11.

8. On European activities and interests in Asia and Africa prior to 1500, a relatively neglected topic in comparison with the period after 1500, see, for example, J. R. S. Phillips, *The Medieval Expansion of Europe* (Oxford: Oxford Univ. Press, 1988); and Jean-Paul Roux, in collaboration with Sylvie-Anne Roux, *Les explorateurs au Moyen Age* (Paris: Fayard, 1985). Also useful in this context are two quite different studies: Archibald R. Lewis, *Nomads and Crusaders A.D. 1000-1368* (Bloomington, Ind.: Indiana Univ. Press, 1988), which considers the development of and the relations amongst Latin Christendom and "those other great civilizations of medieval times —the Byzantine-Russian, the Islamic, the Indic, and the East Asian," emphasizing in particular "geographical, demographic, economic, technological, military, naval, and maritime factors" rather than "political, religious, and cultural elements" (pp. vii-viii); and Denys Hay, *Europe: The Emergence of an Idea*, rev. ed. (Edinburgh: Edinburgh Univ. Press, 1968).

9. Henri Baudet, *Paradise on Earth: Some Thoughts on European Images of Non-European Man*, trans. Elizabeth Wentholt (New Haven: Yale Univ. Press, 1965), p. 6; see also pp. 9, 23, 74-75. Lack of contact with "Indian" civilization was an important factor in Latin Christendom's view of it as naturally good, according to Thomas Hahn, "Indians East and West: Primitivism and Savagery in English Discovery Narratives of the Sixteenth Century," *Journal of Medieval and Renaissance Studies* 8 (1978): 77-114 (see esp. p. 110).

10. *Orientalism* (1978; repr. New York: Vintage, 1979), pp. 12 (emphasis in original), 24. For two helpful critiques of Said's analysis of "Orientalism," both from an anthropological point of view but with quite different emphases, see James Clifford, *The Predicament of Culture: Twentieth-Century Ethnography, Literature, and Art* (Cambridge, Mass.: Harvard Univ. Press, 1988), pp. 255-76, and James A. Boon, *Other Tribes, Other Scribes: Symbolic Anthropology in the Comparative Study of Cultures, Histories, Religions, and Texts* (Cambridge, Eng.: Cambridge Univ. Press, 1982), p. 280, n. 10. More generally, Boon's chapter 2 offers the student of medieval culture an interesting reexamination of medieval ethnology by turning it against Enlightenment thought, reversing

the usual practice in intellectual history, although not to rehabilitate
medieval ethnology in itself; Boon's aim is rather to show how later
ethnology was no more able than medieval ethnology to represent
other peoples *as such*, apart from its own (over-)simplifying cultural
categories (cf. the essay by Flint cited below, n. 15).

11.   The most useful source of information on manuscripts and editions in
the various languages is still Josephine Waters Bennett, *The Redis-
covery of Sir John Mandeville*, The Modern Language Association of
America Monograph Series 19 (New York: MLA, 1954), especially
Appendixes 1 and 2, but this should be supplemented by the
bibliographies in Ralph Hanna, III, "Mandeville," in *Middle English
Prose: A Critical Guide to Major Authors and Genres*, ed. A. S. G.
Edwards (New Brunswick, N.J.: Rutgers Univ. Press, 1984), pp. 129-
32; and Christian K. Zacher, "Travel and Geographical Writings," in
A Manual of the Writings in Middle English 1050-1500, gen. ed.
Albert E. Hartung (New Haven: The Connecticut Academy of Arts and
Sciences, 1986), 7:2452-54, 2456, the latter making reference to
editions in all the languages, not just in English. On the French
manuscripts, see also Guy De Poerck, "La tradition manuscrite des
'Voyages' de Jean de Mandeville," *Romanica Gandensia* 4 (1955):
125-58. On their descent in England, see M. C. Seymour, "The
Scribal Tradition of Mandeville's *Travels*: The Insular Version,"
Scriptorium 18 (1964): 34-48. The forty-three extant manuscripts
(including epitomes and fragments) of the English versions of
Mandeville's Travels represent six separate recensions, including
four prose versions (Bodley, Cotton, Defective, and Egerton), a
metrical version, and a stanzaic fragment; only the Defective version
has not been printed in a critical edition. Though not the earliest or
the best English rendering, the Cotton version cited throughout the
present essay has the advantage of offering a full text and being a
direct translation from the French—specifically from the *Insular*
French version. Though even farther from the French original, the
Egerton version offers the best English text from a literary point of
view; volume 1 of *Mandeville's Travels*, ed. Letts, contains a
modernized text of this version, which was first published as *The
Buke of John Maundeuill. being the Travels of John Mandeville,
Knight 1322-56. A Hitherto Unpublished English Version from the
Unique Copy (Egerton Ms. 1982) in the British Museum . . . together
with the French Text, Notes, and an Introduction*, ed. George F.
Warner (London: Roxburghe Club, 1889). Unfortunately, there is
still no critical edition of any French text; volume 2 of *Mandeville's
Travels*, ed. Letts, prints, amongst other things, the French text of
the earliest dated manuscript (Paris, Bibliothèque Nationale,
MS Nouv. Acq. Franç. 4515; copied in 1371), a text of the
Continental version already showing signs of change in

transmission, while Warner prints an Anglo-French text (a copy of the Insular version).

There is a short summary of the *Mandeville*-author's sources in *Mandeville's Travels*, ed. Seymour, pp. 276-78; for much fuller information, see Albert Bovenschen, "Untersuchungen über Johann von Mandeville und die Quellen seiner Reisebeschreibung," *Zeitschrift der Gesellschaft für Erdkunde zu Berlin* 23 (1888): 177-306; and the introduction and notes to Warner's edition. For William of Boldensele's *Itinerarius*, see C. L. Grotefend, ed., "Die Edelherren von Boldensele oder Boldensen," *Zeitschrift des historischen Vereins für Niedersachsen* (1855 [for 1852]): 209-86 (the text is printed on pp. 237-86). For Odoric of Pordenone's *Relatio*, see Anastasius van den Wyngaert, ed., *Itinera et Relationes Fratrum Minorum Saeculi XIII et XIV*, vol. 1 of *Sinica Franciscana* (Quaracchi-Florence: Collegium S. Bonaventurae, 1929), pp. 413-95; and Henry Yule, ed. and trans., "The Eastern Parts of the World Described," in vol. 2 of his *Cathay and the Way Thither, Being a Collection of Medieval Notices of China*, 2nd ed., rev. Henri Cordier, 4 vols., Hakluyt Society, 2nd ser. 33, 37, 38, 41 (London: Cambridge Univ. Press, 1913-16). For a brief but indispensable survey of the large and heterogeneous body of writing to which *Mandeville's Travels* and several of its sources belong, see Jean Richard, *Les récits de voyages et de pèlerinages*, Typologie des sources du Moyen Age Occidental 38 (Turnhout: Brepols, 1981).

The best literary study of the *Travels* is that by Donald R. Howard, "The World of Mandeville's Travels," *Yearbook of English Studies* 1 (1971): 1-17, reprinted in a slightly shorter version in his *Writers and Pilgrims: Medieval Pilgrimage Narratives and Their Posterity* (Berkeley: Univ. of California Press, 1980), pp. 53-76. Mary B. Campbell, *The Witness and the Other World: Exotic European Travel Writing, 400-1600* (Ithaca: Cornell Univ. Press, 1988), pp. 122-61, offers a stimulating reading of the book as the "first" instance of "realistic prose fiction . . . since Petronius" (p. 122).

12. On the question of authorship generally, see Rita Lejeune, "Jean de Mandeville et les Liégeois," in *Mélanges de linguistique romane et de philologie médiévale offerts à Maurice Delbouille*, 2 vols. (Gembloux: J. Duculot, 1964), 2:409-37, who summarizes the protracted debate. Lejeune holds what she considers to be the majority view: "le véritable nom de l'auteur des *Voyages* était celui d'un ANGLAIS, Jean de Mandeville, qui avait vécu à Liège sous le nom de Jean à la Barbe" (p. 434). Among those who have argued that the *Mandeville*-author was personally acquainted with at least the Near East, one of the most recent is Dorothee Metlitzki, *The Matter of Araby in Medieval England* (New Haven: Yale Univ. Press, 1977), pp. 220-39; unfortunately, Metlitzki never raises the question implied by her argument: why should we assume that what has as yet

no known source in another text must therefore derive from the author's own personal experience of a place?

Insofar as it is possible to do so I intend to distinguish the book's author (whom I have been calling the *Mandeville*-author) from its narrator (whom I shall call "Sir John"). The indiscrimate use of "Mandeville" for author and narrator alike has led to some confusion in many studies; I have even seen "Mandeville" receive credit for the work of translators and scribes. Take, for example, this scribe's or translator's interpolation which is regarded as coming from the author himself: "Nothing more about the author appears in the text, but in order to disarm any charges against his veracity he alleges that he visited the papal curia in Rome (*recte* 'the court of Rome', that is at Avignon, if the work was actually composed when claimed), and showed the pope his book" (Phillips, *Medieval Expansion*, p. 206). This particular account of the book's examination at Rome during the "author's" return blatantly contradicts the next paragraph of the book ("And now I am comen hom. . . . And thus takynge solace in my wreched reste recordynge the tyme passed I haue fulfilled theise thinges and putte hem wryten in this boke. . . ." [p. 229; Letts, p. 411]), and is "found only in the English versions and one late-fifteenth-century Latin manuscript written in England" (*Mandeville's Travels*, ed. Seymour, p. 257, note to 228/27). More surprisingly, Scott Douglas Westrem, after rightly praising the book's account of its "author's" homecoming as a "stunning innovation," treats the papal interpolation as though it had come from the author's own hand, even though he points out that the "French manuscripts omit the interview with the Pope": *A Critical Edition of Johannes Witte de Hese's* Itinerarius, *the Middle Dutch Text, an English Translation, and Commentary, together with an Introduction to European Accounts of Travel to the East (1240-1400)* (Ph.D. diss., Northwestern Univ., 1985), pp. 246-47.

Clearly, whatever its source, the account is not authorial. As a compilation by an unknown author, *Mandeville's Travels* raises in an acute way a number of important questions in the study of medieval writing, amongst them the problem of the "book-author unit," as it is called by C. S. Lewis, *The Discarded Image: An Introduction to Medieval and Renaissance Literature* (1964; repr. Cambridge: Cambridge Univ. Press, 1967), p. 210. This, however, is not the place to deal with such questions; I have touched on some of them briefly in the first chapter of my doctoral dissertation, "The World of a Book of the World: *Mandeville's Travels* in Middle English (British Library MS Cotton Titus C.xvi." (Harvard, 1988), which I am currently revising for publication as a study of the Middle English versions generally.

13. *The World, the Text, and the Critic* (Cambridge, Mass.: Harvard Univ. Press, 1983), pp. 170-71. Borrowing the concept of "elaboration" from Antonio Gramsci, Said notes that "Gramsci's insight is to have recognized that subordination, fracturing, diffusing, reproducing, as much as producing, creating, forcing, guiding, are all necessary aspects of elaboration" (p. 171). Particularly important for the sort of fracturing, reproducing, and diffusing that the *Mandeville*-author was engaged in was the twelfth-century development of the book as a tool like any other—"le livre devient [désormais] un outil comme un autre" (Roux, *Les explorateurs*, pp. 58-59)—since this allowed a great many more genuine and armchair travelers to read, write, and be read.

14. "Rank . . . imposture": Zoltán Haraszti, "The Travels of Sir John Mandeville," *Boston Public Library Quarterly* 2 (1950): 311; "romance of travel": Bennett, *Rediscovery*, chapter 3; "marvel-monger": J. R. Hale, *Renaissance Exploration* (New York: Norton, 1968), p. 32; "summa": Howard, "World," p. 2; "rich index": Christian K. Zacher, *Curiosity and Pilgrimage: The Literature of Discovery in Fourteenth-Century England* (Baltimore: The Johns Hopkins Univ. Press, 1976), p. 6; and "realistic prose fiction": Campbell, *Witness*, p. 122.

15. Douglas R. Butturff, "Satire in *Mandeville's Travels*," *Annuale Mediaevale* 13 (1972): 155-64, argues from passages like this one that "the world of the East" in *Mandeville's Travels* "is in fact antipodal to that of the West" and hence is used "for satiric inversion" (p. 157); although I would generally agree with Butturff's claim that *Mandeville's Travels* is a satire on Latin Christendom, I believe that his use of "antipodal" here betrays some confusion ("antipodal" does not necessarily mean "upsidedown" morally, etc.), and that his reading of *Mandeville's Travels* is far too monologic—in his view *everything* in the book serves a satiric end. The problem of the Antipodes, incidentally, was not necessarily connected to discussions of the earth's shape, but rather to questions of Christianity's dissemination in the world and of Christian tolerance for others, especially the so-called monstrous races; two useful discussions of this problem are Valerie I. J. Flint, "Monsters and the Antipodes in the Early Middle Ages and Enlightenment," *Viator* 13 (1984): 65-80; and John Carey, "Ireland and the Antipodes: the Heterodoxy of Virgil of Salzburg," *Speculum* 64 (1989): 1-10; see also below, n. 19.

16. Yule, *Cathay*, 2:117-32, and Wyngaert, *Itinera*, pp. 424-39.

17. Yule, *Cathay*, 2:209, n. 1 ("very confused"), 316 (Latin text), 316, n. 7 (interpolation, which may not be an interpolation, since a

translator or scribe unwilling to imagine pygmies with rational souls may have deleted this remark from the family of texts that lack it); see also Wyngaert, *Itinera*, pp. 468-69; Yule, *Cathay*, 2: 207-09 (English text; translation modified slightly).

18. Jean le Long's Odoric is printed in Louis de Backer (or Baecker; he used both spellings), *L'Extrême Orient au moyen-âge d'après les manuscrits d'un flamand de Belgique Moine de Saint-Bertin à Saint-Omer et d'un Prince d'Armenie Moine de Prémontré à Poitiers* (Paris: Leroux, 1877), p. 119; Jean le Long dates his translation on p. 90 (cf. p. 124). See also Yule, *Cathay*, 2:209, n. 1. Warner and Campbell both err in ignoring this statement in the French texts of Odoric, Warner suggesting that the *Mandeville*-author "no doubt drew from other sources than Odoric" (*Buke*, p. 204), Campbell claiming that "he develops a whole cultural being for the pygmies, and one that includes an irony so pungent in relation to Odoric that one must wonder if Mandeville's text is at open war with its source" (*Witness*, pp. 155-56). Campbell's stimulating study of medieval travel writing is unfortunately sometimes a little too unaware of the complexity of intertextual relations in a manuscript culture, but the forcefulness of her statement sent me back to Odoric's *Relatio* as well as to the brief reference to this passage in my dissertation, where I make a similar error in attributing the change to the *Mandeville*-author (*World*, p. 72).

19. There are of course certain exceptions and limits to the *Mandeville*-author's sympathy. Some of the monstrous races, for example, are described as being of "cursed kynde" (p. 147; Letts, p. 343); on the monstrous races, which appear only infrequently in *Mandeville's Travels*, see the excellent study by John Block Friedman, *The Monstrous Races in Medieval Art and Thought* (Cambridge, Mass.: Harvard Univ. Press, 1981); although he offers no extended discussion of the *Travels*, Friedman's scattered remarks place the book in the context of the larger medieval concern with these creatures and are notable for their judiciousness and insight. The most obvious exception to the author's sympathy is the Jews, who receive uniformly hostile treatment throughout the book; since it deserves more extensive treatment than I can give it here, I will not discuss the book's anti-Semitism in the present essay.

20. Studies of the legend and *Letter* of Prester John are legion. Two useful starting points are Igor de Rachewiltz, *Prester John and Europe's Discovery of East Asia*, The Thirty-Second George Ernest Morrison Lecture in Ethnology (Canberra: Australian National Univ. Press, 1972); and Vsevolod Slessarev, *Prester John: The Letter and the Legend* (Minneapolis: Univ. of Minnesota Press, 1959).

21. Yule, *Cathay*, 2:244-45; see also Wyngaert, *Itinera*, p. 483. For a useful account of most of the travelers mentioned in this paragraph, see Leonardo Olschki, *Marco Polo's Precursors* (Baltimore: The Johns Hopkins Univ. Press, 1943); see also chapters 1-11 in Westrem, *Critical Edition*, whose careful and wide-ranging discussion of European accounts of travel to the East from 1240 to 1400 is one of the few studies of medieval travel writing to acknowledge the difficulties posed by the nature of medieval authorship and manuscript transmission.

22. See below, n. 27.

23. Most of the *Mandeville*-author's discussion of the "Saracens" and their laws, into which this colloquy is set, was borrowed from William of Tripoli's *De statu Saracenorum . . .* (1273). On William's tract, see Benjamin Z. Kedar, *Crusade and Mission: European Approaches toward the Muslims* (1984; repr. Princeton: Princeton Univ. Press, 1988), pp. 180-82, an invaluable study of Latin Christian views of Islam; for a brief discussion of the *Mandeville*-author's use of William see Eric John Morrall, "Der Islam und Muhammad im späten Mittelalter: Beobachtungen zu Michel Velsers Mandeville-Übersetzung und Michael Christans Version der 'Epistola ad Mahumetem' des Papst Pius II," in *Geschichtsbewusstsein in der deutschen Literatur des Mittelalters*, ed. Christoph Gerhardt, Nigel F. Palmer, and Burghart Wachinger, Tübinger Colloquium 1983 (Tübingen: Max Niemeyer, 1985), pp. 147-61.

24. Not quite two centuries later, Martin Luther put to different use a similar argument about the excellent moral behavior of Muslims in comparison with Christians, insisting in his *Libellus de ritu et moribus Turcorum* (1530) that Christianity is a matter of faith not morals; see George Huntston Williams, "Erasmus and the Reformers on Non-Christian Religions and *Salus Extra-Ecclesiam*," in *Action and Conviction in Early Modern Europe: Essays in Memory of E. H. Harbison*, ed. Theodore K. Rabb and Jerrold E. Seigel (Princeton: Princeton Univ. Press, 1969), pp. 319-71.

25. Christopher Dawson, intro. *Mission to Asia*, Medieval Academy Reprints for Teaching 8 (Toronto: Univ. of Toronto Press, 1980), p. xxxiv. Dawson's book was originally published under the title *The Mongol Mission* (London: Sheed and Ward, 1955), and was first reprinted as *Mission to Asia* in 1966 (New York: Harper and Row).

26. This passage is displaced slightly in the Egerton version, occurring in chapter 23 (*Mandeville's Travels*, ed. Letts, p. 153) rather than chapter 25 (Letts, pp. 169-70); since he seems unaware that the two passages are the same, Letts's notes to them are misleading.

27.   In a comment on the manuscript version of this essay, Scott Westrem notes that "all this is in the context of what sounds very like an appeal for missionaries because the attention turns to what these people *don't* know, but could—if only a crusade of priests would move East" (his emphasis). A knowledge of God through "natural reason" was commonly ascribed by medieval thinkers to the peoples of distant Asia; see Thomas Hahn, "The Indian Tradition in Western Medieval Intellectual History," *Viator* 9 (1978): 213-34, and his "Indians East and West" (above, n. 9), both of which deal in passing with *Mandeville's Travels* and therefore nicely supplement the present essay.

Arguing that humanity uses time, as "a carrier of significance," to define the relations between self and other, Johannes Fabian distinguishes the medieval, Christian "vision of Time"—the "inclusive or incorporative" "Time of Salvation"—from the Enlightenment vision of "temporal relations as exclusive and expansive," a distinction that has obvious consequences: whereas "the pagan was always *already* marked for salvation, the savage is *not yet* ready for civilization": *Time and the Other: How Anthropology Makes its Object* (New York: Columbia Univ. Press, 1983), pp. ix, 26 (his emphasis). Though perhaps overschematic, Fabian's distinction does seem to be borne out in the "other" worlds represented both on the encyclopedic *mappaemundi* and in *Mandeville's Travels*: in them time is almost always a matter of space and even the most distant creatures are capable of salvation.

28.   *The Vision of Piers Plowman: A Critical Edition of the B-Text*, ed. A. V. C. Schmidt (London: Dent; New York: Dutton, 1978), Prol., lines 48-49.

29.   On Menocchio generally, see Carlo Ginzburg, *The Cheese and the Worms: The Cosmos of a Sixteenth-Century Miller*, trans. John and Anne Tedeschi (1980; repr. Harmondsworth, Eng.: Penguin, 1982); "new world" (pp. 13, 77, 81); "causes of my errors"—from a letter to his judges, quoted in full by Ginzburg—(p. 88); "majesty of God" (p. 51).

The Nature of the Infidel:
The Anthropology of the Canon Lawyers

James Muldoon

An historian who should have known better, Henry Steele Commager, once observed that "sixteenth-century Europeans had no compunction about killing Indians because the Indians had no souls."[1] Such an opinion is not, unfortunately, restricted to American historians. It has something of the popular modern myth about it. The massive population decline among the inhabitants of the Americas, which the conquistadores observed and modern scholars have analyzed in great detail, suggests that the Spanish invaders had no interest in the people they encountered because they did not see them as human in the first place.[2]

The view that Europeans judged non-European peoples as non-human or, at the very least, sub-human, seems to rest largely on analysis of literary and polemical texts. We often see European attitudes toward non-Europeans illustrated in chronicles that were composed hundreds of miles from any border by monks who never saw a Mongol or a Saracen.[3] These chroniclers were anxious to record contemporary responses to the horrifying tales of conquest and death associated with the terrifying invaders of Christendom. A related purpose of such discussions was to inspire Europeans to meet the dangers that would soon approach from the most distant corners of Europe unless men roused themselves from their lethargy and confronted the enemy. Other expressions of late-medieval European attitudes toward non-Europeans

James Muldoon is Professor of History at Rutgers University, Camden College of Arts and Sciences (see Notes on Contributors, p. 222).

conjured up literary images of Wild Men (and Women), creatures such as werewolves, and other forms of beings who, at the very least, were incompletely human.[4] Here the medieval writers' goal was titillation, and so the strange folk were described in the most grotesque terms.

In all of these cases, accurate, informed descriptions of the peoples beyond Europe had no place. The purpose of describing the non-European in terrifying or grotesque terms was to appeal to the emotions—not the minds—of readers or hearers. Furthermore, such descriptions did not reflect first-hand experience of the non-European world, but rather second- or third-hand observations at best. They even echoed not contemporary experience but ancient experience as medieval writers drew upon a narrative tradition that ran back to Herodotus.[5] As a result, any serious discussion of medieval attitudes toward real non-European peoples as opposed to the inhabitants of a world of fantasy and imagination must begin elsewhere, away from the literary and the artistic representations of the non-European. Such discussions must also keep away from the moralists, the grotesqueness of whose descriptions of the non-European was in inverse proportion to their experience of them and to the willingness of the European warrior aristocracy to fight them.

One way to determine what medieval men really thought of non-Europeans is to examine the writings of those who actually dealt with such peoples. It might be pointed out that, while there were indeed medieval Europeans who did have a realistic view of the non-Europeans, there were too few of them and their information reached too few people to be of any significance. Margaret Hodgen argues similarly in her important book, *Early Anthropology in the Sixteenth and Seventeenth Centuries*. Discussing the works of Marco Polo and two nearly contemporary Franciscan missionaries, Hodgen concludes:

> Strange to say, and significant as were the reports of the three intrepid travelers for the history of European thought, they were all but forgotten in the West during the centuries that followed. The relatively truthful account written by Marco Polo attracted less attention in the later Middle Ages than the mendacious romance which appeared under the name of Sir John Mandeville.[6]

While it is true that more copies of Mandeville's *Travels* have survived than have copies of Marco Polo's book, this does not necessarily prove that Mandeville's fanciful work was more important in shaping European attitudes toward the non-European than was Marco Polo's realistic one.[7] A more important question is: who held realistic as opposed to fanciful conceptions of non-European peoples and what were the implications, if any, of that knowledge? I wish to suggest that realistic evaluations of the humanity and the rationality of non-Europeans were more common than the circulation of Mandeville's work suggests and that these realistic appraisals were of more long-term significance than were the opinions of Mandeville and similar writers.

To illustrate this argument, I wish to examine a few well-known documents from the mid-thirteenth century, materials connected with the Mongol Mission of Pope Innocent IV (1243-1254). The most important of these materials are a legal commentary, written by Innocent IV in his capacity as a canon lawyer, and two letters that as pope he addressed to the Mongol khan. The final piece of evidence is John of Plano Carpini's report of his journey to the Mongols, in the course of which he delivered the pope's letters and received in turn a response from the khan. What makes these materials important is that they contain the views, implicit and explicit, of men who actually had dealings with non-Europeans. Furthermore, the views of Innocent IV shaped ecclesiastical and legal responses to the non-European world long after his death, enjoying an important revival in the early sixteenth century as Europeans began to wrestle with the implications of the discovery of the New World and its inhabitants.[8]

Innocent IV dealt with the nature of the non-European, non-Christian in his commentary on a letter of his predecessor, Innocent III (1198-1216). The letter, *Quod super his* (X.3.34.8), was included in the second collection of canon law, the *Decretales*, in a chapter on vows. In the original letter, Innocent III dealt with what must have been a common problem, the inability of an individual who had taken an oath to go on a crusade to fulfill his vow because he was too old, too ill, or too constrained by circumstances beyond his control to travel to the Holy Land. What was to be done? Innocent III resolved the matter expeditiously, outlining a procedure for allowing the would-be crusader to compound for his vow so that a suitable warrior could replace him. After all, there was nothing to be gained by sending an old or sick man to fight.[9]

When Innocent IV came to write his commentary on the *Decretales*, he paid little attention to the actual circumstances that generated the letter and raised instead the question of the right of Christians to wage war against infidels at all.[10] He began by accepting the legitimacy of wars to regain possession of the Holy Land. This was simply an exercise of defence and recuperation, in which the Christian inhabitants of the Holy Land were legally permitted to fight Muslims who had unjustly attacked them and unjustly dispossessed them of their lands.[11]

Of greater interest was the question of whether Christians had the right to invade, conquer, and govern any and all lands that infidels held. Innocent IV's answer was that God, who made the world and everyone in it, has so ordered matters that all men, believers and infidels alike, can legitimately possess land and property and can select their own rulers. Such "things were made for every rational creature" and so "it is not lawful for the pope or for the faithful to take sovereignty or jurisdiction from infidels, because they hold without sin. . . ."

According to Innocent IV, it was the very rationality of all mankind that meant that every human being was subject to papal jurisdiction and thus possibly subject to invasion by Christians acting under papal warrant. If, according to Innocent IV, "a gentile, who has no law except the law of nature [to guide him], does something contrary to the law of nature, the pope can lawfully punish him. . . ." For example, according to this line of argument, "if they [infidels] worship idols [the pope can judge and punish them] for it is natural for a man to worship the one and only God, not creatures." The pope cannot command the forced baptism of legitimately conquered infidels, but he "can order infidels to admit preachers of the Gospel in the lands that they administer, for every rational creature is made for the worship of God. . . ."

The emphasis upon the rationality of the infidels is important, not only because, paradoxically, it provides a justification for the legitimate conquest of the infidels, but also because it means that believer and non-believer possess the same human nature. The believer alone has the Gospel to guide him in the ways of righteousness, but both believer and non-believer possess the capacity to know the natural law through the operation of human reason alone and so are subject to its terms.

The theme of the rationality that all men share appeared fully developed in the two letters Innocent IV addressed to the leader of the Mongols. Parenthetically, let me note here that we do not know when Innocent IV wrote specific sections of his commentary on the *Decretales*. It does not matter for the purposes of this discussion, however, whether he wrote the legal commentary on the common rationality of mankind before or after he sent these two letters. What is important is that the documents, taken together, demonstrate that Innocent IV thought seriously about and acted purposefully on the view that mankind shared a common rationality.

The letters that John of Plano Carpini brought to the Great Khan had different themes. The first provided an introduction to Christian doctrine, while the second focused on the pope's desire to stop the Mongol conquests of Christian lands. They shared, however, an emphasis upon the rationality of all men.

The first letter opens with a discussion of human experience that presumably should bring the khan to consider the truth of the Christian faith. The human condition is described as "the unhappy lot of the human race," a situation created by the fall of the first man. As a consequence, God became Man and "showed Himself in a form visible to all men." According to Innocent IV, the Incarnation took place because

> human nature, being endowed with reason, was meet to be nourished on eternal truth as its choicest food, but, held in mortal chains as a punishment for sin, its powers were thus far reduced that it had to strive to understand the invisible things of reason's food by means of inferences drawn from visible things.

Christ became incarnate

> in order that, having become visible, He might call back to Himself, the Invisible, those pursuing after visible things, moulding men by His salutary instructions and pointing out to them by means of His teaching the way of perfection. . . .[12]

The goal of the Incarnation was to replace the penalty of sin, which is death, with eternal life.

The point of this summary of the fundamental Christian mystery as Innocent IV presented it was that everyday experience demonstrates to any rational human being the melancholy state of human existence. He began, in other words, with an appeal to the khan's own experience. Clearly men, endowed as they were with reason, could see that they were meant for more than a short, painful life on earth. That the life men experienced was less happy than what they could imagine was due to the fall of Adam and the consequences of original sin.

Once men realized the nature of their condition, however—that is, once they applied their human reason to analyze their condition and to understand its fundamental flaws, the consequences of original sin—they could then appreciate the Christian message. In other words, faith would develop upon a base of reason. Innocent IV believed that the Mongols, being rational human beings, capable of understanding the human predicament, would come to the baptismal font from a rational appraisal of their situation.

Having discussed the fall of Adam and Christ's incarnation, Innocent IV moved to a discussion of the pope's role in the continuing process of redemption. The pope is the successor of St. Peter, Christ's initial vicar on earth, and the Franciscan friars who bear the papal letters act for him. These men are

> remarkable for their religious spirit, comely in their virtue and gifted with a knowledge of Holy Scripture, so that following their salutary instructions you may acknowledge Jesus Christ the very Son of God and worship His glorious name by practising the Christian religion.[13]

The approach that Innocent IV took to converting non-believers was clearly an essentially rational route. The mind of the infidel listener was to be the means by which his baptism would be secured. There are no threats of eternal damnation, no recitations of the miracles that accompanied conversions elsewhere, no appeals to the emotions. This letter contains an appeal to the infidel mind that foreshadowed Thomas Aquinas's *Summa contra Gentiles*. In both cases, the fundamental assumption is that Christians and non-Christians share a common humanity, one of whose fundamental characteristics is rationality. On account of this shared rationality, the infidel can be led to the true faith through appeals to reason and to experience. In one sense, this assumption transforms religious conversion from a spiritual experience to a rational learning process.

Innocent IV's second letter to the khan focused on establishing peaceful relations between the Mongols and Christian Europe. The theme is the natural desire for peace and harmony among all living creatures. The pope began:

> Seeing that not only men but even irrational animals, nay, the very elements which go to make up the world machine, are united by a certain innate law after the manner of the celestial

> spirits, all of which God the Creator has divided into choirs in the enduring stability of peaceful order, . . . we are driven to express in strong terms our amazement that you . . . have invaded many countries belonging both to Christians and to others and are laying them waste in a horrible desolation, and . . . breaking the bond of natural ties . . . you rage against all indiscriminately with the sword of chastisement.

The pope called upon the Mongols to follow "the example of the King of Peace" who desires "that all men should live united in concord in the fear of God. . . ." If they did not heed this message, end their wars, and "conciliate by a fitting penance the wrath of Divine Majesty," then they faced God's punishment both here and hereafter.[14]

This second letter differed from the first in that it instructed the Mongols to end their reign of terror before God's wrath struck them down. The pope's interest here was not primarily conversion but rather peaceful relations between Christians and Mongols. The two letters did, however, share the theme of human rationality, indeed the rationality and order of the entire universe. By attacking their neighbors, the Mongols were upsetting the natural order of the world, something that they should realize. Again, reason was the instrument the pope employed to obtain his ends. He clearly assumed that the khan, a rational man, would see the error of his ways and follow the directives of the pope because he was only pointing out what should have been obvious to any rational creature.

The last of the documents in this discussion, John of Plano Carpini's *History of the Mongols*, reinforced the conclusion that the thirteenth-century papacy and those who served it saw the infidel, wherever he dwelled, as a rational creature who shared a common humanity with Christian Europeans. The Franciscan's description of the Mongol way of life was critical but not judgmental. That is, he saw good and bad qualities in the Mongols, but his interest lay in describing and understanding various practices rather than condemning them. He recognized that their society was an organized, disciplined one and that they had developed a way of life that, while expansionistic and threatening to their neighbors, nevertheless worked fairly and efficiently for them. At the end of his report, Plano Carpini even pointed to the rationality of the Mongols as a reason for not bringing ambassadors back to Europe with him and his companions. The ambassadors would see the weaknesses and internal divisions that separated the Christians and so upon their return to the khan would encourage an attack upon Europe.[15]

One final issue still requires some discussion. Even if the thirteenth-century papacy appreciated the rational nature of the infidel, of what significance was this perception since the descriptions of wild men, half-men, and other fantastic creatures dominated the European image of the infidel? As has been noted, more copies of Mandeville's fantastic voyage survive, and presumably circulated, than do copies of the more realistic papal materials.

The answer lies in the effect of these various perceptions of the infidel on those who went to seek him from the end of the fifteenth century. From the very beginning of the overseas expansion that began with Columbus's first voyage, missionary activity was an important aspect of the endeavor. Columbus himself emphasized the importance of missionary work, and on his second voyage he brought missionaries with him to begin the work of converting the inhabitants of the Caribbean islands. If these people were not human, such efforts would have been useless. Indeed, they would be unnecessary. Likewise, the letters of Pope Alexander VI that divided the newly discovered lands between the Castilians and the Portuguese in 1493 by means of the famous line of demarcation would have been pointless because the papal right to draw such a line was rooted in the papal responsibility for the souls of the infidel inhabitants of the newly-found lands.[16] If these people had no souls and thus could not accept the salvation that Christ's sacrifice promised, then the papacy would not have expended so much intellectual effort on achieving a solution to the Portugese/Castilian conflict.

In fact, papal and other ecclesiastical interest in the New World was rooted in the perception of the infidels as rational human beings, just like Europeans. In the fifteenth and sixteenth centuries, when ecclesiastics considered the infidel, they saw not the fantastic creatures described by Mandeville and others but rather rational creatures like themselves, for whom Christ had suffered and died. They perceived the infidel this way not from personal experience but from the line of argument that began with Innocent IV and John of Plano Carpini. It is worth noting that while Plano Carpini's manuscript may not have circulated widely, the commentary of Innocent IV on the *Decretales* most certainly did. Canon lawyers from the thirteenth- to the sixteenth-century continuously cited his discussion of the rights of infidels and with it his defense of their essential humanity.[17] In the sixteenth century, the entire Spanish debate about the legitimacy of the conquest of the Americas was carried on in the terms of Innocent IV's commentary. In the 1500s, as in the 1200s, there was no doubt about the humanity or the rationality of the inhabitants of what to the West was a new world. The issue was not that they were somehow morally or intellectually deficient but rather that they did have souls, which it was the responsibility of Christians to save.

NOTES

1. Henry Steele Commager, "Should the Historian Make Moral Judgments?" *American Heritage* 17[2] (Feb. 1966): 27, 87-93 at 91.

2. On the debate about the biological effects of the discoveries, see Alfred W. Crosby, *The Columbian Exchange: Biological and Cultural Consequences of 1492* (Westport, Conn.: Greenwood, 1972), and *Ecological Imperialism: The Biological Expansion of Europe, 900-1900* (Cambridge, Eng.: Cambridge Univ. Press, 1986).

3. See, for example, Charles W. Connell, "Western Views of the Origins of the 'Tartars': an Example of the Influence of Myth in the Second Half of the Thirteenth Century," *Journal of Medieval and Renaissance Studies* 3 (1973): 115-37.

4. See Richard Bernheimer, *Wild Men in the Middle Ages* (Cambridge, Mass.: Harvard Univ. Press, 1952); Edward Dudley and Maximillian E. Novak, eds., *The Wild Man Within: An Image in Western Thought from the Renaissance to Romanticism* (Pittsburgh: Univ. of Pittsburgh Press, 1972); and John Block Friedman, *The Monstrous Races in Medieval Art and Thought* (Cambridge, Mass.: Harvard Univ. Press, 1981).

5. "If antiquity confers respectability, some of Mandeville's stories came from the most impeccable sources, the cream of the flamboyant anthropogeography of Pliny, Solinus, Mela, and Isidore. . . . There are the Albanians, who made their first bow to the European reading public in the pages of Herodotus." See Margaret Hodgen, *Early Anthropology in the Sixteenth and Seventeenth Centuries* (1964; repr. Philadelphia: Univ. of Pennsylvania Press, 1971), p. 70.

6. Hodgen, *Early Anthropology*, p. 103.

7. Scholars differ on the number of manuscripts involved. A recent editor of Mandeville's work declares that "some three hundred" manuscripts

of the work have survived while "only about seventy" of Polo's work
have survived. See *The Travels of Sir John Mandeville*, trans.
C. W. R. D. Moseley (Harmondsworth, Eng.: Penguin, 1983), p. 10.
Other writers indicate that as many as 138 copies of Polo's manuscript
survive; see Boies Penrose, *Travel and Discovery in the Early
Renaissance* (Cambridge, Mass., 1955; repr. New York: Atheneum,
1962), p. 22.

8. On the later use of Innocent IV's legal opinion, see James Muldoon,
   *Popes, Lawyers, and Infidels: The Church and the Non-Christian
   World 1250-1550.* (Philadelphia: Univ. of Pennsylvania Press,
   1979), esp. ch. 7; and Kenneth J. Pennington, "Bartolome de Las
   Casas and the Tradition of Medieval Law," *Church History* 39 (1970):
   149-61.

9. James A. Brundage, *Medieval Canon Law and the Crusader* (Madison:
   Univ. of Wisconsin Press, 1969), p. 77.

10. Innocent IV, *Commentaria Doctissima in Quinque Libros Decretalium*
    (Turin: apud haeredes Nicolai Beuilaque, 1581), fols. 176-77.

11. For a fuller discussion of Innocent IV's commentary, see Muldoon,
    Popes, Lawyers, and Infidels, ch. 2. The most important discussion of
    the just war tradition is Frederick H. Russell, *The Just War in the
    Middle Ages* (Cambridge, Eng.: Cambridge Univ. Press, 1975).

12. *Mission to Asia*, ed. Christopher Dawson, Medieval Academy
    Reprints for Teaching 8 (Toronto: Univ. of Toronto Press, 1980),
    p. 73; this work was originally published as *The Mongol Mission*
    (London: Sheed and Ward, 1955), and was reprinted for the first time
    in 1966 as *Mission to Asia* (New York: Harper and Row). The original
    texts are in: *Epistolae saeculi XIII e registis pontificum romanorum*,
    ed. G. H. Pertz and C. Rodenberg, MGH, *Epistolae*, 3 vols. (Berlin:
    Weidmann, 1883-94), 2:72-3 (nu. 102) and 2:74-5 (nu. 105).

13. Pertz and Rodenberg, *Epistolae*, 2:75.

14. Pertz and Rodenberg, *Epistolae*, 2:75, 76.

15. Pertz and Rodenberg, *Epistolae*, 2:68.

16. See James Muldoon, "Papal Responsibility for the Infidel: Another
    Look at Alexander VI's *Inter Caetera*," *Catholic Historical Review* 64
    (1978): 168-84.

17. Muldoon, *Popes, Lawyers, and Infidels*, pp. 141-45.

Ptolemaic Influence on Medieval Arab Geography:
The Case Study of East Africa

Marina Tolmacheva

Claudius Ptolemy made a profound impression on the development of Arabic geographic science which goes far beyond mere translations of his *Geography*. From as early as the ninth century to as late as the fifteenth century, most Arabic authors writing in the genres of descriptive and mathematical geography echoed Ptolemy as a source for systematic description of the habitable earth. The major areas in which Ptolemaic influence made an impact on Islamic scholars include geographic data (description of continents and seas, as well as the coordinates of settlements and of topographic features), geographic theory, and cartography. (Ptolemaic mathematics and astronomy are not discussed here.)

This paper reexamines the nature and extent of the Greek influence traditionally ascribed to Ptolemy on early medieval Arabic works which demonstrate a recognized familiarity with Ptolemy on each of these levels, including writings by the early mathematician, astronomer, and geographer Muhammad ibn Musa al-Khorezmi (d. c. A.H. 232/A.D. 846-847), and his less well-known editor Suhrab (first half of the tenth century A.D.), and the *Kitab al-zij al-Sabi'* by the astronomer al-Battani (d. A.H. 317/A.D. 929). Data relevant to the historical geography of East Africa will be explored below. In addition, questions of general methodology of interpreting data derived from Arabic manuscript sources will be considered.

Marina Tolmacheva is Associate Professor of History at Washington State University (see Notes on Contributors, p. 223). Research for this paper was supported by grants from the American Philosophical Society and the Washington State University Graduate School.

Although the general extent of Arab geographical borrowing
from Ptolemy has been well explored,[1] the case of East Africa deserves
particular attention especially in view of the still unresolved
"Ptolemaic" cartographic convention which extends the African mainland south of the equator all the way east to form the southern shore of
the Indian Ocean. The fact that Arab geographers of the Islamic era also
show this convention while drawing on Ptolemy has allowed modern
scholars to regard Arabic geographic sources as carrying on Ptolemy's
tradition during the centuries when his work was lost to Europe. Maps
which reappear in the West in the fifteenth century are commonly attributed to Ptolemy in part because they share this cartographic feature
of medieval Arabic texts and maps. A sketch-map of the East according
to Ptolemy appears in Figure 1 (following page 128).

A few preliminary observations are in order regarding the extent
of Ptolemaic influence on Arab authors in general and on descriptions
of East Africa in particular. First, a brief comment on the coordinates of
latitude and longitude. Inasmuch as Ptolemy is considered to be the
earliest geographer to apply coordinates systematically,[2] all Muslim
geographers who employ them may be considered as having known and
accepted his method to some degree. It may be worth noting that such
authors represent a numerical minority in the field of Islamic geography, however significant their output may have been. Second, the use
of coordinates by some authors does not guarantee their acceptance of
Ptolemy's figures or even of his method of computing the coordinates;
this is especially true of longitude. The nature of discrepancies and
some of the reasons for them are discussed below. Third, some authors
acknowledge their debt to Ptolemy, yet they do not use his degree coordinates but rather transform his cartographic projection while filling the
map and text with contemporary data. Fourth, no "pure" Ptolemy can
be found in Arabic texts. Even the works regarded as translations of the
Geography, such as al-Khorezmi's *Kitab surat al-ard* and Suhrab's *Kitab
ᶜadja'ib al-aqalim al-sabᶜa* do not contain a complete Arabic version of
the Greek text or tables; they also differ from the book structurally.[3] In
addition, already in the ninth century al-Khorezmi is thought to have
corrected and augmented Ptolemy's data with new information then being obtained through scholarly efforts sponsored by the early Abbasids.
Fifth, the Greek latitudinal system of the division of habitable earth
into seven zones ('climes'; Arabic *iqlim*) is introduced into Arab
geography with al-Khorezmi's reworking of Ptolemy[4] and, despite the

parallel existence of at least two other systems in the early centuries of Islam, becomes dominant in later sources even where no other Greek influence is noticeable. Sixth, although Ptolemy's early impact is clearest in, and almost limited to, works of mathematical geography, his major concepts concerning the continents and the surrounding sea, the seven climes, and the configuration of Africa penetrate the genre of descriptive geography, dictionaries, and encyclopedias. Seventh, within the widely accepted cartographic and conceptual framework, the proportion of descriptive and coordinate data traceable directly to Ptolemy falls drastically from its highest point in the ninth- and tenth-century works of the "Greek school" to its lowest in about the middle of the eleventh.

The Greeks and the Arabs knew only the coastal area of East Africa. Sailing from Aromata promontory, the ancients came to Azania, traveling with the south wind as far as Rhapta and Prasum. Aromata emporium, at 83° longitude and 6° latitude N, lies only 2° west of Opone, firmly identified as Ras Hafun on the Horn of Africa; Rhapta, "metropolis of Barbaria," is placed by Ptolemy at 71° longitude and 7° latitude S. The farthest African location east and south is the island of Menuthias at 85° longitude and 12° 30' latitude S.[5]

Of all these and other less significant and mostly unidentified locations in *Geography*, for which almost twenty sets of coordinates are provided, al-Khorezmi retains five, restructuring his table not to follow the outline of the coast, as Ptolemy does, but to begin with the south-ernmost part beyond the first clime. Thus, *Rafata* (Arabic for 'Rhapta') comes first, and *al-Tib* (Arabic for 'Aromata') follows in the section on the first clime. Two out of five coastal cities are designated merely as *madina ʿala 'l-bahr* ('town by the sea')[6] with no transcription of the Greek toponym presumably listed in the original. Although coordinates are given, their significant and generally inconsistent disagreement with Ptolemy's make identification of place-names impossible. The fifth remaining toponym, which it is possible to place on the eastern, rather than northern, coast of the Horn, is *Qanana*. In the discussion below Qanana is held to be identical with Acanna, which Ptolemy mentions in *Geography* IV,7. For conjectural locations of cited Greek and Arabic toponyms, see Figure 2 (following page 128).

Following Ptolemy, the Arab translators of *Geography* list longitude first and latitude second. Al-Khorezmi's text seems to describe a map, with the sequence of coordinates following the topography of the coast; the general direction of the narrative moves to the east and

south. The tables follow the clime division south to north and west to
east. The system is repeated in Suhrab's work cited above. Al-Battani's
reworking of Ptolemy, descended from a different translation, contains a
condensed introduction and tables of selected locations listed by the
region rather than according to precise coordinates, although the west-
to-east sequence is roughly observed. Only one of Ptolemy's East
African toponyms is retained here.[7] The combined list of named locations, increasing in distance from the Red Sea, with their coordinates
from Ptolemy and the three Arabic sources is offered in Table 1.

TABLE 1

*Named Locations and Their Coordinates in Ptolemy and
Three Medieval Arabic Sources*

	Acanna (Qanana)		Aromata (al-Tib)		Rhapta (Rafata)	
Ptolemy	82°	7° N	83°	6° N	71°	7° S
al-Khorezmi (table)	72°30'	2°45' N	72°	4°30' N	65°	8° S
al-Khorezmi (text)	72°30'	2°20' N	69°30'	6°10' N	66°	7°30' S
al-Battani			82°	4°30' N		
Suhrab (table)	73°30'	3°45' N				
Suhrab (text)	72°30'	2°20' N	69°30'	6°10' N	65°05'	7°30' S

Certain questions arise in regard to these figures. First of all, data
cited by the same Arabic author in tables and in the text do not always
coincide; this is not the case in Ptolemy. The examined texts do not
contain discussion of itineraries or distance measurements in other units
which might be compared against the degrees. The nature of the
narrative, which describes what appears on the map rather than unequiv-
ocally citing location coordinates, allows for some discrepancy between
the table listings and data extrapolated from the text. For instance,
Kitab surat al-ard offers slight variations in the coordinates of all three
named East African locations, while the literal reading of the text does
not claim mathematical precision:

> The boundary of the Green Sea . . . passes under a city at
> 69°30' longitude and 6°10' latitude. Then it curves like a pot
> near (the place) below the city of al-Tib and adjoins (the
> place) under the city of Qanana at 72°30' longitude and 2°20'
> latitude. . . . It passes under the city of Rafata at 66°00'
> longitude and 7°30' latitude beyond the equator. . . . [8]

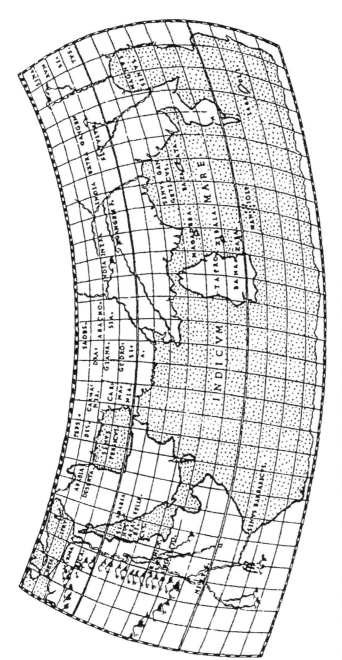

Figure 1. The East according to Ptolemy (after the Venice, 1561 edition).
The Indian Ocean is completely enclosed.

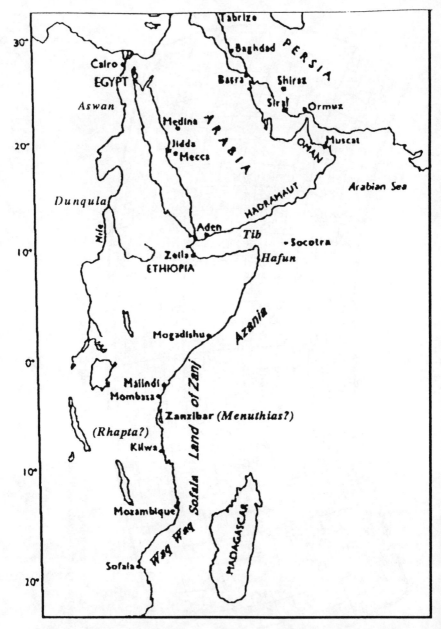

Figure 2. Conjectural locations of Greek and Arabic toponyms in East Africa, the Arabian peninsula, and Persia. Italics indicate locations cited in Ptolemy and Arabic authors.

Although the apparent graphic approximation might excuse the inconsistency in the coordinates, the problem deserves further attention. To begin with, the coordinates contained in the quotation above, as well as the much longer text of nearly uniform nature from which it is excerpted, are very closely followed in Suhrab's version. In fact, despite the distancing effect that time, editing a new version, and copying may have had on the original data, the narrative parts of al-Khorezmi's and Suhrab's works are closer to each other than the text data of al-Khorezmi to his own tables. This discrepancy has not been noted in the literature, and, since the confusion obviously does not originate in Ptolemy, it requires an explanation which will take into account the nature of Arabic geographic works. Ideally, we could inquire as well into the transmission process, examining the transfer of data from one language and numerical system to another; unfortunately, although we know that many Greek texts were translated into Arabic through Syriac or Hebrew, no intermediary versions are extant.[9] The following comments therefore treat the data as if they were, indeed, a direct translation from Ptolemy; this study compares coordinates within the source, among the sources of the selected group, and between these sources and Ptolemy. This discussion also elaborates on the value of the coordinates, the manner and format of their presentation, and the implications of these for Greek-Arabic geographical theory and cartography, as well as manuscript-derived numerical data.

Regarding the differences between the coordinates cited by Ptolemy and those allegedly derived from him found in Arabic sources, the prevailing explanation considers the Arabic data to be improvements or corrections resulting from the newer independent observations and calculations made by Arab geographers and astronomers. This theory, however, does not hold for the above examples, since in the ninth century the Arabs did not have independently-obtained measurements for the old Greek toponyms in the region; their post-Islamic acquaintance with the East African coast must have quickly revealed that names like Rhapta no longer existed there, and a new inventory of place-names began to be compiled, making Ptolemy's lists irrelevant.[10]

Further, it has long been observed that the greatest discrepancies among the Arabic coordinates, whether Ptolemaic in origin or not, occur in the longitudes. These discrepancies are usually of two kinds: one reflects the random variation in magnitude explained as mistakes occasioned by the difficulty of establishing the longitude in pre-modern times; the other originates in the difference of 10° built into the practice of placing the prime meridian at the Canary Islands rather than at the westernmost point of Africa. Mistakes also occur in latitude data but are usually less disparate.[11]

As Table 1, on page 128, shows, in our case variations occur both in longitude and in latitude. Taking the longitude first, as did both the Arabs and Ptolemy, we may assume that al-Battani follows the prime meridian chosen by Ptolemy while al-Khorezmi's prime meridian differs from both by close to 10°; the latter is also apparently adopted by Suhrab. However, in a wider context it turns out that al-Khorezmi and al-Battani do not diverge consistently. In fact, *Kush al-dakhila* (Ethiopia Interior) has the identical 50° longitude in both sources. Another example from Eastern Africa (not found in Ptolemy) is *Dunqula* (Dongola), the capital of Nubia, which al-Khorezmi places at 53° longitude, and al-Battani at 93°.[12] Similarly, for Aswan (also not in Ptolemy) the longitude is given as 55°30' and 95°, respectively.[13] Clearly, a consistent mistake of 40 degrees by the author or even by the translator is doubtful. Surveying the sources makes it evident that in each case the discrepancy is significant due to positional mathematical value of the "translated" decimal components; an explanation needs to be sought in the numerical notation used in Arabic sources.

The Islamic system for marking the numbers originating in sexagecimal computation, such as the 360 degrees of the circle, uses Arabic characters assigned numerical value in an antiquated order which made transcribing Greek alphanumeric data both easy and convenient. However, a carelessly scripted character could be misread and incorrectly copied by another scribe; considering the graphic specificity of Arabic characters, a resulting mathematical mistake in this system could potentially vary in magnitude from 1 to 90 in a single digit (considering the range of longitude measurements). The important point to keep in mind is that such a mistake would have nothing to do with (mis)calculation or fundamental differences in method: its origin would lie purely in orthographical confusion.

Let us return for a moment to the apparent 40-degree disagreement between al-Khorezmi and al-Battani (who followed a different translation of Ptolemy). Using the notation accepted in the Arab East, the two longitudes for Dunqula are represented as follows: al-Khorezmi gives *nun-jim* (or 53°; this is in the table—the text reads 52°20'), while al-Battani gives *sad-jim* (or 93°). This difference may be quickly reduced to only 10° if the maghribi notation is assumed in the latter case: then *sad* equals 60, and we are back to the prime meridian differential of 10°. This notation, however, does not apply in the case of al-Battani, whose published text contains *nun* for 50° as the longitude of *Kush al-dakhila* (Ethiopia Interior). Immediately above and below Kush in the table other toponyms have tens of degrees marked with ligatures apparently containing *sad*. Thus it is logical to seek the source of the huge disparity not in the method of measurement or in the value of symbols adopted for notation, but in the graphics of the symbols themselves. Because *nun* is used consistently for 50 in astronomical data, it seems logical to conclude that the transformation of *nun-jim* in al-Khorezmi into *sad-jim* in al-Battani is a consequence of scribal distortion. Similar reasoning would apply in the case of Aswan's longitudes (*nun-ha* for 55 in al-Khorezmi versus *sad-ha* for 95 in al-Battani). Mathematical values of the eastern system of notation are consistently followed here; the possibility that the scribe vacillated between two systems of notation—"eastern" and "maghriban"—which would have allowed the substitution of *sad* for *nun* may be considered but cannot be confirmed here.

Once the probability of graphic distortion is accepted, it becomes possible to treat the disagreement between al-Khorezmi's and al-Battani's longitude for Aromata/al-Tib also as a graphic mistake that confuses sources that were originally coherent with each other and with Ptolemy. Specifically, in the case of al-Khorezmi's apparent disparity with Ptolemy's longitude for Aromata (72° as opposed to 83°), the proximity to the 10-degree difference between two prime meridians ceases to be inviting once the resemblance between the Arabic symbols is taken into consideration. The *ayn-ba* combination for 72 is very close to the contours of the *fa-ba* ligature for 82. (The potential for confusing 2 and 3—or 72 [for 82] and 83—is discussed below.) Moreover, once the intrusion of the "prime meridian factor" into Greek-Arabic coordinates is eliminated or at least suspended for sources under discussion, it becomes possible to view in the same light the disparate degrees of latitude cited for identical locations.

Aromata promontory, at 6° N according to Ptolemy, is inconsistently placed at 4°30' N in al-Khorezmi's table but at 6°10' N in the accompanying text. It appears that al-Battani's figures agree with those of al-Khorezmi's table, while Suhrab follows al-Khorezmi's text. This observation may be of some significance in determining the precise (Syriac?) versions of Ptolemy used for different Arabic redactions. Regardless of the later authors' exact source of borrowing, al-Khorezmi's data may be easily reconcilable, considering the graphic resemblance between *waw* for 6 and *dal* for 4.

There are other examples of digit confusion might easily have originated. The letters *jim* and *ha* have the same body and are distinguished only by the presence or absence of a dot; in the sexagecimal system, confusing the two means variation from 3 to 8. Records show that *jim* was occasionally scripted without a dot and even with its tail left off, to prevent its (then most likely) confusion with *ha*.[14] This could—and evidently did—open further possibilities of confusing the truncated, dotless *jim* with other characters.

Qanana offers an obvious instance of inconsistent citations for latitude, which is given variously by al-Khorezmi at 2°45', Suhrab's table at 3°45', and Suhrab's text at 2°20' (Ptolemy locates Acanna at 7°). It may be observed that the first and second measurements differ by a magnitude of 1°, the first and third differ in minutes, and the second and third in both the degree and minute components. The letters *ba* for 2 and *jim* for 3 are both normally scripted with a diacritical dot underneath, and may be corrupted or confused if carelessly written. Compare, for instance, the transformation of 53° (*nun-jim*) in al-Khorezmi's table into 52° (*nun-ba*) in his own text for Dunqula. It is more difficult to explain in graphic terms the transformation of 45' into 20' (*mim-ha/kaf*), but it may be observed that both the degree and minute components of all-Khorezmi's figure reappear separately in Suhrab. Therefore the difference among the coordinates as cited need not be regarded as an intended correction but may instead be a corruption.

We can find further support for this conclusion by casting the net wider among non-Ptolemaic toponyms related to eastern Africa. The capital of Nubia, Dunqula, has the following listings of latitude: 2° (*ba*) in al-Khorezmi, 14°15' (*ya-dal ya-ha*) in al-Battani, 14°05' (*ya-dal ha*) in Suhrab's text, and 14°30' (*ya-dal lam*) in Suhrab's table. Since al-Khorezmi's and Suhrab's coordinates for Aswan coincide completely (55°30' longitude, 22°30' latitude), these discrepancies again do not seem intended. The latitude of 2° N is inconsistent not only with the other authors' figures but even with al-Khorezmi's own data for other locations as well as with Dunqula's placement in the sequence of listed toponyms (generally moving north from the equator). Because both numbers are commonly transcribed with characters marked with diacritical dots underneath, we may see in al-Khorezmi's published figure another instance of scribal corruption of the digit.

The discussion here is limited to the East African group of toponyms, but further examples of a similar nature may be found among both Ptolemaic and non-Ptolemaic data relating to Africa and other locations. The point is that what scholars have taken to be a mathematical discrepancy may in fact be no more than scribal error; even if the extant manuscript copies from which published editions were prepared are carefully written and appear to be plainly legible,[15] the mistake may have occurred at an intermediate stage. This is an important factor in the evaluation and interpretation of geographic and astronomic data, especially those derived from the same original source or, in E. S. Kennedy's words, "families of sources." Most important, this factor operates in records of both latitude and longitude. Therefore, our awareness of it should serve to temper the willingness to explain away mistakes in longitude by focusing on geographical theory while dissociating the mathematical content from the system of notation.

Data included above demonstrate that the minute component of the coordinates is subject to variation and corruption no less frequently than the degree numbers. There is, however, one pattern of variation which occurs in the minute component at a rate that suggests special vulnerability. Three types of numbers are involved: zero minutes (00'), tens of minutes, and fractions ending in 5. Again, this discussion needs to be divorced from modern Arabic-numeral notation and focused on sexagecimal Arabic characters. The "zero minutes" notation, absent in Ptolemy, uses the Indian zero, while the tens are all transcribed with a single character; therefore the mistake, if such is the cause of variation, might involve graphic confusion between the cipher and one out of several numerical characters sufficient for expressing the above group of fractions.

For the most part these are easily distinguishable even in handwriting. Reviewing our selected examples, however, we notice that the variation, even within this limited pool of numbers, is not between the "zero minutes" and "tens of minutes" components but rather effects changes from "zero minutes" to "$n + 5$ minutes" and from "tens of minutes" to "$n + 5$ minutes" (or vice versa). Compare 20'/45' for Qanana, 00'/05' for Rafata among the Ptolemy-derived data, and 00'/15'/30' for Dunqula from the non-Ptolemaic. The apparently Greek-derived Ptolemaic city of Tiyas(?) on the Red Sea has a latitude varying from 17°00' in al-Khorezmi to 17°05' in Suhrab's table.[16] Since Suhrab's text mentions the integer 17° with no reference to minutes, it is likely that here again Suhrab did not intend to correct data but that a scribe made a mistake in the process of transmitting astronomical data through alphabetic notation. The particular culprit here is the cipher, easily confused in its medieval full-round form with the letter *ha* (= 5) in its unattached or final scripted form. No locations are listed with the latitude or longitude of 0°, so confusion between the cipher and whole-degree coordinates is much less likely to occur; in fact, I have seen no examples of such confusion.

This examination also confirms that al-Battani and Suhrab were editing, copying, or otherwise revising Ptolemaic data in an Arabic—rather than a Greek or Syriac—text, because the nature of digital corruption is tied so closely to the particular script used. There is no reason to challenge the accepted view that al-Khorezmi's *Surat al-ard* served as the source for both authors. Moreover, mistakes in the minute component of the coordinates were unlikely to originate in the process of translation from the Greek for two reasons: Ptolemy's tables do not mark 00', and the Greek text frequently employs fraction designations that are not carried over in Arabic versions—1/2° for 30', 1/4° for 15', and 1/2° + 1/4° for 45'. Moreover, Arabic scribes themselves recognized the potential for confusing the symbols for 0 and 5: in some manuscripts the zero was marked in red to distinguish it from the 5.

The sequencing of toponyms in the text and tables plays an important role in controlling the precision of transmission. Ptolemy's regional divisions of Africa were known to his Arab editors, but their texts seem to follow a map rather than a systematic narrative. Their tables also differ in content organization, both from Ptolemy and among each other. The most significant distinction is in the sequencing of the place-names in the tables by clime, the unit first used by Eratosthenes; it is not used by Ptolemy in the existing version of *Geography*. In this system, locations in the First Clime are generally listed beginning from the south, in the order of increasing longitude; the latitudes for the most part, but not consistently, increase as well. The lists for the Second Clime start again in the west and south and proceed toward the east and north, and so on. Since the earliest Arabic version—al-Khorezmi's—offers a fully integrated and competent handling of the clime system in all three formats (text, tables, and maps) and since the early European Ptolemaic maps retain it as well, we may assume that a version of Ptolemy's *Geography* incorporating the clime grid predates the ninth century and was available to early Arab scholars. Regrettably, there are no surviving maps of East Africa by the three authors. The only known manuscript of al-Khorezmi contains four maps of which one shows the Nile but not the rest of Africa; there is no world map. (Figure 3, following page 136, gives an example of a later, round world map of the "Greek" school.) The precise nature of the map which the texts of al-Khorezmi and Suhrab seem to be describing has not been established, nor has its exact provenance. The theoretical discussion of the seas, continents, and measurements found in Ptolemy is missing in both. Suhrab's close paraphrasing of al-Khorezmi suggests that his book merely repeats al-Khorezmi's description of the lost map and does not describe another map similar to the former.

Unlike al-Khorezmi and Suhrab, al-Battani includes a description of the earth and, particularly, the seas. Although also organized as *zij* (i.e. astronomical tables), this work follows the *Geography*'s structure somewhat more faithfully, incorporating Ptolemy's system of listing the ninety-four inhabited areas in Book VIII, which is missing in al-Khorezmi and Suhrab. In the geographical introduction al-Battani does not suggest that he based his work on a map but offers systematic comments on the location and size of the seas, division of the continents, and possibilities of navigation.

The issue of maps acquires special significance because historians of European cartography disagree about whether Ptolemy himself mapped the east coast of Africa to extend to the east opposite Asia, as late medieval maps show, and whether he conceived of the Indian Ocean as an open or closed sea. The text and tables of *Geography* do not answer these questions. On the one hand, Ptolemy's description of Ethiopia limits the extent of Barbaria to the east by the Bay of Arabia, the Red Sea, and the Barbaricus Sea (IV,7). On the other hand, he notes that the land mass of Ethiopia bounded by the Great Bay of the Outer Sea is "terminated . . . by the unknown land toward the west and the south" (IV,8).

The controversy over the closed contour of the Indian Ocean does not apply to Arab geography since no text or map currently in existence, of whatever school of thought in Islamic scholarship, suggests that the waters of the Indian Ocean are separate from the mass of the ocean. Furthermore, the suggestion that printing and color confusion may have played a role in the proliferation of European maps of the "closed-sea" pattern[17] has no bearing on Arab cartography because it is the product of a tradition which preceded the revival of Ptolemy in Europe by centuries; the earliest extant world maps to show the Indian Ocean—or *Bahr al-Hind*—[18] beginning with al-Istakhri's (tenth century A.D.), were not of the Greek school. After al-Khorezmi, Greek-Arabic cartography takes a leap to al-Idrisi (mid-twelfth century A.D.) whose most detailed maps show the African mainland extended east, with the Indian Ocean open to the Surrounding Ocean (*al-Muhit*) to the extent of its full "width" from north to south. If, therefore, historians of European cartography look toward Arabic sources for confirmation of the "open-sea thesis," they will find adequate substantiation from narrative and illustrative Islamic data, originating both in Ptolemy and elsewhere.

The cartographic reconstruction of the East African coastline from Ptolemy's data, attempted early in the twentieth century, is difficult and involves a great deal of guesswork.[19] However, the eastward curve of the littoral may be guessed at from al-Khorezmi's narrative, which describes a map bearing place-names and the markings for degrees and minutes of longitude and latitude:

> The coastline . . . passes below the city of Rafata at 66°00' longitude and 7°30' latitude beyond the equator, reaching to the longitude of 68°00' and the latitude of 13°00'. The latitudes we refer to are beyond [i.e. south of] the equator, and if [the coastline] recrosses [the equator] we shall point that out. [The coastline then proceeds] to the longitude of 72°00' and the latitude of 14°00' and reaches the longitude of 112°00' and latitude of 14°00'. . . .[20]

Suhrab's text is nearly identical, differing only by slight omissions and the variation in coordinates from 00' to 05' as discussed above. Characteristically, nothing is described and no locations are listed for the longitudes between 72° and 112°. Thus the mainland's location so far east is implied rather than stated or substantiated.

It has been argued that Ptolemy did not make it his business to describe *unknown* places and, therefore, whatever his ideas of continental contours, he was unlikely to create a visual representation of a southern *Terra Incognita*.[21] The Arabic versions suggest that a Ptolemaic representation did exist of an Africa distorted eastward. In fact, the case would be more doubtful if the Arabic text did not base itself on a map: in the awkward phrasing of al-Khorezmi it is easy to lose track of the correct noun, causing one to understand that the sea,

Figure 3. A round map of the world by al-Idrisi (after the Cairo codex).

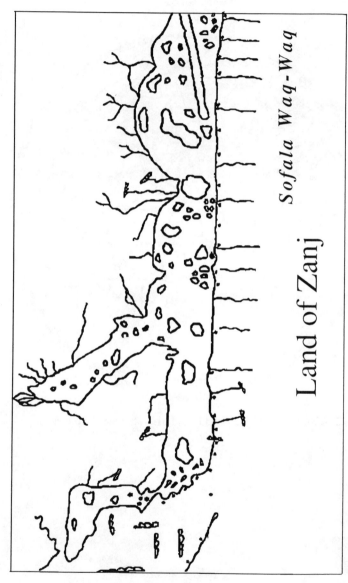

Land of Zanj

Sofala   Waq-Waq

Figure 4. East Africa, according to al-Idrisi (mid-12th century). "Land of Zanj" is the coastal area south of Somalia. "Sofala" was the remote part of Zanj adjoining the land of Waq-Waq, identified as both Madagascar and southeast Asian islands.

rather than the coast, reaches to 112° E. Two factors argue against this possibility. First, the reiteration of 14° latitude at both "ends" of the coastline suggests that a *line* was indeed drawn between the cited meridians on the map being described. Second, later works belonging to the al-Idrisi school of geography—such as the authoritative Ibn Saʿid al-Maghribi—return to the use of coordinates which, when superimposed on the African coast, seem to reconfirm Ptolemaic notions at a time when Arab navigation to East Africa flourished. (Figure 4, opposite this page, illustrates al-Idrisi's view of Africa and the Indian Ocean.) True, Ibn Saʿid, who wrote in the latter half of the thirteenth century, no longer includes the Greek toponyms, but he willingly recognizes his theoretical source in Ptolemy.

The very different narrative of al-Battani focuses on the seas and the equator, rather than on continents or the coastline, which also suggests a system where the Asian landmass north of the equator symmetrically faces another landmass across the sea, south of the equator. This landmass is Africa: "It is claimed that the equator crosses east to west the space between India and Ethiopia. . . ."[22] Al-Battani gives the Indian Ocean an elongated contour, citing a length west to east of 8,000 miles and a width of 2,700 miles.

Nevertheless, al-Battani includes statements which imply a much greater southward extent of the Indian Ocean than either Ptolemy or other Greek-Arabic geographers indicate: "They have measured Bahr al-Hind and stated that it . . . stretches beyond the island where night equals day [i.e. beyond the equator] in the direction of the south for one thousand and nine hundred miles. . . ."[23] If measured in degrees at the so-called al-Ma'mun equivalent of 1° = 56 2/3 miles, this would extend the ocean to approximately 34° S latitude.[24] If other equivalents are used (Ptolemy's 66 2/3 miles or the Syrian 75 miles per degree; the latter seems to have been used by al-Idrisi[25]), the difference as compared to 14° S in al-Khorezmi is even more dramatic. Suhrab's texts (as indicated above) do not contain mile measurements which otherwise might allow a comparison with or verification of al-Battani's figures. Al-Idrisi, on the other hand, cites distances in cubits, miles, and *farsakhs* (one unit of which equals 3 miles) but has no corresponding figures in degrees. Although he cites Ptolemy for his description of the seas, he quotes no dimensions for the whole of the Indian Ocean (he estimates the length of the Red Sea to be 1,400 miles).[26]

While this limited evidence is inconclusive, it would be difficult to dismiss al-Battani's figures altogether: the numbers, however round and therefore easily suspect, are carefully written out as words and thus cannot be explained as orthographical corruptions. Although the dimensions found in the latter quotation tend to contradict al-Battani's own numbers in the preceding passage, it is important to see that Greek-Arabic geography may have allowed for a more realistic conceptualization of the Indian Ocean, however imperfectly it may have been measured and visualized cartographically.

To limit the discussion of Ptolemy's influence on Arab geographers to three early works may appear to restrict the pool of data unnecessarily. However, the sources chosen here represent not only the most complete and faithful exposition of Ptolemy's information in Arabic, but they are also among the most carefully edited and extensively examined pieces in medieval Arabic geographic literature. Not only the later Muslim authors but also geographers of medieval Europe drew on these tables and descriptions, especially those of al-Battani.[27] Under the name *Kitab rasm al-rub^c al-ma^cmur* ('Design of the Inhabited Quarter'), al-Khorezmi's *Kitab surat al-ard* ('Geography' or 'Image of the Earth') was quoted in the fourteenth century by Abu 'l-Fida'; occasionally he cited al-Khorezmi's coordinates anonymously.[28] By the 1300s, however, East African toponyms known to the Arabs were different from those transcribed or translated from Ptolemy. The coordinates, when provided, were attached to new and different names; the continuity between ancient and medieval knowledge was broken. The cartographic tradition, although still inclined to imitate old authorities, underwent a dramatic transformation at the hands of al-Idrisi, who was imitated from then on by descriptive geographers. New translations of Ptolemy were made by Islamic geographers in the late-fifteenth century. They resulted, however, from access gained by Turks to Greek manuscripts; thus they bypass the medieval Arabic tradition altogether.

NOTES

1. See, for example, I. Iu. Krachkovskii, *Arabskaia geograficheskaia literatura*, vol. 4 of *Izbrannye sochineniia* (Moscow-Leningrad: Akademiia Nauk SSSR, 1957), ch. 3. Consult also the Arabic translation by S. A. D. 'Uthman Hashim (Cairo, 1963); J. H. Kramers, "La littérature géographique classique des musulmans," in J. H. Kramers, *Analecta Orientalia* (Leiden: Brill, 1954), 1:172-204; and

S. Maqbul Ahmad's entry under "Kharita" in vol. 4 of the *Encyclopædia of Islam*, 2nd ed. (Leiden: Brill; London: Luzac, 1978).

2. G. J. Toomer, "Ptolemy," *Dictionary of Scientific Biography* (New York: Scribners, 1975), 11:198.

3. See discussions in Ernst Honigmann, *Die sieben Klimata und die πόλεις ἐπίσεμοι* (Heidelberg: Winter, 1929), esp. pp. 120-25, 133, 155; Krachkovskii, *Arabskaia geograficheskaia literatura*, esp. pp. 79-82, 94; and Carlo A. Nallino, "Al-Huwarizmi e il suo rifacimento della geografia di Tolomeo," *Raccolta di scritti editi e inediti* (Rome, 1944), 5:458-532.

4. On *iqlim* in Arab geography, see the entry by André Miquel in *Encyclopædia of Islam*, 2nd ed.; and Honigmann, *Die sieben Klimata,* esp. pp. 92-93, 117-18, 161-62. Al-Khorezmi's manner of placing the *iqlim* boundaries is unique (see Krachkovskii, *Arabskaia geograficheskaia literatura*, p. 95).

5. Consult C. F. A. Nobbe, *Claudii Ptolemaei Geographia* (Leipzig, 1843-45; repr. Hildesheim: Olms, 1966), esp. 1:9, 14, 17 and 4:7, 8. Edward L. Stevenson's English translation, *Geography of Claudius Ptolemy* (New York: New York Public Library, 1932), is used here. For attempts at identification, see Hans von Mžik, "Afrika nach der arabischen Bearbeitung der Γεωγραφικὴ ὑφήγησις des Claudius Ptolemaeus von Muhammad ibn Musa al-Hwarizmi," *Wiener Zeitschrift fur die Kunde des Morgenlandes* 43 (1916); and Bernhard Struck, "Rhapta, Prasum, Menuthias," *Zeitschrift der Geschichte für Erdkunde zu Berlin* 5/7 (1921): 188-96.

6. See Hans von Mzik, *Das Kitāb Sūrat al-Ard des Abū Ga'far Muhammad ibn Mūsā al-Huwārizmī*, Bibliothek Arabischer Historiker und Geographen 3 (Leipzig: Harrassowitz, 1926), pp. 3-6.

7. Suhrab's work was originally published in 1930 by Mžik, and al-Battani's *zij* was published by Nallino in 1904. Both are cited here as they appear in the edition by L. E. Kubbel' and V. V. Matveev, *Arabskie istochniki VII-X vekov* (Moscow: Akademiia Nauk SSSR, 1960), pp. 301, 296-97.

8. Mžik, *Kitab Surat al-Ard*, p. 75.

9. At least two intermediate versions, in Syriac only, are hypothesized for Ptolemy; four Arabic versions of *Geography* were produced. See Krachkovskii, *Arabskaia geograficheskaia literatura*, pp. 79, 81, 86, 97, 100, 105.

10. On the early degree measurements and the updating of Ptolemaic place-names, see Krachkovskii, *Arabskaia geograficheskaia literatura*, pp. 82-88. On early Arab contact with East Africa, see George Fadlo Hourani, *Arab Seafaring in the Indian Ocean in Ancient and Early Medieval Times* (Princeton: Princeton Univ. Press, 1951).

11. For a concise summary of variation patterns in astronomic coordinates, see Mary H. Regier, "Kennedy's Geographical Tables of Medieval Islam: An Exploratory Statistical Analysis," in *From Deferent to Equant: A Volume of Studies in the History of Science in the Ancient and Medieval Near East in Honor of E. S. Kennedy* (New York: New York Academy of Sciences, 1987), pp. 357-72.

12. Mžik, *Kitāb Sūrat al-Ard*, p. 4; Kubbel' and Matveev, *Arabskie istochniki*, p. 297.

13. Mžik, *Kitāb Sūrat al-Ard*, p. 108; Kubbel' and Matveev, *Arabskie istochniki*, p. 297.

14. Rida A. K. Irani, "A Sexagecimal Multiplication Table in the Arabic Alphabetical System," *Studies in the Islamic Exact Sciences, [Symposium] by E. S. Kennedy, Colleagues and Former Students*, ed. David A. King and Mary Helen Kennedy (n.p.: American University of Beirut, 1983): 511-12.

15. I was unable to inspect manuscript versions of the texts under discussion here.

16. Mžik, *Kitāb Sūrat al-Ard*, p. 9; Kubbel' and Matveev, *Arabskie istochniki*, p. 302.

17. Wilcomb E. Washburn, "A proposed explanation of the Closed Indian Ocean on some Ptolemaic Maps of the Twelfth-Fifteenth Centuries," *Revista da Universidade de Coimbra* 33 (1985): 435-37.

18. *Encyclopædia of Islam*, 2nd ed. (see above, n. 1): s.v. "Bahr al-Hind," by D. M. Dunlop; and "Djughrafiya," by S. Maqbul Ahmad.

19. Ptolemaic cartographic reconstructions of the East African coastline were attempted by Mžik in 1916 and Honigman in 1929 (see above, nn. 3 and 5). See also Gabriel Ferrand, *Relations de voyages et textes géographiques arabes, persans et turks relatifs à l'Extréme-Orient du XIII-e au XVIII-e siècles* (Paris: Leroux, 1916), 2:590-95.

20. Mžik, *Kitāb Sūrat al-Ard*, p. 75.

21. Washburn, "A proposed explanation," pp. 3-4.

22. Kubbel' and Matveev, *Arabskie istochniki*, p. 296.

23. Kubbel' and Matveev, *Arabskie istochniki*, p. 296.

24. Krachkovskii, *Arabskaia geograficheskaia literatura*, p. 84.

25. Al-Idrisi, *Opus geographicum: sive "Liber ad eorum delectationem qui terras peragrare studeant"* (Naples: Istituto universario orientali di Napoli, 1970), p. 8.

26. Al-Idrisi, *Opus geographicum*, p. 10.

27. Krachkovskii, *Arabskaia geograficheskaia literatura*, pp. 100-01.

28. Krachkovskii, *Arabskaia geograficheskaia literatura*, p. 93.

Rhetoric and
Aristotelian Natural Philosophy

Laurie Shepard

Studies of medieval rhetorical practice are defined as much by the dominance of Christian doctrine as by the decline of the political and forensic institutions that had promoted the rhetorical art in antiquity. The medieval orator, we tend to assume, strove "to express more effectively the truth already possessed," because Holy Scripture and a small body of *auctores* contained all truth vital to faith and human knowledge.[1] In fact, of the three parts of the ancient rhetorical art that were retained in the Middle Ages—*inventio, dispositio*, and *elocutio*— only *ornamentatio*, a subtopic of *elocutio*, received much serious elaboration in the composition manuals or *artes dictaminis* of the twelfth and early-thirteenth centuries.[2]

Rhetoric was influenced by intellectual pursuits in other fields. The study of classical literature at Chartres in the twelfth century fostered a rhetoric from the region that was embellished and molded by allusions and quotations from ancient poets. The renewal of legal studies in the twelfth century promoted a more logically structured rhetoric. Maxims from the Justinian law code and the canonical decretals gave form to legal documents. A third example of the influence of intellectual inquiry on rhetoric is found in the simpler, less ornamental language used in Paris around 1200, the result of scholastic investigation of language inspired by the Aristotelian texts on logic.[3]

Laurie Shepard is Assistant Professor of Romance Languages at Boston College (see Notes on Contributors, p. 223).

This paper examines some of the rhetorical implications of the discovery and assimilation of Aristotle's *Posterior Analytics*, an event that would eventually promote an epistemological reorientation in Latin Europe. The *Posterior Analytics* presents the philosopher's definition of apodictic (or scientific) demonstration. Scientific demonstration depends on the establishment "in precise language not only *that* things are so, . . . but also *why* they are, . . . and why they have to be that way."[4] Rhetorical argument, on the other hand, is based on the probable and not the certain. When something is demonstrated scientifically and conclusively, a rhetorical argument that is aimed at gaining the adherence of the public becomes superfluous. The two types of argument are theoretically distinct, but I believe that the epistemological challenge of apodictic demonstration influenced rhetorical practice in the thirteenth century.

There is some evidence that medieval professors of rhetoric pondered the importance of scientific demonstration to their field of expertise. Boncompagno, a professor of rhetoric at Bologna in the first half of the thirteenth century, does so in defense of the claim that his *Rhetorica novissima* is indeed very new.[5] Richard McKeon raised the issue in its converse form in a seminal article written half a century ago. McKeon states that the difference between the types of proof, which is fundamental to Aristotle's epistemology, was disregarded through the twelfth century, and that rhetorical and dialectical modes of thought tended to obscure the definition of the principles. He adds that "even after the thirteenth century scientific method was in constant danger of being assimilated to dialectic, the *Posterior Analytics* to the *Topics*."[6]

The present study will focus not so much on the specific implications of the *Posterior Analytics* as on the more general influence of a series of texts that elaborate and apply Aristotle's theory of apodictic demonstration. I refer to Aristotle's texts of natural philosophy.[7]

The discovery of Aristotle's texts of natural philosophy had profound repercussions in the Latin West. For the first time the Christian mystical-symbolic conception of nature was challenged by a probing, systematic, and necessary explanation of natural processes that was conceived as readily accessible and comprehensible to the human mind. Aristotelian natural philosophy presented a unified explanation of human, animal, and vegetable life. The autonomy of nature and of the laws that structure it was particularly emphasized in the Averroist commentaries that were disseminated in the Latin West in the first half of the thirteenth century along with the texts of Aristotle.

Ecclesiastical authorities immediately perceived a danger and condemned certain Aristotelian concepts (not all from the field of natural philosophy), including the eternity of matter and the mortality of the individual soul. Despite the censure of specific concepts, the systematic approach to nature found in the Aristotelian texts had a gradual but pervasive and profound impact on thirteenth-century man's modes of perceiving and interpreting his environment.

The ability of the mind to understand creation and human motivation independently of Holy Scripture and exegetic guidance was reclaimed. The impact of the new mode of understanding and interpreting was rhetorical as well as epistemological. While the truth of the Bible was often shrouded in figurative language, the necessary truths of the natural world could be directly investigated and demonstrated using non-figurative language.

Dante, at the beginning of the fourteenth century, makes an explicit connection between Aristotle's method in the *Physics* and the correct mode of interpretation of the *canzoni* in the *Convivio*. Dante insists on the absolute priority of the literal sense of a text for understanding because the literal contains within it the other levels of meaning.[8] To proceed otherwise, according to Dante, would be irrational:

> Whence, as the Philosopher says in the first book of the Physics, nature desires that one proceed in an orderly manner in our knowledge, that is proceeding from that which we know better to that which we don't know so well; I say that nature wants this, in that this way of knowing is by nature innate in us.[9]

Dante is not, of course, discounting the importance and verity of the allegorical interpretation of the text. But he is addressing the medieval exegetic tendency to value the spirit over the letter and emphatically insisting on the authority of the literal reading of the text. The literal sense of the text, like material reality, is not merely a medium through which the truth might be attained. The literal, non-figurative reading of the text, like the created world, is the starting point of human knowledge and reason. And to argue his case Dante alludes to the methodological instruction of the *Physics*.

One thirteenth-century milieu in which the Aristotelian texts of natural philosophy were zealously studied was the court of Frederick II of Hohenstaufen. The court at Palermo was, because of its geographical location and the history of conquest of Sicily, a point at which the Latin and Greek Christian cultures and the Arabic Muslim culture converged. Frederick's Norman predecessors maintained Latin, Greek, and Arabic divisions in their chancery through the twelfth century. Sicily was an important center for the translation of Greek texts into Latin.[10]

Frederick II conceived his imperial dignity in universal terms. He consciously embraced the symbols of power, the refined luxuries, and the scientific and philosophical traditions of the East and West. He invited Arab, Christian and Jewish philosophers to converse and to study in his court, he maintained a Muslim colony in Sicily, and he sometimes traveled with a menagerie of exotic animals.

In his time Frederick was referred to as *stupor mundi*—the 'wonder of the world'—and damned as the Antichrist. Modern historians tend to avoid such sensationalist epithets but recognize Frederick's talent in the fields of administration, law, diplomacy, agriculture, architecture, natural philosophy, poetry, and linguistics, among others.

Frederick wrote a work of ornithology, *De arte venandi cum avibus*, which is considered to be one of the great empirical works of the Middle Ages. Michael Scot served as scientist and astrologer at the court from about 1227 until his death sometime before 1236. Scot is credited with the translation from Arabic into Latin of numerous Aristotelian texts and Averroistic commentaries.[11]

The discovery of the Aristotelian science of nature at Frederick's court influenced the perception, description, and justification of human affairs, and in turn it influenced rhetorical practice. Superficially the rhetoric of imperial letters resembles the papal style of the period: in both papal and imperial documents rhythmic and phonic repetition and grand-sounding phrases enhance the prestige of the prose. But the arguments of imperial letters, in contrast to papal documents, indicate a much greater reliance on the presentation of contingent circumstances as causes of events and imperial responses to events. Providential interpretation of events, citation of authority, ornament, and emotional appeals are less evident and less important than in the papal documents.

Many of the letters from the papal and imperial chanceries are also legal documents. In ecclesiastical legal documents the facts or circumstances of a case are presented in order to prove or disprove a charge, as required by canon law. But the church tended to treat questions as moral issues.[12] The rhetoric of a church document that was circulated, for example, to move a community to reject an excommunicate aimed most often at portraying that man as a sinner and the community at risk, whatever the facts or legal implications of the case. The appeal was usually emotional and featured long lists of allusions to the sinner's failings, a rhetorical device that does not encourage analysis on the part of the public.

A brief example of the difference between imperial and papal rhetoric is provided by an exchange between the chancery and the Roman curia in 1227, the year in which Pope Gregory IX first excommunicated Frederick.[13] The emperor is an excommunicate by law because he has broken his vow to lead a crusade within a prescribed period of time. The Roman curia dedicates most of its encyclical to condemning the emperor as a degenerate who is not fit to serve as secular leader of the Christian people and protector of the church. Papal proof of the inadequacy of Frederick's authority depends on a moral and traditional Christian interpretation of an historical event. According to Pope Gregory, the Crusaders' defeat in the Holy Land signifies the emperor's improbity. Failure is an expression of God's anger at his people who have elected an immoral man to lead them in the Crusade, a recreant who reneged on his duty as defender of the Church.

By contrast, in his letter of defense, the emperor strips away the moral interpretation of events in the Holy Land. Failure to achieve the desired end is attributed to incompetence and lack of adequate preparation. The Christian defeat was due to misdirection: "imprudently led, the Crusaders fell into a pit or rather a trap, without warning."[14] The meaning of the defeat has a clear circumstantial explanation which is demonstrated by the events as they were played out and is not symbolic of anything. The Christian defeat is the necessary and predictable consequence of poor leadership.

In Aristotle's studies of natural philosophy, human, animal, and plant behavior is removed from the realm of the providential and is explained mechanistically and systematically. Fundamental to the study of nature is the concept of necessity. The necessity of nature, of the sublunar world of generation and decay, of human society, is contingent necessity, also referred to as hypothetical or teleological necessity. Michael Scot translated the term in the first book of *De partibus animalium*, the methodological introduction to the biological sciences: "necessity means that which is is not unless because of something."[15] This concept of necessity is not absolute or eternal but based on the principle of cause and effect.

From the point of view of rhetoric, the Aristotelian concept of hypothetical necessity is of utmost consequence. The persuasive thrust of imperial documents is in the recitation of contingent circumstances interpreted as determinant causes of an imperial response. In the sublunar world over which a prince rules, actions are not defended by moral or spiritual considerations or by logical deductions from biblical or legal texts; instead, actions are the necessary responses to the contingencies of a situation in view of the prince's mandate to restore justice and to maintain peace. The Aristotelian texts provided a cognitive model and a mode of argument appropriate to the secular sphere of human affairs.

At the Frederican court the development of a new rhetoric was motivated by a convergence of cultural and political interests. Frederick II sought to establish the autonomy of the secular sphere in relation to the papacy. The *Prooemium* to the Constitutions of Melfi of 1231 is Frederick's most prominent statement of the ideology of imperial office, and in it necessity functions as a fundamental justification for the creation of the empire.

Biblical, classical, and Aristotelian scientific language resound in the opening of the *Prooemium*.

> After Divine Providence had formed the universe [*machinam mundi*] and had distributed primordial matter [*primordialem materiam*] by favor of a better nature into images of things, he, who had foreseen what should be done, looked at what he had done and was satisfied with what he saw. He made man in his own image and likeness, the worthiest creature of the creatures below the globe of the lunar circle [*globo circuli lunaris inferius hominem, creaturam dignissimam*]. . . .[16]

Phrases such as the *primordialis materia* and the *officio naturae melioris conditionis* have distinct Aristotelian overtones. The description of man as *creaturam dignissimam* is Aristotelian.[17] The omission of the creation of primordial material *ex nihilo*, a reference to the problematic Aristotelian concept of the eternity of matter, seems almost meant to bait theologians at the Roman curia.

The *Prooemium* continues with an explanation of the creation of princes. The emperor's intention to stake out an autonomous sphere of influence is manifest. When man transgressed the divinely prescribed law, when society became chaotic and sinful, God made princes to restore law to the society of fallen man. It is the duty of the prince to maintain peace and justice among men.

> Therefore, by this compelling necessity of things and not less by the inspiration of Divine Providence, [*rerum necessitate cogente nec minus divine provisionis*] princes of nations were created through whom the license of crimes might be corrected. . . . They should protect her [the church] from attacks of public enemies by power of the secular sword, and they should, if possible, preserve peace, and, after the people have been pacified, justice, which embrace each other like two sisters.[18]

For the present discussion this is the most important passage of the *Prooemium*. *Necessitas*, nature's *modus operandi*, is named in association with Divine Providence as the creator of princes. The imperial court is rooting its statement of ideology of empire in the two principles proper to scientific demonstration: why the empire is and why it is necessarily so.[19] There is nothing casual about the inclusion of the necessary origins of imperial power in the *Prooemium*.

Two brief texts, both composed in 1237 at the imperial chancery, serve to demonstrate the profound difference between the traditional, moralistic rhetoric of the period and the "scientific" rhetoric of chancery.[20] (Although there are numerous extant texts to illustrate this, most of a polemical nature are very long.) They also show that while the imperial court often found it useful to employ a rational mode of interpretation, it did not abandon ornamental and emotional modes of gaining the adherence of its public. The rhetorical choice of the chancery was determined by its perception of the culture of the public it was addressing.

The letters belong to a spate of letters dispatched by the emperor following the most important military victory of his reign, the defeat of the Milanese at Cortenuova in December 1237. They aim to persuade the public of the justice of an act already completed. The first letter is addressed to the German princes and prelates and the second to the Earl of Cornwall.[21]

The first letter no doubt reflects the chancery's recognition of the traditional moralistic and ecclesiastic culture of the German princes and prelates. The battle is described as a struggle of light against darkness.

The Lombards are a cowardly lot, morally and physically corrupt: they are the sons of Belial, Satanic offspring who rose in revolt against the Davidic line of kings.[22] They dare not show their faces to the light but sow tares in the fields by night. Their end is recorded in the Gospel according to Matthew.[23]

The descriptions of the battle are almost operatic in their drama and musicality. It is the awful voice of the ancient prophets:[24]

> Oh how great were the ranks of soldiers, how great the multitude of warriors! Here pride beat the drum, passion sounded the horn, struck the zithers, plucked the lyre: and thus the field of passion was bristling with bright banners of shame.[25]

Frederick, the new Solomon, comes to Lombardy to bring peace. But the sons of the Devil will not be subdued. Finally the emperor, whose victory is guaranteed by the heavens, dons his cuirass, arms himself, and, accompanied by the angelic army of the Lord, enters into the fray like a giant:

> and the voice of thunder and stupor was heard, "Euge! Euge! the swift-footed Frederick flies towards the Milanese." Hearing this, the rash Milanese were frozen by fear. The cymbals of the assembly sounded, arms were donned, and with great trepidation anyone who could took up a sword in his right hand. Each man implored silently in his breast, "Heu! Heu! my soul, why do you torture me so terribly and unmercifully with the cruel and ruthless Frederick?" And the instruments sounded: "Alas! Alas! for you, wretched Lombardy!" What more? the old man was slaughtered, the child torn to pieces, the youth sacrificed like calf, the fields drenched in blood and strewn with the wealth of the vanquished.

Frederick, the patient and omnipotent peacemaker, wields a sword that thirsts for blood and devours flesh. The letter concludes in the same hyperbolic tone: a description of the defeated sinners is juxtaposed to the portrait of the German princes, luminous in mind, noble in reason, rich in virtue. The emperor, the almighty soldier of Christ, invites the princes to share the glory of the magnificent victory.

In contrast, the Battle of Cortenuova is described without the attendant figurative readings of events in the letter sent to Richard, Earl of Cornwall. Each act is explained as the consequence of well or poorly laid plans or pure chance.

The letter opens with a condensed allusion to the justice of an imperial act. The foolhardy and wicked temerity of the Lombards who have long defied imperial rule in Italy is condemned. The situation has caused suffering in the region and is known in distant lands. Other remedies having proved inadequate, the emperor is finally moved by necessity to resort to arms in order to curb the adversary's criminal conduct.

> How audacious and rash have been the proceedings of the Ligurians . . . in rebelling against our royal person. . . . And we think that you are not unaware of what the world knows, namely that our constant system of passing over their offenses has continued so long, that, if we were to do so any further, our endurance would lose the name of true patience, and would incur the stigma of vile pusillanimity, instead of the honourable name of virtue. Considering, then, after some little time, that wounds which do not feel any effect from the application of fomentations, ought to be cut with the knife, we of necessity resorted to arms. . . .[26]

The analogy between medical intervention and the emperor's necessary dependence on arms is traditional but also very appropriate to the appeal in the letter. The concept of necessity is clearly that which is conditioned by the situation in view of a positive good, i.e. the establishment of imperial rule (peace and justice) in the region.

The battle between the imperial and Lombard forces is not divinely ordained or monitored. It is by chance, "casualiter tamen feliciter," that a small imperial advanced guard sets up camp on the shore of the Oglio River opposite the Milanese. Sight of the imperial band puts the Milanese to flight.

At this point the main corps of the imperial army, apparently including the emperor, makes haste to join the advanced guard, but its way is impeded by the debris of the Milanese army: unmanned battle horses, corpses of enemy knights, enemy infantry who have been bound together and abandoned by the officers.

> The Milanese and their allies, not being able to stay any longer in their hiding-places, owing to the scarcity of necessaries, crossed the river Oglio by the fords and bridges, and came into the open plain, thinking to escape from us by a secret flight, and perhaps not imagining that we were so near. When, however, they knew of our proximity, fear and terror fell on them like a clap of thunder from heaven, and at

> sight of the advanced guard of our imperial army . . . they turned to flight before us . . . and, as we believed that it was necessary for us to hasten to the assistance of the auxiliary troops, who had proceeded in advance in a small body, we marched after them with all speed with the strength of our army. . . . At length we discovered their *carrocium*, near the walls of Nuova Croce [Cortenuova], surrounded by trenches, and protected by an immense body of knights and all their foot soldiers, who fought wonderfully in its defense. . . . The shades of night, however, coming on, which our men ardently wished for, we desisted from the attack till the following morning early. . . . To make a short account of the matter, almost ten thousand men were said to have been taken or slain; among whom a great many nobles and chiefs of the Milanese faction fell.

There is no indication that the emperor ever engaged in battle.

The dissimilarity between the two letters could not be more striking. The melodramatic and moralistic fervor of the letter to the Germans leads to flagrant distortions, the most obvious being the transformation of the emperor into a battlefield titan and Old Testament hero. There is a timeless, epic quality to the first letter that is absent in the second, in which events are presented chronologically and the emperor's military adventurism is introduced as a necessary remedy to a destabilizing situation. In the second text events are explained in terms of typical human behavior: the Milanese leave their hideouts due to a scarcity of supplies, unaware of the proximity of the imperial advance guard. The few rhetorical flourishes do not distract from an essentially sober account of the battle which includes praise for the courage of the enemy infantry.

In the letter to Richard, moral interpretations do not provide the key to explain the success or failure of human endeavors. The battle is recounted and its outcome explained on the basis of a knowledge of human nature and of contingent circumstances as causes. Military intervention is justified as necessary to correct a situation that threatened the imperial mandate to administer justice and to preserve peace.

Frederick II sought to portray himself as a rational lord of an autonomous secular sphere. By borrowing techniques of argument and interpretation from Aristotelian science, his chancellors authorized modes of persuasion that were independent of the Christian categories of morality and appropriate to the sublunar, natural world of coming-to-be and the ever-changing world of human affairs.

NOTES

1. P. Albert Duhamel, "The Function of Rhetoric as Effective Expression," in *Philosophy and Argumentation*, ed. Maurice Natanson and Henry W. Johnson, Jr. (University Park, Penn.: Pennsylvania State Univ. Press, 1965), p. 81.

2. As Bene of Florence explains in his *Candelabrum* 1.4.16: "Unde ars ista, que dictatoria nuncupatur, non est ipsa rethorica sed pars eius elocutio nominata." (Bene Florentini, *Candelabrum*, ed. Gian Carlo Alessio [Padua: Antenore, 1983], p. 6.)

3. Hans Martin Schaller, "Die Kanzlei Kaiser Friedrichs II. Ihr Personal und Ihr Sprachstil" [Part II], *Archiv für Diplomatik* 4 (1958): 264-325 (esp. pp. 273-78).

4. John Herman Randall, Jr., *Aristotle* (New York: Columbia Univ. Press, 1960), pp. 33-34.

5. Boncompagnus, "Rhetorica novissima," in *Scripta anecdota glossatorum*, ed. Augusto Gaudenzi (Bologna: Virano, 1892): "Preterea philosophi et naturali scientia redimiti contra me possent magis verisimilem et rationabilem proponere questionem in hunc modum: Ille qui dicit se novissimam rhetoricam invenisse, tenetur assignare causas principales et materias inductivas, pro quibus tam arduum tentavit subire laborem. Tales namque obiectores dignis possum laudibus commendare: unde illorum teneor satisfacere questioni ex eo quod a rationabili motu nature procedi" (p. 252).

6. Richard McKeon, "Rhetoric in the Middle Ages," *Speculum* 17 (1942): 1-32 (quotation from p. 8). In the same article McKeon notes that in the previous century "John of Salisbury found the *Posterior Analytics* . . . difficult or even unintelligible" (p. 8).

7. I am defining natural philosophy as the study of that which "comes into being and passes away," to borrow a phrase from Randall, *Aristotle*, p. 164. This includes Aristotle's investigation of nature in the *Physics* and his works on biology, especially *Parts of Animals* (which I refer to by its Latin title, *De partibus animalium*), *Generation of Animals*, and *History of Animals*, as well as some brief monographs. The *De anima* is, in part, a work of natural philosophy, as are some of the studies of the heavens.

8. "E in dimostrar questo, sempre lo litterale dee andare innanzi, sì come quello ne la cui sentenza li altri sono inchiusi. . . ." See Dante Alighieri, *Il Convivio*, ed. Maria Simonelli (Bologna: Patron, 1966), p. 32 (2.1.8).

9. "Onde, sì come dice lo Filosofo nel primo de la Fisica, la natura vuole che ordinatamente si proceda ne la nostra conoscenza, cioè procedendo da quello che conoscemo meglio in quello che conoscemo non così bene; dico che la natura vuole, in quanto questa via di conoscere è in noi naturalmente innata"; Dante, *Il Convivio*, p. 33 (2.1.13).

10. See, for example, Aurelio Roncaglia, "Le corti medievali," in *Il letterato e le istituzioni, Letteratura italiana* (Turin: Einaudi, 1982), 1:33-147; Thomas Curtis Van Cleve, *The Emperor Frederick II of Hohenstaufen, Immutator Mundi* (Oxford: Clarendon Press, 1971); and the more modest assessment of Frederick's achievements in David Abulafia, *Frederick II, A Medieval Emperor* (London: Penguin, 1988).

11. Lynn Thorndike, *Michael Scot* (London: Nelson, 1965), pp. 22-31. Although there is some disagreement among scholars on whether or not Michael Scot was the first to translate all of the following works into Latin, the Aristotelian texts that are generally credited to him include: *De celo et mundo*, completed after 1217 and accompanied by the "great commentary" by Averroës; the *De partibus animalium*, the *De generatione animalium*, and the *Historia animalium* (all three translated at Toledo before 1220); and the *Physics* with a commentary by Averroës. Scot composed a Latin *Compendia* of the *Parva naturalia*; he translated the *De anima* and the accompanying commentary by Averroës, as well as parts of the *Metaphysics*, with an Averroës commentary. He dedicated another work, Avicenna's *Abbreviatio de animalibus*, based on the Aristotelian *Liber de animalibus,* to Frederick II. According to Thorndike, Scot "has been held largely responsible for the introduction of Averroism into western Christian Europe" (p. 24). *De arte venandi cum avibus* has been edited by Carl A. Willemsen, *Friderici Romanorum Imperatoris Secundi "De arte venandi cum avibus,"* 2 vols. (Leipzig: Insula, 1952). It was translated into English by Casey A. Wood and Marjorie G. Fyfe, *The Art of Falconry being the "De arte venandi cum avibus" of Frederick II of Hohenstaufen* (Stanford: Stanford Univ. Press, 1943). In Edward Grant, *A Source Book in Medieval Science* (Cambridge, Mass.: Harvard Univ. Press, 1974), the work is described as "one of the great scientific treatises of the Middle Ages." That Aristotle's method was more important to Frederick than his compilation of data is made clear in the following passage from the preface to *De arte venandi*, which is quoted by Grant: "We discovered by hard-won experience that the deductions of Aristotle, whom we followed when they appealed to our reason, were not entirely to be relied upon. . . . In his work, the *Liber animalium* . . . we find many quotations from other authors whose statements he did not verify and who, in their turn, were not speaking from experience. Entire experience of the truth never follows mere hearsay" (pp. 657-59).

12. The most significant example of this is provided by *Novit*, a letter which Pope Innocent III addressed to the bishops of France in April 1204. The pope justifies his intervention in the war between Philip II and King John of England by declaring the war to be an issue of sin and not a feudal matter, as Philip asserted: "Let no man, therefore, imagine that we intend to diminish or disturb the king's jurisdiction and power. . . . For we do not intend to judge concerning a fief, judgment on which belongs to him, . . . but concerning sin [*sed decernere de peccato*], a judgment which unquestionably belongs to us, and which we can and should exercise against anyone. . . . Though we are empowered to proceed thus in respect of any criminal sin so that we may recall the sinner from error to truth and from vice to virtue, yet we are specially so empowered when it is a sin against peace. . . ." The letter is included in the decretals; see C. R. Cheney and W. H. Semple, ed. and trans., *Selected Letters of Pope Innocent III* (New York: Nelson, 1953), pp. 63-68.

13. For the papal encyclical of excommunication, see J.-L. A. Huillard-Bréholles, *Historia diplomatica Friderici Secundi* (Paris: Plon, 1852-61), 3:23-30; the imperial response is on pp. 37-48.

14. Huillard-Bréholles, *Historia diplomatica*: "incaute ductus populus incidit in lacum, immo laqueum, improvisum . . ." (p. 38).

15. According to Gonville and Caius College [Cambridge] MS 109/178, fol. 60v: "Et necessitas significat quod hoc quod est non est nisi propter quid." This thirteenth-century manuscript contains a copy of Michael Scot's translation from the Arabic.

16. "Post mundi machinam providentia divina firmatam et primordialem materiam naturae melioris [conditionis] officio in rerum effigies distributam qui facienda providerat facta considerans [et] considerata commendans a globo circuli lunaris inferius hominem, creaturarum dignissimam, ad imaginem propriam effigiemque formatam. . . ." The text of the *Prooemium* is from Hermann Conrad, Thea von der Lieck-Buyken, and Wolfgang Wagner, ed., *Die Konstitutionen Friedrichs II. von Hohenstaufen für sein Königreich Sizilien* (Cologne: Böhlau, 1973), p. 2. The translation is by James M. Powell, ed. and trans., *The "Liber Augustalis" or Constitutions of Melfi, Promulgated by the Emperor Frederick II for the Kingdom of Sicily in 1231* (Syracuse: Syracuse Univ. Press, 1971), pp. 3-4.

17. Thea Buyken, "Über das Prooemium der Constitutionen von Melfi," *Revista Portuguesa de História* 14 (1941): 161-76.

18. "Sicque ipsa rerum necessitate cogente nec minus divinae provisionis instinctu principes gentium sunt procreati, per quos possit licentia scelerum coerceri; . . . et ut ipsam (sacrosanctam ecclesiam) ab hostium publicorum incursibus gladii materialis potentia tueatur atque pacem populis eisdemque pacificatis iustitiam, quae velut duae sorores se invicem amplexantur, pro posse conservet": Conrad et al., *Die Konstitutionen*, pp. 2-4.

19. "We think we understand a thing *simpliciter* . . . whenever we think we are aware both that the explanation because of which the object is is its explanation, and that it is not possible for this to be otherwise." *Posterior Analytics* 1.2.71b10. For the English translation, see Jonathan Barnes, ed. and trans., *Aristotle's Posterior Analytics* (Oxford: Clarendon Press, 1975), p. 2.

20. I discuss these two letters in my dissertation, "Rhetorical Innovation in the Chancery of Frederick II of Hohenstaufen and Its Reception by Vernacular Poets of the Thirteenth Century" (Ph.D. diss., Boston College, 1985), pp. 86-91.

21. The letter to the German princes appears in Huillard-Bréholles, *Historia*, 5: 147-49. The letter to Richard of Cornwall is found in Huillard-Bréholles, *Historia*, 5: 132-34.

22. See 2 Chronicles 13:6-17. My thanks to Scott Westrem for pointing out the political importance of the epithet.

23. Matthew 13:24-30.

24. Compare, for example, Joel 2.

25. "O quanta erat multitudo militum! quanta numerositas et universitas bellatorum! Ibi superbia pulsavit tympanum, voluptas tuba concinit, resonat cythara, plaudit lyra: et sic voluptatis ager cum pudendi decoris insignibus pullulavit. . . . [E]t audita est vox tonitrui et stuporis: 'Euge! euge! ad Mediolanenses impiger advola Friderice.' Quo audito, Mediolanensis protervitas statim fuit perterrita: compagnie projiciunt cimbala, sumunt arma: et dum a trementi cujuslibet dextera retineri vix poterat gladius, quilibet mutus in suo pectore tacitos vertit questus: 'Heu! heu! anime nostre: quid sic torques nos acriter atrox et immisericorditer immisericors Friderice?' Fit clamor ad sydera: 'Ve! ve! tibi misera Lombardia.' Quid plura? mactatur senex, puer diripitur, juvenis ut vitulus immolatur, campi madescunt sanguine, ac interfectorum exuberant ubertate" (Huillard-Bréholles, *Historia*, 5:147-49).

26. The translation of Matthew Paris's *Chronicle* is by J. A. Giles, ed. and trans., *English History from the Year 1235-1273* (New York: Bohn, 1852), 1:93-95. The Latin reads: "Quante audacie quanteque temeritatis sint Ligurum excellentie nostre rebellium factiones, . . . nec latere vos credimus, nec mundus ignorat tam longe nostre dissimulationis constantiam circa eos, ut tolerantia nostra verum patientie nomen amitteret et vitiose notam pusillanimitatis incurreret pro decore virtutis. Animadvertentes postmodum quod ferro secanda sunt vulnera, que fomentorum non sentiunt medicinam, necessario nos ad arma convertimus. . . . Et sic cum in cavernis morari diutius ultra flumen, rerum ipsos arcente penuria, non valerent, Mediolanenses et socii per pontes et vada fluminis Olei transeuntes, in apertam planiciem exiverunt, credentes se nobis per subsidium occulte fuge subripere, dum nos adeo prope consistere forsitan non putarent. Sed cum de adventu nostro terror et fremitus tanquam de celo tonitruum ipsis intonuit, ad premissas nostre celsitudinis acies . . . in fugam sic subito a facie nostra contriti se converterunt. . . . Et dum auxiliares acies, et post eas nos cum nostrorum agminum robore, gressibus festinatis, hiis qui in levi manu precesserant necessario cursu succurrere crederemus, . . . ad carrochium tandem quod juxta muros municipii Curtis Nove fossatorum vallis circumdatum et immensa militum copia et suorum omnium peditum mira defensione pugnantium munitum invenimus applicantes. . . . Supervenientis autem noctis umbrosa caligine, quam nostrorum vota longissimam suspirabant, tentatum aggressum tantisper obmisimus usque mane sequenti. . . . Et ut multa sub compendio concludamus, tum capti tum mortui, inter quos multi Mediolanensis factionis primates et principes corruerunt, decem milia fere numero computantur" (Huillard-Bréholles, *Historia*, 5:132-34).

"Gaainable Tere":
Symbolic Appropriation of Space and Time in Geoffrey of Monmouth and Vernacular Historical Writing

Monika Otter

The phrase *gaainable tere* in the title is borrowed from Denis Piramus's *Vie Seint Edmund le Rei*, a late-twelfth-century Anglo-Norman saint's life which will be examined later in this paper. It appears in the title because it conveniently sums up several of the aspects of *tere*, or 'territory', with which this study is concerned. The phrase has a precise technical meaning: it means 'arable land', land that can be cultivated and turned to profit.[1] But given the contexts in which *gaainable* appears, one is tempted to hear a trace of another meaning of *gaagner*—'to win, to acquire'—in the phrase as well: the word occurs three times in the *Vie Seint Edmund*, each time as someone is conquering a land or taking possession of it. In addition, Denis uses "gaainable" consistently side by side with more affective terms, in describing the richness, sweetness, and delightfulness of the land: "Le païs trovent delitable / E la tere bien gaainable" (lines 219-20); or "Riche païs e gaainable / E bon e douz e delitable" (lines 403-04).[2] These juxtapositions give the word overtones of 'lovely, attractive, desirable'. Therefore, we may read *gaainable tere* not only as 'arable land' but also as 'available, conquerable' and 'desirable' or 'coveted' land. While this reading of the phrase may appear somewhat idiosyncratic, it is not without warrant in the context of Denis's poem and related texts.

Monika Otter is a Ph.D. candidate at Columbia University (see Notes on Contributors, p. 222).

The theme of *gaainable tere* in this wider sense was first developed by Geoffrey of Monmouth in his *Historia regum Britanniae*. The motif is not isolated: geography is an important element in the *Historia*, and the many uses of place names, topography, and space form a resonant, coherent motif pattern which I believe is an important key to Geoffrey's historiography. Here, however, the focus will be on the *gaainable tere* motif alone. The three vernacular writers whom I will discuss briefly—Denis Piramus, the anonymous author of the romance *Fouke le Fitz Waryn*, and the early Middle English poet Laȝamon—are all clearly familiar with Geoffrey's work and influenced by it, either directly, or through Wace's or Gaimar's French versions of it, or both. *Gaainable tere*, in fact, seems to be one of the more prominent aspects of Geoffrey's influence. Other writers eagerly pick up the theme and adapt it creatively to their own purposes.

Geoffrey develops *gaainable tere* out of an older tradition. In imitation of Orosius's geographical introduction, many early British historians like to begin their work with a *descriptio Britanniae*, a brief topographical description and panegyric of Britain: the sixth-century historian Gildas, Bede in the eighth century, and the ninth-century *Historia Britonum* commonly attributed to "Nennius" all follow this tradition, as does, for instance, Geoffrey's contemporary Henry of Huntingdon.[3] The function of the *descriptio* and its relationship to the work as a whole are different in each case. But certain distinctive features remain constant. All the *descriptiones*, including Geoffrey's, emphasize the beauty and, above all, the convenience and utility of the land, its suitability for farming, and its rich natural resources: "It pro-vides in unfailing plenty everything that is suited [*congruit*] to the use of human beings," says Geoffrey.[4] In keeping with medieval notions of aesthetics, the panegyrists stress harmony, measure, balance. They have a predilection for clear-cut numbers: two (or three) major rivers; four (or five) nationalities; twenty-eight ("twice-ten and twice-four") major towns. Unstructured, untouched nature is not described, and the land seems unthinkable apart from its use and cultivation by humans.

What distinguishes the *Historia* from all previous instances of the topos is that Geoffrey integrates the *descriptio* of the desirable land into his historical narrative. In the *Historia*, the *descriptio* is no longer merely prefatory and no longer static. Geoffrey sets it in motion, as it were. Even as he unfolds the laudatory description, he inserts small dia-chronic movements and gestures towards narrative. The whole passage not only leads directly, seamlessly, into the narrative proper, but appears to launch and motivate it. Most significant, the *descriptio* is recalled in various echoes and transformations as part of the narrative. These correspondences between auctorial, editorializing comment and the narrative proper create important parallels between the characters' actions (especially Brutus's) and the narrator's activity in arranging and commenting on his narrative.

Geoffrey culls his *descriptio* from Gildas and Bede, but he changes its emphasis and function in an innovative way. He adopts the key concepts of his sources: plenitude (*fertilitas, fecundus, ubertas*) and suitability (*aptus, congruere, conuenire*). Like Gildas and Bede, he lists "perfect numbers" (three principal rivers, five nations), but he soon swerves from the course suggested by his sources. With the mention of "twice-ten and twice-four" cities, he suddenly leaves the synchronic plane—the map, as it were—and launches into narrative:

> In earlier times Britain was graced by twenty-eight cities. Some of these, in the depopulated areas, are now mouldering away, with their walls broken. Others remain whole and have in them the shrines of saints, with towers built up to a noble height, where religious communities of men and women offer praise to God according to the Christian tradition.[5]

This emphasis on historical change is a new element in the essentially synchronic *tableau* offered in Geoffrey's sources.

Similarly, his mention of the "five nations" that inhabit Britain (Normans, Britons, Saxons, Picts, and Scots) immediately gives rise to a narrative start that leads right into the history proper:

> Of these the Britons once occupied the land from sea to sea, before the others came. Then the vengeance of God overtook them because of their arrogance and they submitted to the Picts and the Saxons. It now remains for me to tell how they came and from where, and this will be made clear in what follows. (Thorpe, p. 54; Griscom, p. 222)

Bede, too, has a historical excursus at this point, but the differences are instructive. Bede's historical note is retrospective and explanatory: it serves merely to explain how the current distribution of Celtic peoples came about. In the body of the work, this material is not taken up again. Moreover, Bede emphasizes harmony and unity: Latin is a language common to all; the study of Truth is a common pursuit that unifies the disparate ethnic groups.[6] Geoffrey, by contrast, deliberately injects a note of conflict, creating a starting point for narrative development. His passage is proleptic: his narrative, as he says, will serve to expand this short preview.

The next step in the narrative transformation of the *descriptio* is the episode in which the expatriate Trojans, under Brutus's leadership, consult the ancient oracle of Diana on the island of Leogetia (Thorpe, pp. 64-66; Griscom, pp. 237-40). The island is deserted; its towns and temples are in ruins. This not only harks back to the twenty-eight towns of the initial *descriptio*, but anticipates the repeated mention of destroyed, rebuilt, rededicated temples, a major image of change and continuity in the *Historia*.[7] In response to Brutus's elaborate ritual, Diana promises Brutus a land "once occupied by giants. Now it is empty and ready [*apta*] for your folk. Down the years [*in aeuum*] this will prove an abode suited [*locus aptus*] to you and to your people; and for your descendants it will be a second Troy" (Thorpe, p. 65; Griscom, p. 239). This obviously prepares and legitimizes Brutus's appropriation of Britain, in terms that are already familiar and will be echoed again later on. The word *aptus* appears twice, but it has become somewhat more pointed in meaning: it describes not merely the land's general suitability for various agricultural and economic pursuits, but its fitness, even predestination, for this specific conqueror and his people, "in aeuum," forever. This is a kind of "manifest destiny" reasoning, here sanctioned by divine authority and—through the strong Virgilian flavor of the entire episode—classical literature. It comes as no surprise that the island is described as "deserted," its only inhabitants being "giants," that is, non-human creatures whose very nature disqualifies them from having a serious moral or legal claim to the land.

The extraordinarily rich and dense passage that describes Brutus's arrival in Britain and his taking possession of the land is a succinct account not only of a conquest and its legitimization, of settlement and cultivation, but also of a different kind of appropriation: the process by which the settlers make the land morally, or shall we say historically, their own. The Trojans land and deal with what little resistance they encounter from the "few giants." They settle and cultivate the land, spontaneously instituting a kind of feudal system, by which Brutus apportions lands to his retainers ("Patriam donante duce sortiuntur").[8] Brutus names the land for himself ("Britannia"). Corineus, his second-in-command, does the same for his portion of land ("Corinea," or Cornwall), and kills the giant Goemagog. Brutus then chooses a site for his capital, builds it, and names it New Troy, a name suggested by the Diana oracle (Thorpe, pp. 72-74; Griscom, pp. 249-53).

Many aspects of this account deserve comment. Again, the semantic field of *aptus* is represented, in terms like *amoenus, congruus, perspicuus*. But now there is an even stronger emphasis on the persons to whom the land is thus 'attractive' or 'suitable'. This emphasis is created in part by the characters' movements in space. Brutus and his followers travel around the new country, surveying, appreciating, parceling it: an obvious gesture of taking possession. But their active participation is not limited to accepting what makes itself available to them. They are also engaged in a quest: the ideal location for the capital does not simply present itself by destiny, but has to be sought out in order for the ideal site and its predestined conqueror to come together. The process is given affective coloring in a new key word to complement *aptus*: *affectus*. The beauty and suitability of the land immediately induces "affectus habitandi" in the travelers—the desire to inhabit it. Soon after, "*affectauit* brutus ciuitatem edificare. *Affectum* itaque suum exequens circuiuit totius patrie situm. ut congruum locum inueniret" ("Brutus desired to build a city. Therefore, carrying out his desire, he traveled over the whole country to find an appropriate site" [Griscom, p. 251, emphasis added; my translation]). "Aptitude," an objective quality of the place, is now matched by the *affectus* of the settler, the perceiving and appropriating subject.

The settlers immediately begin to cultivate the land and build houses on it; that is, they begin to civilize it. This theme is a necessary part of the "empty land" justification, which argues that the conquerors acquired a right to the territory by being the first to put it to civilized use (unlike the giants, or whatever other natives they might find). But, interestingly, Geoffrey pushes this civilizing act back in time, supplementing Diana's future prophecy, "in aeuum," with a backwards-looking "ab euo": ". . . so that in a short time you would have thought that the land had always [*ab euo*] been inhabited" (Thorpe, p. 72; Griscom, p. 249). The Trojans, as it were, establish their right retroactively. This also explains why the land is immediately referred to as "patria," a term that otherwise makes little sense for first-generation immigrants just off the boat. The usage clearly echoes Virgil, but whereas the *Aeneid* makes the transference of *patria* from Troy to Italy an explicit and emotional issue, Geoffrey makes the switch quite casually, appropriating the new land for his settlers not only for the present and future, but for the past as well.[9]

While all this bears an almost uncanny resemblance to colonialist rhetoric of later ages,[10] the purpose here would seem to be somewhat different. The conquest, as the parallel between the narrator and his warrior characters implies, is at least in part a metaphoric one. Geoffrey doubles the initial *descriptio*, repeats it at the level of character action, and turns the static, taxonomic description into a dynamic account of historical development; thus he creates verbal and thematic parallels between the narrator's and the characters' perspectives. The parallel, I believe, says something about Geoffrey's understanding of himself as a historian. Early twelfth-century historians, such as Eadmer or William of Malmesbury, are highly self-conscious about their roles; Geoffrey, whose work, in a sense, parodies his contemporaries' methods and narrative stance, is more self-conscious than most.[11] Many of them express their awareness that they are pioneering unto new historiographical territory: no history of any magnitude had been attempted since Bede, as William points out; and Geoffrey, of course, takes his history back in time before the period covered by Bede.[12] "Historiographical territory" is not necessarily an imported metaphor here: some twelfth-century writers do speak of history in almost spatial terms. These historians seem to have a strong sense of linearity in history: they are not so much concerned with showing typological patterns in history or providing a store of *exempla* for contemporary conduct, but with presenting an uninterrupted line of development, a "series temporum."[13] Gaps in chronology disturb them profoundly: William is concerned that English history "limps" in the middle, having nothing to support it for the entire long stretch from Bede to Eadmer, and he promises to "patch up the interrupted sequence of time" ("interruptam temporum seriem sarcire").[14]

Geoffrey himself, it is true, does not offer any such picturesque metaphors in his prologue; but he, too, presents himself as filling in gaps, as extending the line of historical knowledge farther backwards than had been previously attempted (Thorpe, p. 51; Griscom, p. 219). He is, therefore, a kind of explorer or conqueror himself, and occasionally a ruthless one at that. His historical fictions are sometimes so audacious that even some skeptical contemporaries, whose means of verifying his claims were naturally limited, accused him of lying.[15] In his dedicatory prologue, Geoffrey makes a much-imitated and much-discussed claim: he says he has discovered his history in a "very ancient book [*liber uetustissimus*] written in the British language" (Thorpe, p. 51; Griscom, p. 219). Thus, his narrative is not invented, not even compiled, but has been waiting as a self-contained whole to be discovered by an enterprising (and linguistically privileged) translator. He shrewdly strengthens the fiction by peppering his narrative with *effet de réel* elements: there are numerous loose ends and incomplete casual references of the kind one might expect to find in a chronicle that was compiled at a different time. In an "old book," one would naturally come across events and names for which one can no longer supply the context. Geoffrey appears to "antique" his narrative deliberately by artificially creating such remnants. For instance, he twice cryptically alludes to the "eagle of Shaftesbury" (Thorpe, pp. 80, 283; Griscom, pp. 261, 534), a legend that, to my knowledge, has never been traced, and which stumped even his first translators, Wace and Laȝamon.[16]

The very boldness of these tricks suggests that they may be not so much an attempt to deceive as a playful challenge to the reader to enter into the game of making up history retroactively; that, at any rate, seems to be how many of his readers used Geoffrey.[17] In any case, one metaphorical implication of the "liber uetustissimus" should have become clear by now: like his prototypical settler Brutus, Geoffrey seeks out the territory that has been waiting only for him; he covets, then occupies his *gaainable tere*; he makes himself at home in it and boldly pretends that he has always possessed it. The Diana oracle is another emblem for this attitude: it has been waiting for many years in a deserted island, "si forte ab aliquo peteretur," in case somebody were to seek it out (Thorpe, p. 64; Griscom, p. 238). Reactivating traditions, real or pretended (rededicating temples, or naming places after an abandoned homeland, or inventing a national history) is an activity common to both the historian and his hero.

At the same time, there is an implied awareness, or at least an uneasy hunch, that the land thus appropriated is not in fact quite the conqueror's for the taking. The uneasiness is illustrated by the fact that the giants in Britain are not completely vanquished but driven underground (Thorpe, p. 72; Griscom, p. 249)—an unstable solution at best, given both the giants' mythological associations and other instances in the *Historia* of unsuccessful containment of trouble "underground."[18] Geoffrey repeatedly draws attention to the extreme, and in many cases gratuitous, violence of the conquerors; that would seem to be one of the major functions of the semi-comical character Corineus. Corineus willfully provokes a bloody and ultimately quite useless war in Gaul, and he engages in giant-killing because he enjoys it as a sport (Thorpe, pp. 67-68, 72-73; Griscom, pp. 241-42, 250). While one may perhaps enjoy the slapstick humor of the scene, one is not allowed to forget that the conquerors have victims.[19]

There is no such thing, it seems, as an unoccupied territory. In fact, the literary imagination of the historians seems unable to conceive of untouched land; it is always imagined as already cultivated, or at least so "apta" to cultivation that it has no true existence apart from the cultivators and their desires. In extending their histories backwards, the twelfth-century historians not only have to draw on earlier literary models (Virgil, the Bible), but they are also imposing their post-conquest, school-trained literary sensibilities and scholarly needs on an earlier, indigenous historical culture that they use and describe, but whose separate value and importance they have to deny. Geoffrey, who, as R. William Leckie has shown, skilfully exploits both narrative traditions and gaps in earlier historiography to insert his own account, is presumably quite aware of the process.[20] The historian is a pioneer, but the land is not entirely pristine; appropriating a space of one's own involves both exploitation and denial of what came before.[21] The "liber uetustissimus" which Geoffrey claims to be using embodies this dual awareness. Geoffrey's work is both innovative and derivative; he "discovers," or invents, history, but he imagines it as already in book form.[22]

Geoffrey's imaginative use of *gaainable tere* seems to have struck a sympathetic chord in several historiographers who read and imitated him. It is striking, but perhaps not surprising, that such imitations occur most often when the writers' objective is to rewrite history, to claim a more or less open space in accepted chronology, and to splice their own story into the opening.[23] Geoffrey, by his own bold and almost explicit appropriation of territory, not only encourages others to do their own retroactive historicizing, but he has thrown himself open to appropriation by others to their own purposes. The three examples that I have chosen to concentrate on come from three quite different spheres; this suggests the flexibility and range of applicability of the topos. Furthermore, they are interesting as vernacular transformations of Geoffrey's motif. Since I am arguing here that *gaainable tere* has poetological significance, one might expect to find different accentuations of the theme in the different poetological situation of vernacular historical writing; and in two of the three texts, this would indeed appear to be the case. In the remainder of this article I shall sketch very briefly a monastic and hagiographic version of *gaainable tere* (Denis Piramus's *Vie Seint Edmund le Rei*); a secular, baronial version (the thirteenth-century Anglo-Norman romance *Fouke le Fitz Waryn*); and what I believe to be a more purely poetological version (Laȝamon's *Brut*).

It is appropriate to begin with Denis's *Vie Seint Edmund le Rei*, which, after all, contributed the phrase and notion of *gaainable tere* to this discussion. In order to understand Denis's use of the motif, it is necessary to be aware of the important role the Edmund legend played in the rhetoric and politics of Denis's monastic house, the influential abbey of Bury St. Edmunds. As one of the major landlords in East Anglia, the monastery used the figure of its patron saint to establish and defend its land claims, its jurisdiction, its royal privileges, and its independence from the diocesan bishops. Hence its virtual obsession with the "terra Sancti Edmundi" in its historiography and documents. The fact that Edmund was a king as well as a saint proved eminently useful in this enterprise. By carefully legitimizing Edmund's right to the land—after his death as well as before—the monks bolstered their claim to spiritual as well as political "ownership" of their lands.[24]

Part of the long-term hagiographic project at Bury, besides developing the Edmund legend internally, was to fit it into known and accepted historiography. There are beginnings of this in the earliest major hagiography of St. Edmund, the tenth-century *passio* of the saint by Abbo of Fleury, which begins with a brief historical introduction and a short version of the familiar *descriptio Britannie*.[25] Denis has no *descriptio* at the beginning, but instead carefully places his *vita* into a large historical context derived not only from Abbo but from Geoffrey as well. What is more, he turns the *descriptio* of his source into a full-fledged, quite complex Geoffreyan appropriation topos with important structural and thematic functions.

The phrase *gaainable tere*, as has been mentioned before, always occurs in connection with conquests. Denis uses it to set up an interesting pattern of parallels and contrasts in his story. The first invasion he describes is that of the Saxons. (Brutus is only briefly alluded to.) The Saxons arrive at a time when the Britons have left their land because of a famine; therefore, they find the land empty. The stages of the appropriation are by now familiar: "They find the country delightful, and the land very *gaainable*."[26] Before long, the Saxons begin to build fortifications, then a town. They successfully cultivate the land. (It should be noted that the Britons, who were forced into exile by a famine, apparently were unable to do this.) When the Britons return to reclaim "lur dreit et lur heritage" ("their right and their heritage" [line 259]), the Saxons explain that their right to "lur tere e lur conquest" ("their land and their conquest" [line 278]) supersedes the Britons', "for, when they entered the country, they found neither man nor woman there who lodged any protest or asked for any justification; for at that time, neither man nor woman nor child lived in the land."[27] The Saxons' victory in a fair battle confirms this interpretation and settles the question once and for all. As the conquered land is divided among the victors, the story zeroes in on the part that will be important for the further development of the story—East Anglia—and dutifully repeats the steps of appropriation for this "rich and *gaainable*, good, sweet, delightful land" (lines 403-04).

Edmund's arrival as the designated successor of the childless King Offa is entirely peaceful. But it strikingly echoes that of the military invaders: he lands on a plain that is "pleasing and beautiful and green and delightful" ("acceptable / E bele e vert e delitable" [lines 1503-04]). Like other newcomers, he "cultivates" and improves the land to make it his own, but after his own fashion: on his arrival, he kneels and prays, with the effect that the area, to this very day, is "more *gaainable* and more plentiful in all good things" ("plus gaainable / E de tuz biens fusunable") than the surrounding territory (lines 1515-16). Like Brutus, he travels his new land, and he marks his territory by leaving miraculous transformations in his wake. Denis goes out of his chronological way to tell us that later, immediately after his coronation, Edmund builds a hall and a chapel—a secular and a religious building— near his landing place (lines 1541-50). He is elected king peacefully and unanimously, since there is no legitimate heir (lines 1589-1756): again, not unlike the Angles and Saxons, he gains power by default, takes over an unclaimed realm.

The viciously brutal Danish raids that lead to Edmund's martyrdom read like a cruel, semi-comic parody of the Saxons' legitimate conquest and Edmund's peaceful arrival. The raiders are driven not so much by greed as by their envy of Edmund's effortless "conquest," the nature of which they thoroughly misunderstand: King Lothebroc taunts his sons with Edmund's achievement (lines 1949-92), and they proceed to take the land by force, slaughter its inhabitants, and execute the legitimate ruler, King Edmund.

This series of "conquests" is only the beginning of the careful legitimization of Edmund's rights to the land. His reign does not end with his death. Denis could hardly make this point more clearly than when he reports that East Anglia was without a king for a while after Edmund's death, because no one dared to take "segnurie": "They acknowledged in their hearts that he well ought to be king and lord of the land where he suffered martyrdom, for he had well deserved it before the Lord God."[28]

There are, however, legitimate successors of two kinds: first, those kings who respect Edmund's lordship and are endorsed by him; second, the religious community that forms around the martyr's burial place. Edmund continues his church-building activities after death. It is his body that brings the scattered English back together after the devastating raids. In the most famous episode of the Edmund legend, they scour the forest for Edmund's severed head, and the head assists them in their search by shouting "her, her, her" (lines 2665-2744). The body, like the community, miraculously comes back together (lines 2819-26), and Edmund's incorrupt body is later found to be free of any wounds, except for a thin red line around the neck (lines 2997-3005). One is tempted to interpret this as a parallel to the hagiographer's enterprise: he is, after all, trying to close gaps in the history of his house, to create a seamless account.

The chapel that is constructed above Edmund's tomb (lines 2828-30) is soon felt to be inadequate. The next step is to house the *corseint* better. A second search is mounted that is not unlike the search for the head—and not unlike Brutus's search for the ideal spot to found Troia Nova: "They searched throughout the land, they asked and inquired, until they found an pleasing, good, beautiful place in a great royal city."[29]

As Brutus the conqueror must find (and earn by his painstaking search) the place that is "aptus" for him, so St. Edmund's followers find a regal city for their royal saint, one that is "convenable." The remainder of the poem emphasizes the growth and continuity of the early ecclesiastical establishment around the relics of the saint, his almost-live presence within it—"in flesh and bones, as if he were alive" ("en char, en os, cum il fust vifs" [line 3024])—and his continued influence on daily life as defender, ruler, and judge.

On a much more modest scale, the thirteenth-century Anglo-Norman verse romance *Fouke le Fitz Waryn* is a secular counterpart to Denis's narrative.[30] *Fouke*, of which only a fourteenth-century prose version survives, is one of the so-called "ancestral romances."[31] The story traces the early history of the Fitz Waryns, an influential family in the Welsh march and, by implication, of the Welsh border barons in general. *Fouke* begins with the Norman Conquest: the Conqueror, in a gesture familiar from Brutus, travels through the region, dotting it with castles and with loyal barons (pp. 3-4). There is considerable genealogical detail to show that several contemporary families descend from these early barons. Since most of the families named do not in fact go back as far as William the Conqueror, this is in itself a bit of retroactive historicizing, similar to Geoffrey's observation that one might have thought the settlers had been on the land forever.[32]

But that is by no means the only Geoffreyan reminiscence. Like many ancestral romances, *Fouke* pillages other well-known texts for narrative motifs and works the scraps into a wild and playful pastiche of literary echoes and real-life history and topography. *Fouke*'s chief quarry is Geoffrey of Monmouth. In the course of the Conqueror's first land-taking trip, Payn Peverel, a Fitz Waryn ancestor, performs a replay of Corineus's fight with Geomagog in a deserted and haunted city called La Blaunche Launde (pp. 4-7). This is not just an indirect allusion: we are explicitly told that Payn's adversary is an evil spirit in Geomagog's body. To make sure that Geoffrey's account is present to us in all relevant details, a local peasant reminds the conquerors (and readers) of Geoffrey's original episode. First the peasant, later the ghost himself, vanquished by Payn and interrogated at sword-point, fill us in on the intervening history: Corineus won the place by his victory, but after his death, demons reclaimed it. King Bran attempted to rebuild the city, but the devils continually destroyed his buildings overnight. St. Augustine was more successful in appropriating the land by building a chapel on it, but again, the devils were able to take it back. It is now, as the ghost all but admits, high time for Payn Peverel to take over. La Blaunche Launde, or Whittington, becomes the Fitz Waryns' pet property—a hard-won possession, wrested from the forces of evil, that is, therefore, morally as well as legally theirs.

Although the precise political context of *Fouke* is open to debate, its general drift is clear enough: the Payn episode, like much else in the story, legitimizes the land claims of the Marcher Lords in general, and perhaps of one family in particular.[33] The poetological side of the "appropriation" is less obvious. I believe, however, that it may be found in the very derivativeness, the crazy-quilt character of *Fouke*. The text not only does not disguise, it flaunts its artificiality: the allusions to the Tristan story, to Geoffrey, and to other texts are so obvious that the pleasure of recognizing them and observing their almost grotesque transformations must account for part of the effect of *Fouke*. There is one odd detail in Payn's interrogation of the ghost that seems to speak to this fact. The giants, says the ghost, have left behind a buried treasure of golden animal figures. Payn demands to be led to the site, but the ghost warns him not to attempt it: the treasure is not meant for him but for someone yet to come (pp. 5-6). That is all; the motif is dropped here and never picked up again. This treasure—another possession left unclaimed, waiting to be taken—might be an image not only of the riches awaiting the Fitz Waryns, but also of the narrative possibilities open to a romance like *Fouke*. There are parallels—similar "golden worlds," underground treasures of ambiguous moral origin and difficult accessibility—in Latin historiography, clearly with poetological significance.[34] The *Fouke* narrator may be describing himself, through the Geoffreyan echo, as a latecomer on the romance scene: while implying, with sly self-mockery, that all good stories have been told before, he also suggests something about the riches available to him who can find the treasure. He, too, is appropriating an earlier literary tradition, but, given the looser demands and different ambitions of vernacular romance writing, appears to do so with little anxiety and little need for concealment; he can afford to be frank and playful about his borrowings, and, as it were, to establish his story's "genealogy" along with that of the Fitz Waryns.

Vernacular adaptation and appropriation in a different spirit can be seen in Laȝamon's *Brut*, dated variously between c. 1185 and 1275, a work whose immediate audience, patronage, and literary context remain hard to determine.[35] But Laȝamon's version of the *gaainable tere* motif might help to throw some light on his view of himself and his position as a poet. The *Brut* is, of course, the most directly "Geoffreyan" of the texts studied here: it is the English adaptation of Wace's French adaptation of Geoffrey's *Historia*. Laȝamon does not have a *descriptio Britanniae*—not surprisingly, since Wace does not have it either. But there is a beautiful appropriation passage; we see Brutus lovingly surveying the country he has brought under his control—much like the Creator, seeing that it was good:

> Brutus looked out upon this multitude; he beheld the fair, tall mountains, the broad meadows, the rivers, the wild game, the fish, the birds, the pastures, and the lovely forests. He saw how the woods flowered and the grain grew; all he gazed at in that land was dear to his heart (p. 50).[36]

This contemplation makes him so nostalgic for Troy that it induces him to found "Troye þe Newe" (line 1017). Like Geoffrey's Brutus, he is led by his *affectus* to reestablish an interrupted tradition, to close a gap in his history. Laȝamon's prologue material is, as I said, quite unlike Geoffrey's: there is no *descriptio*. But, as in Geoffrey, this *gaainable tere* or *affectus habitandi* passage harks back to the Prologue: Brutus looking at his land sounds strikingly like Laȝamon looking at his books. Laȝamon, too, has had to travel and search to find his treasured possessions: "Laȝamon traveled widely throughout the land acquiring the honored books he used as exemplars." Then, "Laȝamon laid open these books, turned their leaves, and viewed them fondly— may the Lord be merciful to him. [He took] a pen with his fingers and [wrote] on parchment" (p. 33).[37]

Again, as in *Fouke*, it is interesting to consider Laȝamon's "conquest" in terms of his self-conscious role as a vernacular writer. The priest-turned-historian is surveying his "territory," with an unmistakable, almost sensuous *affectus*. Like Geoffrey's Brutus, Denis's Edmund, or William the Conqueror in *Fouke*, he immediately proceeds to make this land his own by leaving his mark on it—in this case, with a quill. Through this image, Laȝamon casts himself as a clerkly narrator, as a facilitator or mediator who researches the sources and makes learned materials available to a less literate, or even illiterate, audience. In view of this mediating position, it is not, perhaps, without significance that he refers to three books: a Latin, an English, and a French one—and that the French one is placed between the other two, as if to mediate between literate Latin and popular English, which by Laȝamon's time had been virtually stripped of all literate and written functions and thus had become more radically "vernacular," more radically oral than French (p. 33; lines 16-23).

At the same time, especially in the long Arthurian section of the poem, La3amon stresses his close links to an oral, bardic tradition. Although he is in fact following a written source fairly closely, he refers to a wealth of oral tales, suggesting that he is collecting these stories and consolidating them into a written work, not unlike Chrétien in the *Erec* prologue or Thomas in his *Tristan*, who portray themselves as making a similar transition from oral traditions to a new vernacular literacy.[38] In contrast to these writers, however, La3amon does his job without any polemics or any assertions of superiority. There is no contempt for the lesser efforts of "cil qui de conter vivre vuelent,"[39] or competition for the correct version of the story. Arthurian history is a collaborative venture. La3amon's Round Table is not so much a school for courtly civility, as is Wace's, but a Eucharist for bards:

> Thus was it prophesied by the famous Merlin before Arthur's birth that a king would come of Uther Pendragon, and that bards would make a table of that king's breast at which noble poets would eat their fill before going hence; from this king's tongue they would draw wine and drink to make merry the days and nights in game as long as the world endures (p. 215).

> Gleemen will artfully sing of him, noble poets will eat of his breast, and knights will be intoxicated by his blood (p. 184).[40]

The bookish La3amon, in another guise, is also not unlike a bard: in a second start, after his clerkly prologue, he begins, Caedmon-like: "NV sei∂ mid loft-songe þe wes on leoden preost. / al swa þe boc speke∂ . . ." ("Now speaks with lofty song he who was priest in the land / all that the book speaks" [lines 36-37]).[41] Occupying a middle ground between bard and cleric, using learned written sources yet "saying" and "singing" what his sources "speak," he could be said to officiate as the priest at the Round Table Eucharist. In order to do that, he, like Brutus, and like all the other authors, has to seek out, conquer, and appropriate his own space as a historian and narrator, his own *gaainable tere*.

NOTES

1. Tobler-Lommatzsch, *Altfranzösisches Wörterbuch* (Wiesbaden: Steiner, 1960), s.v. "gaaignable"; *Anglo-Norman Dictionary*, ed. Louise W. Stone, William Rothwell, and T. B. W. Reid (London: Modern Humanities Research Association, 1983), s.v. "gainable."

2. Denis Piramus, *La Vie Seint Edmund le Rei*, ed. Hilding Kjellman (Göteborg: Elanders, 1935). Subsequent references to this edition will appear as line numbers in the text.

3. Gildas, *The Ruin of Britain and other works*, ed. and trans. Michael Winterbottom (London: Phillimore; Totowa, N.J.: Rowman and Littlefield, 1978), pp. 89-90; *Bede's Ecclesiastical History of the English People*, ed. Bertram Colgrave and R. A. B. Mynors (Oxford: Clarendon, 1972), pp. 14-21; *Nennii Historia Britonum*, ed. Joseph Stevenson (London: English Historical Society, 1938), pp. 6-7; Henry of Huntingdon, *The History of the English*, ed. Thomas Arnold, Rolls Series 74 (London: Longmans, 1879), pp. 5-13; *Pauli Orosii Historiarum adversum Paganos libri VII*, ed. Carl Zangemeister, CSEL 5 (Vienna, 1882; repr. New York: Johnson Reprint Corporation, 1966), pp. 28-30.

4. Geoffrey of Monmouth, *The History of the Kings of Britain*, trans. Lewis Thorpe (Harmondsworth, Eng.: Penguin, 1983), p. 53. The Latin text used is *The Historia Regum Britanniae of Geoffrey of Monmouth*, ed. Acton Griscom (London: Longmans, 1929); for the quotation here, see p. 221. Subsequent references to both editions will appear in the text.

5. Thorpe, *History*, p. 54; Griscom, *Historia*, pp. 221-22. I have slightly adapted Thorpe's translation here, which seems to contain a distorting misprint.

6. Bede, *Ecclesiastical History*, pp. 16-19.

7. Examples include the rededication of the British temples through Faganus and Duvianus, and Aurelius's pledge, during his campaign against Hengist, to rebuild the destroyed temples as soon as he is victorious (Thorpe, *History*, pp. 124-25, 189; Griscom, *Historia*, pp. 328-30, 401-02).

8. Thorpe's translation ("with the approval of their leader they divided the land among themselves") does not quite capture the force of the Latin "donante duce," which implies that Brutus grants the land, rather than merely sanctioning his followers' choices.

9. On Virgil's use of *patria*, see Lee Patterson, *Negotiating the Past: The Historical Understanding of Medieval Literature* (Madison: Univ. of Wisconsin Press, 1987), p. 173.

10. For examples and discussions of early modern explorers' narratives, see Mary B. Campbell, *The Witness and the Other World: Exotic European Travel Writing, 400-1600* (Ithaca: Cornell Univ. Press, 1988), esp. ch. 5, "'The End of the East': Columbus Discovers Paradise"; and Annette Kolodny, *The Lay of the Land: Metaphor as Experience and History in American Life and Letters* (Chapel Hill: Univ. of North Carolina Press, 1975), esp. ch. 2, "Surveying the Virgin Land."

11. Eadmer, *Historia Novorum in Anglia*, ed. Martin Rule, Rolls Series 81 (London: Longmans, 1884), p. 1; William of Malmesbury, *De Gestis Regum Anglorum*, ed. William Stubbs, Rolls Series 90 (London: Longmans, 1887), 1:1-2. On Geoffrey's "parody," see Robert W. Hanning, *The Vision of History in Early Britain* (New York: Columbia Univ. Press, 1966), pp. 123-36; and Valerie I. J. Flint, "The *Historia Regum Britanniae* of Geoffrey of Monmouth: Parody and Its Purpose. A Suggestion," *Speculum* 54 (1979): 447-68.

12. William of Malmesbury, *De Gestis*, 1:1.

13. Patterson shows how Virgil and the whole *translatio imperii* idea supplied a linear model of history, if a problematic one, to the twelfth century (*Negotiating*, pp. 160-61, 201-02). On genealogy and linear history, see Gabrielle M. Spiegel, "Genealogy: Form and Function in Medieval Historical Narrative," *History and Theory* 22 (1983): 43-53.

14. William of Malmesbury, *De Gestis*, 1:2.

15. For contemporary critics of Geoffrey, see Antonia Gransden, *Historical Writing in England c. 550 to c. 1307* (Ithaca: Cornell Univ. Press, 1974), pp. 212-13, 246, 264-65.

16. On the Eagle of Shaftesbury, see J. S. P. Tatlock, *The Legendary History of Britain: Geoffrey of Monmouth's* Historia Regum Britanniae *and Its Early Vernacular Versions* (Berkeley: Univ. of California Press, 1950), p. 44. Wace admits that he knows nothing about the bird or the content of its prophecies (*Le Roman de Brut*, ed. Ivor Arnold [Paris: S.A.T.F., 1938], vol. 1, lines 1616-18). La3amon makes a feeble attempt to invent a plausible "prophecy"; see *La3amon: Brut*, ed. G. L. Brook and R. F. Leslie, EETS, o.s. 250 (London: Oxford Univ. Press, 1963), 1:72 (lines 1411-16); *Layamon's Brut: A History of the Britons*, trans. Donald G. Bzdyl (Binghamton, N.Y.: Center for Medieval and Early Renaissance Studies, 1989), p. 57.

17. The *Historia Monasterii de Abingdon* (late twelfth century), for instance, uses the general outline of Bede's and Geoffrey's histories to insert the figure of the monastery's own legendary founder, "Abennus," and a foundation myth concerning the finding of the "Black Cross." This episode is of course modeled on St. Helen's Finding of the True Cross, which, on Geoffrey's authority, is connected to England; it is also embedded in a description of the monastery's site that sounds distinctly like *gaainable tere* (*Chronicon Monasterii de Abingdon*, ed. Joseph Stevenson, Rolls Series 2 [London: Longmans, 1858], 1:6-7). The twelfth-century hagiographer William of St. Albans even acknowledges Geoffrey's influence as he uses a similar source fiction ("Alia Acta SS Albani, Amphibali et sociorum . . . ," *Acta Sanctorum*, June 22, Junii Tomus Quintus [Paris: Palme, 1867], p. 129). In the mid-thirteenth century, St. Albans's most famous historian, Matthew Paris, takes the book image one step further by having his predecessors literally dig up an ancient book "antiquo Anglico, vel Britannico, idiomate" in the ruins of an old Roman town; see *Gesta Abbatum Monasterii Sancti Albani*, ed. Henry Thomas Riley, Rolls Series 28[4] (London: Longmans, 1867), 1:26-27. The example of *Fouke le Fitz Waryn* is discussed below.

18. The dragons underneath Vortigern's tower immediately come to mind (Thorpe, *History*, pp. 169-72; Griscom, *Historia*, pp. 382-83); see also Patterson, *Negotiating*, p. 202. Closer in time to the Brutus story is Locrinus's attempt to keep his adultery hidden, and harmless, by banishing his mistress underground (Thorpe, *History*, pp. 76-78; Griscom, *Historia*, pp. 255-56).

19. There are similar accents in the story of Belinus and Brennius: "Brennius stayed on in Italy, where he treated the local people with unheard-of savagery" (Thorpe, *History*, p. 99; Griscom, *Historia*, p. 290).

20. R. William Leckie, Jr., *The Passage of Dominion: Geoffrey of Monmouth and the Periodization of Insular History in the Twelfth Century* (Toronto: Univ. of Toronto Press, 1981), p. 20 and passim.

21. See Patterson on Virgil's "literary exorcism" (*Negotiating*, p. 162).

22. Edmundo O'Gorman's reflections on "discovery" and "invention" are interesting in this context; see *The Invention of America* (Bloomington, Ind.: Indiana Univ. Press, 1961), pp. 9-47 (and p. 9, n.).

23. See above, n. 17. See also Patterson, *Negotiating*, pp. 202-10.

24. For illuminating accounts of the political context of Bury hagiography prior to Denis, see Antonia Gransden, "Baldwin, Abbot of Bury St. Edmunds, 1065-1097," *Proceedings of the Battle Conference on*

Anglo-Norman Studies 4 (1981): 65-76; Barbara Abou-el-Haj, "Bury St. Edmunds Abbey Between 1070 and 1124: A History of Property, Privilege, and Monastic Art Production," *Art History* 6 (1983): 1-27.

25. Abbo, "Life of St. Edmund," in *Three Lives of English Saints*, ed. Michael Winterbottom (Toronto: Pontifical Institute of Mediaeval Studies, 1972), pp. 69-70.

26. Denis Piramus, *Vie*, lines 219-20 (see above, pp. 157 and 172 n. 2). All translations from the *Vie Seint Edmund le Rei* are my own.

27. Kar, kant il en la tere entrerent,
    Homme ne femme n'i troverent
    Ki de rien lur contredeïst,
    Ne qui a reisun les meïst,
    Kar en la tere dunc vivant
    N'out homme ne femme n'enfant. (lines 279-84)

28. Kar en lur curages noterent
    Que bien deit estre e reis e sire
    Del païs ou suffrit martire,
    Kar mult l'en aveit deservi
    Vers Dampnedeu e bien meri. (lines 3338-42)

29. Tant unt cerchié par le païs,
    Tant unt demandé e enquis,
    Qu'il unt trové liu acceptable
    E bel e bon e convenable
    En une grant vile real. (lines 2895-99)

30. *Fouke Le Fitz Waryn*, ed. E. J. Hathaway, P. T. Ricketts, C. A. Robson and A. D. Wilshere, Anglo-Norman Text Society 26-28 (Oxford: Blackwell, 1975). References to this edition will appear in the text. Although the only extant text of this romance is a fourteenth-century prose "remaniement," we can be fairly certain that the passage under discussion here was in the thirteenth-century French verse romance seen and described by John Leland in the sixteenth century: a sizable part of the passage (the ghost's prophecy) is in verse and can be shown to be a remnant of the old text; the editors also point out several rhymes in the prose text that point to the underlying verse model (*Fouke*, p. 67; see also "Introduction," pp. xix-xxvi).

31. On "ancestral romance," see M. Dominica Legge, *Anglo-Norman and Its Backgrounds* (Oxford: Clarendon, 1963), pp. 139-75 (on *Fouke*, pp. 171-74); Susan Crane, *Insular Romance: Politics, Faith, and Culture in Anglo-Norman and Middle English Literature* (Berkeley: Univ. of California Press, 1986), pp. 53-91 (on *Fouke*, pp. 16-18, 57-58).

32. *Fouke*, p. 63 (note for p. 3, line 17).

33. Crane challenges the widespread notion that ancestral romances—and *Fouke* in particular—served as propaganda for specific noble families; she instead ties them to the political interests of the entire baronial class (see above, n. 31). For other views on *Fouke*'s political context, see the introduction to the edition by Hathaway et al. (above, n. 30), pp. ix-xv and xxvii-xxxii; Louis Brandin, "Nouvelles Recherches sur *Fouke Fitz Warin*," *Romania* 55 (1929): 17-44; and E. A. Francis, "The Background to 'Fulk FitzWarin'," *Studies in Medieval French Presented to Alfred Ewert* (Oxford: Clarendon, 1961), pp. 322-27.

34. In William of Malmesbury's *De gestis regum Britanniae*, for instance, there is an apparently unmotivated pair of anecdotes about gold treasures found in caves that are protected from unauthorized intruders by several fantastic mechanisms. Gerald of Wales has a touching story of a boy who for many years has access to an underground fairyland but loses it when he attempts to steal one of its many golden objects. See William of Malmesbury, *De Gestis*, 1:196-201; Giraldus Cambrensis, *Itinerarium Kambriae et Descriptio Kambriae*, ed. James F. Dimock, Rolls Series 21[6] (London: Longmans, 1868), pp. 75-78. For further stories of the same type, see Arturo Graf, *Roma nella memoria de nelle immaginazioni del medio evo* (Turin: Chiantore, 1923), pp. 119-42. For a thorough and stimulating discussion of William of Malmesbury's treasure episodes and some closely related stories, see Massimo Oldoni, "'A fantasia dicitur fantasma.' Gerberto e la sua storia, II, prima parte," *Studi Medievali*, 3rd ser. 21 (1980): 493-622. The findings of this fully-documented study are summarized in Massimo Oldoni, "*Imago* e *Fan-tasma*: l'incantesimo storiografico di Gerberto," in *Gerberto: scienza, storia e mito: Atti del Gerberti Symposium (Bobbio 25-27 luglio 1983)*, ed. Michele Tosi (Bobbio: Archivi Storici Bobiensi, 1985), pp. 755-61.

35. The most recent edition (in two volumes but to date unfinished) is *Laȝamon: Brut*, ed. G. L. Brook and R. F. Leslie, EETS, o.s. 250 and 277 (London: Oxford Univ. Press, 1963, 1978). The only readable full translation is Bzdyl's *Layamon's Brut* (see above, n. 16). Subsequent references to both the edition and the translation will appear in the text: page numbers refer to Bzdyl's translation; line numbers refer to the "Caligula" text, on the left-hand side of Brook's and Leslie's parallel text edition. Criticism on the *Brut* and its literary and social context is summarized and discussed by Francoise H. M. Le Saux, *Laȝamon's Brut: The Poem and Its Sources* (Cambridge, Eng.: D. S. Brewer, 1989). She makes many plausible suggestions on Laȝamon's sources and political outlook (summarized on pp. 228-30), but does not address the question of possible patronage or audience. She also attempts to narrow down the dating of the poem to the earlier part of

the range proposed by earlier critics: 1185-1216 (pp. 1-10). For a recent discussion of La3amon's political position, see Daniel Donoghue, "La3amon's Ambivalence," *Speculum* 65 (1990): 537-63.

36. Brutus hine bi-þohte   & þis folc bi-heold.
    bi-heold he þa muntes   feire & muchele.
    bi-heold he þa medewan   þat weoren swiðe mære.
    bi-heold he þa wateres   & þa wilde deor.
    bi-heold he þa fisches   bi-heold he þa fu3eles.
    bi-heold he þa leswa   & þene leofliche wode.
    bi-heold he þene wode hu he bleou   bi-heold he þat corn hu hit greu.
    al he iseih on leoden   þat him leof was on heorten. (lines 1002-09)

37. La3amon gon liðen   wide 3ond þas leode.
    & bi-won þa æðela boc   þa he to bisne nom. (lines 14-15)

    La3amon leide þeos boc   & þa leaf wende.
    he heom leofliche bi-heold   liþe him beo Drihten.
    Feþeren he nom mid fingren   & fiede on boc-felle. (lines 24-26)

38. *Erec et Enide*, ed. Mario Roques, vol. 1 of *Les Romans de Chrétien de Troyes*, Les Classiques Français du Moyen Age (Paris: Honore Champion, 1952), lines 1-25; *Le Roman de Tristan par Thomas*, ed. Joseph Bedier (Paris: Firmin Didot, 1902), vol. 1, lines 2107-56.

39. *Erec et Enide*, line 22.

40. swa him sæide Merlin   þe wite3e wes mære.
    þat a king sculde cume   of Vðere Pendragune.
    þat gleomen sculden wurchen burd   of þas kinges breosten.
    and þer-to sitten   scopes swiðe sele.
    and eten heore wullen   ær heo þenne fusden.
    and winscenches ut teon   of þeos kinges tungen.
    and drinken & dreomen.   daies & nihtes.
    þis gomen heom sculde i-lasten   to þere weorlde longe.
    (lines 11492-99)

    of him scullen gleomen.   godliche singen.
    of his breosten scullen æten   aðele scopes.
    scullen of his blode   beornes beon drunke. (lines 9410-12)

41. I have here substituted my own very literal translation, since Bzdyl's (p. 35) is too free to capture the tone of this poetic opening and to reproduce the subtle play of the "oral" terms "seið," "songe," and "spekeð" against the source reference, "þe boc."

The Geography of Escape and Topsy-Turvy Literary Genres

Louise O. Vasvari

I. *The geography of escape*

The escape from reality in popular fantasy is a universal need of mankind manifested not only in wishes and dreams but also in taletelling. One popular form of what might be called the "geography of escape" is the depiction of the fabulous earthly and earthy *mundus inversus* of gluttony and idleness, most often called *Cockaigne* or *Schla(u)raffenland*. In this paper I shall attempt to show how the interrelated motifs of *Cockaigne*, as well as the whole alternate world it depicts, can best be understood as part of the carnivalesque. I shall also discuss how in a number of medieval literary works these motifs are raised to a literary level, with hilarious results.

Cockaigne is not a nostalgic depiction of a lost fantasy world of the past, as is the Golden Age, nor the promise of a rationally constructable ideal world achievable in a historical future, as is a Utopia, but an unchristian Neverland, often located somewhere far off in the sea, perhaps "west of Spain," or "three miles west of Christmas, [and] to the left of Paradise."[1] To reach it one may have to wade in pig excrement or in snot, or to eat one's way through a mountain of

Louise O. Vasvari is Professor of Comparative Literature and Linguistics at the State University of New York at Stony Brook (see Notes on Contributors, p. 223). The research for this paper was supported by a Senior Research Fellowship from the National Endowment for the Humanities during 1987-88.

porridge for seven miles or for seven years. But the lucky few who do reach Cockaigne are rewarded by having all their erotic and alimentary fantasies met with no effort on their part.

Depictions of Cockaigne are a series of interrelated motifs describing a topsy-turvy alimentary and consumer's paradise where all material needs are automatically met in excess. Cockaigne is also an edible world, where rivers flow with milk or brand-name wines, both white and red; where it rains honey and snows sugar and almonds; and where houses and fences are made from what is most popular in the local diet, from bratwurst to waffles. Roasted fowl fly into open mouths, mules may shit figs, and horses lay eggs. Other material goods, like clothes, may also grow on trees, drop from the vast storehouse of heaven, or be distributed free by merchants. Cockaigne may also contain a fountain of youth which turns everyone thirty, a prison for those who want to work, and a calendar full of holidays. If people don't grow on trees like fruit, women may give birth dancing, and people die laughing, if they die at all. Men can have unlimited access to willing women, whom they can change daily or weekly.

Cockaigne puts the highest value on inertia, laziness, and sleep. Typical are the following lines from *Li pais a non Coqaigne*:

> qui plus i dort, plus i gaaigne
> cil qui dort jusq'a miedi
> gaaigne cinq sols et demi.
>
> [whoever sleeps the longest earns the most / whoever sleeps until noon / earns five and a half sous.]

In this land, where laziness is the greatest virtue, lying is the highest creative art form, so that whoever can tell the biggest lie for virtuosity's sake is crowned king of the whole land, or abbot of a monastery of idle monks, while whoever tells the truth may have his head bashed in.[2]

This cluster of secondary motifs is part of the central motif of the Land of Cockaigne, of the inverted, or upside-down, world. The description of this fantastic world masquerades as a "true" personal narrative, or *memorate*, told by a first-person narrator, who pretends to have returned from a trip there; this technique is a familiar feature of imaginary voyage literature, which also had its greatest vogue in the same centuries. The narrator recounts his tale with ludicrous lying, or, more precisely, by tall tale-telling, which involves not merely unusual or unlikely events but exaggeratedly impossible ones. Unlike the narrator in imaginary travel literature, however, the I-speaker purposely shatters the illusion of the credibility of his narrative either by declaring outright that he is lying or, conversely, by exaggerated insistence on his truthfulness.

It is evident from the mode of narration that Cockaigne, unlike a Utopia, is not prized for its mythic elements—that is, features, however fanciful, that its audience would consider to be ultimately truthful—but rather for its quality of verbal artifice. The audience of a Cockaigne narrative will evaluate it for the skill and effectiveness of its telling. The exaggerated tale-telling and agonistic verbal games that are essential motifs of most descriptions of Cockaigne consist of the weaving together of incongruous elements whose essential feature is their absurdity and discord. The narrator strings together absurd and comical inversions and exaggerations of many kinds, in which his lies must top all others by their illogic and excess, or, as one Hungarian poet put it: "Now I'll tell such a lie that I don't believe it myself."[3] In an age of residual orality in which verbal facility was greatly valued, most important was not who had the best case but who could argue it most eloquently, or with the quickest wit. Therefore, in the typical "lying as a game" agonistic structure, the inevitable winner was the one who could tell the most ridiculously implausible or the most bawdy story.

Cockaigne is related to the concept of Carnival in that it is a vision of life as one endless Carnival, which in turn is a kind of temporary Cockaigne, with the same emphasis on excess and reversals. In addition, Carnival can be considered not only in opposition to Lent but also as representative of the ritual "world upside down" desacralization of official hierarchical culture of the rest of the year. Both Cockaigne and Carnival offer a temporary world of freedom and abundance, which through mockery, mimicry, and parody seeks to expose and degrade the values of official culture. Their alternate worlds are a means through which the ideal, the spiritual, and the abstract are all deflated to the level of material reality.

The interchange of motifs between Carnival and Cockaigne is extensive. Contests of lying and the performance of farces with a lying structure were an integral part of Carnival festivities, as were mock sieges, lawsuits, sermons, and weddings. The typical alimentary motif of Cockaigne in which prepared dishes function both as inert materials, such as roofs and fences, and in which animals appear simultaneously roasted and alive is paralleled in the mock battles of Meat (or Mardigras) and Lent, where cooked meats armed with pots and platters as shields fight the vegetal or fishy armies of Lent.

In both Carnival and Cockaigne alterity is immediately marked by what Mikhail Bakhtin calls the carnivalization of language.[4] This refers to the lying contests, and the non-sense of *impossibilia*, already mentioned, which by their intentionally absurd verbal combinations release signifier from signified, to enjoy a momentary play period of complete freedom; but this carnivalization of language also includes the free play of verbal aggression, or ritualized insults, as well as the use of crude humor in general. Particularly central is the reinterpretation of the central metaphors on the three major symbolic levels of Carnival—food, sex, and violence—but always ending up as a gross sexual *double entendre*, so that, for example, an *andouille* ('tripe sausage'), which features prominently in all carnivals, may be, simultaneously, an item of edible link fence, a soldier who fights in the armies of Mardigras covered with mustard, or in carnivalesque phallic hagiography *Saint Andouille* ('Saint Sausage/Phallus'), whose martyrdom, recounted in a burlesque sermon, consists of being roasted over coals and then cut up and stuffed inside young women.[5]

Lying tales were an enormously popular genre under a number of different names in different languages, such as the German lying couplets (or *Spruche*) and the French *fatras(ie)*, *resverie*, and *sotte chanson*. Essentially all lying tales are totally stereotyped according to a few interrelated types. Some of the most common categories include: ludicrous hierarchical reversals of sex, age, or social categories, as well as of the natural order of human-animal or animate-inanimate reversals; images of the edible world; exaggerations of size; and feats of impossible strength or acrobatic ability.

In the following section I will discuss a number of literary uses of the Cockaigne-Carnival motif cluster, from the simplest lying *couplets* in a number of languages, to early French and English descriptions of Cockaigne, to motifs in *Aucassin et Nicolette*, the *Voyage* (or *Pèlèrinage) de Charlemagne*, the *Libro de buen amor*, Boccaccio's *Decameron*, and, finally, several somewhat later French farces.

II. *Topsy-turvy literary genres*

The oldest documented lying tale is the eleventh-century Latin *Modus florum*, which begins "I'll sing you a tall tale, which should make you laugh. . . ." The poet tells of a king who announces that he will grant his daughter's hand to whomever is the greatest master in lying. A Swabian peasant, a stock comic character, takes on the king's challenge and proceeds to recount an absurd story about catching a hare, out of whose ears honey flows (note the gastronomic connection with the Land of Cockaigne). The peasant claims that inside the tail of the animal he found a message saying that the king is his subject. The king replies "the hare lied, and so do you" and accepts him as a son-in-law.[6]

The first known medieval example of the lying tale in the vernacular attributable to a specific poet is by the Provençal poet Arnaut Daniel ("I am Arnaldo who collects the wind, hunts the hare with the ox, and swims against the current . . ."), but the tenacity of the images can be illustrated by the very similar anonymous version in several Galician traditional songs collected in the nineteenth century:

> Pol-a mar andavan as levres,
> pol-o monte andan as troitas;
> Si che parece mentira,
> Come esta haiche moitas!

> [The hares ran in the sea, the trout in the mountain, / If all this seems a lie, / There are many [more] where these came from.][7]

The fourteenth-century German "So ist diz von lügenen" is another typical example of the genre.[8] The poet immediately marks the unreliability of his narrative by beginning: "Ich sach eins males in der affen zit . . . " ("I once saw in monkey/fool's time"). The sixty-four verse poem is a concatenation of *impossibilia*, one every two or three verses, each signaled with *ich sach* or *da sach ich* (varied once with *da hörte ich*), and interrupted once, eliciting a progress report from his fictive audience with: "ist daz niut gelogen genouc?" ("[How am I doing?/] Have I lied enough?"). The wonders recounted represent all the categories of *impossibilia* described above: a legless man running to catch a fast horse; a young donkey hunting two quick hares; a linden tree on which hot pancakes grow; a one-year-old throwing four millstones from Regensburg to Trier, and from Trier to Salzburg; a river of honey located in a valley on top of a hill; two mosquitos making a bridge; two doves plucking a wolf; two mice consecrating a bishop; two cats scratching out a bear's tongue; a snail killing two lions; a shearer shearing a woman's beard; and more.

The earliest surviving complete description of Cockaigne, the French *Li pais a non Coqaigne* (c. 1250), is little more than another catalog of marvels. The poem is in part a parody of a pilgrimage, in which the poet claims in the introductory verses that he went to Rome to receive absolution and that the Pope sent him to do his penance in Cockaigne. The description of the land includes brief reference to the laziness motif, the calendar of many holidays, and the fountain of youth, but by far the most details are lavished on the edible and potable world, seconded only by the clothing and shoes handed out free by drapers and shoemakers. The narrative is interrupted by reiterated assurances like "that's the whole truth," "don't think I exaggerate," and "the rest I tell you, without lying." Although sex gets considerably less attention than do material needs, there is the stock topsy-turvy "women on top" theme, which describes how in this land women are enhanced rather than diminished in reputation by sexual experience, and if a woman takes a fancy to a man she can make the first move, in Sadie Hawkens Day style ("she accosts him in the middle of the road, and has her way with him and thus they both do each other good").[9]

The English *Land of Cockaygne*, preserved in Harley MS 913 (first quarter of the fourteenth century), is a much more imaginative work than the earlier Old French version. It is a monk's paradise, a parody of the tradition of the *paradisus claustralis*, of the contemplative life of the cloister as paradise. After specifically denouncing the comparative boredom of the Christian Paradise ("What is there in Paradise to see / But grass and flowers and greenery?"), it describes a marvelous land with the usual details, from lack of strife and immortality, to the availability of garlic goose hot off the spit and a cloister with edible walls. However, the second half of the poem turns into a Bosch-like surrealist fantasy describing the totally dis-ordered life led by the monks, who fly about and are called back at mealtime by their abbot, who beats on the white backside of a maiden. Meanwhile, the inhabitants of the nunnery next door go boating and swimming in a river of sweet milk, simultaneously an allusion to the potable rivers of Cockaigne, to sexuality, and to heavenly iconography, until the monks sweep them away: "And techith the nunnes an oreisun / With iambleue up and dun."

These verses, as well as the ones about the young girl's behind being used as a drum, have generally been left without commentary, mistranslated, or expurgated by editors of the text. *Iambleue* comes from the French *jambe lever*—'raise one's legs'—showing that the *oreisun* ('prayer') the monks plan to teach the nuns is a very sacrilegious one in the carnivalesque tradition of *parodia sacra*, where the whole semantic field of the cult becomes reinterpretable in terms of eating and/or copulation. In this monk's paradise the one who can perform as a "good stallion" is allotted twelve wives a year, and the one who can sleep the best will soon be named abbot. Unfortunately, whoever wants to come to this land must undergo the difficult penance of wading through swine dung up to the chin for seven years.[10]

Two French works, *Aucassin et Nicolette* and the *Pèlèrinage de Charlemagne*, both of which have generally been interpreted as serious works, are each a patchwork of Cockaignesque motifs. The first, which has been called everything from a serious allegory to a touching romance of innocent young love, is a humorous pastiche, full of allusions to other literary genres, particularly romance and epic, all held together by a topsy-turvy depiction of life, of which only a few can be mentioned here. Like the narrator in the English *Land of Cockaygne*, the hero, Aucassin, denounces Paradise as being the dull abode of the old and sick; he would much rather go to Hell and be with all the young and beautiful people. Aucassin's relationship with his beloved Nicolette is a stock sex role reversal, where he just sits around and mopes, while she does everything to be with him, from escaping from jail to crossing the seas masquerading as a male troubadour. Most interesting is that while Aucassin's and Nicolette's adventures are already full of topsy-turvy motifs, at one point in the tale they end up in an even more Cockaignesque land called *Turelure*, where the king stays in *couvade* for a month while his wife is out fighting a war with cheeses and vegetables, and where Aucassin beats up the king for his lack of manliness. Significantly, *Turelure* is not simply a funny-sounding nonsense name (in the character of other alliterative and reduplicate nonsense names for topsy-turvy worlds, such as *Kurru Murre* or *Guckel Gemur*) but has carnivalesque sexual connotations. From the twelfth century, *turelu(ru)* is documented in burlesque refrains. *Turelure(ette)* also imitates the sound of the fife and hence comes to stand for the instrument itself, a stock carnivalesque phallic symbol which often appears in the hands of medieval fools. At the same time, *Robin turelure* or *Jenin turelurette* are cuckolds, and the *roi de Torelore* or *de la Cornemuse* is the king of Carnival, illustrating once more that Cockaigne and Carnival are inseparable entities.[11]

Le Voyage de charlemagne à Jerusalem et Constantinople, a grotesque simulacrum of the *chanson de geste*, is a work whose every aspect has elicited even more contradictory opinions than has *Aucassin et Nicolette*; scholars even dispute its proper title. The brief *Voyage*, variously dated anywhere from the second half of the eleventh century to the second half of the thirteenth, is one of the earliest surviving imaginary travel accounts. The story opens with a preening Charlemagne ludicrously praising his kingly trappings to his wife in front of all his court and rather childishly boasting: "With my spear I shall still conquer many cities!" She jokingly retorts that he holds himself in too high esteem and that she knows a king, King Hugo of Constantinople, who is greater than he. Charlemagne counter-challenges her, threatening to have her beheaded if she is proven wrong, and immediately sets out with a great army in search of Hugo. In defiance of geography (or at least of common sea routes), the Frenchmen journey first to Jerusalem, where Charlemagne receives many relics from the local patriarch. A partial list includes: a nail from the Cross, the Holy Shroud, the Virgin's Shift, the infant Jesus's swaddling clothes, one of Simeon's arms, eight thorns from the Crown of Thorns, and a fragment of the True Cross. Several critics have argued that such relics would have been taken seriously by the audience of the time because they were venerated in a number of shrines. This ignores the fact that their very enumeration smacks of ludicrous excess. Furthermore, the relics will be used later in the story most inappropriately to try to save Charlemagne's and his twelve peers' skins after they have made some very foolish boasts.[12]

When, after four months in Jerusalem, Charlemagne finally remembers the purpose of his trip and moves on to Constantinople, he finds Hugo incongruously tilling his land with a golden plow. The king's magic palace rotates like a mill when struck by wind on the western side. Before they realize it, the Frenchmen, in most unknightly fashion, fall all over the place, covering their heads in fear.

After much feasting and drinking, Charlemagne and his peers amuse themselves at bedtime and get revenge for their humiliation in the castle by engaging in *gabs*, a series of ritual boasts combined with mockery. The *gab* is a variant of the infantile self-aggrandizement of the lying tales, as can be seen by the boasts of the peers, which involve such implausible feats of strength or dexterity, that they could only serve to show who could tell the most outrageous lie. To cite only two examples, Ernaut of Gironde brags that if he is encased in molten lead he will break out after it has hardened, and Berenger vows that he will throw himself from the tallest tower onto upturned blades of the swords of all of Hugo's knights, which will all shatter and splinter while his skin won't even be scratched. The most outrageous is Olivier's *gab*, who claims he will take the King's daughter one hundred times in one night—and that she will testify to it.

While Olivier does not manage more than thirty successes with Hugo's daughter, she has become so enamored of him that she agrees to stretch the truth to her father. Two more peers make good their boasts, one almost destroying the palace with a kind of giant bowling ball and the other causing an enormous flood. And so, with the aid of God, our heroes go home victorious, having substituted circus tricks and sexual "tricks" for knightly combat. It is evident that both the *gab* episode and the different kinds of exaggerations and *impossibilia* in the *reliques* and in the magic castle episodes are all motifs of the lying tale.[13]

Within Spanish literature I have recently demonstrated several references to *Cockaigne* in the fourteenth-century *Libro de buen amor*.[14] In one episode, structured as a lying tale, two lazy men, one of whom claims to be lame and the other one-eyed, vie in verbal combat for the hand of an aristocratic lady, in a burlesque *mélange* of popular and courtly genres. The lady tells her suitors that she will marry the laziest, so the two try to outdo each other in describing their lethargy, couched in a parody of epic and lyric style. One, for example, says he went blind in one eye because he was once lying in bed with water dripping on him and was too slothful to turn his head. The other reports that he fell in love one spring day but lost the girl when, standing in front of her, he was too lazy to wipe the snot running down from his nose. Though the two could well qualify for nobility in Cockaigne, both on the merits of their laziness and on the incongruity of two cripples being courtly lovers, the tale is not really about two unambitious men but about two highly skilled and competitive tellers of tall tales. The point is not to determine which of the two is the lazier but which one can demonstrate the greatest virtuosity by inventing the most outrageous *mentira* on the set topic of laziness. Their ultimate triumph is in their verbal skill in the expression of their lumpen Cockaigne ideas in a grotesquely inappropriate courtly register.

The earliest documented descriptions of Cockaigne in Italian literature appear in the *Decameron*. In one tale (VI.10) a charlatan peddler of false relics and champion yarnspinner with the alimentary name Fra Cipolla ('onion'), pretends that some parrot's feathers are the feathers that remained in the Virgin's room at the Annunciation and that certain bits of charcoal are the coals used to roast St. Lawrence. He describes his supposed pilgrimage to the Holy Land in search of treasures (in which he actually describes certain Florentine streets and inhabitants in exotic terms), first to the lands of *la Truffia* and *Buffia* ('Land of Tricks and Pranks'), both well populated lands, and from there to the Land of *Menzonga* ('Land of Lies'), where many clerics live.

Another *novella* in the *Decameron* (VIII.3), structured as a lying tale, clearly labels as an idiot anyone credulous enough to believe in the fantasy of Cockaigne. One Maso del Saggio, having heard of the simpleton Calandrino, decides to play *alcuna beffa* on him and make him believe in the existence of a city called *Bengodi* ('Good Time/Perpetual Carnival'), located in Basque country—which during the Middle Ages was considered exotic since it was difficult of access and its inhabitants spoke a totally unintelligible language. The alimentary centerpiece of the fantasy is replete with local color: a mountain of grated Parmesan cheese, on top of which people did nothing but cook *maccheroni* and *raviuoli* in capon broth and then used them as missiles to throw into a rivulet of *vernaccia*, an excellent white wine. This image is, of course, a funny elaboration on the stock motif of edible nature with the carnivalesque use of foods as implements of war.

The sympathetic image of the grated cheese mountain is repeated and elaborated in other Italian works of the later Middle Ages and early Renaissance. According to one, from around 1500, on top of a giant mountain of grated cheese, an autonomous giant kettle constantly cooks macaroni and then ejects them so that they will roll down the hill to be covered all over with cheese. As if all this *abbondanza* of pasta were not enough, in this land it also rains ravioli, and the king is not only the laziest, biggest, and fattest man, but he has himself become an alimentary image, shitting manna, spitting marzipan, and having fish instead of lice in his hair. The poet concludes by offering to show the way to whomever in the audience wants to go to this land: he should sail over the "Liar's sea" and if he gets there, he'll be in the Land of Fools, which is the poet's way of saying, "April Fool, folks!"[15]

Several French farces from the fifteenth century are also essentially lying descriptions of Cockaigne. In the *Farce . . . de Jenin Landore*, a wife laments her husband's death while the priest consoles her that he died of thirst while asking for a drink. Jenin (a stock name for 'fool'), however, is "resuscitated" forthwith and claims he came from Paradise and has passed through Purgatory. With the priest playing straight man, Jenin describes in vulgar terms and with the most outrageous tall tales the goings on in Paradise, all the while insisting that they are all *tout aussy vray que je le dis* ("as true as I'm telling you"). Perhaps his wildest invention is a description of St. Lawrence torturing Swiss mercenaries who have overrun Paradise by roasting them on a grill—"just as one roasts sausages in a tavern in winter!"

Lying tales are closely tied to the theme of deception. Liars can be tricksters, like Muso in the *Decameron*, who dupe others for the sheer fun of it, but they can also be professional con artists who lie for a living, like Fra Cipolla, and other barkers, beggars, or wandering peddlers. Lists of relics which must stretch the credulity of even the most faithful came to be associated with lying tales, as we have already seen in the *Pèlèrinage* and in Fra Cipolla's tale. The *Farce . . . d'un pardonneur, d'un triacleur et d'une tavernière* also makes use of the same stock of ludicrous relics. It starts off as a lying contest between a patent medicine salesman and a pardoner, actually a peddler of false relics. The two mutually accuse one another of being a liar and a cheat but end up with grudging admiration for each other's virtuosity in lying, and they go off to drink together at the expense of the credulous tavern keep, on whom they pawn off a pair of old breeches as a saint's relic.

The pardoner claims in his harangue that he brings relics from several onomastically genital saints: *Saint Boudin* ('Saint Blood Sausage/Phallus'), *Sainte Fente* ('Sainte Split/Crack'), *Saint Couille-bault, confesseur*, which is homonymous with *couille + con + fesseur* ('nice balls + cunt + ass[man]'), and the latter's "sister" *Sainte Velue* ('saint hairy'), among whose miracles is that she gave back a woman her virginity. The relics themselves are no less carnivalized; one of them—"the crest of the cock which crowed in Pilate's house"—simultaneously has phallic connotations and is also an allusion to the exclamation *coquelicoq* ("cockscrest / I know you just told a big lie") with which the contenders interrupt each other in many lying tales. The patent medicine hawker's wares are even more outrageously impossible, such as Prosperina's beard, the fruit of a chestnut tree from the deepest sea in Spain, and a monk's egg laid in Barbarie, another stock name for *Cockaigne*.

In the *Farce* . . . *des coquins a cinq personnes*, three *coquins* ('tricksters/fools') have a contest describing lands of monstrous inhabitants they have supposedly visited. One describes a place where the population has horns, goes about nude, and eats people raw, a combination apparently predicated only on the easy rhyme of *cornus / nus /* and *crus*. A second *coquin* counters with a description of a people whose teeth are hairier than a bear and who walk backwards and have only one eye in their back. Another describes people so small that over two hundred could fit under a leaf. The first, taking another turn, in the ultimate twist on the central alimentary image of Cockaigne and worthy of a painting by Archimboldo, tells of a land in a valley where gold grows, whose population has eyelids of apples, eyebrows of frozen cabbage, and eyes of peeled onions, and where everyone dresses in lanterns (a symbol of Carnival).[16]

Certain literary modes—like parody, pastiche, and burlesque—are defined by their refusal to grant privileged status to official, hierarchical truth. All these ludic forms flourished during the Middle Ages in pageants, processions, irreverent church festivals, and the many genres, from the residually literate to the highly literary, of playfully inverted verbal games discussed in this study. They could be valued for the pleasurable escape from reality they afforded through laughter and virtuoso display. While the topsy-turvy world might be considered to be a simple bundle of motifs, it can more profitably be placed in the category of anti-genre, given its deliberate attempt to empty the meaning from every primary genre with which it comes into contact. Its rise in the thirteenth century coincided with that of other festive, escapist genres, including farce, fabliaux, secular theater, and imaginary travel narratives.

NOTES

1. On the contrast between Cockaigne and other utopias, see A. Cioranescu, "Utopie: Cocagne et age d'or," *Diogène* 75 (1971): 86-123; Guy Demerson, "Cocagne, utopie populaire?" *Revue Belge de Philologie et d'Histoire* 59 (1981): 529-53; see also the special issues of *Daedalus* (Spring 1965), *Revue des sciences humaines* 155[8] (1974), and *Littérature* 21 (1976). Other important studies are: Mircea

Eliade, "Paradis et Utopie: Géographie Mythique et Eschatologie," *Eranos Jahrbuch* 32 (1963): 211-13; Frank E. and Fritzie P. Manuel, "Sketch for a Natural History of Paradise," *Daedalus* 101 (1972): 83-127; Juliette De Caluwé-Dur, "L'anti-Paradis du pays du Cocagne," in *Marche romane: Mélanges de philologie et de littératures romanes offerts à Jeanne Wathelet Willem* (Liège: Cahiers de l'A.R.U., 1978), pp. 103-23.

2. For the quote and discussion of Cockaigne, see E. M. Ackermann, *Das Schlaraffenland in German Literature and Folksong* (Ph.D. diss., Univ. of Chicago, 1944); see also Giovanna Angeli, *Il mondo rovesciato* (Rome: Bulzoni, 1977); Guiseppe Cocchiara, *Il paese di cuccagna e altri studi di folklore* (Turin: Boringhieri, 1980), and *Il mondo alla rovescia* (Turin: Boringhieri, 1981); and Dieter Richter, *Schlaraffenland: Geschichte einer populären Phantasie* (Cologne: Diederich, 1984). For more detailed bibliography, see my "The Two Lazy Suitors in the *Libro de buen amor*: Popular Tradition and Literary Game of Love," *Anuario Medieval* 1 (1989): 181-205, where, as in this article, I treat Cockaigne motifs raised to a literary level. Another study along similar lines, which came to my attention only after the completion of this article, is Jean-Charles Payen, "Fabliaux et Cocagne. Abondance et fête charnelle dans les contes plaisants du XIIe et du XIIIe siècles," in *Epopée animale, fable, fabliau. Actes du IVe Colloque de la Société Internationale Renardienne, Evreux, 7-11 sept., 1981*, ed. Gabriel Bianciotto and Michel Salvat (Paris: PUF, 1984): 435-48.

3. On tall tale-telling and *impossibilia* of all sorts, see Gustav Roethe, ed., *Die Gedichte Reinmars von Zweter* (Leipzig: Hirschfeld, 1887); A. I. Langfors, *Deux receuils de sottes chansons* (Helsinki, 1945; repr. Geneva: Slatkine Reprints, 1977); Karl Müller-Frauereuth, *Die deutschen Lügendichtungen bis auf Münchhausen* (Halle, 1881; repr. Hildesheim: Olms, 1965); Sarah Westphal-Wihl, "Quodlibets: Introduction to a Middle High German Genre," in *Genres in Medieval Literature*, ed. Hubert Heinen and Ingeborg Henderson (Göppingen: Kümmerle, 1986), pp. 157-74.

Modern versions of the form, sometimes called *whoppers* or *talking trash* have been studied in more detail, although never in historical context. See, for example, Gustav Henningsen, "The Art of Perpendicular Lying," *Journal of the Folklore Institute* 2 (1965): 180-219; Brunhilde Biebuyck-Goetz, "This is the Dyin' Truth: Mechanisms of Lying," *Journal of the Folklore Institute* 14 (1977): 73-95; Kay L. Cotwan, "Talking Trash on the Okefenoke Swamp Rim, Georgia," *Journal of American Folklore* 87 (1974): 340-56; and Carolyn S. Brown, *The Tall Tale in American Folklore and Literature* (Knoxville: Univ. of Tennessee Press, 1987).

4. *Rabelais and his World* (Cambridge, Mass.: MIT Press, 1968).

5. For a detailed analysis of the polysemy of metaphors of food, sex, and violence, see my "Amor, pecado, y muerte carnavalizados en el *Libro de buen amor*," forthcoming in *Amor, pecado, y muerte en la edad media*, ed. Nicasio Salvador Miguel (Madrid: Turner/Universidad Complutense, 1991).

6. For the *Modus florum* see Müller-Frauereuth, *Lügendichtungen*, p. 86; see also pp. 5-6, 12-13, 25-26 for other examples. A more accessible version (with English translation) is in *Vagabond Verse: Secular Poems of the Middle Ages*, ed. and trans. Edwin H. Zeydel (Detroit: Wayne State Univ. Press, 1966).

7. Théophile Braga, *Cancionero popular gallego* (Madrid: Ricardo Fe, 1886): 1:196.

8. Ackerman, *Schlaraffenland:*, pp. 143-44; Richter, *Schlaraffenland*, pp. 181-85 (see above, n. 2).

9. Ed. Veikko Väänänen, "Le fabliau du Cocagne," *Neuphilologische Mitteilungen* 4 (1957): 3-36.

10. See Ackermann, *Schlaraffenland*, pp. 147-50; Howard R. Patch, *The Other World, According to Descriptions in Medieval Literature* (Cambridge, Mass.: Harvard Univ. Press, 1950), esp. pp. 7-22, 134-74; T. J. Garbáty, "The Land of Cokayne in the Kildare MS," *Franziskanische Studien* 45 (1963): 139-53; and Wolfgang Biesterfeld and Marlis H. Haase, "The Land of Cokkaygne: eine englische Version des Märchens vom Schlaraffenland," *Fabula* 25 (1984): 76-82. For a particularly egregious misreading, see Clifford Davidson, who claims that the jests are meant to shock audiences into understanding that "each man's life ought to imitate Christ" ("The Sins of the Flesh in the Fourteenth-Century Middle English Land of Cokaygne," *Ball State University Forum* 11 [1970]: 21-26).

11. *Aucassin et Nicolette*, ed. Mario Roques (Paris: Champion, 1963); Tony Hunt, "La parodie médiévale: le cas d'*Aucassin et Nicolette*," *Romania* 101 (1980): 433-81.

12. See Ronald C. Finucare, *Miracles and Pilgrims: Popular Beliefs in Medieval England* (Totowa, N.J.: Rowman and Littlefield, 1977), who discusses medieval beliefs about relics and saints and the bizarre relic inflation and relic forgeries by unscrupulous laymen and clerics alike (pp. 31, 222), where, for example, some Western churches claimed to possess Christ's breath, tears, or blood, or Mary's milk, in a bottle. Some relics ranged on the pornographic, such as the display of the six breasts of St. Agatha and the two penises of St. Bartholomew.

13. For a history of the scholarship, see, most recently, John D. Niles, "On the Logic of *Le Pèlèrinage de Charlemagne*," *Neophilologische Mitteilungen* 81 (1980): 208-16; and Jean-Louis Picherit, *The Journey of Charlemagne to Jerusalem and Constantinople* (Birmingham, Ala.: Summa, 1984). Olivier's *gab* was so offensive to one translator that he simply left it out: Paul Aebischer demotes the most offensive verse to a footnote and tries to prove that the "original" poet didn't really say it. He is so upset by Olivier's portrayal as a "monstrous Don Juan," by Hugo's willingness to prostitute his daughter, by her lubricity, and by God's consecration of such obscenity, that he wants to "cleanse French medieval literature of this blemish, not only to morals but to good taste" (see "Le gab de Olivier," *Revue Belge de Philologie et d'Histoire* 38 [1956]: 659-70, esp. pp. 660-61).

14. See Vasvari, "Two Lazy Suitors," passim.

15. *Storia di Campriano contadino* (c. 1500), and in the sixteenth-century *Capitolo qual narra l'essere di un mondo novo trovato nel mar oceano* (Piero Camporesi, *La maschera di Bertoldo. G. C. Croce e la letteratura carnevalesca* [Turin: Einaudi, 1976], pp. 309-11).

16. For *Jenin Landore*, see M. Viollet le Duc, *Ancien Théatre Français* (Paris: Jannet, 1854), pp. 21-34. The similar *Resurrection Jenin a Paulme* is even more outrageous. See Gustav Cohen, *Receuil de farces françaises inédites du XVème siècle* (Cambridge, Mass.: The Medieval Academy of America, 1949), pp. 405-11. For *Pardonneur . . . triacleur*, see Viollet le Duc, pp. 50-63; for *Farce . . . des coquins*, see Cohen, pp. 433-46.

"Out upon Circumference": Discovery in Dante

Peter S. Hawkins

I saw no Way—The Heavens were stitched—
I felt the Columns close—
The Earth reversed her Hemispheres—
I touched the Universe—

And back it slid—and I alone—
A Speck upon a Ball—
Went out upon Circumference—
Beyond the Dip of Bell—
—Emily Dickinson

In the first book of the *Convivio*, a work that sets out to explore and celebrate the human desire to know, Dante gives the reader a portrait of himself not as a philosopher secure in his academy, but rather as a displaced person. Writing in the early years of his exile from Florence, he describes himself as unjustly thrown out into the world, forced to wander as a man without a country, "peregrino, quasi mendicando" (1.3). "Truly," he says, "I have been a ship without a sail and without a rudder, cast about to different harbors and inlets and shores by the dry wind of wretched poverty."[1]

Elsewhere he attempts to turn this nightmare into a sign of his universality, boasting in the *De vulgari eloquentia* that in fact because of his displacement, and as a result of reading widely in the volumes of poets and other writers, he has come to know all the world's diverse

---

Peter S. Hawkins is Associate Professor of Religion and Literature at Yale University Divinity School (see Notes on Contributors, p. 222).

regions. He is, therefore, "one for whom the world is fatherland as the sea is for fish" ("cui mundus est patria velut piscibus equor" [1.6]).

And yet for all this bravado, with its transparent effort to portray an uprooted Tuscan landsman as a happy *gyrovagus* of the world's seas, the metaphor which appeals to him most deeply in his exile is that of the sailor coming home to port—the metaphor which he deploys, in fact, at the end of the *Convivio*. There, thinking about the fourth and final stage of human life, he imagines the soul as a navigator who negotiates his way through the waters of our three score and ten, seeking to come home to God at the end of his days—to the God who is that safe harbor from which the soul set forth at birth.[2]

This miniature allegory is, of course, none other than the one Dante will expand into the narrative of his *Commedia*, where he takes a Neoplatonic commonplace—the progress of the soul as a sea voyage—and turns it into a figure that drives forward the hundred cantos of his poem. But instead of having the good mariner hoist up his sails in old age, "in years that bring the philosophic mind," he will present himself at the outset of the *Inferno* as someone shipwrecked in the middle of the journey of our life, "as one who with laboring breath has escaped from the deep to the shore [and] turns to look back upon the dangerous waters" (to recall the *Commedia*'s first simile).[3] He will show himself to be a desperate *homo viator*, who sails his way into a heavenly port at the end of his journey, but only after undergoing the crisis of conversion and an arduous passage across the landscapes of sin and purgation.

The journey Dante describes is neither a dream nor a vision but what the poet claims from start to finish to have been an actual "historical" event—an exploration of what his *Letter to Can Grande* calls the "state of souls after death."[4] Because in the early fourteenth century both hell and purgatory could still be treated as matters of geographical, or at least cosmological, science—that is, treated as actual terrestrial sites—Dante was able to show much of the hereafter as occupying the topography of the here and now; he could situate his exploration of the life to come in unknown and inaccessible regions of this life. For all but the final stage of his journey, therefore, he is seen discovering territory which, if strictly off-limits to flesh and blood, was nonetheless capable of being charted in the material heavens or located on an earthly map. Indeed, what the *Commedia* essentially unfolds for the reader is a literary *mappa mundi*, a complex map of words that builds upon (and by and large reflects) a contemporary cartographer's notion of the world and its position in the cosmos. The general picture holds few surprises. As might be expected, it is drawn not from observation but from reading, and from a stock of familiar authorities that includes Orosius, Albertus Magnus, Alfraganus, Isidore of Seville, and (more immediately) Brunetto Latini.[5] Dante views the earth as a ball, a "palla," that is largely covered by ocean—what he refers to in *Paradiso* 9.84 as "quel mar che la terra inghirlanda." The dry land thus "engarlanded" by water is restricted to the northern hemisphere; it is also kept within clear bounds. As he writes in the *Quaestio de aqua et terra* (delivered in 1320, the year before his death, and his solo flight as a professional geographer): "It is commonly held by all that this habitable earth extends in longitude from Gades, which lies on the western boundaries of Hercules, and as far [east] as the mouths of the Ganges, as Orosius states."[6]

Although Dante was well aware of the diversity of opinion on the possibility of life at the antipodes, he follows Augustine's lead in rejecting it outright. Even if there were dry land there, no one could ever have navigated the waters stretching between the hemispheres, across what Augustine describes with a shudder as "Oceani immensitate traiecta."[7] Because of this impassable gulf, the existence of people in the southern hemisphere would require another father than Adam, and therefore be of another kind of humanity altogether. Such an idea for Dante is not only utterly false according to our faith ("appo la nostra fede"); it is also against the ancient law and belief of the Philosopher: "And doubtless Aristotle would laugh heartily if he heard speak of two different species of human generation, as if we were talking about horses and asses: for they who hold this opinion (may Aristotle forgive me) might well themselves be called asses" (4.15).[8]

In all these regards, the "prose" Dante follows a conventional, and in several matters conservative, line. But when on the other hand we come to the *Commedia*, his picture of the world changes radically in one major regard. It is almost as if in the relatively few years between the breaking off of the *Convivio* and his writing of the poem he had made a geographic discovery that warranted a revision of the world's map. All of a sudden, in what had formerly been taken as the utterly vacant waters of the southern hemisphere, he describes a solitary landmass, an "isoletta," or small island, located at the antipodes from Jerusalem's Mount Sion. From its shores there rises up a mountain of almost incalculable height.

It takes an effort of the imagination to consider what effect the appearance of this "dilettoso monte" would have had on Dante's first readers. For what he does in the *Commedia* is report a "discovery" that no other writer before him had made, a discovery that at once purported to resolve not only the ancient and vexed question of the whereabouts of the Garden of Eden—in the *De vulgari eloquentia* he had placed it (as had many others) "in oris orientalibus" (1.8)— but that also settled the debated location of Purgatory. With the confidence of the traveler who has seen it all for himself first hand, he shows both sites to occupy the same mountain, the one atop the other, and precisely on the other side of the globe from the holy city where Christ died.

To be sure, elements of this new configuration are to be found elsewhere.[9] The Earthly Paradise was often represented (in text and map) as an island, as inaccessible because of a wall of fire or a stretch of ocean, even as "planted" (according to the Venerable Bede) on a mountain so high it touched the sphere of the moon. Likewise Purgatory was occasionally imagined as insular (as in the *Voyage of St. Brendan* and the legend of St. Patrick), or as hidden within the depths of a mountain, be it in Scotland or the wastes of Norway. Purgatory had even been linked allegorically to Eden by virtue of an association made by Ambrose and Rupert of Deutz, an interpretative bridge that joined the cherubs' flaming swords of Genesis 3:24 and the refining fires spoken of by St. Paul in 1 Corinthians 3:12-15.[10]

Nonetheless, as even the most cautious of the *studiosi* have had to admit, Dante seems indeed to have reworked these traditions with striking originality, and in the process discovered more than one new thing under the sun. Singlehandedly, as it were, he removed Eden to the southern hemisphere and discovered within it not the requisite four rivers of Paradise but two—and two that no one had ever placed there: Lethe, flowing out of Virgil's Elysian Fields, and Eunoe, flowing entirely out of Dante's imagination.[11] He also brought Purgatory up from the horrors of the underworld and delivered it into the bright light of day. No one before him had ever joined these two locations so concretely (or described them in such unforgettable detail); no one had placed them together at the antipodes to Jerusalem; and certainly no one else records the *felix culpa* of their genesis.

I am referring to the origin of the mountain as related in the last canto of the *Inferno* (and apparently Dante's total invention)[12]: the story of how, when Satan was expelled from heaven, he plummeted to earth,

plunged through its surface at the antarctic pole, and buried himself at
the dead center of the universe. At his impact the dry land which once
covered the southern hemisphere fled to the north, while the land at the
core of the earth not only shrank from his presence (thereby creating the
pit of hell around him), but also rushed upward to fill the watery
vacuum at the southern pole. The result was a mountain "which rises
highest from the sea" ("che si leva più da l'onda" [*Par.* 26.139]). With
Eden planted at its peak, that mountain became the birthplace of
humanity; after Adam's sin, an unpeopled world off limits to mortals.
But with the redemption of Christ, its steep slopes and garden summit
again took on life, not as a place where flesh and blood were permitted
to return, but as a purgatory where the penitent souls of the dead might
work their way up the mountain, through sin and into virtue; where
they might reenter Eden en route to the celestial paradise.

What we find in this extraordinarily dense act of myth-making is
a blend of topography, sacred history, and belief—a treatment of
geography as a kind of scriptural exegesis—that links Dante to the
cartographers of the *mappaemundi*.[13] In the art of both, theology
generates landscape, and faith has the power to invent mountains as
well as to cast them into the midst of the sea. No space is neutral.
Rather, it becomes the occasion for Christian doctrine to take on a local
habitation and a name; for event to become place. Or to put it another
way, because the second Adam redeemed the first Adam's sin, so
"Christs Crosse and Adams tree" are seen as standing at the antipodes
from one another on the globe of Dante's imagining. Jerusalem and
Eden share a common horizon line so that geography can show the
redeeming link between one testament of scripture and another.

The purpose of Dante's map-making, however, is more than a
description of the physical world as shaped by Christian theology; the
purpose of the poem is the charting of pilgrimage. From the opening
canto of the *Inferno* Dante is told that his itinerary through Hell and
Purgatory has as its purpose the destination of God's heavenly city.
When in the last cantos of the *Paradiso* he finally arrives there, it is
quite explicitly as "a pilgrim who is refreshed within the temple of his
vow as he looks around, and already hopes to tell again how it was"
(31.43-45). He compares himself open-mouthed in the Empyrean to
some barbarian from the north come for the first time to Rome,
"wonder-struck" upon seeing St. John Lateran rising up "above all

mortal things" (31.34-35); he is like a bumpkin from Croatia who gapes in wonder at the sacred image of Veronica's Veil (31.103-05).

In forging this likeness, of course, Dante is relating the actual travel experience of contemporary pilgrims to his own arrival in the Empyrean—"quella Roma onde Cristo è romano" (*Purg.* 32.102).[14] He goes out of his way to establish this correspondence by setting the poem's journey in Holy Week of 1300, the Jubilee year when the plenary indulgence offered by Pope Boniface VIII could make a pilgrimage to Rome as spiritually efficacious as one to the Holy Land.[15] Thus while the poem presents Dante as having been given the unexampled opportunity to go from an infernal Egypt to a heavenly Jerusalem before his death (*Par.* 25.55-57)—the chance, as he puts it elsewhere, to leave Florence in order to discover, outside space and time, a people "giusto e sano" (*Par.* 31.39)—the effort of the *Commedia* is to underscore a commonality between his unique pilgrimage and those undertaken, at home or abroad, by any other Christian. Whether from Croatia to the Lateran, or from a "selva oscura" to the heavenly Jerusalem, the journey to which Dante calls attention is an *itinerarium mentis ad Deum*. Indeed, the poem offers itself to the reader as an allegorical invitation to precisely this spiritual voyage. To turn its pages is to set sail for God.

Given this, it is striking that within the *Commedia* Dante should feature so prominently an account of a voyage (and the identity of a voyager) totally at odds with his personal enterprise. Over against all the characteristics of his own pilgrimage—the finding of a "vera via," the need for guidance along the way, a known (not to mention sacred) destination, a return home with the fruits of the experience—over against pilgrimage itself, Dante offers the counter-example of Ulysses.[16] In a poem that defines Adam's original sin as a "trapassar del segno" (*Par.* 26.117), an overpassing of a boundary, Ulysses is used not only to reenact the primal trespass against mortal limitation, but to do so specifically in the form of a navigational transgression, as if in deliberate refutation of that "good mariner" described in the fourth book of the *Convivio*. Rather than venturing out in order to return home to the soul's safe harbor in God, Ulysses exemplifies the choice to take another direction entirely, to sail off the map of the known world and into forbidden seas. He breaks boundaries without looking back, making a voyage that goes "out upon Circumference— / Beyond the Dip of Bell—"

The account of this journey is given in the twenty-sixth canto of the *Inferno* (and in the circle of the fraudulent counselors) when at Dante's passionate and repeated request, Virgil engages the tormented soul of Ulysses in conversation, asking him to "tell where he went, lost, to die" ("dove, per lui, perduto a morir gissi" [84]).[17] What follows is a spell-binding narration that utterly takes over the canto and, without interruption, brings it to a close. Ulysses describes how, when he left Circe after more than a year's stay, none of the familial loves or civic obligations that should have drawn him home could in fact conquer the deeper longing within him: an ardor to gain experience of the world, and of human vice and worth. And so, taking with him one boatload of faithful (if aged) companions, he sets forth on the open sea of the Mediterranean, "per l'alto mare aperto" (100). But rather than sailing eastward to Ithaca, he heads instead for the western edge of the known world, to "that narrow outlet where Hercules set up his markers, so that man should not pass beyond" ("dov' Ercule segnò li suoi riguardi / acciò che l'uom più oltre non si metta" [108-09]). Poised at the paradigmatic threshold of Gibraltar, the geographical boundary that represents the spiritual limits to human aspiration and knowledge, Ulysses then urges his men to break through the *ne plus ultra* ("più oltre non" [109]). Speaking lines that are so often quoted out of context simply because they defy the infernal setting in which they ring out, he says to his crew at the moment of their indecision:

> "O frati," dissi, "che per cento milia
> perigli siete giunti a l'occidente,
> a questa tanto picciola vigilia
>
> d'i nostri sensi ch'è del rimanente
> non vogliate negar l'esperïenza,
> di retro al sol, del mondo sanza gente.
>
> Considerate la vostra semenza:
> fatti non foste a viver come bruti,
> ma per seguir virtute e canoscenza." (112-20)

["O brothers," I said, "who through a hundred thousand dangers have reached the west, to this so brief vigil of our senses that remains to us, choose not to deny experience, following the sun, of the world that has no people. Consider your origin: you were not made to live as brutes, but to pursue virtue and knowledge."]

Such was the power of this little speech, this "orazion picciola" (122), that Ulysses's companions lose their will in his, refusing even to wait for favorable winds to set out upon the open seas. Instead, as he remembers, "we made of our oars wings for the mad flight" ("de' remi facemmo ali al folle volo" [125]). Turning their boat's stern to the morning and gaining always on the left—that is, sailing due southwest—they find themselves come to the other side of the equator, traveling under the stars of the southern hemisphere. After five months of navigating through the unfathomed waters of this "alto passo" (132), they suddenly (and with the joy of all mariners) discover land. Before them is a mountain, dark in the distance, and rising up from the ocean higher than anything seen in our world. Ulysses calls it, after the fashion of discoverers, "la nova terra" (137). But even as he and his companions rejoice to sight this new found land, a storm whips up from its shore, striking the boat three times and whirling it in the waters for a fourth and final spin. "[It] lifted the stern aloft and plunged the prow below, as pleased Another, till the sea closed over us" ("a la quarta levar la poppa in suso / e la prora ire in giù, com' altrui piacque, / infin che 'l mar fu sovra noi richiuso" [140-42]). With these words the canto comes to its end, in the recollection of Ulysses and his men shipwrecked at landfall. Having discovered the antipodes of the southern hemisphere—the same mountain Dante will climb in *Purgatorio*—they are prevented by Another's pleasure from gaining experience of its "mondo sanza gente." Over their enterprise death has the last word: "richiuso."

It is possible that behind this canto there stands an actual event in the history of navigation: the ill-fated expedition of the Vivaldi brothers, who in search of India set sail from Genoa in 1291, and passed through the straits of Gibraltar into the waters of the Atlantic. They were never to be heard from again.[18] Twenty years after Dante's death, Alfonso IV of Portugal would sail the same route, discover the Canary Islands, and safely return to tell the tale in 1341. But this latter event (although nearly contemporaneous with the *Commedia*) took place in what was indeed another world from the one in which Dante lived. Nor is there the slightest indication anywhere in his writings that he would conceive of such a sailing "out upon circumference" as anything other than what in fact he has Ulysses call it—a "folle volo," a mad flight.[19]

It is also important to add that this "madness" has a great deal less to do with actual navigational transgression than it does with other kinds of voyaging and other kinds of trespass. Had Dante wanted simply to ground humanity within geographical boundaries he could have easily followed his general practice in the *Inferno* and chosen contemporary Italians like the Vivaldi brothers to make the point. Instead he chose Ulysses. Why?

Although Dante did not have direct access to Homer's poetry— the text of the *Odyssey* was not rediscovered in the West until 1362— he had inherited a complex notion of Ulysses, the man skilled in all ways of contending, that in turn informs the complexity (some have called it ambivalence) of his own account.[20] For instance, Virgil, Ovid, and Statius all treat the worker of Troy's ruin as a brilliant scoundrel in the Greek (which is to say, duplicitous) mode: he is a wordsmith of deceit—"fandi fictor"—to Virgil; "fallax," "audax," "experiens" in Ovid; an inciter to evil deeds—"hortator scelerem"—for Statius.[21] At the same time, however, there is also a rich allegorical tradition that treated him as a model of wisdom and fortitude: "nobis exemplar Ulixen." Transformed by the Stoics into a figure of wisdom—into a man skilled in all ways of *knowing*—Ulysses is praised (by Seneca) for riding out the storms of the spirit, for being so fixed on the high calling of *sapientia* (according to Horace) that he could hold his own against a sea of troubles in order to return home.[22] Nor is this *in bono* allegorization limited to pagans; for many patristic writers Ulysses became, as Hugo Rahner has shown, a type of the Christian *homo viator*, who sails in the ship of the church, bound to the mast of the cross, able finally to reach the port of heaven, his true *patria*.[23] To be Ulysses, in this view, was to be a pilgrim.

But not for Dante. Aware, even without having Homer's text, of Ulysses's determination to sail home, he rewrites an ancient script of return and in so doing rejects a venerable allegorical tradition. The experienced navigator, piloted by wisdom and valiantly keeping his course, becomes in Dante's hands a shipwrecked madman. Some of the finest Dante scholarship of the last three decades has stressed the medieval orthodoxy of this boldly revisionary move: its repudiation of *curiositas*, of wandering, of philosophical presumption, of rhetorical power when it is cut off from a commitment to truth and community, of the wisdom of this world which knows nothing of the wisdom of God. John Freccero has even suggested that Dante's sabotage of Ulysses in the *Commedia* may be a palinode on his own philosophical ambitions in the *Convivio*; that is, a rejection of philosophy as the pole star and a chastened look back on the foundering of Dante's own "ship without a sail and without a rudder."[24] What all of these readings examine in their various ways is how Dante places the intellectual boundary-breaker within bounds, even as he pockets Ulysses in the eighth *bolgia* of lower hell. As on earth, so in the mind: there are mountains meant to be "frightful, sheer, no-man-fathomed."

There can be no doubt that the *Commedia* intends the reader to see Dante's voyage as an explicit correction of the wanderer; as the triumph of pilgrimage over sheer exploration.[25] In the first canto of the *Purgatorio*, for instance—and just before Dante is girded with the reed of humility—we are told that he came on "to the desert shore, that never saw any man navigate its waters who afterwards had experience of return" ("in sul lito diserto, / che mai non vide navicar sue acque / omo, che di tornar sia poscia esperto" [130-32]). The comparison implicit in these lines is unmistakable: he lands where Ulysses could not and has returned to tell the tale.

While there are other such recollections along the way (*Par.* 13.136; 26.61-63), certainly the most explicit contrast between pilgrim and wanderer comes in *Paradiso* 27, when Dante looks down through the universe from his lofty vantage in the heaven of the Fixed Stars. Sighting the puny semblance of the earth's globe at the still center of the cosmos, he sees the whole of the habitable world and at its western extremity, beyond Cadiz, "il varco / folle d'Ulisse" (82-83)— the mad track of Ulysses. From this celestial perspective the ambition of the explorer "to gain experience of the world, and of human vice and worth" is meant to seem small, or at least to appear infinitely less than the "esperïenza piena" (*Inf.* 28.48) that Dante has come to know in the course of his journey to God. Instead of a "folle volo"—a madness that indeed he feared in himself before beginning his journey ("temo che la venuta non sia folle" [*Inf.* 2.35])—divine grace has afforded him an "alto volo" (*Par.* 25.50), a lofty flight into regions of knowledge beyond the grasp even of high fantasy. Ulysses burned to see the unpeopled world and he failed; but Dante, soaring above the mark of that desire, claims to have seen God face to face, and lives to tell what he can remember of that vision.

Given all this, it is possible to see Dante connecting the dots of tradition in a new but essentially reassuring way; to watch him break some boundaries (narrative and exegetical) in order to reinforce others. But at the same time that we can assert the "orthodoxy" of his handling of Ulysses—the containment of the wanderer within the poetic structure of pilgrimage—it is important not to lose sight of the provocative audacity of the treatment itself: the fact that Dante is at his most inventive and exploratory exactly when he is upholding the importance of limit. Although in *Inferno* 26 the poet is overtly controlling the impulse to cut loose and go it alone, he is also at this very same moment performing an act of extraordinary authorial daring. Not only does he give us the revolutionary "discovery" of Ulysses's final voyage—a tale told by no one else—but he has his navigator shipwrecked off the shores of a mountain in the southern hemisphere that is utterly his own invention, that is *his* "nova terra." Dante places the boundary breaker within infernal bounds, yes; but it is also true that the circumference of legitimacy is drawn by him alone; that in some absolute sense *he* is that Other who wills that Ulysses should drown on the brink of discovery.

If the *Commedia* presents a clear dichotomy between the success of one voyager and the disaster of the other, in other words, the poet's settling of his own account is both more complicated and more fraught. For the danger of a "trapassar del segno," an overpassing of a boundary, is not entirely disposed of by the narrative triumph of pilgrimage over exploration. There is still the precarious nature of Dante's whole poetic enterprise to deal with, especially as the claims for the "poema sacro" (*Par.* 25.1) escalate with the move into the final canticle. In the dedicatory epistle to Can Grande, Dante violates a fundamental barrier between God's Book and any human text by claiming that the *Paradiso* (and by extension his entire work) can be read according to a fourfold exegesis held to be uniquely applicable to Scripture. In the opening of the *Paradiso* itself he swears to have been enraptured like St. Paul into the "third heaven" of God's presence; then, quite unlike St. Paul, he breaks the interdiction of silence that guards the ineffable words. He does this, moreover, in a vernacular poetry that had not been deemed worthy of philosophy, let alone theology—an Italian rich in neologisms, as sublime as Latin, which is in effect Dante's own linguistic "discovery."[26]

No wonder, then, that in the *Paradiso* our attention is shifted away from the arduous journey of the pilgrim and turned more and more to the voyage of the poet, to his literary navigation of new and dangerous waters. In the extended address to his readers that opens the second canto of the *Paradiso*, for instance, Dante returns again to the same nautical metaphor he used for himself at the outset of the *Purgatorio* (1.1-3), but which had also been prominent among his personal tropes as early as the *De vulgari eloquentia* and the *Convivio*: the metaphor of himself as a sailor and of his poetic career as a ship at sail.[27] Speaking to his readers as if he were the captain of a diverse crew, not all of whom might prove to be seaworthy, he announces a literary expedition into fathomless waters, a voyage into depth and danger ("in pelago," "per l'alto sale"), in which the text of the *Paradiso* becomes the forbidden ocean stretching out beyond the straits of all previous literature.[28]

> O voi che siete in piccioletta barca,
>   desiderosi d'ascoltar, seguiti
>   dietro al mio legno che cantando varca,
>
> tornate a riveder li vostri liti:
>   non vi mettete in pelago, ché forse,
>   perdendo me, rimarreste smarriti.
>
> L'acqua ch'io prendo già mai non si corse;
>   Minerva spira, e conducemi Appollo,
>   e nove Muse mi dimonstran l'Orse.
>
> Voialtri pochi che drizzaste il collo
>   per tempo al pan de li angeli, del quale
>   vivesi qui ma non sen vien satollo,
>
> metter potete ben per l'alto sale
>   vostro navigio, servando mio solco
>   dinanzi a l'acqua che ritorna equale.
>
> Que' glorïosi che passaro al Colco
>   non s'ammiraron come voi farete,
>   quando Iasón vider fatto bifolco. (1-18)

[O you that are in your little bark, eager to hear, following behind my ship that singing makes her way, turn back to see again your shores. Do not commit yourselves to the open sea, for perchance, if you lost me, you would remain astray. The water which I take was never coursed before. Minerva breathes and Apollo guides me, and nine Muses point out to me the Bears.

You other few who lifted up your necks betimes for bread
of angels, on which men here subsist but never become sated
of it, you may indeed commit your vessel to the deep brine,
holding to my furrow ahead of the water that turns smooth
again. Those glorious ones who crossed the sea to Colchis,
when they saw Jason turned plowman, were not as amazed as
you shall be.]

In this prolonged confrontation with his audience, Dante reminds
his readers that they stand on a threshold and then asks them to consider
what it will mean, what it will cost, to step over. Echoing within this
text, moreover, is Ulysses's speech to his men in *Inferno* 26.112-20:
that "orazion picciola" delivered at the Pillars of Hercules and meant to
turn the oars of aging sailors into wings for the mad flight. Indeed,
Dante's description of his "ship that singing makes her way" ("mio
legno che cantando varca" [3]) not only uses vocabulary closely associated with the wanderer—"legno," "varca"—but presents the singing
poet (like Ulysses himself) as a kind of siren. Except that *this* Ulysses
does not use his powers of language to seduce his audience unawares;
instead he shows himself employing a full array of rhetoric to enjoin a
choice. Rather than asking his readers to consider the seed from which
they spring (as opposed to considering the danger of the voyage "ne
l'alto passo"), Dante warns his crew—who like Ulysses's men are
"eager to hear"—that there are the real consequences to going further.
Those readers who are not capable of the *Paradiso* should look back to
the shore of the second canticle and hold off committing themselves to
the open seas ("pelago") of the third. Should they decide to proceed,
they must be wary of the danger they face in getting lost ("smarriti").
That the words of Dante's warning here ("pelago," "smarriti") recall the
poem's prologue scene, and with it the spiritual shipwreck of the
pilgrim, suggests that reading may in fact be dangerous, a matter of risk
and potential loss.

And yet, of course, the poet's address to his readers shows more
than concern for the well-being of those who follow in his wake. It is
also a strategy calculated to heighten the importance of the final
canticle, its author, and that "fit audience though few" who decide to
take what is presented as a voyage of unprecedented discovery. For quite
as important as Dante's insistence on the danger of the *Paradiso*'s
enterprise is his announcement that it is an exploration of virgin
territory. As Ulysses himself might have said, "The water which I take

was never coursed before." The claim is characteristically bold, and perhaps even outrageous. Certainly there had been other portrayals of the blessed, elegantly drawn in Virgil's Elysian Fields, crudely in some vernacular accounts of the thirteenth century.[29] But of course Dante is laying claim to direct experience, is speaking where St. Paul remained resolutely silent, and is in the process of inventing an illustrious Italian vernacular to explore that "great sea of being" (*Par.* 3.86) who is God.

On the brink of his narrative ascent, then, the poet takes the occasion to insist on his absolute novelty, on the charting of unexplored ocean and "nova terra." It is as if the Ulysses who could not deny experience had lived to tell the tale of its acquisition. Except that rather than breaking boundaries of his own volition, Dante wants to insist that he has been piloted all the way. Minerva breathes wisdom into him, Apollo gives him guidance, and all "nove Muse"—the Muses of the new[30]—help him navigate the stars toward the divine love that moves them. Anticipating the claim of *Paradiso* 25.1-2 that his sacred poem has been at least partly the result of heaven's hand, he undergirds his authority from the outset of the canticle by stating where that authority comes from; by announcing that his poetic voyage, like the pilgrimage it describes, has been the response to a divine call.

To those readers who crave the "bread of angels," who are driven by that "inborn and perpetual thirst" for God (*Par.* 2.20-21), the poet says, "you may indeed commit your vessel to the deep salt sea, holding close to my furrow ahead of the water that turns smooth again." On the last leg of the journey there are those capable of following the leader into the sea; capable, that is, of following a layman and poet, who speaks the *arcana verba* of theology—in Italian rather than in Latin—starting in this very canto with Beatrice's weighty discourse on the moon spots. Referring to his poem as if it were the great ocean itself, Dante asks his readers to watch the path he inscribes in his wake before the surface of the sea once again turns calm. This is not only a suggestion that they should hold on tight to his intellectual lead. It is also an invitation to marvel over the poetics of the *Paradiso*: to catch its brilliant metaphors in the brief moment of their articulation, before they dissolve once again into the silence beneath the surface ripples of language, below and beyond the mark of his boat. Dante knows that in the final canticle he is writing on water.

He also makes it clear that the proper response to this evanescent script is nothing less than wonder. And so at the end of the address he rewrites the disaster of Ulysses and his men by associating his own effort with that of another ancient sailor and another crew. He compares his readers to "those glorious ones who crossed the sea to Colchis" and himself, of course, to Jason. E. R. Curtius speculates that Dante received the story of the Argonauts through a complex line of literary transmission that runs from Pindar, through Latin poetry (Valerius Flaccus, Statius), and into the *Roman de la Rose*. But he judges Ovid's account in the *Metamorphoses* to be the most likely direct source, with its story of the Argonauts' journey "over an unknown sea in that first ship to seek the bright gleaming fleece of gold" ("vellera cum Minyis nitido radiantia villo / per mare non notum prima petiere carina" [*Metam.* 6.721]).[31]

It is easy to recognize the appeal of this epic story of innovation to the poet of the *Paradiso*. As the hero who (unlike the Dantean Ulysses) succeeds in returning home, Jason is an appropriate exemplar for the pilgrim; as the first navigator of the "mare non notum," he also prefigures Dante's poetic voyage through waters never coursed before, in a poem that wants to present itself as being the first boat, the "prima carina." But instead of explicitly underscoring the thematic of discovery—and without emphasizing the crucial fact that Jason came back from the unknown sea alive, with the Golden Fleece in tow—Dante chooses to let these associations remain implicit and to focus instead on one incident in Ovid's extended narrative, the moment "when . . . Jason turned plowman" ("quando Iasón vider fatto bifolco").

The reference here is to one of the ordeals put upon Jason in his quest for the Fleece. Harnessing the fierce iron-tipped bulls of King Aeëtes, he "made them draw the heavy plow and cut through the field that had never felt steel before" ("suppositosque iugo pondus grave cogit aratri / ducere et insuetum ferro proscindere campum" [7.118-19]). Ovid says that the local onlookers were amazed at the feat ("mirantur Colchi, Minyae clamoribus augent / adiciuntque animos" [120-21]). Dante transfers this wonder to the Argonauts themselves and therefore to the heroic readers of his *Paradiso*, who will not only equal the astonishment of the ancient worthies but even (or so they are told) surpass it: "Those glorious ones who crossed the seas to Colchis . . . were not as amazed as you shall be." Not only does the poet sail waters never navigated before; he also cultivates ground not yet touched by pen. As Dante plays with a commonplace metaphor that turns plowing into writing, he allows his own identification with Jason "fatto bifolco" to draw our

attention once again to the novelty of his final canticle.[32] Reaching far
beyond the georgic poet's cultivation of well-known fields, he is instead
an epic plowman whose pen makes one "versus" after another, and in so
doing breaks open *terra incognita*, canto by canto. He is the unabashed
master of the new.

In the final canto of the *Paradiso*, however, Dante dramatizes the
limits of that mastery as he discovers with poignancy an outer
circumference beyond which nothing can be remembered or said. At the
end of the journey the poet confesses his own failure, the dissolution of
his literary achievement, as "in the wind, on the light leaves, the
Sibyl's oracle was lost" ("al vento ne le foglie levi / si perdea la
sentenza di Sibilla" [33.65-66]). Nonetheless, even as the *Commedia*
seems to self-destruct in the very moment of its completion, the poet
sails on, describing the pilgrim's initial vision of God as a "volume" in
which all the scattered pages of the universe are bound together with
love. He tells us that the vision behind this metaphor lasted but an
instant; it was "un punto solo" (94). And in trying to remember it
"now," at the present point of recollection and writing, his sense of the
oblivion stretching between him and that rapturous sight—now lost
except as metaphor—seems greater even than the twenty-five centuries
that stand between his poetic efforts and "the enterprise that made Neptune wonder at the shadow of the Argo" ("la 'mpresa / che fé Nettuno
ammirar l'ombra d'Argo" [95-96]).

At the end of the *Paradiso* as in its beginning, Dante remembers
Jason and once more associates his own literary boat with the maiden
voyage of the Argo. As in the address to his readers in *Paradiso* 2, he
again underscores the appropriate reaction to such achievement by
repeating the same verb of wonder used earlier: *ammirare*. He also
continues and refines the metaphorical play between sailing, plowing,
and writing. Punning on the word *impresa*, 'enterprise'—a noun used
three other places in the *Commedia*, twice in reference to the
pilgrim's journey (*Inf.* 2.41, 47) and once to describe the poet's writing
(*Inf.* 32.7)—Dante also asks us to imagine the venture of the Argo as
an imprint ("impressa"; cf. *Par.* 33.59), a watery script no more sub-
stantial or enduring than a shadow or "ombra" cast on the sea. Thus the
earlier metaphor of the poem as a boat whose rudder incises the blank
surface of the ocean ("mio solco / dinanzi a l'acqua che ritorna equale"
[*Par.* 2.14-15]) here dematerializes into a metaphor of even greater
evanescence—the poem as an "ombra" floating on water. By the

hundreth canto of Dante's *Argonautica*, the text is hardly on the page; the mighty venture barely leaves an impression.

It is when we note the identity of the admiring onlooker, moreover, that the poet's handling of this navigational scenario becomes almost as remarkable as his claims. For the one who stares in astonishment at the voyage of the Argo (and thus the one who beholds the final canto of the poem with equal amazement) is none other than a god! From the depths of the sea Neptune looks up to behold a new thing, sailing high above him and skimming the surface of waters never coursed before; he sees the trespass of the explorer. At the beginning of the *Paradiso* a human audience would suffice, but here at the end Dante will settle for nothing less than a god—and for yet another *tour de force* of innovation. The tradition of the Argo had always included the element of astonishment, be it that of the Olympian deities and nymphs of Pelion (Apollonius), of the Nereids (Catullus), or of Thetis (Statius). But never before had wonder been assigned to Neptune, for whom (as Curtius has shown) the tradition chose instead to reserve the emotion of wrath.[33] Dante converts this divine opposition by a daring fiat of mythic revision. He makes it pleasing to the divine Other not to rage against the interloper upon his seas, not to shipwreck the shadow that has presumed so much. Whereas the "mad flight" of Ulysses ended in disaster, "com' altrui piacque," Dante shows his pilgrim sailing on to safe harbor in the Empyrean. So too the poet of the *Paradiso*, who, in the midst of imagining the beatific vision *per verba*,[34] gives us the image of a god looking up in wonder—at him.

Nine cantos earlier, in the autobiographical disclosure of *Paradiso* 25.1-12, Dante imagined himself returning to Florence after his extraordinary journey through the Other World, as if he were a triumphant (if travel-worn) Jason, bearing the Golden Fleece of the *Commedia* in his hand: "con altra voce omai, con altro vello / ritornerò poeta" (7-8). Until this moment in the poem the title "poeta" had been reserved for the masters of antiquity. But here he claims it for himself, as if in recognition of his own vernacular voice ("voce") and the hundred-canto Fleece ("vello") that is his prize. What seems to matter most in the strategic identification with Jason, however, is the sheer fact of the traveler's return. Because it is not the going out upon circumference alone that Dante emphasizes in the end, but the going out and coming back—his return, that is, to the "monstrous races" of his own countrymen, for whom this journey to the unpeopled world of the after life might serve as a map for pilgrimage, an invitation to the voyage of conversion.

We do Dante a disservice, however, if we simplify the enterprise he himself refused to uncomplicate. For while it is true that the Ulysses within him—the transgressor against the sign—is openly reined in throughout the *Commedia*, the impulse to explore nonetheless pulls the poem along, beyond established boundaries, in order to discover what is possible for a self-proclaimed poet of the new. Even Dante's turn in the end to Jason as a counter to Ulysses does not resolve the problem of his own identity as a boundary-breaker; on the contrary, it keeps that identity intensely problematic. To be sure, Jason's status as the first to sail or to plow *nova terra* marks the legendary hero as a master of novelty— an epoch-maker—and therefore as an apt model for both pilgrim and poet. But it is also true that in Virgil and Ovid alike the innovations of boat and plow are associated quite specifically with the passing away of the Golden Age, and therefore with a "fall" into experience, history, and loss. The Argo's accomplishment, if indisputable, is also tainted; its *ombra* an ambiguous foreshadowing.[35] So too (according to Ovid in *Metam.* 7.121-42) Jason "turned plowman" no sooner opens up virgin territory than he sows the serpent's teeth and reaps a harvest of destruction. His heroism comes with a price.

Nor in the *Commedia* does Dante present Jason exclusively in triumph. When the captain of the Argo actually appears in the poem, it is not in the *Paradiso*'s figural context of success and wonder—as the first sailor of the first ship, the plowman of virgin territory, and the cause of Neptune's wonder. It is, rather, as one of the damned, imprisoned in the second ditch of Malebolgia. Although retaining his regal bearing even in lower hell, Jason is nonetheless placed in the vile company of the seducers, among those who made a career of deception specifically through their artful use of language, "con segni e con parole ornate" (*Inf.* 18.91). "With him," says Virgil, "go all who practice such deceit" ("Con lui sen va chi da tal parte inganna" [97]).

It is customary in Dante studies to separate one Jason from the other, so that the seducer of Hypsipyle remains discretely in hell, with no particular relevance to pilgrim or poet, while the voyager after the Golden Fleece—Dante's exemplar—takes his symbolic place in paradise, in another world of discourse altogether. Certainly the placement of these references seems to enjoin such a distinction, with one Jason in the first canticle, observed in passing, and the other in the *Paradiso* where (as we have seen) Dante twice claims him as an avatar of himself. The poem, however, does not necessarily work so neatly. Rather than moving from a Jason *in malo* to another *in bono*, we may instead be confronting in a single figure an ambiguous confusion of possibilities meant to be experienced at once, a "polysemous" mixture of seduction and discovery that the poet condemns in Ulysses, makes ambiguous in Jason, and celebrates in himself.

Giuseppe Mazzotta has suggested, in fact, that Dante does not ignore a comparison of himself with Jason the seducer, but in *Paradiso* 25.7-8 deliberately marks the radical difference between Jason's "signs and ornate speech" and his own Golden Fleece, an alterity signified by the poet's description of himself as having an "*altra* voce" and an "*altro* vello."[36] The point is well taken, and yet the marking of difference can also be seen as the masking of a perceived identity, the veiled exposure of ambivalence. In any case, condemnation and wonder seem to sail together in the *Commedia*, with the poem's judgment on exploration paradoxically authorizing its own discoveries. Jason offers the example of a successful homecoming, but carries with him liabilities of association that Dante may have wanted to exploit rather than avoid in the development of his own highly complex persona.

This is not to say, of course, that either "fair words" or the artful speaker are inevitably undermined. On the contrary, Dante goes out of his way to establish from the outset of the *Commedia* that even pagan poetry can be commissioned by heaven to do God's work, as when Beatrice goes to Virgil in Limbo and asks him to use his "parola ornata" (*Inf.* 2.67)—the same phrase used to describe Jason's seductions—in order to save the pilgrim. But Dante's larger point seems to be that all language, all the tokens and fair words of poetry, are by nature as ambiguous (and as perilous) as discovery itself. For as the poem shows in its contrast between Ulysses and the pilgrim, a voyage beyond mortal boundaries can either be an act of transgression or a journey to God. So too the poet as siren can seduce us into an epic of narcissism or call us away from whatever "Florence" we call home, to come instead to a way of life more "just and sane" (*Par.* 31.39).

Dante neither shipwrecks the reader in a sea of indeterminacy nor allows his text to wander unmoored. Instead, he makes discovery not only the subject but the nature of his poem. Interpretation becomes navigation, and the poem not so much a map to be followed blindly as one to be read critically, vigilantly—read even against its author.

Inveighing constantly against the peril of overreaching, Dante at once conceals and confesses his own presumption. He establishes his authority as a seaworthy guide by the sheer force of his claim, and yet includes strategically within his poem the necessary critique of that authority. Perhaps nowhere more powerfully than through the figure of Ulysses, he issues a warning against the demonic possibilities of his own talent: a warning that words, whether spoken or written, have the power to create worlds no less dangerous than one in which we live and through whose waters we navigate our course. The *Commedia* asks to go out upon circumference in order to see the center; but it does so all the while alerting us to the risks of the enterprise, to the shadowy nature of all language—even that of a "sacred poem."

NOTES

1. *Convivio* 1.3: "Veramente io sono stato legno sanza vela e sanza governo, portato a diversi porti e foci e liti dal vento secco che vapora la dolorosa povertate." All citations of Dante's prose works are taken from the *Opere di Dante* (Florence: Società Dantesca Italiana, 1921); citations from the *Commedia* are from *The Divine Comedy*, trans. (with a commentary) Charles S. Singleton, Bollingen Series 80 (Princeton: Princeton Univ. Press, 1970-75).

2. In *Convivio* 4.28, where Dante is speaking about the fourth (and final) stage of life, he refers to the soul's return to God, "sì come a quello porto onde ella si partio quando venne ad intrare nel mare di questa vita. . . ." He goes on to develop this metaphor of navigational return at some length, as he will (at large) in the *Commedia*, but perhaps most provocatively in *Inferno* 26-27. For Dante's use of nautical metaphors in general, see Ernst Robert Curtius, *European Literature and the Latin Middle Ages*, trans. Willard R. Trask, Bollingen Series 36 (New York, 1953; repr. Princeton: Princeton Univ. Press, 1973), pp. 128-30.

3. "E come quei che con lena affannata
      uscito fuor del pelago a la riva,
      si volge a l'acqua perigliosa e guata,

   così l'animo mio, ch'ancor fuggiva,
      si volse a retro a rimirar lo passo
      che non lasciò già mai persona viva." (lines 22-27)

Introduced into the lexicon of the poem in this first simile are two words ("pelago" and "passo") that will both gather weight as the *Commedia* progresses and continually point the reader back to this opening moment of Dante's spiritual "naufragio."

4. Mary B. Campbell, in *The Witness and the Other World: Exotic European Travel Writing, 400-1600* (Ithaca: Cornell Univ. Press, 1988), suggests that the literary situation of the traveler who writes is "a limit case for such intertwined literary issues as truth, fact, figure, fiction, even genre. How, for instance, does one *distinguish* fact from fiction, either as writer or as reader, in the case of unverifiable records of private experience taking place in profoundly unfamiliar surroundings?" (p. 2). Her question can be used to examine the literal truth claims of the *Commedia* quite apart from any discussion of the "allegory of the theologians"; that is, as an absolute "limit case" in the history of travel literature.

5. For the most extensive study of Dante's geography, see Edward Moore, *Studies in Dante, Third Series* (Oxford: Clarendon Press, 1903), pp. 108-43. A concise appendix on the subject is in George H. T. Kimble, *Geography in the Middle Ages* (London: Methuen, 1938), pp. 240-44. See also Patrick Boyde's chapter, "Land and Sea," in *Dante Philomythes and Philosopher* (Cambridge, Eng.: Cambridge Univ. Press, 1981), pp. 96-111.

6. *Quaestio de aqua et terra* 19: "Nam, ut comuniter ab omnibus habetur, hec habitabilis extenditur per lineam longitudinis a Gadibus, que supra terminos occidentales ab Hercule positos ponitur, usque ad hostia fluminis Ganges, ut scribit Orosius." (See *Par.* 27.80-87, where, from the heaven of the Fixed Stars, Dante surveys the "whole arc which the first climate makes from its middle to its end" ["tutto l'arco / che fa dal mezzo al fine il primo clima"]). The *Quaestio* purports to be a disquisition delivered by Dante in January of 1320, a "scientific" inquiry into the relative levels of land and water on the surface of the globe. Dante concludes that the elevation of heavy earth above lighter water is a result of the attraction of the stars. Although the authenticity of the *Quaestio* has been challenged, it is now largely accepted as being Dante's work. See Manlio Pastore Stocchi's entry in the *Enciclopedia Dantesca* 4:761-65, which includes a bibliography. Also Paget Toynbee, *A Dictionary of Proper Names and Notable Matters in the Works of Dante*, rev. Charles S. Singleton (Oxford: Clarendon Press, 1968), pp. 534-35; and David Alexander, "Dante and the Form of the Land," *Annals of the Association of American Geographers* 76[1] (1986): 38-49.

7. St. Augustine, *De civitate Dei*, CCSL 48 (Turnhout: Brepols, 1955), p. 510 (16.9): "Quoniam nullo modo scriptura ista mentitur, quae

narratis praeteritis facit fidem eo, quod eius praedicta conplentur, nimisque absurdum est, ut dicatur aliquos homines ex hac in illam partem, Oceani immensitate traiecta, nauigare ac peruenire potuisse, ut etiam illic ex uno illo primo homine genus institueretur humanum."

8. *Convivio* 4.15: "E sanza dubbio forte riderebbe Aristotile udendo fare spezie due de l'umana generazione, sì come de li cavalli e de li asini; che, perdonimi Aristotile, asini ben si possono dire coloro che cosi pensano."

9. A standard overview of Dante's Terrestrial Paradise in relation to the larger tradition can be found in Howard R. Patch, *The Other World According to Descriptions in Medieval Literature* (New York: Octagon, 1970), pp. 184 ff. A fuller account is offered by Edoardo Coli, *Il paradiso terrestra dantesco* (Florence: Carnesecchi, 1897), who discusses at length Dante's peculiar positioning of Eden and Purgatory on the same invented mountain; see pp. 189-90. Bruno Nardi has explored this territory in even greater depth in his impressively erudite essay, "Intorno al sito del Purgatorio e al mito dantesco dell' Eden," first published in 1922 and then in *Saggi di Filosofia dantesca* (Milan: Società Anonima Editrice Dante Alighieri, 1930), pp. 349-74. See also Boyde, *Dante Philomythes*, pp. 96-111, who underscores the originality of Dante's conception. The poet's "remaking" of Purgatory is discussed by Jacques LeGoff in *The Birth of Purgatory*, trans. Arthur Goldhammer (Chicago: Univ. of Chicago Press, 1981), pp. 334-55.

10. Nardi, "Intorno al sito del Purgatorio," pp. 352-54 quotes from Ambrose, *Enarratio in Psalm. 118* (17.1) and Rupert of Deutz, *De Trinitate* (1.32-33).

11. Nardi, "Intorno al sito del Purgatorio," pp. 372-73, masks the sheer surprise of Eunoe by saying that Dante was led ("fu condotto") to imagine a companion stream to Virgil's Lethe, whose name (as well as whose existence) he "coined." The point is that Eunoe is Dante's own discovery, what LeGoff refers to as the poet's "invention" (*Birth of Purgatory*, p. 479), and what Patch calls "an astonishing change for Dante to make from the traditional picture of Eden, a point in his originality and in the classical influence to which he was subject" (*The Other World*, p. 185). See Vittorio Russo's entry "Eunoe" in the *Enciclopedia Dantesca* 2:765-66; Charles S. Singleton, *Dante Studies 2: Journey to Beatrice* (Baltimore: The Johns Hopkins Univ. Press, 1977), pp. 159-83, who discusses Eunoe as "a striking departure from scriptural authority"; and Peter Dronke, *The Medieval Poet and His World* (Rome: Edizioni di Storia e Letteratura, 1984), pp. 402-04, who wonders if an observation by Pliny regarding two fountains in Boethia (*Nat. hist.* 31.11) may be the source of Dante's "originality."

12. Both Moore, *Studies in Dante*, pp. 119-20, and Kimball, *Geography*, pp. 241-42 (see above, n. 5) attribute the origin of the mountain to Dante's invention, as does the commentary tradition in general. A more extensive consideration (and the argument that Dante's account grew out of three biblical texts: Isaiah 14:11-16, Revelation 12:7-16, and Luke 10:18) is made by Bruno Nardi in a monograph, *La Caduta di Lucifero e l'autenticità della 'Quaestio de Aqua et Terra'* (Turin: Società Editrice Internazionale, 1959).

13. An excellent discussion of the *mappaemundi* as "largely exegetic" is given by David Woodward, "Medieval *Mappaemundi*," in vol. 1 of *The History of Cartography*, ed. J. B. Harley and David Woodward (Chicago: Univ. of Chicago Press, 1987), pp. 283-370. See also the first chapter of John Block Friedman's *The Monstrous Races in Medieval Art and Thought* (Cambridge, Mass.: Harvard Univ. Press, 1981). When Friedman notes that the medieval map was "likely to be a hodgepodge of biblical, classical, and fabulous history mixed with the names of true places, cities, and peoples" (p. 38), he is in fact describing the "hodgepodge" of the *Commedia* itself.

14. The thesis of John G. Demaray, in *The Invention of Dante's 'Commedia'* (New Haven: Yale Univ. Press, 1974), is that "Dante's long pilgrimage throughout the *Commedia* is an imitation of an earthly pilgrimage made by countless medieval Christians to holy stations located in the Near East and Italy" (p. 4). While I find Demaray's reconstruction of pilgrimage routes interesting as one of the poem's many "subtexts," his effort to demonstrate that the Great Circle Route (Rome-Egypt-Sinai/Jerusalem-Rome) is "mirrored centrally" in the tripartite structure of the poem forces him into making strained correlations.

15. See the explicit reference to the "anno del giubileo" in *Inferno* 18.28-33, where Dante compares the movements of panderers and seducers in the Malebolgia to crowds of pilgrims going back and forth over the Tiber to the Vatican. Despite the bitter irony of the reference (not to mention his general opinion of the Pope), Dante seems to uphold the legitimacy of the indulgence granted by Boniface in *Purgatorio* 2.97-99. See LeGoff's discussion, *Purgatory*, pp. 330-31.

16. For a full-scale treatment of the tension between pilgrimage and wandering, see the second and third chapters of Christian K. Zacher's *Curiosity and Pilgrimage, The Literature of Discovery in Fourteenth Century England* (Baltimore: The Johns Hopkins Univ. Press, 1976). Zacher discusses Dante's Ulysses as "probably the most striking medieval depiction of the *curiosus* as wanderer" (p. 35). See also Gerhart B. Ladner, "*Homo Viator*: Mediaeval Ideas on Alienation and Order," *Speculum* 42 (1967): 233-59 (esp. p. 251).

17. The bibliography on Dante's treatment of Ulysses is extraordinarily extensive. For an overview of the figure himself, see W. B. Stanford's *The Ulysses Theme, A Study in the Adaptability of a Traditional Hero,* 2nd ed. (Ann Arbor: Univ. of Michigan Press, 1976), ch. 14. A masterful summary of critical work up through the 1960s can be found in John A. Scott's brilliant essay, *"Inferno* XXVI: Dante's Ulysses," *Lettere Italiane* 23 (1971): 145-86. Franco Fido brings the bibliography more up to date in "Writing Like God—or Better? Symmetries in Dante's 26th and 27th Cantos," *Italica* 63 (1986): 262-63. See also Mario Fubini's entry on "Ulisse" in *Enciclopedia Dantesca* 5:803-09, which surveys critical positions and also provides a bibliography. The introduction to canto 26 offered by Umberto Bosco and Giovanni Reggio in their commentary on *Inferno* is excellent *(Dante Alighieri, La Divina Commedia* [Florence: Le Monnier, 1979], 1:376-81); see also Hermann Gmelin, *Kommentar I: Die Hölle,* vol. 1 of *Die Göttliche Komödie* (Stuttgart: Ernst Klett, 1949-57), pp. 380-95.

18. That the ill-fated expedition of the Vivaldi brothers may have been in Dante's mind when he told his version of the Ulysses story has become something of a commonplace among commentators. But there is at least one exclusive study of the subject—Francis M. Rogers, "The Vivaldi Expedition," *Dante Studies* 73 (1955): 31-45—that maintains a reverse order of influence: Dante's Ulysses framed the way in which the Vivaldi expedition came to be treated. "In other words, just as the Dante passage has inspired many later poets, so there is a reminiscence of the *Divina Commedia* in historical scholarship concerning European exploration and discovery" (p. 45).

19. Ever since Francesco De Sanctis, in the late nineteenth century, it has been *de rigeur* among Italian critics of a certain stripe to see Ulysses as anticipating (and perhaps even inspiring) what we call the "Age of Discovery." Thus De Sanctis says of Ulysses's speech to his men: "we feel that burning curiosity to know which assailed the men of that era. We seem to be taking part in a voyage of Columbus: sin becomes virtue. Dante the logical Ghibelline puts the besieger and traitor of Troy into Hell, for Troy was the root of the Holy Roman Empire, but Dante the poet raises a statue to this forerunner of Columbus, who stretches wide his arms to new seas and new worlds" *(History of Italian Literature,* trans. Joan Redfern [New York: Harcourt, Brace, 1931], 1:208).

20. Against this Romantic identification of Ulysses (and Dante, his maker) as Renaissance world explorers *avant la lettre,* John A. Scott demonstrates impressively, by a broad look at Dante's works, that there is nothing in the poet himself "of the intrepid explorer, another Marco Polo, let alone a precursor of Columbus" (*"Inferno* XXVI," p. 157); that Dante clearly acknowledged limitations to the habitable

world (p. 164); and that he respected restraints on human intellect: "The idea of exceeding certain natural or divinely-appointed limitations is basic to Dante's view of human nature and one which is implied in the use of the term *follia*" (pp. 167-68). See Umberto Bosco, "La 'follia' di Dante," in *Dante vicino* (Rome: Salvatore Sciascia Editore, 1966), pp. 55-76; also Bruno Nardi, "La Tragedia d'Ulisse," in *Dante e la cultura medioevale*, ed. Paolo Mazzantini (Bari: Laterza, 1983), pp. 125-34.

20. There is a superbly comprehensive treatment of the Ulysses traditions available to Dante in Giorgio Padoan's essay, "Ulisse 'Fandi Fictor' e le vie della sapienza," *Studi danteschi* 37 (1960): 21-61. Ernest Barker covers some of the same source material in "Dante and the Last Voyage of Ulysses," *Traditions of Civility* (Cambridge, Eng.: Cambridge Univ. Press, 1948), pp. 53-73, as does John Freccero in "The Prologue Scene" and "Dante's Ulysses," both collected in *Dante, The Poetics of Conversion*, ed. Rachel Jacoff (Cambridge, Mass.: Harvard Univ. Press, 1986). See also David Thompson, *Dante's Epic Journeys* (Baltimore: The Johns Hopkins Univ. Press, 1974), who argues (pp. 43-50) that Dante would have known of Ulysses's return even without Homer's text, through allusions in Latin literature as well as in the works of medieval mythographers and commentators.

21. For Virgil, Ovid, and Statius on Ulysses, see Padoan, "Ulisse 'Fandi Fictor'," pp. 22-33.

22. In attempting to reconstruct the possible sources for Dante's novel conception of Ulysses, critics point us in a number of directions. There is, for instance, the suggestion in Cicero's *De finibus* (5.18) that Ulysses might have held knowledge dearer than home, while Seneca in *Epist. mor.* 88.7 is sure that he must have traveled outside the known world. Ovid, moreover, concludes his account of Ulysses in the *Metamorphoses* by reporting his departure from Circe without a specified destination; there is only "the dubious pathways of the sea, their vast extent, and all the desperate perils yet to come" ("ancipitesque vias et iter Titania vastum / dixerat et saevi restare pericula ponti" [14.438-39]). Perhaps most important as a source, however, is the first chapter of Augustine's *De beata vita*, as has been suggested by Padoan,"Ulisse 'Fandi Fictor'," pp. 41-42; and Freccero, "The Prologue Scene," pp. 20-24. There we find sailors wandering at sea, forgetful of their *patria*, and an immense mountain that "throws them back into the darkness and snatches away the home they so much desired and almost in sight" ("eisque in tenebras revolutis, eripiat luculentissimam domum, quam pene iam viderant"). Hugh Shankland, "Dante *Aliger* and Ulysses," *Italian Studies* 32 (1977): 21-38, offers Augustine's meditation on Psalm 138:9 (quoted on pp. 37-38) as another possible subtext.

23. Hugo Rahner, "Odysseus at the Mast," *Greek Myths and Christian Mystery*, trans. Brian Battershaw (New York: Harper and Row, 1971), pp. 328-86.

24. In his essay, "Dante's Ulysses," Freccero (p. 146) writes: "[It] seems safe to presume that the figure of Ulysses, for all of its apparent historicity, is at the same time a palinodic moment in the *Divine Comedy*. As Bruno Nardi once suggested, it implies a retrospective view of Dante himself both as poet and as man, when with confidence and *ingégno* he embarked upon the writing of the *Convivio*, a work never completed, which began by stating that all men desire to know and that ultimate happiness resides in the pursuit of knowledge. Ulysses would then stand for a moment in the pilgrim's life . . . for the disastrous prelude to the preparation for grace, a misleading guide before the encounter with Virgil."

25. Shankland shows how linguistic similarities in certain details of the journeys of Ulysses and Dante constantly contrast the "folle volo" of one with the "alto volo" of the other ("Dante *Aliger* and Ulysses," pp. 28-31).

26. Erich Auerbach in *Literary Language and its Public in Late Latin Antiquity and in the Middle Ages*, trans. by Ralph Mannheim, Bollingen Series 74 (Princeton: Princeton Univ. Press, 1965), pp. 94-320, maintains that Dante merged all the forms of his Latin heritage into his own vernacular and made Italian "(not as such but as one of the vernacular languages) into the language of the European spirit" (p. 314). See Curtius, *European Literature and the Latin Middle Ages* (pp. 350-57) on Dante's fusion of Latin and the vernacular.

27. Major studies of Dante's addresses to the reader are found in Hermann Gmelin, *Deutsches Dante-Jahrbuch* 29/30 (1951): 130-40; Leo Spitzer, *Italica* 32 (1955): 143-65; and Erich Auerbach, *Romance Philology* 7 (1953-54): 268-78, and *Literary Language*, pp. 296-301. All touch on the opening of *Paradiso* 2, which is well studied in the commentaries of Attilo Momigliano, Gmelin, and Bosco and Reggio.

28. In their commentary on *Par.* 2.5, "non vi mettete in pelago," Bosco and Reggio restrict the reference of "pelago" to the high seas of the Mediterranean and deny that it can apply to the ocean itself, "because a voyage in the ocean was for Dante inconceivable: only Ulysses ventured forth there, contravening divine prohibition" (*La Divina Commedia*, 3:29; see above, n. 17). I am suggesting that the final canticle is not speaking of navigation but of writing, and that it announces itself as a trespass from the outset, before then going on to claim that its literary venture is a discovery made licit by virtue of divine call. See also Piero Boitani, *The Tragic and the Sublime in*

Medieval Literature (Cambridge, Eng.: Cambridge Univ. Press, 1989), pp. 250-78.

29. Bosco and Reggio, *La Divina Commedia*, 3:25, mention the thirteenth-century vernacular descriptions of the blessed by Giacommino da Verona and Bonvesin de la Riva as precedents (in Italian) for the waters that Dante was coursing in the final *cantica*. They then go on to assert that the poet's *novità* lies in his taking on theological and philosophical issues so boldly (and with such sophistication). Perhaps the most ardent defense of Dante's novelty, however, is offered by Benvenuto da Imola in his commentary on the *Commedia*, written between 1373 and 1380 (Florence: Barbera, 1887). Beginning his lengthy gloss on Dante's claim in *Par.* 2.7 to travel uncharted seas, he asks, "Quis enim unquam excogitavit facere unum coelum artificiale, quale hic poeta mirabilis?" His answer is, no one else.

30. Natalino Sapegno, *Dante Alighieri, La Divina Commedia* (Florence: La Nuova Italia, 1984), 3:19, notes that since Daniello's 1568 commentary the "nove Muse" have often been taken to refer not to all nine Muses, but to new and Christian (rather than antique pagan) revelation. But following on the assertion that "L'acqua ch'io prendo già mai non si corse," the poet may well be playing with the full range of the adjective "nove." The Muses invoked, therefore, may not only be nine in number or Christian in inspiration, but themselves new, never before called upon—the muses of novelty invoked to help the poet express what is presented as a "vista nova" (*Par.* 33.136).

31. E. R. Curtius, "The Ship of the Argonauts," *Essays on European Literature*, trans. Michael Kowal (Princeton: Princeton Univ. Press, 1973), pp. 486-92. The citation of Ovid is from *Metamorphoses*, trans. Frank Justus Miller, Loeb Classical Library (Cambridge, Mass.: Harvard Univ. Press, 1916).

32. For the metaphor "writing" as "ploughing," see Curtius, *European Literature and the Latin Middle Ages*, pp. 313-14.

33. Curtius, "The Ship of the Argonauts," p. 491; see also Peter Dronke, *The Medieval Poet and His World*, p. 436. Robert Hollander, *The Allegory of Dante's 'Commedia'* (Princeton: Princeton Univ. Press, 1968), pp. 220-32, gives an important and extensive reading of the Jason material in *Paradiso*. He does not, however, consider the conversation of the sea god's traditional wrath. Instead he emphasizes Jason and Neptune as two figural identities of Dante, Pilgrim and Poet (pp. 230-31). Boitani, in *Tragic and the Sublime*, discusses the sublimity of Dante's poetic navigation but not its trespass (pp. 275-78).

34. In *Par.* 1.70-72, the poet proclaims the impossibility of conveying "transhumanized" experience *per verba*. For an analysis of these important lines as emblematic of the poetics of the *Paradiso* as a whole, see my essay, "Dante's *Paradiso* and the Dialectic of Ineffability," in *Ineffability, Naming the Unnamable from Dante to Beckett*, ed. Peter S. Hawkins and Anne H. Schotter (New York: AMS Press, 1984), pp. 8-9.

35. Virgil's *Eclogue* 4.31-40 refers to the *vestigia fraudis* in terms of sailing the seas and cleaving the earth. With the return of the Golden Age, however, "even the trader will quit the sea, nor shall the ship of pine exchange wares"; "the earth shall not feel the harrow." Likewise in *Metam.* 1.89-100, Ovid defines the Golden Age as free of navigation and of plowing. See also Curtius, "The Ship of the Argonauts," pp. 490-91.

36. Giuseppe Mazzotta, *Dante, Poet of the Desert* (Princeton: Princeton Univ. Press, 1979), p. 142. Hollander, *Allegory of Dante's 'Commedia'*, glosses *Par.* 25.7-9 as meaning "not only that Dante, the lamb, will have another pelt, but that Dante, the poet, shall return from heaven with a new Fleece, not the Golden Fleece of Jason, but the true *vello*, granted by the Grace of God" (p. 224).

Notes on Contributors

MARY B. CAMPBELL, Assistant Professor of English and American Literature at Brandeis University, is the author of *The Witness and the Other World: Exotic European Travel Writing, 400-1600*; she is co-editor, with Mark Rollins, of *Begetting Images: Studies in the Art and Science of Symbol Production*, which contains her essay "Imaginary Facts: Columbus's Letter to Sanchez and the Image of Paradise." Two essays on Renaissance discovery literature are forthcoming: "Carnal Knowledge: Fracastoro's *De Syphilis* and the Discovery of America," in *Crossing Cultures: Essays in the Displacement of Western Civilization*, ed. Harry Liebersohn and Daniel Segal; and "The Illustrated Travel Book and the Birth of Ethnography: Part I of De Bry's *America*," in *New Explorations, Old Texts*, ed. David G. Allen and Robert A. White. She is at work on *Wonder and Science*, a book about late-medieval and Renaissance science, science fiction, and protoethnography.

VINCENT DIMARCO, Professor of English at the University of Massachusetts at Amherst, has written on medieval imaginative travel and discovery literature in connection with the Middle English *Letter of Alexander to Aristotle* and Chaucer's "Squire's Tale," for which he wrote the explanatory notes in the *Riverside Chaucer*. His essay, "The Historical Basis of Chaucer's Squire's Tale," appeared in *Edebiyât* n.s. 1 (1989). He is now writing a book on the subject of medieval Amazons.

GREGORY G. GUZMAN, Professor of History at Bradley University, is the author of more than ten articles on Vincent of Beauvais's *Speculum historiale* and medieval European contacts with the Mongols. He founded and edits the annual *Vincent of Beauvais Newsletter*. Two major projects occupy him at present: *Monumenta Latina rerum Mongolorum*, a compendium of references to Mongols in thirteenth- and fourteenth-century Latin sources, and a book on reports of cannibalism in Inner Asia that circulated in the West during the Middle Ages.

PETER S. HAWKINS, Associate Professor of Religion and Literature at Yale University Divinity School, is the author of *The Language of Grace: Flannery O'Connor, Walker Percy, Iris Murdoch* and *Getting Nowhere: Christian Hope and Utopian Dream*. He has published over twenty scholarly articles, many of them on Dante, including one in *Civitas: Religious Ideas of the City*, a book he edited, and one in *Ineffability: Naming the Unnamable from Dante to Beckett*, which he co-edited with Anne H. Schotter. He is currently working on a book-length investigation of Dante's relationship to the Bible.

IAIN HIGGINS, Assistant Professor of English at the University of British Columbia, is revising for publication his dissertation, "The World of a Book of the World: *Mandeville's Travels* in Middle English (British Library MS Cotton Titus C.xvi)" (Harvard University, 1988). He is especially interested in considering Middle English versions of the *Travels* as both literary texts and cultural documents.

JAMES MULDOON, Professor of History at Rutgers University (Camden College of Arts and Sciences), edited *The Expansion of Europe: The First Phase*; he is also the author of *Popes, Lawyers, and Infidels: The Church and the Non-Christian World, 1250-1550*, and numerous articles on medieval canon law. He is now studying the application of medieval legal theories of human rights to the inhabitants of the New World, especially as they were developed by Spanish lawyer and imperial official Juan de Solórzano Pereira (1575-1654). His article, "Solórzano's *De Indiarum Iure*: Applying a Medieval Theory of World Order in the Seventeenth Century," is forthcoming in the *Journal of World History*.

MONIKA OTTER, a Ph.D. candidate in English and Comparative Literature at Columbia University, is finishing her dissertation on spatial images in twelfth- and thirteenth-century English historiography.

JAMES ROMM, Assistant Professor of Classics at Bard College, is particularly interested in the Indian-wonders tradition in Western literature. His article "Aristotle's Elephant and the Myth of Alexander's Scientific Patronage" is published in the *American Journal of Philology* 110 (1990). His book, tentatively entitled *The Edges of the Earth in Ancient Thought: Geography, Exploration and Fiction*, is forthcoming from Princeton University Press.

LAURIE SHEPARD, Assistant Professor of Romance Languages and Literatures at Boston College, teaches medieval Italian literature and has completed a book on modes of argument in thirteenth-century political literature.

MARINA TOLMACHEVA, Associate Professor of History at Washington State University, has written numerous articles on Arab cartography, geography, and topography for academic journals in Africa, Europe, and North America. She is an editor and translator of *Arabskie istochniki XII-XIIIvv* [Arabic Sources of the Twelfth through Thirteenth Centuries], volume 3 in the series *Drevnie i srednevekovye istochniki po etnografii i istorii narodov Afriki iuzhnee Sakhary* [Ancient and Medieval Sources for the Ethnography and History of the Peoples of Africa South of the Sahara], published by the Institute of Ethnography of the USSR Academy of Sciences.

LOUISE O. VASVARI, Professor of Comparative Literature and Linguistics at the State University of New York at Stony Brook, has produced two books on the work of the fifteenth-century Spanish writer, Juan de Mena, as well as some four dozen publications on medieval romance literature and linguistics. Recent and forthcoming articles include: "A Tale of 'Taillying': Aesop Topsy-Turvy in the *Libro del Arcipreste,*" *Journal of Interdisciplinary Hispanic Sciences* 2 (1990); and "Amor, pecado, y muerte carnivalizados en el *Libro de buen amor,*" in *Amor, pecado, y muerte en la edad media*, ed. Nicasio Salvador Miguel (1991).

SCOTT D. WESTREM, Assistant Professor of English at Lehman College of The City University of New York, has an article, "Two Routes to Pleasant Instruction in Late Fourteenth-Century Literature," forthcoming in *New Explorations, Old Texts*, ed. David G. Allen and Robert A. White. His book, *Johannes Witte de Hese's* Itinerarius: *A Fourteenth-Century Extension of the Medieval Pilgrim's Horizon*, is also forthcoming. He is finishing a book-length study and English translation of the geographical section (Book 1) of Honorius Augustodunensis's *Imago mundi*, and is preparing a critical edition and translation of William of Boldensele's *Itinerarium ad terram sanctam*.

Bibliography

Primary Sources

Abbo. "Life of St. Edmund." In *Three Lives of English Saints*. Ed. Michael Winterbottom. Toronto: Pontifical Institute of Mediaeval Studies, 1972.

Adam of Bremen. *Gesta Hammaburgensis ecclesiae pontificum*. Ed. G. Waitz. In MGH SS rer. Germ. Hanover: Bibliopolii, 1876.

-----. *History of the Archbishops of Hamburg-Bremen*. Trans. Francis J. Tschan. New York: Columbia Univ. Press, 1959.

Adamnan. *Adamnan's De locis sanctis*. Ed. and trans. Denis Meehan. Scriptores Latini Hiberniae 3. Dublin: Dublin Institute for Advanced Studies, 1958.

Aethicus Ister. *Cosmographia*. Ed. Heinrich Wuttke. In *Die Kosmographie des Istrier Aithikos im lateinischen Auszüge des Hieronymus*. Leipzig: Dyk, 1853.

d'Ailly, Pierre. *Imago mundi, de Pierre d'Ailly . . . texte latin et traduction française des quatre traites cosmographiques de d'Ailly et des notes marginales de Christophe Colombe*. Ed. Edmond Buron. 3 vols. Paris: Maisonneuve frères, 1930.

Alexander Legend/Letter: See Boer, Budge, Engelmann, Feldbusch, Foster, Gunderson, Pseudo-Callisthenes, Smithers, and Thomas of Kent.

Alighieri, Dante. *Opere di Dante*. Florence: Società Dantesca Italiana, 1921.

-----. *Il Convivio*. Ed. Maria Simonelli. Bologna: Patron, 1966.

225

Alighieri, Dante. *The Divine Comedy.* Trans. [with commentary] Charles S. Singleton. Bollingen Series 80. Princeton: Princeton Univ. Press, 1970-75.

Annales Burtinenses. Ed. Pauli. MGH SS. Hanover: Hahn, 1885.

Annales de Burton, (A.D. 1004-1263). In *Annales Monastici.* Ed. Henry Richards Luard. *Rerum Britannicarum Medii Aevi Scriptores* 36 (1864).

Aristotle. *The Basic Works of Aristotle.* Ed. Richard McKeon. New York, Random House, 1941.

-----. *Posterior Analytics.* Ed. and trans. Jonathan Barnes. Oxford: Clarendon Press, 1975.

Aucassin et Nicolette. Ed. Mario Roques. Paris: Champion, 1963.

Backer [Baecker], Louis de. *L'Extrême Orient au moyen âge d'après les manuscrits d'un flamand de Belgique Moine de Saint-Bertin à Saint-Omer et d'un Prince d'Armenie Moine de Prémontré à Poitiers.* Paris: Leroux, 1877.

Bacon, Roger. *The Opus Majus of Roger Bacon.* Ed. John Henry Bridges. 2 vols. with supplement. Oxford, 1897; repr. Frankfurt, Minerva, 1964.

-----. *Opus majus.* Ed. Robert B. Burke. New York: Russell and Russell, 1962.

Beazley, C. Raymond. *The Dawn of Modern Geography.* 3 vols. 1897-1903; repr. New York: Peter Smith, 1949.

-----. *The Western Texts and Versions of John de Plano Carpini and William de Rubruquis.* Hakluyt Society, extra ser. 13. London: Hakluyt Society, 1903.

Bede, Venerable. *Bede's Ecclesiastical History of the English People.* Ed. Bertram Colgrave and R. A. B. Mynors. Oxford: Clarendon Press, 1972.

Boer, Walther W. *Epistola Alexandri ad Aristotelem ad Codicum Fidem Edita.* The Hague: Excelsior, 1953.

Bridia, C. de: See Skelton.

Budge, Ernest A. Wallis, trans. *The History of Alexander the Great, being the Syriac version of the Pseudo-Callisthenes.* Cambridge, Eng., 1889; repr. Amsterdam: Philo Press, 1976.

-----, trans. *The Life and Exploits of Alexander the Great, being a Series of Ethiopic Texts.* London: Clay, 1896.

-----, trans. *Book of the Cave of Treasures.* London: Religious Tract Society, 1927.

-----, trans. *The Alexander Book in Ethiopia: The Ethiopic Versions of Pseudo-Callisthenes.* London: Oxford Univ. Press, 1933.

Charlesworth, J. H., ed. *The Old Testament Pseudepigrapha.* 2 vols. Garden City, N. Y.: Doubleday, 1983.

Cockaigne, Land of: See Väänänen.

Columbus, Christopher. *Epistola de insulis nuper inventis.* Rome: S. Plannck, after April, 1493.

Dante: See Alighieri.

Dawson, Christopher, ed. and intro. Trans. "a nun of Stanbrook Abbey." *Mission to Asia: Narratives and Letters of the Franciscan Missionaries in Mongolia and China in the Thirteenth and Fourteenth Centuries.* Medieval Academy Reprints for Teaching 8. Toronto: Univ. of Toronto Press, 1980. Originally published as *The Mongol Mission.* London: Sheed and Ward, 1955. An earlier reprint as *Mission to Asia.* New York: Harper and Row, 1966.

Dörrie, Heinrich A., ed. "Drei Texte zur Geschichte der Ungarn und Mongolen." *Nachrichten der Academie der Wissenschaften.* Göttingen philologisch-historischen Klasse 6 (1956).

Eadmer. *Historia Novorum in Anglia.* Ed. Martin Rule. Rolls Series 81. London: Longmans, 1884.

Egeria. *Itinerarium Egeriae.* Ed. E. Franceschini and R. Weber. Corpus Christianorum, Series Latina 175. Turnhout: Brepols, 1953.

-----. *Egeria: Diary of a Pilgrimage.* Trans. George Gingras. Ancient Christian Writers: The Works of the Fathers in Translation 38. New York: Newman Press, 1970.

Engelmann, Helmut. *Der griechische Alexanderroman Rezension Γ Buch II.* Beiträge zum klassischen Philologie 12. Meisenheim am Glan: Hain, 1963.

Eusebius. Extracts from *Historia ecclesiastica* in "The Churches of Constantine at Jerusalem." Ed. and trans. John H. Bernard. Library of the Palestine Pilgrims' Text Society 1. London, 1890; repr. New York: AMS Press, 1971.

Feldbusch, Michael. *Der Brief Alexanders an Aristoteles über die Wunder Indiens.* Beiträge zur klassischen Philologie 78. Meisenheim am Glan: Hain, 1976.

"Fermes." *Letter to Hadrian.* Ed. Henri Omont. *Bibliothèque de l'école des Chartres* 74 (1913): 507-15.

Foster, Brian, ed. *The Anglo-Norman Alexander (Le Roman de toute chevalerie) by Thomas of Kent.* London: Anglo-Norman Text Society, 1976.

Fouke Le Fitz Waryn. Ed. E. J. Hathaway, P. T. Ricketts, C. A. Robson, and A. D. Wilshere. Anglo-Norman Text Society 26-28. Oxford: Blackwell, 1975.

Frederick II [Hohenstaufen]. *Historia diplomatica Friderici Secundi.* Ed. J.-L. A.Huillard-Bréholles. 10 vols. Paris: Plon, 1852-61.

-----. *The "Liber Augustalis" or Constitutions of Melfi, Promulgated by the Emperor Frederick II for the Kingdom of Sicily in 1231.* Ed. and trans. James M. Powell. Syracuse: Syracuse Univ. Press, 1971.

-----. *Die Konstitutionen Friedrichs II. von Hohenstaufen für sein Königreich Sizilien.* Ed. Hermann Conrad, Thea von der Lieck-Buyken, and Wolfgang Wagner. Cologne: Böhlau, 1973.

Geoffrey of Monmouth. *The Historia Regum Britanniae of Geoffrey of Monmouth.* Ed. Acton Griscom. London: Longmans, 1929.

-----. *The History of the Kings of Britain.* Trans. Lewis Thorpe. Harmondsworth, Eng.: Penguin, 1983.

Gerald of Wales. *Itinerarium Kambriae et Descriptio Kambriae.* Ed. James F. Dimock. Rolls Series 21[6]. London: Longmans, 1868.

Gildas. *The Ruin of Britain and other works.* Ed. and trans. Michael Winterbottom. London: Phillimore; Totowa, N.J.: Rowman and Littlefield, 1978.

Gosman, Martin, ed. *La Lettre du Prêtre Jean: édition des versions en ancien français et en ancien occitan.* Groningen: Bouma, 1982.

Grotefend, C. L., ed. "Die Edelherren von Boldensele oder Boldensen." *Zeitschrift des historischen Vereins für Niedersachsen.* (1855 [for 1852]): 209-86. (William of Boldensele's *Itinerarium* appears on pp. 237-86.)

Gunderson, Lloyd L. *Alexander's Letter to Aristotle about India.* Beiträge zum klassischen Philologie 110. Meisenheim am Glan: Hain, 1980.

Hayton of Armenia: See Backer.

Henry of Huntingdon. *The History of the English.* Ed. Thomas Arnold. Rolls Series 74. London: Longmans, 1879.

Herodotus. *History of the Persian Wars.* Trans. A. D. Godley. Loeb Classical Library. 1921; repr. Cambridge, Mass.: Harvard Univ. Press, 1971.

-----. *The Persian Wars.* Trans. G. Rawlinson. New York: Modern Library, 1942.

Honorius Augustodunensis. "Honorius Augustodunensis. *Imago mundi.*" Ed. Valerie I. J. Flint. *Archives d'Histoire Doctrinale et Littéraire du Moyen Age* 57 (1982): 7-153.

Hrabanus Maurus. *De Universo.* Ed. J. P. Migne. *PL,* 2nd ser. 111. 1852; repr. Paris, 1964.

Hugh of Strassburg. *Compendium theologicae veritatis.* In vol. 34 of *B. Alberti Magni opera omnia.* Ed. S. C. A. Borgnet. Paris: Ludovicum Vines, 1895.

al-Idrisi. *Opus geographicum: sive "Liber ad eorum delectationem qui terras peragrare studeant."* Naples: Istituto universario orientali di Napoli, 1970.

Innocent IV. *Commentaria Doctissima in Quinque Libros Decretalium.* Turin: apud haeredes Nicolai Beuilaque, 1581.

Isidore of Seville. *Isidori Hispalensis Episcopi Etymologiarum sive Originum Libri XX.* Ed. W. M. Lindsay. 2 vols. 1911; repr. Oxford: Clarendon Press, 1985.

Jacinthus the Presbyter: See Wilkinson.

Jacques de Vitry. *Historia Orientalis.* In vol. 1 of *Gesta Dei per Francos.* Ed. Jacques Bongars. Hanover: Typis Wechelianis apud Ioan. Aubrii, 1611.

Jacques de Vitry. *Historia Iherosolymitana*. Trans. Aubrey Stewart (*The History of Jerusalem A.D. 1180 by Jacques de Vitry*). Library of the Palestine Pilgrims' Text Society. London, 1896; repr. New York: AMS Press, 1971.

-----. *La Traduction de l'Historia Orientalis de Jacques de Vitry*. Ed. Claude Buridant. Paris: Klincksieck, 1986.

Jean le Long: See Backer.

Jerome, St. "Letter XLVI." In vol. 2 of *Saint Jerome: Lettres*. Ed. and trans. Jerome Labourt. Paris: Société d'Éditione "Les Belles Lettres," 1951.

-----. *S. Hieronymi Presbyteri opera*. Pars I, opera Exegetica IV of *Commentariorvm in Hiezechielem libri XIV*. Corpus Christianorum, Series Latina 75. Turnhout: Brepols, 1964.

----- *S. Hieronymi Presbyteri opera*. Pars I, opera Exegetica V of *Commentariorvm in Danielem libri III<IV>*. Corpus Christianorum, Series Latina 75a. Turnhout: Brepols, 1964.

John of Plano Carpini. See Beazley, Dawson, and Wyngaert.

Jordan of Severac. *Mirabilia Descripta: The Wonders of the East*. Ed. and trans. Henry Yule. Hakluyt Society, 1st ser. 31. London, 1863; repr. New York: Franklin, 1970.

Jordanes. *The Gothic History of Jordanes*. Trans. Charles Christopher Mierow. Cambridge, Eng.: Speculum Historiale; New York: Barnes and Noble, 1966.

Josephus. *Complete Works*. Trans. William Whiston. Grand Rapids, Mich.: Kregel, 1960.

Justin. *Justin, Cornelius Nepos, and Europius*. Trans. John Selby Watson. London: George Bell, 1890.

al-Khwarazmi. *Das Kitāb Sūrat al-Ard des Abū Ga'far Muhammad ibn Mūsā al-Huwārizmī.* Ed. Hans von Mžik. Bibliothek Arabischer Historiker und Geographen 3. Leipzig: Harrassowitz, 1926.

Lambert of St. Omer. *Liber floridus colloquium.* Ed. Albert Derolez. Ghent: Story-Scientia, 1973.

Laȝamon. *Brut.* Ed. G. L. Brook and R. F. Leslie. EETS, o.s. 250 and 277. London: Oxford Univ. Press, 1963, 1978 (unfinished).

-----. *Layamon's Brut: A History of the Britons.* Trans. Donald G. Bzdyl. Binghamton, N.Y.: Center for Medieval and Early Renaissance Studies, 1989.

Mandeville, John. *[Itinerarium] Iohannes von Monteuilla, Ritter.* Trans. Otto von Diemeringen. Strassburg: Johann Pruss, 1488.

-----. *The Buke of John Maundeuill. being the Travels of John Mandeville, Knight 1322-56. A Hitherto Unpublished English Version from the Unique Copy (Egerton Ms. 1982) in the British Museum . . . together with the French Text, Notes, and an Introduction.* Ed. George F. Warner. London: Roxburghe Club, 1889 (Egerton version).

-----. *Mandeville's Travels: Texts and Translations.* Ed. Malcolm Letts. 2 vols. Hakluyt Society, 2nd ser. 101-02. London: Hakluyt Society, 1953 (French text in vol. 2).

-----. *Mandeville's Travels.* Ed. M. C. Seymour Oxford: Clarendon Press, 1967 (Cotton version).

-----. *The Metrical Version of Mandeville's Travels.* Ed. M. C. Seymour. EETS, o.s. 269. London: Oxford Univ. Press, 1973 (Metrical version).

-----. *The Travels of Sir John Mandeville: Facsimile of Pynson's Edition of 1496, with an Introduction by Michael Seymour.* Exeter: Univ. of Exeter, 1980 (Defective version).

Mandeville, John. *The Travels of Sir John Mandeville.* Trans. C. W. R. D. Moseley. Harmondsworth, Eng.: Penguin, 1983.

-----. *The Travels of Sir John Mandeville: A Manuscript in the British Library.* Ed. Josef Krása. Trans. Peter Kussi. New York: Braziller, 1983.

Matthew Paris. *Matthew Paris's English History.* Trans. J. A. Giles. New York: Bohn, 1852. Also published as *English History from the Year 1235-1273.* 3 vols. London: George Bell, 1853.

-----. *Chronica Majora.* Ed. Henry Richards Luard. In *Rerum Britannicarum Medii Aevi Scriptores* 57[4] (1877).

Morris, Richard, ed. *Prick of Conscience (Stimulus Conscientiae).* Berlin: Asher, 1864.

Musper, H. Th., ed. *Der Antichrist und die fünfzehn Zeichen: Faksimile-Ausgabe des einzigen erhaltenen chiroxylographischen Blockbuches.* Munich: Prestel-Verlag, 1970.

Nennius. *Nennii Historia Britonum.* Ed. Joseph Stevenson. London: English Historical Society, 1938.

Odoric of Pordenone: See Backer, Wyngaert, and Yule.

Orosius, Paulus. *The Seven Books of History against the Pagans.* Trans. Roy J. Deferrai. The Fathers of the Church 50. Washington, D.C.: Catholic Univ. of America Press, 1964.

-----. *Pauli Orosii Historiarum adversum Paganos libri VII accedit eiusdem liber apologeticus.* Ed. Carl Zangemeister. CSEL 5. Vienna, 1882; repr. New York: Johnson Reprint Corporation, 1966.

-----. *The Old English Orosius.* Ed. Janet Bately. EETS, s.s. 6. London: Oxford Univ. Press, 1980.

Otto of Freising. *The Two Cities: A Chronicle of Universal History to the Year 1146 A.D. by Otto Bishop of Freising.* Ed. Austin P. Evans and Charles Knapp. Trans. Charles Christopher Mierow. New York: Columbia Univ. Press. 1928.

Palestine Pilgrims' Text Society. 14 vols. (with index). London, 1887-1897; repr. New York: AMS Press, 1971.

Paula [and Eustochium]: See St. Jerome and Stewart.

Peter, Archbishop of Russia: See Dörrie.

Pfister, Friedrich. *Der Alexanderroman des Archipresbyter Leo.* Heidelberg: Winter, 1913.

Piacenza Pilgrim: See Wilkinson.

Piramus, Denis. *La Vie Seint Edmund le Rei.* Ed. Hilding Kjellman. Göteborg: Elanders, 1935.

Pliny. *Natural History.* Trans. H. Rackham. Loeb Classical Library. 1938; repr. Cambridge, Mass.: Harvard Univ. Press, 1942.

Prester John, Letter of: See Gosman.

Pseudo-Callisthenes. *Historia Fabulosa.* Ed. Karl Müller. In *Arriani Anabasis et India.* Ed. Fr. Dubner. 1846; repr. Paris: Ambrusia Firmin-Didot, 1877.

-----. *Historia Alexandri Magni (Pseudo-Callisthenes).* Trans. W. G. Kroll. 2nd ed. Berlin: Weidmann, 1928.

-----. *The Life of Alexander of Macedon.* Trans E. H. Haight. Loeb Classical Library. New York: Longmans, Green, 1955.

-----. *History of Alexander the Great, being the Syriac version of the Pseudo-Callisthenes.* Trans. Ernest A. Wallis Budge. Cambridge, Eng., 1889; repr. Amsterdam: Philo Press, 1976.

Pseudo-Methodius. *Methodii Revelationes.* Ed. Ernst Sackur. In *Sibyllinische Texte und Forschungen.* Halle: Niemeyer, 1898.

Ptolemy, Claudius. *Claudii Ptolemaei Geographia.* Ed. C. F. A. Nobbe. Leipzig, 1843-45; repr. Hildesheim: Olms, 1966.

-----. *Geography of Claudius Ptolemy.* Trans. Edward L. Stevenson. New York: New York Public Library, 1932.

Rabanus Maurus: See Hrabanus Maurus.

Sacrobosco, Johannes. *The Sphere of Sacrobosco and Its Commentators.* Ed. and trans. Lynn Thorndike. Chicago: Univ. of Chicago Press, 1949.

Simon de Saint-Quentin. *Historia Tartarorum.* In *Simon de Saint-Quentin: Histoire des Tartares.* Ed. Jean Richard. Paris: Libraire Orientaliste Paul Geuthner, 1965.

Skelton, R. A., Thomas E. Marston, and George D. Painter. *The Vinland Map and the Tartar Relation.* New Haven: Yale Univ. Press, 1965.

Smithers, G. V., ed. *Kyng Alisaunder.* EETS, o.s. 227. London: Oxford Univ. Press, 1952.

Solinus. *C. Iulii Solini Collectanea Rerum Memorabilium.* Ed. Theodor Mommsen. 1895; 3rd ed., Berlin: Weidmann, 1958.

-----. *The Excellent and Pleasant Worke Collectanea Rerum Memorabilium.* Ed. George Kish. Gainesville, Fla.: Univ. of Florida Press, 1955. (A facsimile of Arthur Golding's English translation of 1587.)

Solomon of Basra. *Book of the Bee.* Vol. 1, part 2 of *Anecdota Oxoniensia.* Trans. and ed. Ernest A. Wallis Budge. Oxford: Clarendon Press, 1886.

Stewart, Audrey, trans. "The Letter of Paula and Eustochium to Marcella about the Holy Places." Library of the Palestine Pilgrims' Text Society 1. London, 1889; repr. New York: AMS Press, 1971.

Strabo. *The Geography of Strabo.* Ed. and trans. Horace Leonard Jones. Loeb Classical Library. London: Heinemann; New York: Putnam, 1928.

Thomas of Cantimpré. *Eine altfranzösische moralisierende Bearbeitung des Liber de Monstruosis Hominibus Orientis aus Thomas von Cantimpré, De naturis rerum nach der einzigen Handschrift (Paris, Bibl. Nat. fr. 15106).* Ed. Alfons Hilka. In *Abhandlungen der Gesellschaft der Wissenschaften zu Göttingen.* Philologisch-historische Klasse, 3rd ser. 7. Berlin: Wiedmann, 1933.

-----. *Thomas Cantimpratensis Liber de natura rerum.* Ed. H. Boese. 2 vols. Berlin: de Gruyter, 1973.

Thomas of Kent. *The Anglo-Norman Alexander (Le Roman de toute chevalerie) by Thomas of Kent.* Ed. Brian Foster. 2 vols. London: Anglo Norman Text Society, 1976.

Trevisa, John. *On the Properties of Things: John Trevisa's Translation of Bartholomaeus Anglicus De Proprietatibus Rerum.* Gen. ed. M. C. Seymour. Oxford: Clarendon Press, 1975.

Väänänen, Veikko, ed. "Le fabliau du Cocagne." *Neuphilologische Mitteilungen* 4 (1957): 3-36.

Velislai Biblia Picta. Ed. Karel Stejskal. Prague: Pragopress, 1970.

Westrem, Scott Douglas. "A Critical Edition of Johannes Witte de Hese's *Itinerarius*, the Middle Dutch Text, an English Translation, and Commentary, together with an Introduction to European Accounts of Travel to the East (1240-1400)." Ph.D. diss., Northwestern Univ., 1985.

Wilkinson, John. *Jerusalem Pilgrims before the Crusades.* Warminster, Eng.: Aris and Phillips, 1977.

William of Boldensele: See Grotefend.

William of Malmesbury. *De Gestis Regum Anglorum.* Ed. William Stubbs. Rolls Series 90. London: Longmans, 1887.

William of Rubruck. See Beazley, Dawson, and Wyngaert.

Wyngaert, Anastasius van den, ed. *Itinera et Relationes Fratrum Minorum Saeculi XIII et XIV.* Vol. 1 of *Sinica Franciscana.* Quaracchi-Florence: Collegium S. Bonaventurae, 1929.

Yule, Henry, ed. and trans. *Cathay and the Way Thither, Being a Collection of Medieval Notices of China.* 2nd ed. Rev. by Henri Cordier. 4 vols. Hakluyt Society, 2nd ser. 33, 37, 38, 41. London: Cambridge Univ. Press, 1913-16.

Secondary Sources

Abulafia, David. *Frederick II, A Medieval Emperor.* London: Penguin, 1988.

Ackermann, E. M. "Das Schlaraffenland in German Literature and Folksong." Ph.D. diss., Univ. of Chicago, 1944.

Aerts, W. J., E. R. Smits, and J. B. Voorbij, ed. *Vincent of Beauvais and Alexander the Great.* Groningen: Forsten, 1986.

Aerts, W. J., J. M. Hermans, and E. Visser, ed. *Alexander the Great in the Middle Ages. Ten Studies on the Last Days of Alexander in Literary and Historical Writing.* Symposium Interfacultaire Werkgroep Mediaevistiek, Groningen, 12-15 October 1977. Nijmegen: Alfa, 1978.

Alexander, David. "Dante and the Form of the Land." *Annals of the Association of American Geographers* 76[1] (1986): 38-49.

Anderson, Andrew Runni. "Alexander at the Caspian Gates." *Transactions of the American Philological Association* 59 (1928): 130-63.

-----. "The Arabic *History of Dulcarnian* and the Ethiopian *History of Alexander.*" *Speculum* 6 (1931): 434-45.

-----. *Alexander's Gate, Gog and Magog, and the Inclosed Nations.* Cambridge, Mass.: Mediaeval Academy of America, 1932.

Anderson, Benedict. *Imagined Communities: Reflections on the Origin and Spread of Nationalism.* London: Verso, 1983.

Angeli, Giovanna. *Il mondo rovesciato.* Rome: Bulzoni, 1977.

Arens, William. *The Man-Eating Myth: Anthropology and Anthropophagy.* Oxford: Oxford Univ. Press, 1979.

Arentzen, Jörg-Geerd. *Imago Mundi Cartographica: Studien zur Bildlichkeit mittelalterlicher Welt- und Ökumenekarten unter besonderer Berücksichtigung des Zusammenwirkens von Text und Bild.* Münstersche Mittelalter-Schriften 53. Munich: Fink, 1984.

Auerbach, Erich. *Mimesis: The Representation of Reality in Western Literature.* Trans. Willard R. Trask. 1953; repr. Princeton: Princeton Univ. Press, 1968.

-----. *Literary Language and its Public in Late Latin Antiquity and in the Middle Ages.* Trans. Ralph Mannheim. Bollingen Series 74. Princeton: Princeton Univ. Press, 1965.

Ayalon, David. "The Great Yasa of Chingiz-Khan: A Reexamination." *Studia Islamica* 34 (1971): 97-140(A) and 150-180(B).

Bakhtin, Mikhail. *Rabelais and his World.* Cambridge, Mass.: MIT Press, 1968.

Barker, Ernest. "Dante and the Last Voyage of Ulysses." In *Traditions of Civility.* Cambridge, Eng.: Cambridge Univ. Press, 1948.

Bataillon, Marcel. "The Idea of the Discovery of America Among the Spaniards of the Sixteenth Century." In *Spain in the Fifteenth Century, 1369-1516*. Ed. [John] Roger [Loxdale] Highfield. Trans. Frances M. López-Morillas. London: Macmillan, 1972. 426-64.

Baudet, Henri. *Paradise on Earth: Some Thoughts on European Images of Non-European Man*. Trans. Elizabeth Wentholt. New Haven: Yale Univ. Press, 1965.

Beazley, C. Raymond. *The Dawn of Modern Geography*. 3 vols. London, 1897-1903; repr. New York: Peter Smith, 1949.

Bennett, Josephine Waters. *The Rediscovery of Sir John Mandeville*. The Modern Language Association of America Monograph Series 19. New York: MLA, 1954.

Berg, B. "An Early Source of the Alexander Romance." *Greek, Roman and Byzantine Studies* 14 (1973).

Bernheimer, Richard. *Wild Men in the Middle Ages*. Cambridge, Mass.: Harvard Univ. Press, 1952.

Bevan, W. L. and H. W. Phillott. *Mediaeval Geography: An Essay in Illustration of the Hereford Mappa Mundi*. London, 1873; repr. Amsterdam: Meridian, 1969.

Bezzola, G. A. *Die Mongolen in abendländischer Sicht (1220-1270): Ein Beitrag zur Frage der Völkerbegegnungen*. Bern: Francke, 1974.

Bianciotto, Gabriel and Michel Salvat, ed. *Epopée animale, fable, fabliau. Actes du IVe Colloque de la Société Internationale Renardienne, Evreux, 7-11 sept., 1981*. Publications de l'Université de Rouen 83. Paris: Presses Universitaires de France, 1984.

Biesterfeld, Wolfgang and Marlis H. Haase. "The Land of Cokkaygne: eine englische Version des Märchens vom Schlaraffenland." *Fabula* 25 (1984): 76-82.

Boitani, Piero. *The Tragic and the Sublime in Medieval Literature.* Cambridge, Eng.: Cambridge Univ. Press, 1989.

Boner, Georg. "Ueber den Dominikanertheologen Hugo von Strassburg." *Archivium Fratrum Praedicatorum* 24 (1954): 269-86.

Boon, James A. *Other Tribes, Other Scribes: Symbolic Anthropology in the Comparative Study of Cultures, Histories, Religions, and Texts.* Cambridge, Eng.: Cambridge Univ. Press, 1962.

Bosco, Umberto. "La 'follia' di Dante." In *Dante vicino.* Rome: Salvatore Sciascia Editore, 1966.

Bosco, Umberto and Giovanni Reggio. Commentary on *Dante Alighieri, La Divina Commedia.* Florence: Le Monnier, 1979.

Bousset, Wilhelm. *The Antichrist Legend.* Trans. A. H. Keane. London: Hutchinson, 1896.

Bovenschen, Albert. "Untersuchungen über Johann von Mandeville und die Quellen seiner Reisebeschreibung." *Zeitschrift der Gesellschaft für Erdkunde zu Berlin* 23 (1888): 177-306.

Boyde, Patrick. "Land and Sea." In *Dante Philomythes and Philosopher.* Cambridge, Eng.: Cambridge Univ. Press, 1981.

Brandin, Louis. "Nouvelles Recherches sur *Fouke Fitz Warin.*" *Romania* 55 (1929): 17-44.

Brincken, Anna Dorothee von den. "Mappa mundi und Chronographia." *Deutsches Archiv für die Erforschung des Mittelalters* 24 (1968): 118-86.

-----. "Die Mongolen im Weltbild der Lateinen um die Mitte des 13. Jahrhunderts unter besonderer Berücksichtigung des 'Speculum Historiale' des Vincenz von Beauvais OP." *Archiv für Kulturgeschichte* 57 (1975): 117-40.

----- "Gog und Magog." In *Die Mongolen.* Ed. W. Heissing and Cl. C. Muller. Innsbruck: Pinguin und Umschau, 1989.

Brundage, James A. *Medieval Canon Law and the Crusader*. Madison: Univ. of Wisconsin Press, 1969.

Buyken, Thea. "Über das Prooemium der Constitutionen von Melfi." *Revista Portuguesa de História* 14 (1941): 161-76.

Campbell, Mary B. *The Witness and the Other World: Exotic European Travel Writing, 400-1600*. Ithaca: Cornell Univ. Press, 1988.

Caprotti, Ermino. "Animali Fantastici in Plinio." In *Plinio e la natura*. Ed. A. Roncoroni. Como: Camera di commercio, industria, artigianato e agricoltura di Como, 1982.

Cary, George. *The Medieval Alexander*. 1956; repr. Cambridge, Eng.: Cambridge Univ. Press, 1967.

Casson, Lionel. *Travel in the Ancient World*. London: Allen and Unwin, 1974.

Céard, Jean. *La Nature et les Prodiges*. Travaux d'Humanisme et Renaissance 158. Geneva: Droz, 1977.

Chaunu, Pierre. *European Expansion in the Later Middle Ages*. Trans. Katherine Bertram. Europe in the Middle Ages Selected Studies 10. Amsterdam: North Holland Publishing, 1979.

Ch'en, Paul Heng-chao. *Chinese Legal Tradition Under the Mongols: The Code of 1291 as Reconstructed*. Princeton: Princeton Univ. Press, 1979.

Cioranescu, A. "Utopie: Cocagne et age d'or." *Diogène* 75 (1971): 86-123.

Cocchiara, Guiseppe. *Il paese di cuccagna e altri studi di folklore*. Turin: Boringhieri, 1980.

-----. *Il mondo alla rovescia*. Turin: Boringhieri, 1981.

Cohen, Gustav. *Receuil de farces françaises inédites du XVème siècle.* Cambridge, Mass.: The Medieval Academy of America, 1949.

Coli, Edoardo. *Il paradiso terrestra dantesco.* Florence: Carnesecchi, 1897.

Connell, Charles W. "Western Views of the Origins of the 'Tartars': an Example of the Influence of Myth in the Second Half of the Thirteenth Century." *Journal of Medieval and Renaissance Studies* 3 (1973): 115-37.

Cosman, Madeleine Pelner, ed. *Machot's World: Science and Art in the Fourteenth Century.* New York: New York Academy of Sciences, 1978.

Cox, Edward G. *A Reference Guide to the History of Travel.* 3 vols. University of Washington Publications in Language and Literature 9-11. Seattle: Univ. of Washington Press, 1938.

Crane, Susan. *Insular Romance: Politics, Faith, and Culture in Anglo-Norman and Middle English Literature.* Berkeley: Univ. of California Press, 1986.

Crosby, Alfred W. *The Columbian Exchange: Biological and Cultural Consequences of 1492.* Westport, Conn.: Greenwood, 1972.

-----. *Ecological Imperialism: The Biological Expansion of Europe, 900-1900.* Cambridge, Eng.: Cambridge Univ. Press, 1986.

Cross, S. H. "The Earliest Allusion in Slavic Literature to the Revelations of Pseudo-Methodius." *Speculum* 4 (1929): 329-39.

Curtius, Ernst Robert. *European Literature and the Latin Middle Ages.* Trans. Willard R. Trask, Bollingen Series 36. New York, 1953; repr. Princeton: Princeton Univ. Press, 1973.

-----. *Essays on European Literature.* Trans. Michael Kowal. Princeton: Princeton Univ. Press, 1973.

Czégledy, K. "Kaukázusi Hunok, Kaukázusi Avarok" [Caucasian Huns, Caucasian Avars]. *Antik Tanulmányok* 2 (1955): 121-40.

-----. "The Syriac Legend concerning Alexander the Great." *Acta Orientalia* 7 (1957): 231-49.

Davidson, H. R. Ellis. *The Viking Road to Byzantium.* London: Allen and Unwin, 1976.

De Caluwé-Dur, Juliette. "L'anti-Paradis du pays du Cocagne." *Marche romane: Mélanges de philologie et de littératures romanes offerts à Jeanne Wathelet Willem.* Liège: Cahiers de l'A.R.U., 1978. 103-23.

Demaray, John G., *The Invention of Dante's* Commedia. New Haven: Yale Univ. Press, 1974.

Demerson, Guy. "Cocagne, utopie populaire?" *Revue Belge de Philologie et d'Histoire* 59 (1981): 529-53.

De Poerck, Guy. "La tradition manuscrite des 'Voyages' de Jean de Mandeville." *Romanica Gandensia* 4 (1955): 125-58.

Dihle, Albrecht. *Antike und Orient.* Heidelberg: Winter, 1984.

Donoghue, Daniel. "Laȝamon's Ambivalence." *Speculum* 65 (1990): 537-63.

Dudley, Edward and Maximillian E. Novak, ed. *The Wild Man Within: An Image in Western Thought from the Renaissance to Romanticism.* Pittsburgh: Univ. of Pittsburgh Press, 1972.

Ehrenberg, Victor. *Alexander and the Greeks.* Oxford: Blackwell, 1938.

Emmerson, Richard K. *Antichrist in the Middle Ages: A Study of Medieval Apocalypticism, Art, and Literature.* Seattle: Univ. of Washington Press, 1981.

Fabian, Johannes. *Time and the Other: How Anthropology Makes its Object.* New York: Columbia Univ. Press, 1983.

Fernández-Armesto, Felipe. *Before Columbus: Exploration and Colonization from the Mediterranean to the Atlantic, 1229-1492.* Philadelphia: Univ. of Pennsylvania Press, 1987.

Ferrand, Gabriel. *Relations de voyages et textes géographiques arabes, persans et turks relatifs à l'Extréme-Orient du XIIIe au XVIIIe siècles.* Paris: Leroux, 1916.

Festugière, André-Jean. "Trois rencontres entre la Grèce et l'Inde." *Revue de l'histoire des réligions* (1942-43): 32-57.

-----. "Grecs et sages orientaux." *Revue de l'histoire des réligions* (1945): 29-41.

Filliozat, Jean. "La valeur des connaissances greco-romaines sur l'Inde." *Journal des Savants* (1981): 97-136.

Finucare, Ronald C. *Miracles and Pilgrims: Popular Beliefs in Medieval England.* Totowa, N.J.: Rowman and Littlefield, 1977.

Flint, Valerie I. J. "The *Historia Regum Britanniae* of Geoffrey of Monmouth: Parody and Its Purpose. A Suggestion." *Speculum* 54 (1979): 447-68.

-----. "Monsters and the Antipodes in the Early Middle Ages and Enlightenment." *Viator* 13 (1984): 65-80.

Francis, E. A. "The Background to 'Fulk FitzWarin'." *Studies in Medieval French Presented to Alfred Ewert.* Oxford: Clarendon Press, 1961. 322-27.

Freccero, John. *Dante, The Poetics of Conversion.* Ed. Rachel Jacoff. Cambridge, Mass.: Harvard Univ. Press, 1986.

Friedman, John Block. *The Monstrous Races in Medieval Art and Thought.* Cambridge, Mass.: Harvard Univ. Press, 1981.

Garbáty, T. J. "The Land of Cokayne in the Kildare MS." *Franziskanische Studien* 45 (1963): 139-53.

Ginzburg, Carlo. *The Cheese and the Worms: The Cosmos of a Sixteenth-Century Miller.* Trans. John and Anne Tedeschi. 1980; repr. Harmondsworth, Eng.: Penguin, 1982.

Gmelin, Hermann. *Die Göttliche Komödie.* Stuttgart: Ernst Klett, 1949-57.

Goffart, Walter. *The Narrators of Barbarian History (A.D. 550-800).* Princeton: Princeton Univ. Press, 1988.

Goldstein, Thomas. *The Dawn of Modern Science: From the Arabs to Leonardo da Vinci.* Boston: Houghton Mifflin, 1980.

Goossens, Jan and Timothy Sodmann. *Third International Beast Epic, Fable and Fabliau Colloquium, Münster 1979: Proceedings.* Cologne: Böhlau, 1981.

Gotthelf, Allan and James G. Lennox. *Philosophical Issues in Aristotle's Biology.* New York: Cambridge Univ. Press, 1987.

deGraaf, K. *Alexander de Grote in de Spiegel Historiael.* Nijmegen: Alfa, 1983.

Granet, Marcel. *Chinese Civilization.* 1930; repr. New York: Barnes and Noble, 1957.

Gransden, Antonia. *Historical Writing in England c. 550 to c. 1307.* Ithaca: Cornell Univ. Press, 1974.

Grant, Edward. *A Source Book in Medieval Science.* Cambridge, Mass.: Harvard Univ. Press, 1974.

Gregor, Helmut. *Das Indienbild des Abendlandes (bis zum Ende des 13. Jahrhunderts).* Wiener Dissertationen aus dem Gebiete der Geschichte 4. Vienna: Geyer, 1964.

Gumilev, L. N. *Searches for an Imaginary Kingdom: The Legend and Kingdom of Prester John.* Trans. R. E. F. Smith. Cambridge, Eng.: Cambridge Univ. Press, 1987. (Original Russian version published in 1970.)

Guzman, Gregory G. "Simon of Saint-Quentin and the Dominican Mission to the Mongol Baiju: A Reappraisal." *Speculum* 46 (1971): 232-49.

-----. "Simon of Saint-Quentin as Historian of the Mongols and Seljuk Turks." *Medievalia et Humanistica*, n.s. 3 (1972): 155-78.

-----. "The Encyclopedist Vincent of Beauvais and His Mongol Extracts from John of Plano Carpini and Simon of Saint-Quentin." *Speculum* 49 (1974): 287-307.

-----. "Were the Barbarians a Negative or Positive Factor in Ancient and Medieval History?" *The Historian* 50 (1988): 558-72.

Hahn, Thomas. "Indians East and West: Primitivism and Savagery in English Discovery Narratives of the Sixteenth Century." *Journal of Medieval and Renaissance Studies* 8 (1978): 77-114.

-----. "The Indian Tradition in Western Medieval Intellectual History." *Viator* 9 (1978): 213-34.

Hanna, Ralph, III. "Mandeville." In *Middle English Prose: A Critical Guide to Major Authors and Genres.* Ed. A. S. G. Edwards. New Brunswick, N.J.: Rutgers Univ. Press, 1984. 121-32.

Hanning, Robert W. *The Vision of History in Early Britain.* New York: Columbia Univ. Press, 1966.

Harley, J. B. and David Woodward, ed. *Cartography in Prehistoric, Ancient, and Medieval Europe and the Mediterranean.* Vol. 1 of *The History of Cartography.* Chicago: Univ. of Chicago Press, 1987.

Haskins, Charles H. *Studies in the History of Medieval Science.* 1924; repr. New York: Ungar, 1960.

Hawkins, Peter. "Dante's *Paradiso* and the Dialectic of Ineffability." In *Ineffability, Naming the Unnamable from Dante to Beckett.* Ed. Peter S. Hawkins and Anne H. Schotter. New York: AMS Press, 1984)

Hay, Denys. *Europe: The Emergence of an Idea.* Rev. ed. Edinburgh: Edinburgh Univ. Press, 1968.

Heissing, W. and Cl. C. Muller. *Die Mongolen.* Innsbruck: Pinguin und Umschau, 1989.

Hennig, Richard. *Terrae Incognitae: Eine Zusammenstellung und kritische Bewertung der wichtigsten Vorcolumbischen Entdeckungsreisen an Hand der darüber vorliegenden Originalberichte.* 4 vols. 2nd ed. Leiden: Brill, 1944-56.

Higgins, Iain. "The World of a Book of the World: *Mandeville's Travels* in Middle English (British Library MS Cotton Titus C. xvi)." Ph.D. diss., Harvard Univ., 1988.

Hodgen, Margaret. *Early Anthropology in the Sixteenth and Seventeenth Centuries.* 1964; repr. Philadelphia: Univ. of Pennsylvania Press, 1971.

Hollander, Robert. *The Allegory of Dante's 'Commedia.'* Princeton: Princeton Univ. Press, 1968.

Honigmann, Ernst. *Die sieben Klimata und die πολεις επισεμοι.* Heidelberg: Winter, 1929.

Hourani, George Fadlo. *Arab Seafaring in the Indian Ocean in Ancient and Early Medieval Times.* Princeton: Princeton Univ. Press, 1951.

Howard, Donald R. *The Three Temptations: Medieval Man in Search of the World.* Princeton: Princeton Univ. Press, 1966.

-----. "The World of Mandeville's Travels." *Yearbook of English Studies* 1 (1971): 1-17.

Howard, Donald R. *Writers and Pilgrims: Medieval Pilgrimage Narratives and Their Posterity.* Berkeley: Univ. of California Press, 1980.

Howe, Nicholas, ed. *The Old English Catalogue Poems.* Anglistica 23. Copenhagen: Rosenkilde and Bagger, 1985.

Hunt, E. D. *Holy Land Pilgrimage in the Later Roman Empire, A.D. 312-460.* Oxford: Clarendon Press, 1982.

Hunt, Tony. "La parodie médiévale: le cas d'*Aucassin et Nicolette.*" *Romania* 101 (1980): 433-81.

Husband, Timothy B. *The Wild Man: Medieval Myth and Symbolism.* New York: Metropolitan Museum of Art, 1980.

Ijsewijn, Josef and Jacques Paquet, ed. *The Universities of the Late Middle Ages.* Mediaevalia Lovaniensa, 1st ser. 6. Louvain: Louvain Univ. Press, 1978.

Jeanmarie, J. "Le règne de la Femme des derniers jours et le rajeunissement du monde." In *Mélanges Franz Cumont.* Brussels: Université libre de Bruxelles, 1936. 297-304.

Kantorowicz, Ernst H. "The Problem of Medieval World Unity." In *Selected Studies.* Locust Valley, N. Y.: J. J. Augustin, 1965. 76-81. Originally published in the *Annual Report of the American Historical Association for 1942* 3 (1944): 31-37.

Kappler, Claude. *Monstres, démons et merveilles à la fin du Moyen Age.* Paris: Payot, 1980.

Kedar, Benjamin Z. *Crusade and Mission: European Approaches toward the Muslims.* 1984; repr. Princeton: Princeton Univ. Press, 1988.

Kimble, George H. T. *Geography in the Middle Ages.* London: Methuen, 1938.

King, David A. and Mary Helen Kennedy, ed. *Studies in the Islamic Exact Sciences [Symposium] by E. S. Kennedy, Colleagues and Former Students.* N.p.: American University of Beirut, 1983.

Kolata, Gina. "Are the Horrors of Cannibalism Fact—or Fiction?" *Smithsonian* 17 (1987): 150-70.

Kolodny, Annette. *The Lay of the Land: Metaphor as Experience and History in American Life and Letters.* Chapel Hill: Univ. of North Carolina Press, 1975.

Kosto, Adam. "The Other Amazons: East/West Interaction of the Myth of the Amazons in the Middle Ages." Senior honors essay in Humanities, Yale University, 1989.

Krachkovskii, I. Iu. *Arabskaia geograficheskaia literatura.* Vol. 4 of *Izbrannye sochineniia.* Moscow-Leningrad: Akademiia Nauk SSSR, 1957.

Kramers, J. H. "La littérature géographique classique des musulmans." In *Analecta Orientalia.* Ed. J. H. Kramers. Leiden: Brill, 1954.

Kubbel', L. E. and V. V. Matveev. *Arabskie istochniki VII-X vekov.* Moscow: Akademiia Nauk SSSR, 1960.

Labarge, Margaret Wade. *Medieval Travellers.* New York: Norton, 1983.

Lach, Donald. *Asia in the Making of Europe.* 2 vols. in 5. Chicago: Univ. of Chicago Press, 1965-77.

Ladner, Gerhart B. *"Homo Viator:* Mediaeval Ideas on Alienation and Order." *Speculum* 42 (1967): 233-59.

Leake, Jane A. *The Geats of Beowulf.* Madison: Univ. of Wisconsin Press, 1967.

Leckie, R. William, Jr. *The Passage of Dominion: Geoffrey of Monmouth and the Periodization of Insular History in the Twelfth Century.* Toronto: Univ. of Toronto Press, 1981.

Legge, M. Dominica. *Anglo-Norman and Its Backgrounds.* Oxford: Clarendon Press, 1963.

Le Goff, Jacques. *The Birth of Purgatory.* Trans. Arthur Goldhammer. Chicago: Univ. of Chicago Press, 1984. (Original French version published in 1981.)

Lejeune, Rita. "Jean de Mandeville et les Liégeois." In *Mélanges de linguistique romane et de philologie médiévale offerts à Maurice Delbouille.* Gembloux: J. Duculot, 1964. 2:409-37.

Le Saux, Francoise H. M. *Laȝamon's Brut: The Poem and Its Sources.* Cambridge, Eng.: D. S. Brewer, 1989.

Letts, Malcolm. *Sir John Mandeville: The Man and His Book.* London: Batchworth, 1949.

Lewis, Archibald R. *Nomads and Crusaders A.D. 1000-1368.* Bloomington, Ind.: Indiana Univ. Press, 1988.

Lewis, Bernard. *The Muslim Discovery of Europe.* New York: Norton, 1982.

Lewis, C. S. *The Discarded Image: An Introduction to Medieval and Renaissance Literature.* 1964; repr. Cambridge, Eng.: Cambridge Univ. Press, 1967.

Lewis, Suzanne. *The Art of Matthew Paris in the Chronica Majora.* Berkeley: Univ. of California Press, 1987.

Lindberg, David C., ed. *Science in the Middle Ages.* Chicago: Univ. of Chicago Press, 1978.

Lomax, Derek W. *The Reconquest of Spain.* London: Longman, 1978.

Magie, David. *Roman Rule in Asia Minor to the End of the Third Century after Christ.* Princeton: Princeton Univ. Press, 1950.

Manuel, Frank E. and Fritzie P. Manuel. "Sketch for a Natural History of Paradise." *Daedalus* 101 (1972): 83-127.

Mayer, Hans Eberhard. *The Crusades.* 2nd ed. Oxford: Oxford Univ. Press, 1988.

Mazzotta, Guiseppe. *Dante, Poet of the Desert.* Princeton: Princeton Univ. Press, 1979.

McKeon, Richard. "Rhetoric in the Middle Ages." *Speculum* 17 (1942): 1-32.

Merchant, Carolyn. *The Death of Nature: Women, Ecology and the Scientific Revolution.* San Francisco: Harper and Row, 1980.

Merkelbach, Reinhold. *Die Quellen des griechischen Alexanderromans.* 2nd ed. Munich: Beck, 1977.

Metlitzki, Dorothee. *The Matter of Araby in Medieval England.* New Haven: Yale Univ. Press, 1977.

Michael, Ian. "Typological Problems in Medieval Alexander Literature: The Enclosure of Gog and Magog." See Peter Noble, Lucie Polak, and Claire Isoz.

Miller, Konrad. *Mappaemundi: die ältesten Weltkarten.* Stuttgart: Roth, 1896.

-----. *Die Ebstorfkarte, eine Weltkarte aus dem 13. Jahrhundert.* Stuttgart: Roth, 1900.

Moore, Edward. *Studies in Dante, Third Series.* Oxford: Clarendon Press, 1903.

Morgan, D. O. "The Great Yasa of Chinguiz Khan and Mongol Law in the Il Kanate." *Bulletin of the School of Oriental and African Studies* 49 (1986): 163-76.

Morrall, Eric John. "Der Islam und Muhammad im späten Mittelalter: Beobachtungen zu Michel Velsers Mandeville-Übersetzung und Michael Christans Version der 'Epistola ad Mahumetem' des Papst Pius II." In *Geschichtsbewusstsein in der deutschen Literatur des Mittelalters*. Ed. Christoph Gerhardt, Nigel F. Palmer, and Burghart Wachinger. Tübinger Colloquium 1983. Tübingen: Max Niemeyer, 1985. 147-61.

Moseley, C. W. R. D. "The Metamorphosis of Sir John Mandeville." *Yearbook of English Studies* 4 (1974): 5-25.

Muldoon, James. "Papal Responsibility for the Infidel: Another Look at Alexander VI's *Inter Caetera*." *Catholic Historical Review* 64 (1978): 168-84.

-----. *Popes, Lawyers, and Infidels: The Church and the Non-Christian World 1250-1550*. Philadelphia: Univ. of Pennsylvania Press, 1979.

Müller-Frauereuth, Karl. *Die deutschen Lügendichtungen bis auf Münchhausen*. Halle, 1881; repr. Hildesheim: Olms, 1965.

Mžik, Hans von. "Afrika nach der arabischen Bearbeitung der Γεωγραφική ὑφήγησις des Claudius Ptolemaeus von Muhammad ibn Musa al-Hwarizmi." *Wiener Zeitschrift fur die Kunde des Morgenlandes* 43 (1916).

Nallino, Carlo A. "Al-Huwarizmi e il suo rifacimento della geografia di Tolomeo." *Raccolta di scritti editi e inediti*. Rome, 1944. 5:458-532.

Nardi, Bruno. "Intorno al sito del Purgatorio e al mito dantesco dell' Eden." In *Saggi di Filosofia dantesca*. Milan: Società Anonima Editrice Dante Alighieri, 1930. (First published in 1922.)

-----. *La Caduta di Lucifero e l'autenticità della 'Quaestio de Aqua et Terra'*. Turin: Società Editrice Internazionale, 1959.

-----. "La Tragedia d'Ulisse." In *Dante e la cultura medioevale*. Ed. Paolo Mazzantini. Bari: Laterza, 1983.

Nebenzahl, Kenneth. *Atlas of Columbus and the Great Discoveries.* Chicago: Rand McNally, 1990.

Noble, Peter, Lucie Polak, and Claire Isoz, ed. *The Medieval Alexander Legend and Romance Epic: Essays in Honour of David J. A. Ross.* Millwood, N.Y.: Kraus, 1982.

O'Gorman, Edmundo. *The Invention of America.* Bloomington, Ind.: Indiana Univ. Press, 1961. (Original Spanish version published in 1958.)

Olschki, Leonardo. *Marco Polo's Precursors.* Baltimore: The Johns Hopkins Univ. Press, 1943.

Ousterhout, Robert, ed. *The Blessings of Pilgrimage.* Illinois Byzantine Series 1. Urbana, Ill.: Univ. of Illinois Press, 1990.

Padoan, Giorgio. "Ulisse 'Fandi Fictor' e le vie della sapienza." *Studi danteschi* 37 (1960): 21-61.

Patch, Howard R. *The Other World, According to Descriptions in Medieval Literature.* Cambridge, Mass., 1950; repr. New York: Octagon, 1970.

Patterson, Lee. *Negotiating the Past: The Historical Understanding of Medieval Literature.* Madison: Univ. of Wisconsin Press, 1987.

Payen, Jean-Charles. "Fabliaux et Cocagne. Abondance et fête charnelle dans les contes plaisants du XIIe et du XIIIe siècles." See Gabriel Bianciotto and Michel Salvat.

Pearson, Lionel. *The Lost Histories of Alexander the Great.* New York: American Philological Association, 1960.

Pelliot, Paul. "Les Mongols et la Papauté." *Revue de l'Orient Chrétien,* 3rd ser. 23 (1922): 3-30; 24 (1924): 225-335; 28 (1931): 3-84.

Pennington, Kenneth J. "Bartolome de Las Casas and the Tradition of Medieval Law." *Church History* 39 (1970): 149-61.

Penrose, Boies. *Travel and Discovery in the Early Renaissance.* Cambridge, Mass., 1955; repr. New York: Atheneum, 1962.

Pédech, Paul. "Le paysage chez les historiens d'Alexandre." *Quaderni di Storia* 3 (1977).

Pfister, Friedrich. *Der Alexanderroman des Archipresbyter Leo.* Heidelberg: Winter, 1913.

-----. "Studien zum Alexanderroman." *Würzburger Jahrbücher* 1 (1946): 29-66.

-----. *Kleine Schriften zum Alexanderroman.* Beiträge zur klassischen Philologie 61. Meisenheim am Glan: Hain, 1976.

Phillips, J. R. S. *The Medieval Expansion of Europe.* Oxford: Oxford Univ. Press, 1988.

Poesch, Jessie Jean. "Antichrist Imagery in Anglo-Norman Apocalypse Manuscripts." Ph.D. diss., Univ. of Pennsylvania, 1966.

Rachewiltz, Igor de. *Papal Envoys to the Great Khans.* Stanford: Stanford Univ. Press, 1971.

-----. *Prester John and Europe's Discovery of East Asia.* The Thirty-Second George Ernest Morrison Lecture in Ethnology. Canberra: Australian National Univ. Press, 1972.

Rahner, Hugo. "Odysseus at the Mast." *Greek Myths and Christian Mystery.* Trans. Brian Battershaw. New York: Harper and Row, 1971.

Randall, John Herman, Jr. *Aristotle.* New York: Columbia Univ. Press, 1960.

Regier, Mary H. "Kennedy's Geographical Tables of Medieval Islam: An Exploratory Statistical Analysis." In *From Deferent to Equant: A Volume of Studies in the History of Science in the Ancient and Medieval Near East in Honor of E. S. Kennedy.* New York: New York Academy of Sciences, 1987.

Reinink, G. J. "Pseudo-Methodius und die Legende vom Römischen Endkaiser." In *The Use and Abuse of Eschatology in the Middle Ages*. Ed. W. Verbeke, D. Verhelst, and A. Welkenhuysen. Leuven: Leuven Univ. Press, 1988.

Riasanovsky, Valentin A. *Fundamental Principles of Mongol Law*. Uralic and Altaic Series 43. 1937; repr. Bloomington, Ind.: Research Institute for Inner Asian Studies, 1965.

Richard, Jean. *Simon de Saint-Quentin: Histoire des Tartares*. Paris: Libraire Orientaliste Paul Geuthner, 1965.

-----. "The Mongols and the Franks." *Journal of Asian History* 3 (1969): 45-57.

----. *La Papauté et les Missions d'Orient au Moyen Age (XIIIe-XVe siècles)*. Collection de l'École Française de Rome 33. Rome: École Française de Rome, 1977.

-----. "Les Mongols et l'Occident: Deux siècles de contacts, dans 1274." *Année charnière* 558 (1977): 85-96.

-----. *Les récits de voyages et de pèlerinages*. Typologie des sources du Moyen Age Occidental 38. Turnhout: Brepols, 1981.

Richter, Dieter. *Schlaraffenland: Geschichte einer populären Phantasie*. Cologne: Eugen Diederichs Verlag, 1984.

Rogers, Francis M. "The Vivaldi Expedition." *Dante Studies* 73 (1955): 31-45.

-----. *The Quest for Eastern Christians*. Minneapolis: Univ. of Minnesota Press, 1962.

Romm, James. "Aristotle's Elephant and the Myth of Alexander's Scientific Patronage." *American Journal of Philology* 110 (1990): 566-75.

Roncaglia, Aurelio. "Le corti medievali." In *Il letterato e le istituzioni, Letteratura italiana*. Turin: Einaudi, 1982.

Ross, David J. A. "A Check-list of Manuscripts of Three Alexander Texts." *Scriptorium* 10 (1956): 127-32.

-----. "A New Manuscript of Archpriest Leo of Napoli; Nativitas et Victoria Alexandri Magni." *Classica et Mediaevalia* 20 (1959): 98-158.

-----. *Alexander Historiatus.* 1963; 2nd ed., Frankfurt am Main: Warburg Institute, 1988. Supplement in *Journal of the Warburg and Courtauld Institutes* 30 (1967): 283-88.

-----. *Alexander and the Faithless Lady: A Submarine Adventure.* London: Birkbeck College, 1967.

-----. *Illustrated Alexander-Books in Germany and the Netherlands.* Cambridge, Mass.: Modern Humanities Research Association, 1971.

-----. *Studies in the Alexander Romance.* London: Pindar Press, 1985.

Roux, Jean-Paul. *Les explorateurs au Moyen Age.* Paris: Fayard, 1985.

Rowland, Beryl. *Animals with Human Faces: A Guide to Animal Symbolism.* Knoxville: Univ. of Tennessee Press, 1973.

Runciman, Steven. *A History of the Crusades.* 3 vols. Cambridge, Eng.: Cambridge Univ. Press, 1951-54.

Said, Edward W. *Orientalism.* 1978; repr. New York: Vintage, 1979.

Santarem, Vicomte de [Manuel Francisco de Baros]. *Essai sur l'Histoire de la Cosmographie et de la Cartographie pendant le Moyen Age.* Paris: Maulde et Renou, 1850.

Saunders, John J. "John of Plano Carpini: The Papal Envoy to the Mongol Conquerors who traveled through Russia to eastern Asia in 1245-47." *History Today* 22 (1972): 547-55.

Schaller, Hans Martin. "Die Kanzlei Kaiser Friedrichs II. Ihr Personal und Ihr Sprachstil" [Part 2]. *Archiv für Diplomatik* 4 (1958): 264-325.

Scott, John A. "*Inferno* XXVI: Dante's Ulysses." *Lettere Italiane* 23 (1971): 145-86.

Sedlar, Jean W. *India and the Greek World.* Totowa, N.J.: Rowman and Littlefield, 1980.

Seymour, Michael C. "The Scribal Tradition of Mandeville's *Travels*: The Insular Version." *Scriptorium* 18 (1964): 34-48.

Shepard, Laurie. "Rhetorical Innovation in the Chancery of Frederick II of Hohenstaufen and Its Reception by Vernacular Poets of the Thirteenth Century." Ph.D. diss., Boston College, 1985.

Singleton, Charles S. *Dante Studies 2: Journey to Beatrice.* Baltimore: The Johns Hopkins Univ. Press, 1977.

Sinor, Denis. "Les relations entre les Mongols et l'Europe jusqu'à la mort d'Arghoun et de Bela IV." *Cahiers d'histoire mondiale* 3 (1956): 39-62.

-----. "John of Plano Carpini's Return from the Mongols: New Light from a Luxembourg Manuscript." *Journal of the Royal Asiatic Society* (1957): 193-206.

-----. "Foreigner—Barbarian—Monster." In *East-West in Art.* Ed. Theodore Bowie. Bloomington, Ind.: Indiana Univ. Press, 1966. 154-73.

-----. "The Mongols and Western Europe." In *A History of the Crusades.* Ed. K. Setton. Madison: Univ. of Wisconsin Press, 1975.

Sivan, Hagith S. "Holy Land Pilgrimage and Western Audiences: Some Reflections on Egeria and Her Circle." *Classical Quarterly* 38[2] (1988): 528-35.

Skelton, R. A., Thomas E. Marston, and George D. Painter. *The Vinland Map and the Tartar Relation.* New Haven: Yale Univ. Press, 1965

Slessarev, Vsevolod. *Prester John: The Letter and the Legend.* Minneapolis: Univ. of Minnesota Press, 1959.

Soranzo, Giovanni. *Il Papato, l'Europa cristiana e i Tartari: un seculo di penetrazione occidentale in Asia.* Pubblicazioni della Università del Sacro Cuore 12. Milan: Società Editrice 'Vita e Pensiero', 1930.

Southern, R. W. *Western Views of Islam in the Middle Ages.* 1962; repr. Cambridge, Mass.: Harvard Univ. Press, 1978.

Spiegel, Gabrielle M. "Genealogy: Form and Function in Medieval Historical Narrative." *History and Theory* 22 (1983): 43-53.

Stanford, W. B. *The Ulysses Theme, A Study in the Adaptability of a Traditional Hero.* 2nd ed. Ann Arbor: Univ. of Michigan Press, 1976.

Steer, Georg. *Hugo Ripelin von Strassburg.* Tübingen: Niemeyer, 1981.

Strayer, Joseph R., gen ed. *Dictionary of the Middle Ages.* 13 vols. [with index]. New York: Scribners, 1982-89.

Struck, Bernhard. "Rhapta, Prasum, Menuthias." *Zeitschrift der Geschichte für Erdkunde zu Berlin* 517 (1921): 188-96.

Sumption, Jonathan. *Pilgrimage: An Image of Mediaeval Religion.* London: Faber and Faber, 1975.

Tatlock, J. S. P. *The Legendary History of Britain: Geoffrey of Monmouth's* Historia Regum Britanniae *and Its Early Vernacular Versions.* Berkeley: Univ. of California Press, 1950.

Tattersall, Jill. "Anthropophagi and Eaters of Raw Flesh in French Literature of the Crusade Period: Myth, Tradition, and Reality." *Medium Ævum* 57 (1988): 240-53.

Taviani, Huguette, et al. *Voyage, quête, pèlerinage dans la littérature et la civilisation médiévales.* Senefiance 2. Paris: Champion, 1976.

Thompson, David. *Dante's Epic Journeys.* Baltimore: The Johns Hopkins Univ. Press, 1974.

Thorndike, Lynn. *Michael Scot.* London: Nelson, 1965.

-----. *Medieval Technology and Social Change.* New York: Galaxy, 1966.

Toynbee, Paget. *A Dictionary of Proper Names and Notable Matters in the Works of Dante.* Rev. Charles S. Singleton. Oxford: Clarendon Press, 1968.

Van Cleve, Thomas Curtis. *The Emperor Frederick II of Hohenstaufen, Immutator Mundi.* Oxford: Clarendon Press, 1971.

van Bekkum, W. J. "Alexander the Great in Hebrew Literature." *Journal of the Warburg and Courtauld Institutes* 49 (1986): 218-26.

Vasvari, Louise O. "The Two Lazy Suitors in the *Libro de buen amor*: Popular Tradition and Literary Game of Love." *Anuario Medieval* 1 (1989): 181-205.

-----. "Amor, pecado, y muerte carnavalizados en el *Libro de buen amor*." In *Amor, pecado, y muerte en la edad media.* Ed. Nicasio Salvador Miguel. Madrid: Turner/Universidad Complutense, 1991.

Vaughan, Richard. *Chronicles of Matthew Paris: Monastic Life in the Thirteenth Century.* 1984; repr. New York: St. Martin's, 1986.

Vernadsky, George. "The Scope and Contents of Chingis-Khan's Yassa." *Harvard Journal of Asiatic Studies* 3 (1938): 337-60.

Vogelin, E. "The Mongol Orders of Submission to European Powers, 1245-1255." *Byzantium* 15 (1940-41): 378-413.

Washburn, Wilcomb E. "The Meaning of 'Discovery' in the 15th and 16th Centuries." *American Historical Review* 68 (1962): 1-21.

Watts, Pauline Moffitt. "Prophecy and Discovery: On the Spiritual Origins of Christopher Columbus's 'Enterprise of the Indies'." *American Historical Review* 90 (1985): 73-102.

Westphal-Wihl, Sarah. "Quodlibets: Introduction to a Middle High German Genre." In *Genres in Medieval Literature*. Ed. Hubert Heinen and Ingeborg Henderson. Göppingen: Kümmerle, 1986.

Westrem, Scott Douglas. *A Critical Edition of Johannes Witte de Hese's* Itinerarius, *the Middle Dutch Text, an English Translation, and Commentary, together with an Introduction to European Accounts of Travel to the East (1240-1400)*. Ph.D. diss., Northwestern University, 1985.

-----. "Medieval Western European Views of Sexuality Reflected in the Narratives of Travelers to the Orient." *Homo Carnalis, Acta* 14 (1987): 141-56.

Williams, George Huntston. "Erasmus and the Reformers on Non-Christian Religions and *Salus Extra-Ecclesiam*." In *Action and Conviction in Early Modern Europe: Essays in Memory of E. H. Harbison*. Ed. Theodore K. Rabb and Jerrold E. Seigel. Princeton: Princeton Univ. Press, 1969. 319-71.

Wittkower, Rudolf. "Marvels of the East: A Study in the History of Monsters." *Journal of the Warburg and Courtauld Institutes* 5 (1942): 159-97. Reprinted in *Allegory and the Migration of Symbols*. London, 1977; repr. New York: Thames and Hudson, 1987.

Woodward, David. "Medieval *Mappaemundi*." In *Cartography in Prehistoric, Ancient, and Medieval Europe and the Mediterranean*. Vol. 1 of *The History of Cartography*. Ed. J. B. Harley and David Woodward. Chicago: Univ. of Chicago Press, 1987. 286-370.

Woodward, David, ed. *Art and Cartography: Six Historical Essays.* Chicago: Univ. of Chicago Press, 1987.

Wright, John Kirtland. *The Geographical Lore of the Time of the Crusades: A Study in the History of Medieval Science and Tradition in Western Europe.* American Geographical Society Research Series 15. New York: American Geographical Society, 1925. (An expanded reprint was published in 1965.)

Zacher, Christian K. *Curiosity and Pilgrimage: The Literature of Discovery in Fourteenth-Century England.* Baltimore: The Johns Hopkins Univ. Press, 1976.

-----. "Travel and Geographical Writings." In *A Manual of the Writings in Middle English 1050-1500.* Gen. ed. Albert E. Hartung. New Haven: The Connecticut Academy of Arts and Sciences, 1986. 7:2235-54, 2449-66.

Ziolkowski, Jan. "Avatars of Ugliness in Medieval Literature." *Modern Language Review* 79 (1984): 1-20.

Index